PROVIDENCE WATCHING

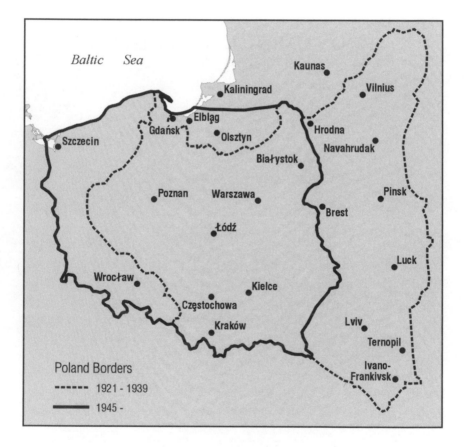

Baltic Sea

Kaunas

Vilnius

Kaliningrad

Elbląg

Gdańsk

Olsztyn

Hrodna

Szczecin

Navahrudak

Białystok

Pinsk

Poznan

Warszawa

Brest

Łódź

Luck

Wrocław

Kielce

Częstochowa

Lviv

Kraków

Ternopil

Ivano-Frankivsk

Poland Borders

----- 1921 - 1939

—— 1945 -

PROVIDENCE WATCHING

Journeys from Wartorn Poland to the Canadian Prairies

Edited by Kazimierz Patalas
Translated by Zbigniew Izydorczyk
Introduction by Daniel Stone

UNIVERSITY OF MANITOBA PRESS

University of Manitoba Press
Winnipeg, Manitoba R3T 2M5 Canada
www.umanitoba.ca/uofmpres
Printed in Canada

Cover design: Kirk Warren
Text design: Sharon Caseburg
Cover photo: Polish soldiers, c. 1946
Maps: Weldon Hiebert

National Library of Canada Cataloguing in Publication

Patalas, K. (Kazimierz), 1925-
  Providence watching : journeys from wartorn Poland to the Canadian Prairies / edited by Kazimierz Patalas; translated by Zbigniew Izydorczyk; introduction by Daniel Stone.

Includes index.
Translation of Przez boje, przez znoje, przez trud.
ISBN 0-88755-674-4

  1. World War, 1939-1945--Personal narratives, Polish.
2. Soldiers—Poland—Biography. 3. Poles—Manitoba—Biography.
I. Izydorczyk, Zbigniew, 1956- II. Title.

D811.A2P38 2003   940.54'81438   ̓C2003-906541-3

The University of Manitoba Press gratefully acknowledges the financial support for its publication program provided by the Government of Canada through the Book Publishing Industry Development Program (BPIDP); the Canada Council for the Arts; the Manitoba Arts Council; and the Manitoba Department of Culture, Heritage and Tourism.

Publication of this book has been made possible through a grant from the Dr. Victor Turek Foundation at the Polish Canadian Congress, Manitoba Division.

CONTENTS

MAPS

PREFACE

In talking to Polish war veterans after the meetings of the Polish Combatants Association (PCA), Chapter #13, in Winnipeg, and listening to their stories in the association's club, I was struck by the richness of experience in their oft-repeated recollections of the Second World War. Those experiences had burnt deeply into their memories and played an important role in their lives. Personal and idiosyncratic as they were, they also contained a wealth of information, shedding unique light on the historical events in which the veterans had participated. The thought that, with the veterans' passing, all that information would also pass into oblivion weighed heavily on my mind. Finally, after some discussions with Tadeusz Gardziejewski, then president of the PCA, a plan was hatched to put together a volume of the veterans' memoirs and preserve them for posterity.

In 1986 we began a series of evening meetings with individual veterans, mainly in my home. We sat in front of a video camera and talked in Polish about the old days. Tadeusz Gardziejewski usually assumed the responsibilities of a host, initiating and maintaining the conversations. After a few minutes, the presence of the camera was completely forgotten, and our guests continued their personal narratives freely and unimpeded. On several occasions, however, I conducted the interviews alone or assisted by my wife, Józefa Patalas, and, in a few instances, by Lech Fulmyk or Antoni Tomszak.

Our guests were the combatants from the PCA, Chapter #13, who came to Winnipeg along various war-swept paths. It was impossible to record memoirs of all the members of the association, so we tried to select those whose experiences were most representative of all the major tracks through war and its aftermath. In this way, we recorded on videotape the memories and reflections of forty-five veterans—over 100 hours of recording time.

The second phase of the project involved transcribing the videotaped accounts into word-processed computer files. Without changing the sense of the stories, I tried to give some shape, coherence, and fluency to the often imperfect spoken Polish of the recorded interviews. In this work, I was greatly assisted by my indefatigable wife, who participated in all aspects of revising and indexing.

These interviews were published in their original Polish in 1996 as *Przez Boje, przez Znoje, przez Trud*, an evocative title suggested by Tadeusz Gardziejewski, which translates as *Through Battles, through Hardships, through Toil.* This publication coincided with the fiftieth anniversary of the combatants' arrival in Canada. It was intended primarily for the combatants themselves and for their families. For the former, so they might retrace the events from the quickly receding past and complete their own memories with those of their friends; for the latter, so they might learn from their fathers or mothers, husbands or wives, what was often the stuff of their silent memories.

The English version of these memoirs, which we are now presenting, is intended for a broader Canadian audience. It will certainly captivate the imagination of the combatants' children and grandchildren, but it will also appeal to those interested in the Polish diaspora and in its contribution to the shaping of the Canadian nation. The first wave of Polish immigrants reached the Canadian prairies at the turn of the twentieth century. The combatants came as the second wave, building on the ethnic strengths of their predecessors and on their own determination to succeed. They had survived Soviet prisons, Siberian taiga, and German POW camps. The history of their painful journey through war and across this country to the expansive landscapes of rural Manitoba is an integral part of Canada's history. For more than fifty years, they and their children have been contributing to the welfare, culture, and history of this province. This book recognizes that our past lies in theirs.

These memoirs often evoke similar events of World War II and of the first years in Canada, but they are related and interpreted differently. Stark historical facts have been filtered through imperfect memories, affected by personal idiosyncrasies, coloured by subsequent experiences. The memoirs do not preserve objective history but living history, history alive in the minds of those who gave it shape. Some of them emphasize the pre-war period; others, the experiences of the war itself; and still others describe in detail the building of new lives after arrival in Canada. The stories clearly reflect the personalities of the tellers, from restrained, even reticent, about the witnessed events, to speculative, given to profuse interpretations, to highly emotional, reflecting the shades and intensity of feelings. When preparing the Polish written text, I made a conscious effort to preserve the individual character of the narrating voices. The variety of narrating styles reminds us that these are true recollections of real people; it also imparts to the book its many human dimensions, which turn a collection of memories into a collective memoir.

This book does not aim to exhaust the subject of Polish post-war immigration to Canada. It may be flawed through minor oversights or misunderstandings. But it will certainly accomplish one goal: it will save from oblivion the memories of forty-five Polish paths to Canada.

I express my thanks to the Dr. Victor Turek Foundation at the Polish Canadian Congress, Manitoba Division, for their encouragement and financial support. In particular, I am thankful to Dr. Joseph Kagan, the chair of the foundation, for his initiative to translate the original Polish book into English, and for his perseverance, without which this book would never have reached the printing press. I also acknowledge the grant received from the Minister of Culture, Heritage and Citizenship for the translation of the book *Przez Boje, przez Znoje, przez Trud.*

TRANSLATOR'S NOTE

Translating this collection of memoirs was both a moving and a challenging experience. The memoirs are ultimately derived from videotaped interviews with the veterans, which K. Patalas transcribed and edited for the Polish book entitled *Przez boje, przez Znoje, przez Trud* (*Through Battles, through Hardships, through Toil*). Their touching, shocking, amusing, and heartbreaking stories drew me to the original tapes, and those tapes certainly left a mark on my translation. In contrast to the more documentary style of the Polish book, I tried—with the editor's permission—to flesh out the personalities of the tellers. Hence, I occasionally included in my translation details, expressions, and anecdotes that do not appear in the Polish text but that, I felt, conveyed a fuller sense of the narrator.

Some of the challenges I encountered in translating these memoirs arose from their oral character. The narratives do not present objective history, but history as it had been lived and was remembered fifty years later by ordinary people. Their memories were vivid, but sometimes scratched and imperfect; the recollections were always genuine, but sometimes coloured by personal idiosyncrasies or obscured by time. It is, therefore, not surprising—in fact, quite natural—that certain inconsistencies crept into these narratives. For example, the narrators occasionally appear to mismatch or misremember dates, localities, military ranks, or details of military hardware. I have made no attempt to correct such discrepancies since they were usually related to the personal circumstances of the narrator, which in most cases cannot be verified.

Another challenge arose in connection with rendering place names. The narrators usually remembered them in their Polish forms or, in the case of small or more remote locations in Asia, in the way they heard and referred to them in Polish. I have not been able to identify all the places mentioned in the memoirs, either because some may have been too small to register on any maps, or because some may no longer exist. However, those places that could be identified are referred to in the following ways:

- large, well-known centres and regions are referred to by their usual English names (e.g., Warsaw, Moscow, Silesia);

- names for lesser known places now in Poland are given in their current Polish forms;

- names for places in eastern Poland before World War II but now in Lithuania, Belarus, or Ukraine are given, on their first appearance in a memoir, in their pre-war Polish forms remembered by the narrators, followed by their current name in brackets;

- names for places in Asia and Middle East that have been changed in the last half-century are given, on their first appearance in a memoir, in the form remembered by the narrators, followed by their current name in brackets.

All current place names are taken from the electronic *Encarta Reference Library 2004,* published by Microsoft.

Translating the memoirs, while intensely gratifying, was also a protracted and arduous process. The final stages of this process were accelerated by the institutional and financial assistance of the University of Winnipeg. Along the way, I was helped by a number of people, but especially by K. Patalas, the editor of this volume, whose enthusiasm for the project was so infectious; by Leszek Wielkopolan, who generously shared with me his knowledge of military terminology; by Murray Evans and Alexandrea Jory, who helped me with various editorial tasks; by Anna Parry, who read the entire manuscript and offered many useful suggestions; and, above all, by Marta, Veronica, Alexander, and Conrad, who put up with me for all the years this translation was in progress.

Zbigniew Izydorczyk

PROVIDENCE WATCHING

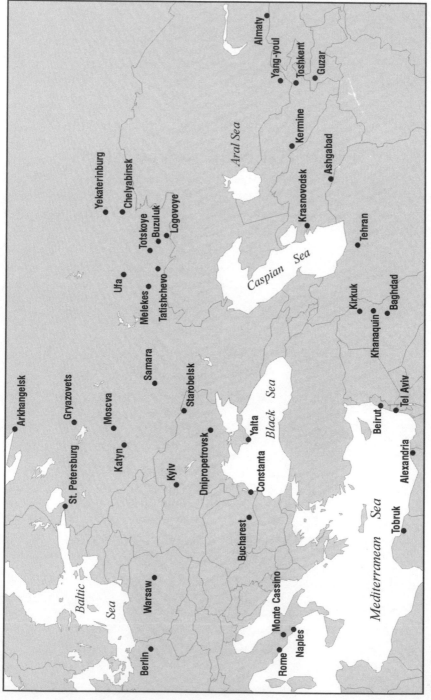

Eurasia

INTRODUCTION

Three hundred and fifty Poles disembarked from the Canadian Pacific Railway train in Winnipeg on November 15, 1946, wearing the khaki battledress adorned with the Polish White Eagles that marked their service in an autonomous command within the British army. They were greeted at the station by 1500 Polish-Manitobans who knew their wartime exploits from Winnipeg's Polish-language press. Anglo-Canadian representatives came, too, such as the commander of the 10th Military District, Brigadier R.O.G. Morton, and his staff. The newcomers went to the Fort Osborne Barracks for military ceremonies, and then to a banquet organized by the Polish community. Seven hundred Polish-Manitobans attended; more would have come, if there had been room.[1]

The veterans looked much the same in their uniforms, and few observers, Anglo- or Polish-Canadian, suspected the unique experiences that lay behind the veterans' smiling faces. Each Polish veteran had his individual story of how he had come from Poland in 1939 to Winnipeg in 1946. These stories frequently were filled with drama, adventure, misfortune, hunger, and death in Europe, Asia, and Africa. Subsequent groups of Polish immigrants arrived over the next decade, women as well as men, bringing similar, yet singular, experiences with them. Settling in Winnipeg, they established the Polish Combatants Association (*Stowarzyszenie Polskich Kombatantow*—SPK, or PCA in English) where they have continued to meet for the last fifty-seven years.

I. PRE-WAR POLAND

When World War II broke out in September 1939, Poland was a new state with ancient roots. Founded in 966 when Duke Mieszko converted from Paganism to Christianity, the Polish state underwent dramatic changes over the next thousand years. It acquired vast territories to the east, primarily through the marriage in 1386 of Princess Jadwiga of Poland with Grand Duke Jogaila of Lithuania.[2] A small country in the twenty-first century, mediaeval Lithuania had absorbed much of modern Ukraine, Belarus, and western Russia. Additional territories were gained and lost (especially in the seventeenth century), but the general outlines remained the same until the Russian, Prussian, and Austrian states annexed portions of Poland-Lithuania and removed it from the map in three partitions, finishing the process in 1795. Poland remained essentially stateless for the next 123 years, although Poles remained Poles and many worked tirelessly, often heroically, to reestablish statehood. World War I led to the defeat of all three partitioning powers, and Poland rejoined the family of states.[3]

Poland was reestablished in 1918 with different borders as new ethnic realities came into play. Many Lithuanians, Belarussians, and Ukrainians developed their own national consciousness in the nineteenth century and wished to form their own states. The Soviet Union vied with Poland to control the lands that lay between them. After two wars and several insurrections, the Polish state held most of ethnic Poland as well as significant, but much less extensive, territories in the east. Lithuania became a small independent country while the Soviet Union integrated major portions of Belarus and Ukraine.

The interwar Polish state was a democratic republic governed by a bicameral parliament; a president fulfilled mainly ceremonial duties. Deep-seated political antagonisms, mostly inherited from rivalries during the struggle for independence, led to sharp political conflict. In 1926, Marshal Józef Piłsudski took power in a coup d'etat, but left many democratic institutions and practices intact. The political atmosphere worsened after Piłsudski's death in 1935 as his followers jockeyed for power. Economic issues played a significant role, as well. The Polish territories had achieved some modern industrial, commercial, and agricultural development before the First World War, but the loss of markets due to border changes, the problems of establishing a new currency, and the Great Depression of the 1930s left the majority of

Polish citizens poor or even desperate. Despite these problems, the Polish Republic made progress in education, urbanization, and even industry before World War II broke out.

Nationality issues posed a serious problem for the interwar Polish state and provide a theme for the life histories included in this book. Approximately 65% of the Polish citizenry were ethnically Polish while 16% were Ukrainian, 10% Jewish, 6% Belarussian, 2.5% German, and 0.5% other. The eastern sections of the Polish state had a non-Polish majority, although Poles provided the most of the richer and better educated classes. Jews made up 30 to 35% of the population of large urban centres and 50 to 90% of the population in many small cities or towns. The large peasantry was about two-thirds Ukrainian and Belarussian and one-third Polish; some Polish villages had existed for centuries while others had been established by the Polish government in the 1920s.[4] The mixture of political, economic, and national problems led to considerable antagonism that played itself out during World War II, as Helena Bator, Tadeusz Gardziejewski, and Henryk Kozubski note, among others.

Ethnic relations were particularly tense in western Ukraine (now part of the Ukrainian Republic) during the interwar period. Austria took the region in the Polish partitions and allowed loyalist Polish nobles to govern on their behalf, particularly after 1871. Ukrainians tried to establish an independent Ukrainian republic in western Ukraine in 1918-19, but lost. The victorious Poles granted the Ukrainians and other national minorities the right to vote, organize political parties, own property, and establish cultural organizations. Nevertheless, the Polish state refused to give Ukrainians the distinct legal identification and state support to which they felt entitled. The underground Organization of Ukrainian Nationalists carried on the struggle through attacks on government buildings and assassinations of Polish officials, mostly around 1930. Anti-terrorist reprisals antagonized Ukrainians, even if they dampened resistance temporarily.[5]

Jews had no separatist aspirations, but numerous Zionists and autonomists saw the Jews as a separate nation and demanded some kind of distinct legal status within the Polish Republic. Others, particularly the Polish-speaking intelligentsia and business elite, subscribed to Polish traditions. Voting patterns suggest that a substantial number of Poles (perhaps 10 to 15%) saw all Jews as an alien threat and wished to restrict or expel them; as in most European and American countries (including Canada), many held passive anti-Jewish attitudes. Others were well-disposed towards Jews and some energetically combatted anti-Semitism.[6] The many observations in this volume about Jews show that interactions varied according to individual situations.

II. WORLD WAR II

The Polish Republic was destroyed when Germany invaded on September 1, 1939, ostensibly to settle a border dispute. The large Polish army had just begun a program of technical modernization and could not match the Germans in aircraft, tanks, artillery, or motorization, no matter how bravely it fought. Poles won some local engagements, including one in which the cavalry destroyed German tanks by galloping up and throwing hand grenades (Kazimierz Klimaszewski and Antoni Jóźwiak), but lost the war quickly. The possibility of regrouping was eliminated when the Soviet Union marched in from the east on September 17 in accordance with a secret agreement signed with Germany to partition Poland again. The Hitler-Soviet Pact of August 23, 1939, gave the Soviets eastern Poland and granted them primacy in the Baltic Republics (Lithuania, Latvia, and Estonia), which they occupied and annexed in 1940.

From September 1939 to June 1941, Poland was split between Nazi Germany and the Soviet Union, leaving half of the memoirists in this collection under Soviet control.[7] The Soviet Union annexed the region after a pro-forma referendum, changed the governing languages into Ukrainian, Belarussian, and Russian, and sovietized all institutions. Nationalized factories, stores, and collective farms replaced private property. Schools taught Marxism-Leninism-Stalinism, and religion was persecuted. Ethnic Poles were the biggest losers because they represented the dispossessed state class, while the aggrieved minorities (primarily Belarussian, Jewish, and Ukrainian youth) greeted the change with some enthusiasm at first.

Reality set in quickly, however. Daily life was extremely difficult under Soviet rule. In addition to losing familiar jobs and institutions, and undergoing material privation, the residents found themselves subject to arbitrary and capricious decisions by Soviet officials who confiscated apartments and possessions, and charged the new Soviet citizens with criminal activities. All groups suffered, although Poles suffered the most. Soviet authorities stereotyped them as counter-revolutionaries, Ukrainians as nationalists, and Jews as speculators. Some individuals from all groups rose within the Soviet system, however.[8]

Mass deportations began in 1939 with the clearing of the border zone. In 1940-41, more than 1.25 million former Polish citizens were sent deep into the Soviet Union, particularly to Kazakhstan as prisoners and "special settlers." Deportations occurred mainly in February 1940 (government workers and small farmers—mostly Polish), April 1940 (tradesmen—mostly Jewish), and June 1940 (merchants and professionals—Jewish and Polish), as well as June 1941 (others including children at summer camp). As many memoirists from this collection recall, conditions were atrocious. The deportees travelled in over-crowded cattle cars with an average load of forty-five persons, without toilets. Very little water was provided and virtually no food, even though the journey often took weeks. Fragmentary statistics suggest that at least 10% of the deportees died and half arrived ill.[9]

Life as a deportee was extraordinarily difficult, as the memoirists show. Although they were not dumped by the side of the track with primitive hand tools as earlier deportees had been, the new arrivals had to find jobs and shelter amidst an impoverished population. Most struggled to make themselves understood in Russian, a related Slavic language, and many had no way of communicating with the Turkic-speaking Uzbeks and Kazakhs of Central Asia. Some deportees found positions that provided some access to food, but others had to buy supplies on the open market, insofar as one existed.[10] Everyone suffered under these conditions, although the degree of suffering varied widely. Helena Bator, for example, would have starved to death on her first Uzbek *kolkhoz* (collective farm) if she had not stolen food, and Lech Fulmyk earned a tolerable living by skinning dead cattle on a Siberian *kolkhoz*. Some young Polish men were drafted into the Soviet army and received equitable treatment; that is to say, they were underfed and subjected to harsh barracks life but could gain promotion according to their merits, as Tadeusz Gardziejewski did.

Many Poles came under Soviet control as interned soldiers or political prisoners. Bolesław Czubak was interned and transferred to camps in the interior. Kazimierz Chmielowicz, Wacław Kuzia, and Stanisław Smoleński Sr. surrendered to the Lithuanians and came under Soviet control in 1940, when the Soviet Union took over this formerly independent country. Still others, such as Konstanty Jackiewicz, were convicted of political crimes by the Soviet regime and sent to camps in the interior. Conditions were generally appalling. Prison cells were overcrowded, often by a factor of five or ten; sanitary facilities, food, and drink were sadly lacking. Prisoners were regularly beaten at interrogations. No one from this group, obviously, shared the fate of the 15,000 Polish officers whom the Soviets executed in 1940, although Kazimierz Chmielowicz and Stanisław Smoleński Sr. found themselves at one of their internment camps somewhat later.[11]

The prisoners and deportees were released from their ordeals after the Germans invaded the Soviet Union in June 1941. Stalin eagerly signed an alliance with Great Britain and willingly concluded another alliance with the Polish government-in-exile that had been established in September 1939 when Poland fell, permitting the Poles to form an army on Soviet soil for eventual joint campaigning. The Soviet refusal to return the lands that had been seized in 1939 created a dilemma for Prime Minister Władysław Sikorski. Eventually, he rejected the advice of many in his cabinet to insist on their return and agreed to leave the point for future resolution in the mistaken hope that circumstances would favour Poland after the war. The treaty helped Poles in the Soviet Union who, as allies, were released from imprisonment and service in the Soviet Army.[12]

News percolated throughout the vast Soviet expanses erratically. Some Poles, like Stanisław Smoleński Sr., were notified and transferred to the Polish army. Others, like Marian Lisowski, applied for transfer, were refused, re-applied, and tried again until they gained admission. Still others, like Tadeusz Gardziejewski, deserted from the Soviet forces in order to enlist. Civilians, too, learned the news in various ways—from official sources and from friends. In general, the journey to reunite Poles was full of difficult adventures and misadventures. Stanisław Smoleński Jr. found out from his father, who had been a Soviet labour camp prisoner. He and his family journeyed across Kazakhstan to meet the father, who had made arrangements with the new Polish authorities. Everyone arrived without incident except Stanisław Smoleński Jr., who missed a connection and hid out without papers for several days until his father came to bring him to camp. Irena Ehrlich was astonished to learn of the Polish-Soviet alliance when she encountered a Polish soldier at an Uzbek railway station. She impulsively joined the army, leaving her mother and sisters. She was allowed onto the Polish army train primarily because she encountered a fellow Pole from her home city of Wilno, but was denied permission to enlist until she ran into another Wilno resident in a position of authority.

Admission to the Polish army in the Soviet Union did not solve the problem of material deprivation.[13] The Polish army had no independent sources of supply and had to rely on the Soviet government. It seems likely that the Poles found themselves on the bottom of Soviet priorities for food and armaments, both of which were in short supply, and suffered accordingly. Henryk Kozubski, for example, weighed only forty-nine kilos when he joined the Polish Army, despite his 181 cm height. Food was scarce and the soldiers shared what they had with Polish civilians. Kozubski was reduced to tears of embarrassment when a cook reproved him for requesting a second helping. Stanisław Kmieć found that his army camp was racked with diseases such as typhus and typhoid, and lacked both doctors and medicines. Many died.

These conditions, as well as profound political differences between Polish and Soviet officials and the suspicious absence of 15,000 Polish officers, led to the departure of the Polish army to Iran (Persia), where they joined the Polish branch of the British army. Thirty-three thousand Polish soldiers and 10,000 civilians left the Soviet Union in March-April 1942, and another 45,000 soldiers and 25,000 civilians left in August 1942.[14] The Poles breathed an enormous sigh of relief when they reached Persia. After Soviet poverty, this Third World country seemed an oasis of plenty. Lech Fulmyk thought that Persia looked like "a land from a fairy tale" while Tadeusz Gardziejewski "wondered if the abundance we saw was real or just an April Fool's Day's joke." Many veterans reported cases of serious overeating that resulted in stomach cramps, hospitalization, or death. Wacław Kuzia reports that one of his comrades might have died from gorging himself on hard-boiled eggs if he had not knocked them out onto the ground and smashed them. The ragged, lice-infested uniforms were burned, and the Polish soldiers underwent disinfection before receiving new, British army issue.

Over the following months, Polish soldiers returned to health and underwent military training under British supervision. Units went on garrison duty in Iran, Iraq, Palestine, and Egypt. Some of the soldiers must have had their first encounter with Winnipeg when they were met by Dr. William Rose, the Minnedosa-born historian who had taught at Wesley College (now the University of Winnipeg) before World War I. Working in Europe in 1914, Rose was interned in Austrian Poland during World War I. After the war, he returned to Poland to work for the YMCA during the 1920s, received his doctorate from the Jagiellonian University in Cracow, and served as Director of the School of Slavonic Studies, University of London (England) from 1939 to 1950. Rose came to Romania in 1939 to meet Polish refugees and, in 1944, spent some time in Palestine addressing Polish troops.[15]

In Palestine, at least half of the 4000 Jewish soldiers deserted from the Polish Army, changed their names, and joined kibbutzim (Jewish communal farms); many went into the anti-British underground, as Feliks Biłos and Henryk Kozubski note. Polish authorities chose not to pursue them except occasionally when the British insisted. Contributing factors include the attraction of the Palestinian Jewish community, the Nazi destruction of the Jewish community in Poland, and anti-Semitic incidents in the Polish army (which the High Command combatted). The most famous absentee, as Kozubski notes, was Menachem Begin, then a Polish corporal and, from 1977 to 1983, Prime Minister of Israel. In a secret deal, the Polish armed forces granted him leave to give anti-Soviet speeches in the United States. Great Britain refused to let Begin leave and he went underground.[16] Some Jews continued to serve, as Kozubski reports. The first Polish soldier decorated in the Italian campaign may have been Jewish.[17]

The Polish army's most important military contribution came in Italy in 1944; it features in many chapters of this volume. The highlight was the Battle of Monte Cassino, the famous Benedictine monastery founded in 529. Held by the Germans, Monte Cassino blocked the route to Rome and threatened the success of the entire Allied campaign. Four Allied assaults had failed to take the heavily fortified monastery; heavy bombing only made matters worse. A major assault in mid-May brought success. The Polish Second Corps took the monastery in "a final and self-sacrificial assault" while French Moroccan irregulars pushed into a nearby valley, forcing the Germans to withdraw their crack, if badly depleted, paratroop regiment before the final assault.[18] The Poles also took part in the Bologna and Ancona campaigns.

The Soviet-Persian-Italian route was not the only way that Poles came west, and the stories of these Polish veterans are equally remarkable. A government-in-exile had been created in France in 1939, and General Władysław Sikorski was appointed both Prime Minister of a broad coalition cabinet and Commander-in-Chief of about 43,000 Polish soldiers, supplemented by about 40,000 volunteers from the large Polish immigrant community in France. After the Fall of France, the government and remnants of the army were evacuated to Britain. The ranks were filled with soldiers like Stanisław Kłoczkowski, who crossed the Polish border into Romania in September 1939 and was interned. He escaped, travelled to France via Beirut, and volunteered for the Polish air force. Similarly, Stanisław Kociołek surrendered to Hungary in 1939, but had little trouble escaping across the border to Yugoslavia, where he found a ship to take him to France. Both made it to Britain after the Fall of France. With General Anders's Second Corps, remnants of the Polish air force and navy, and some later recruiting, the Polish Armed Forces in the West numbered 228,000 at the end of the war, including remnants of the Polish air force and navy at the end of the war.[19]

Germany provided another route to the Polish army, paradoxically. Since Germany annexed the Polish Baltic coast, Alojzy Bach, a Pole, despite his name, was sent to do forced labour in Germany. He reluctantly accepted reclassification as an ethnic German in 1943 to help his family and was drafted into the German army; he fought in its ranks until the Americans captured him. Identifying himself as a Pole forced to do military service, he was permitted to join a Polish regiment. Another Pole from the Baltic Coast, Edmund Kuffel, was drafted for labour when he turned seventeen and was assigned to Italy. He managed to hide while the Germans retreated and joined the Polish army. Antoni Jóźwiak, a soldier in the Polish army, was taken prisoner in 1939 and, after nearly starving in a prisoner-of-war camp, found himself assigned to work on a German farm. Reclassified as a civilian, he attempted to escape to Poland, failed, and went back to prison. Kazimierz Klimaszewski was also taken prisoner in 1939 and put to work as a farm labourer. Injured in an attempt to escape, he spent time in a German army hospital, where he worked with the French resistance. He later escaped and, after encountering American troops in Frankfurt, went back into German confinement to help the prisoners prepare for liberation.

The Polish Resistance was the best developed movement in Nazi-occupied Europe, and three members are represented in this collection. Jerzy Piskor joined a local resistance unit of the *Narodowe Siły Zbrojne*, apparently ignorant of or indifferent to the ultra-nationalistic politics that led to its exclusion from the *Armia Krajowa* (Home Army), the main resistance fighting force. He operated in the Świętokrzyskie (Holy Cross) Mountains and, as the Soviet Army approached in 1944, escaped Poland with his entire unit by agreement with the German army. In what is now the Czech Republic, his unit liberated a German concentration camp, saving, among others, a group of Jewish women who were near death from starvation. The unit surrendered to the Americans just before the war ended. Most of the members were demobilized, although a few with special training, including Piskor, were sent to Italy to join the Polish forces.[20] Janina Popkiewicz was part of the Communications Unit of the Home Army in Lwów, resisting both Soviet and German occupation. After the war, she moved to Cracow and emigrated to Winnipeg in 1957, rejoining her brother who had come here earlier. Tomasz Wielgat served as an explosives expert in the Home Army until his unit was disbanded in 1944. He moved to Czechoslovakia with his Czech wife and escaped west, eventually joining his brother in Canada.

The memoirs reported thus far in this introduction have primarily related the experiences of the men, who made up most of the Polish Armed Forces and, as a result, the majority of authors in this volume. Women's experiences figure only to a minor extent and differ little from men's, in part because the women in this volume were also members of the Polish Armed Forces. Helena Bator and Irena Ehrlich tell stories of their deportation to Siberia and their privations mirror those in men's stories. Janina Popkiewicz gives an account of the Polish resistance, and young Karolina Wiktorowicz documents life in an orphanage and evacuation to Iran. One woman, Helena Bator, learned an atypical skill in the armed forces (airplane mechanic), while two, Irena Ehrlich and Janina Popkiewicz, filled auxiliary roles in the forces (or resistance). There are no reports of rape or other abuse. It is possible (but not certain) that a separate study on women, perhaps conducted by a woman, would uncover something different.

Discussions of women's wartime experiences tend to revolve around the way women coped with the absence of male family members and with abuse.[21] Jan Sajewicz touches on women's experiences in his account of ministering to some of the 20,000 Polish women and children in African refugee camps as a Roman Catholic priest. His account is brief, but it is clear that civilian women made many independent decisions when confronted by wartime problems and played significant roles in administering the refugee camps. The women probably drew on the tradition of Polish women's activism that developed in the nineteenth century, when husbands and fathers were lost during patriotic insurrections against Russian rule. Women played a notable role in the revolutionary movement, too.

Father Sajewicz reports several instances of female activism. In one camp, working women taxed themselves to provide welfare assistance to women in need. He also reports a virtual revolt by women against alleged favouritism by the male camp commander, which forced his transfer; the protest was led by a camp policewoman. Incidentally, Father Sajewicz found teaching morality to refugees from the Soviet Union unusually challenging. It was hard, for example, to condemn theft when a pupil replied that stealing bread "couldn't have been a sin [because a priest] showed us how to do it." Father Sajewicz revealed his own moral concerns as he made it a point to treat the black Africans with a greater sense of equality than the British did, even if he accepted some suggestions to be more "careful" dealing with them.

Both men's and women's narratives show that family was a key value, and both sexes did whatever they could to maintain family ties. Despite their wartime activism, it appears that many women were happy to defer to men, especially priests, in most circumstances. That left the women subject to clerical censorship for their behaviour.

III. POST-WAR

When the European war ended on May 8, 1945, the Polish army in the West was left in limbo. At a series of conferences, especially at Yalta (USSR) in February 1945, the Grand Alliance of the United States, Great Britain, and the Soviet Union agreed to recognize a coalition dominated by Moscow-based communists as the legal government of Poland. The Soviets arrested many non-communist resistance fighters, although they did not force complete communization for several years. Furthermore, the Soviet Union kept eastern Poland, and Poland gained compensation in the west at Germany's expense, thereby establishing the present borders of the Polish state. The Polish soldiers in Italy and Great Britain were deeply distressed, as Edmund Kuffel and Stefan Olbrecht note. Many came from eastern Poland and remembered their bitter experiences with communists. Most would not, under any circumstances, return to Poland as long as it was communist-ruled, even when urged by well-meaning Polonophiles such as William Rose.[22] A few returned, such as Antoni Jóźwiak, who quickly changed his mind and escaped. Presumably, most soldiers, including those represented in this volume, agreed with their commander, General Władysław Anders, who hoped, as a British diplomat noted, "to hold on to his troops until the day when war—in his view inevitable and not too far distant—breaks out between the Soviet Union and the West."[23] Most Polish veterans probably had no intention of remaining permanently in the West.

Great Britain accepted responsibility for its Polish soldiers, although it had no intention of supporting a Polish army that was mobilized for a future war with the Soviets. It offered a refuge for those who chose not to return to Poland, and approached the Commonwealth countries to open their doors. After extensive discussions, Canada accepted 4257 Polish soldiers in 1946-47 to work on Canadian farms for two years and then remain in Canada. Many of the contributors to this volume came here under this program. Canadian agreement was by no means a foregone conclusion because Canada took very few immigrants during the Great Depression of the 1930s and, while it accepted a few hundred Polish engineers and technicians during the war, was still reluctant to reopen its doors until returning Canadian servicemen found jobs. Canada began to open up to immigrants only after 1947.[24]

Both self-interest and altruism led the government to welcome this limited number of Polish veterans in 1946. Canada badly needed farm workers after the war to replace the forced labour of German war prisoners and the interned Japanese-Canadians. Both groups had worked in the Manitoba sugar beet fields. Furthermore, negotiating as an equal with Great Britain over the Polish veterans allowed the Canadian government to assert its sovereignty and emerge from Dominion status as fully sovereign. It impressed world opinion with its responsible behaviour. Finally, and probably least important, it was good politics to respond positively to the well-argued presentations that the Polish-

Canadian community made to the Canadian parliament, notably Winnipeg's Bernard Dubienski. Altruism factored in, as well. Polish fighting men had earned the respect of Canadian diplomats and soldiers during the war. Furthermore, the growth of anti-Soviet sentiment with arrests of Soviet spies in Canada made it attractive to receive resolutely anti-Soviet Polish soldiers.[25]

As a result of the Canadian-British agreement, 4527 Polish servicemen came to Canada. The first 2876 were selected by a Canadian interdepartmental commission that went to Polish army camps in Italy in 1946. The remainder were selected in Britain in 1947. After excluding married men and those who made no claims to agricultural experience, the commissioners took about 65% of some 7000 applicants. Of the rejected applicants, 23% were turned down on medical grounds, 31% on security grounds (suspicion of cooperation with the Germans), and 46% for failing to pass a brief test of agricultural knowledge (memoirists like Henryk Kozubski and Tadeusz Wilton found the test extremely simple). Unfortunately, the Canadians prevailed on the Polish authorities to dissuade Polish-Jewish soldiers from applying; in all, one Jew persisted and came to Canada. The new farm labourers averaged twenty-nine years of age and claimed eight years of farm experience.[26] They arrived by ship in 1946 and 1947. Polish-Canadians greeted them enthusiastically in Halifax and at various stops on the way west.

When they arrived in Winnipeg, the Polish servicemen encountered a community of 36,550 Polish-Canadians (1941 census figures) who made up 5% of Manitoba's population, and 21% of all Polish Canadians.[27] Although the first Poles had arrived with the Selkirk settlers in 1817, the community was really founded during the era of mass migration after 1890 and continued to grow rapidly until Canada imposed strict limits on immigration during the Great Depression. Most immigrants lived on farms in pioneer conditions well into the interwar period, lagging behind other rural Manitobans in family income because the best land had been taken by earlier settlers. Few could afford to hire the Polish veterans who came as farm labourers in 1946-47.

Winnipeg had long held a substantial Polish population and, by 1946, there were more urban Poles than rural in Manitoba. They built a vibrant community, attending the impressive churches that had been constructed before the First World War and joining a network of mutual help societies, credit unions, and cultural groups. Two Polish-language newspapers were established in Winnipeg before the First World War: the *Gazeta Katolicka* (*The Catholic Gazette*) and *Czas* (*The Polish Times*). Most Polish Winnipeggers still worked as unskilled and semi-skilled labourers, although a small middle class emerged during the interwar period, primarily owners of small businesses (usually manual trades) and a few professionals (such as teachers and nurses). Canadian-born children generally graduated from high school; some attended university. Brandon and several smaller cities also contained well-established Polish communities.

When they arrived in 1946-47, the Polish veterans took to life in Canada even though their first experiences were often unsatisfactory. They worked at the farm jobs that the Canadian authorities had identified, signing contracts with individual farmers. Anecdotal accounts from Józef Jankowski and Alojzy Bach recount spare but acceptable conditions and good relations with their employers, but unhappy experiences seem more common. Like Marian Lisowski and Stanisław Kociołek, many veterans complained about poor housing, poor pay, and poor treatment. Within the first fourteen months of the program, the new immigrants sent more than one thousand letters to the newly formed Polish Combatants Association, asking for help in changing jobs. In all, 70% changed jobs, mostly after the authorities rewrote the regulations to allow transfers after one year. Conditions improved in the veterans' second jobs, since they could ask for the higher prevailing wage instead of accepting the $45 per month prescribed in their contracts; they demanded decent housing as well. In Manitoba, 370 veterans worked on farms and ninety received permission to work elsewhere (mostly in forestry and fishing), twenty-two were in hospital, mostly with tuberculosis, four died, twenty went missing, and two bought their own farms. Nevertheless, 97% of Polish veterans moved to urban areas after the two-year contracts expired.[28] They were likely to have been motivated by the declining demand for farm labour caused by mechanization, the inability to buy one's own farm from wages paid to farm labourers, and the desire to associate with other Polish immigrants.

Not all Polish veterans came as farm labourers; some arrived after the Canadian government loosened its immigration restrictions in the late 1940s.[29] The usual immigrant networks came into play when the Poles moved to Winnipeg. Many found jobs through personal contacts in the immigrant community. Konstanty Jackiewicz may have been the first Pole hired at Inland Steel by a sympathetic Canadian army veteran, but he was not the last. In all, nine contributors to this volume found work there. Stanisław Kłoczkowski could not find a job in Montreal and came to Winnipeg when a friend sent him information that McDonald Air was hiring. Friends found Henryk Kozubski a job at Vulcan Iron and Engineering and told him how to answer questions at the interview.

Several established themselves in Britain before moving to Canada to find more opportunity. Stanisław Smoleński Jr. and his family remained in England until "they could see that Britain itself held no future" for them. Following suggestions from Canadian Immigration, the three brothers came first and the rest of the family followed. Lech Fulmyk took a vocational course in leatherwork with the help of a scholarship from the Polish government-in-exile, married, and moved to Canada with his wife, mother, and sister in 1953. Kazimierz Kowaliszyn married a Scottish woman from the Women's Auxiliary Air Force in 1944. They had trouble finding jobs together after the war and came to Canada in 1952. Edmund Kuffel went furthest in Britain. Somewhat younger than other veterans, he took his high school education in London and attended the University of Dublin, where he received his doctorate in 1959. Kuffel came to the University of Manitoba in the late 1960s to teach engineering and served as Dean from 1979 to 1989.

Despite different experiences, backgrounds, and jobs, the contributors to this volume found common ground in the Polish Combatants Association (PCA). Founded in Italy in 1945 and again in England in 1946, the major aims of the association were mutual assistance and opposition to communism in Poland. The association worked on behalf of Polish veterans in disputes with farmers and the Canadian government. Kazimierz Klimaszewski spoke English well and had some experience working with the English authorities, so he was informally assigned by the veterans to work on their behalf. He was so effective that the Department of Labour brought him to Ottawa and put him on the federal payroll. The first Manitoba convention of the PCA was held in Winnipeg in July 1947. Two hundred and fifty veterans travelled an average of 300 kilometres to attend. The first national convention was held in Winnipeg in 1948 with representatives from across Canada; Bolesław Czubak served as first national president.[30]

The combatants became a distinct group within the Canadian-Polish mosaic. Unified by wartime experiences and intense esprit de corps, the veterans stuck together. Simple human needs played a big part. As Józef Jankowski put it, "I have stayed in close touch with my old buddies from the army. We meet every Friday to play cards and talk of the past glory." The veterans were also motivated by what they considered an unsympathetic reaction by part of the established Polish-Canadians community. When the veterans complained about their problems, they often heard that the pioneer generation had endured worse conditions on the land before the Second World War without receiving any support at all from the Canadian government.[31] As a result, some new Polish-Canadians came to feel that it was time for them to go their own way. Nevertheless, the two immigrant generations were not hostile towards each other. Kazimierz Klimaszewski considered that "Winnipeg was a friendly city and a home to many Poles who opened their hearts and homes to Polish veterans." There was extensive overlapping memberships in Polonia organizations such as churches and credit unions.

Virtually every veteran joined the Polish Combatants Association at the start, but membership soon shrank so dramatically that, as Henryk Lorenc reports, the remaining members "debated whether the PCA should continue as an independent organization or whether we should forget our Polish roots and join the Canadian Legion." They not only kept the PCA, but they started a series of social and cultural programs that established it as "one of the best and most prosperous branches in Canada [that could] serve as an example to other branches." In the 1950s, the branch organized a theatre group that performed plays regularly for the Polish-Canadian public across Manitoba and Northwest Ontario, ran a regular radio program, and hosted dignitaries from the London government-in-exile.[32]

Politically, the Combatants Association's ardent opposition to the post-war Polish communist regime became the norm in the Polish-Canadian community. The strong left-wing views of many Winnipeg Ukrainians and Jews had few counterparts among Manitoba Poles.[33] In 1949, the Combatants Association joined the Polish Canadian Congress, a coalition of social, veterans, and other organizations founded in 1944, and combatants quickly rose to high leadership positions. As late as 1985, the Polish Canadian Congress expressed loyalty to the aging and powerless Polish government-in-exile, and called for the return to Poland of the eastern territories that had been lost to the Soviet Union in 1939. And in 1989, the Combatants Association reaffirmed its support for the London government and the pre-1939 eastern borders, while somewhat illogically accepting the expanded 1945 western border awarded to Poland by the Big Three in 1945.[34]

This anti-communist position created strains with the Polish-Canadian community, although Ontario seems to have been more affected than Manitoba. Opposition to the Stalinist government was virtually unanimous within the Polish-Canadian community, but Stalin died in 1953 and Polish communist leader Władysław Gomułka, who came to power in October 1956, relaxed the terror, encouraging personal, cultural, and economic ties with the rest of the world, including Poles abroad. However, Poland remained a one-party state with a largely nationalized economy. The Combatants Association denied that these changes were significant, while some groups (mainly in Ontario) felt it was time to come to terms with a communist government that would not go away. Some of the strains in the late 1950s and early 1960s included debates over whether the historical and artistic treasures from the royal castle in Cracow, Poland, which had been sent to Canada for safekeeping during World War II, should finally be returned; they went home in 1961. As a result, the Polish Alliance, the leading secular Polish organization of the interwar period, withdrew from the Canadian Polish Congress from 1972 to 1981. The alliance insisted on returning the Wawel treasures to Poland, initiated contacts with the non-governmental Catholic University in Lublin, sent their children to courses for Polish-Canadian students at the state-run Jagiellonian University in Cracow, and invited Polish musicians to perform in Canada.[35]

Despite its political anti-communism, the Combatants Association never opposed contact with friends and relatives in Poland, and contributors to this volume began visiting as soon as circumstances permitted. Alojzy Bach stayed in touch with his family and visited in 1958. Kazimierz Chmielowicz also visited Poland in 1958 and maintained close ties after that. His visit provided a pleasant reunion with most of the family, but it caused difficulties for one brother who was an officer in the Polish army. Stanisław Kłoczkowski went to Poland in 1963, married a Polish woman, and brought her back to Canada. Jerzy Piskor maintained ties with his Polish relatives and visited them for the first time in 1968. The combatants welcomed new members such as Janina Popkiewicz, who emigrated in 1957.

The veterans who came to Canada as Poles slowly became Polish-Canadians. An early sign of adaptation may have been the formal association of the Winnipeg branch of the Combatants Association in 1954 with the Royal Canadian Legion, although that may just have been good politics (a looser form of organization occurred earlier).[36] A clearer sign came when they settled into Canadian life, joined immigrant associations, raised families, and passed their feelings of Polishness on to their children. Earlier generations of Polish immigrants based their sense of communal identity on church membership; fraternal organizations were generally church-based. This group of veterans, however, based its identity in the Combatants Association, even though most members are regular churchgoers and many refer to Christian values in these pages. As previously indicated, shared wartime and immigrant experiences drew the veterans together and made them less inclined to socialize with Polish-Manitobans who came to Canada before the Second World War or earlier. Jerzy Piskor noted that veterans "maintained good relations with the local Polish families and were invited to various celebrations" but rarely "married Polish-Canadian girls." Instead, they married recent immigrants like themselves.

Working in Polish-Manitoban organizations provides an important statement for self-identification. For example, Janina Popkiewicz refers to her impressive list of communal activities as working for "the Polish cause." Tadeusz Gardziejewski was active in the Scouting movement as well as with the Combatants Association. Lech Fulmyk devoted himself to *Czas* when it ran into trouble. Kazimierz Chmielowicz helped found the PCA credit union. Father Jan Sajewicz edited *Gazeta Polska* in Winnipeg.

The memoirists philosophically (and attractively) note the three most important achievements by which they measure the success of their own life: earning a decent living, providing for their children, and passing on their Polish heritage. Most of the authors bring this up in formulaic statements at the end of their articles. Jakub Plewa, for example, calls himself "a proud old man now." He is proud of fighting in the Polish army, proud of the Combatants Association, and proud of his children and grandchildren. Stefania Kociołek notes that, after a difficult beginning, "things got better and more plentiful. . . . Our family and our standard of living kept growing. Both our children finished university, both have settled in their careers. After the many tragic events of my youth, the summer and autumn of my life have been normal and quiet and happy." Education is a strong value for this group. As Henryk Kozubski notes, "since the war denied it [education] to them, they wanted to make damn sure that their children could get it."

The veterans are not free of anxiety about the future of the Polish identity that they prize, especially through the Combatants Association that has meant so much to them. Henryk Kozubski says that he

> would like to remain an optimist, yet thoughts about uncertain future weigh heavily on me: unless we manage to reach and appeal to our Polish youth, . . . our organization may become a mere footnote in a history book within a decade or so.

Similarly, Stanisław Kłoczkowski sees that changes will be needed to adapt the Combatants Association for the next generation. Lech Fulmyk stresses that he worked with the Winnipeg Polish newspaper, *Czas*, because "it is our duty to support and maintain that publication for the sake of our Polish past, our present, and particularly our future."

Bicultural identity has become important to the authors. They consider themselves to be both Polish and Canadian, and want their children to belong to both groups. Typically, Stanisław Kociołek is proud that his children and grandchildren "speak Polish well and are not ashamed of their Polish roots"; he is equally proud that his son-in-law is an officer in the Canadian army. Similarly, Wacław Kuzia is proud that "both my children finished university and speak Polish fluently. So does my little grandson." And Stanisław Smoleński Jr. is very proud of his children, who "all speak Polish" and continue to participate in both cultures in which they grew up. Adolf Franciszek Wawrzyńczyk suspects that he has "probably become a typical Canadian" but is invigorated by frequent visits to Poland and other parts of Europe. Janina Lorenc notes that "Canada has treated us well and look forward to our golden years with optimism and peace." Henryk Lorenc summarizes it best, saying that

I am convinced that Canada has benefitted greatly from the arrival of the Polish military immigrants. Statistics show that ninety percent of Polish veterans ensured their children finished university. Today that second generation of Polish Canadians holds many key positions in Canadian industry, commerce, and education. They have prospered in their parents' adoptive homeland and are now making it prosperous, drawing inspiration from their Polish roots and Canadian soil.

Tadeusz Wilton sees that "all my children have done very well for themselves and live much richer lives than I ever did," adding philosophically that "that is how it should be." Similarly, Stanisław Kociołek is "proud that for all those years I was never a burden to Canadians. In fact, I feel that myself and others like me have helped create the Canadian prosperity."

These statements show the distance that the thirty-nine male and nine female memoirists have come, both physically and emotionally. Twenty-one came from eastern Polish lands that were annexed to the Soviet Union, ten from central Poland (mostly around Warsaw), seven from southern Poland, and seven from western Poland. Of the total group, thirteen were deported to non-European parts of the Soviet Union in 1939-41; the men entered the Polish army after 1941, while most of the women and children went into refugee camps in Africa. Seven Poles served in Soviet labour camps, five went to Soviet prisons, three served in the Soviet army. Three served in the German army. Six memoirists left Poland through the Balkans to get to the Polish army in France. Four spent the war in German prisons or doing forced labour. Three served in the Polish underground. One served as a priest in Africa. Of the soldiers, twelve served in the infantry, nine in the motorized cavalry, seven in the artillery, five in the air force, three in the underground; there was one paratrooper and one military policeman. Three women were in the army, one as a nurse. Twenty-three persons served on the Italian Front. Two fought in North Africa and one in Holland. Three participated in the Polish underground.

In Canada, most of these authors worked at first on farms and then moved to the city. The great majority worked in blue-collar occupations: eleven for the Canadian railways, nine worked in machine factories (especially Inland Steel), six entered trades, three worked in garment factories. Several entered white-collar occupations: five laboratory technicians, four clerks, two bookkeepers, one priest, one chemist, and one university professor. None ever took unemployment insurance payments or welfare; when in need, they borrowed from their credit union.

Most memoirists practised Roman Catholicism. Thirty-nine started families; divorces were a rarity. Most bought their own homes and some bought summer cottages. War and immigration prevented most from pursuing higher education, but education was a premium and fifty-nine children finished university while ten took other post-secondary programs. Among the children, there are six doctors, five engineers, two lawyers, and one journalist. None of the memoirists was ever in trouble with the law in Canada.

The journeys of these forty-five memoirists from Poland to Canada were filled with adventure, hazard, and uncertainty, but they finished with finding a new home on the prairies. The presence of the Polish veterans here is largely an accident of war and international politics. None of the authors planned to emigrate in 1939 and the first farm labourers probably had no plans to remain here. In their new home, the veterans undertook new jobs, learned a new language, and mastered a new way of life, while keeping their Polish identity through a con-scious effort to live near other Poles and participate in Polish organi-zations. Starting as Poles in 1939, they eventually became Polish-Canadians, whose children and grandchildren will carry their own adaptations of their dual national loyalties and their rich view of the world into the future. The presence of these new Canadians, like the presence of other new Canadians, adds to the rich texture of Canadian society.

Daniel Stone
University of Winnipeg

1. November 19, 1946, *Czas.* Cited in Kazimierz Patalas, ed., *Przez boje, przez znoje, przez trud. Kombatanckie losy* (Winnipeg: SPK, 1996), 16-7.

2. Daniel Stone, *The Polish-Lithuanian State, 1386-1795* (Seattle: University of Washington Press, 2001).

3. See Norman Davies, *God's Playground. A History of Poland*, 2 vols. (Oxford: Oxford University Press, 1981); Norman Davies, *Heart of Europe. The Past in Poland's Present*, 2nd ed. (Oxford: Oxford University Press, 2001); Jerzy Lukowski and Adam Zawadzki, *A Concise History of Poland* (Cambridge: Cambridge University Press, 2001).

4. *Historia Polski w liczbach* (Warsaw: Glowny Urzad Statystyczny, 1994), 161-64; Lucjan Dobroszycki and Barbara Kirshenblatt-Gimblett, *Image Before My Eyes. A Photographic History of Jewish Life in Poland, 1864-1939* (New York: Schocken, 1977), 257-59.

5. See Orest Subtelny, *Ukraine. A History*, 3rd. ed. (Toronto: University of Toronto Press, 2000), 425-52.

6. Ezra Mendelssohn, *The Jews of East Central Europe Between the World Wars* (Bloomington: Indiana University Press, 1983), 11-83.

7. See Jan T. Gross, *Revolution from Abroad. The Soviet Conquest of Poland's Western Ukraine and Western Belorussia*, 2nd ed. (Princeton: Princeton University Press, 2002).

8. Ibid., 29-35, 146-50ff.

9. Ibid., 196-230.

10. Elena Osokina, *Our Daily Bread. Socialist Distribution and the Art of Survival in Stalin's Russia, 1927-1941* (Armonk, N.Y.: M.E. Sharpe, 2001), 166-75, 212.

11. Gross, *Revolution,* 146-60. See J.K. Zawodny, *Death in the Forest. The Story of the Katyn Forest Massacre* (London; Macmillan, 1971).

12. Władysław Anders, *An Army in Exile* (London: Macmillan, 1949), especially 47-60; Józef Garlinski, *Poland in the Second World War* (London: Macmillan, 1985), 113.

13. Garlinski, *Poland,* 149-62; Edward Soltys, *Road to Freedom* (Toronto: Polish Combatants Association, 1997), 7-8.

14. Anders, *Army in Exile*, 93-115; Garlinski, *Poland* 152, 155-6.

15. Daniel Stone, ed., *The Polish Memoirs of William John Rose* (Toronto: University of Toronto Press, 1975), 225.

16. David Engel, *Facing a Holocaust. The Polish Government-in-Exile and the Jews, 1943-1945* (Chapel Hill, N.C.: University of North Carolina Press, 1993), 97-100, 111-14. See also Garlinski, *Poland*, 231-32, and Jerzy Tomaszewski,

Najnowsze dzieje Żydow w Polsce (Warsaw: PWN, 1993), 373-74. Begin's description of hard labour in the Soviet Gulags contradicts the account given by Bolesław Czubak in this volume. See Menachem Begin, *White Nights* (New York: Harper and Row, 1977), 174.

17. Daniel Stone, "Coverage of the Holocaust in Poland in Winnipeg's Jewish and Polish Press, 1939-1945," *Polin. A Journal of Polish-Jewish Studies*, v. 19 (forthcoming).

18. Anders, *Army in Exile,* 175-85; John Keegan, *The Second World War* (New York: Viking, 1989), 360; B.H. Liddell-Hart, *History of the Second World War* (London: Cassell, 1970), 535; Garlinski, *Poland,* 251-56.

19. Soltys, *Road to Freedom,* 20; Garlinski, *Poland,* 47-60, 87-102.

20. Stefan Korbonski, *The Polish Underground State* (New York: Hippocrene, 1978), 104-107.

21. See, for example, Margaret Randolph Higonnet and others, *Behind the Lines. Gender and the Two World Wars* (New Haven: Yale University Press, 1987); and Marlene Epp, *Women without Men. Mennonite Refugees of the Second World War* (Toronto: University of Toronto Press, 2000).

22. Anders, *Army in Exile,* 376-78; Martin Thornton, *The Domestic and International Dimensions of the Resettlement of Polish Ex-Servicemen in Canada, 1943-1948* (Queenston, ON: Edwin Mellen Press, 2000); Stone, ed., *Memoirs of Rose,* 228.

23. Thornton, *Dimensions of Resettlement,* 125.

24. Ibid., 114. See Donald H. Avery, *Reluctant Host: Canada's Response to Immigrant Workers, 1896-1994* (Toronto: McClelland & Stewart, 1995), esp. 108-69.

25. Thornton, *Dimensions of Resettlement,* 42-45; Patalas, ed., *Przez boje,* 4-13. Henryk Kozubski, in this volume, served with the individual described in Irving Abella and Harold Troper, *None Is Too Many* (Toronto: Lester and Orpen Dennys, 1986), 218.

26. Thornton, *Dimensions of Resettlement,* 187-90ff.

27. Victor Turek, *Poles in Manitoba* (Toronto: Polish Alliance Press, 1967), 57, and elsewhere. Wacław Kuzia, in this volume, recounts having helped Turek immigrate to Canada. See also Edward Walewander, ed., *Leksykon geograficzno-historyczny parafii i kosciołow w Kanadzie,* vol. II (Lublin: KUL, 1982).

28. Soltys, *Road to Freedom,* 13; Thornton, *Dimensions of Resettlement,* 202-10.

29. Avery, *Reluctant Host,* 144-68.

30. July 30, 1947, *Czas.* Cited in Patalas, *Przez boje,* 29-31; Soltys, *Road to Freedom,* 28-9, 53-7.

31. Soltys, *Road to Freedom,* 45.

32. Ibid., 225. See pages 217-25 for a sketch of the Winnipeg branch.

33. Turek, *Poles in Manitoba,* 146-48, 212; Henryk Radecki with Benedykt Heydenkorn, eds., *A Member of a Distinguished Family. The Polish Group in Canada* (Toronto: McClelland and Stewart, 1976), 69-71.

34. See Benedykt Heydenkorn, ed., *A Community in Transition. The Polish Group in Canada* (Toronto: Canadian Polish Research Institute, 1985), especially 37-60, 111-18, 224. Edward Soltys and Benedykt Heydenkorn, *Trwanie w walce. Kulturowa analiza Stowarzyszenia Polskich Kombatantow w Kanadzie* (Toronto: Canadian Polish Research Institute, 1992), 209-10; Soltys, *Road to Freedom,* 98.

35. Radecki and Heydenkorn, eds., *A Community in Transition*, 100-107; Aloysius Balawyder, *The Odyssey of the Polish Treasures* (Antigonish, NS: St. Francis Xavier University Press, 1978).

36. Soltys, *Road to Freedom*, 217.

37. Kazimierz Patalas kindly provided this statistical survey.

ALOJZY BACH

I was born in Pomerania in 1925 into a large family and grew up with eleven brothers and five sisters. My father's first wife died during World War I, and he married my mother, widowed by the same war. Thus ours was a combined family from two marriages. My oldest brother was born in 1901; when the war broke out in 1939, three of my brothers were serving in the army, and I was fourteen.

In December 1939, I was shipped to Germany as a forced labourer. They sent me to a place named Kolesino near Szczecin and placed me on a farm, where I worked for over two years. In the meantime, Pomerania and Silesia were incorporated directly into the Reich, and Nazi authorities pressured local people to sign the Volksdeutsch list.[*] That pressure bordered on harassment if the families had German-sounding names, like ours. In 1942 my mother wrote to me and asked if I would mind her signing the list. We knew that if she signed it, all her children under eighteen would have to do the same; we also knew that I would be conscripted by the Germans. But what could I say? I let her decide what was best for the whole family. "If you think this will help you survive," I wrote back, "and will help my sisters avoid forced labour in Germany, I don't object." And so she signed the list.

I was called before the German recruitment commission in the spring of 1943 and was assigned to infantry. They trained us in

---

[*] Signing the Volksdeutsch list was equivalent to accepting German citizenship.

Konstanz, near the Swiss border. There were many Polish conscripts from Pomerania and Silesia in my unit; some did not know any German, and they really suffered for it. A year later, in May 1944, we were stationed in Holland. There, during some exercises, I had a mishap and badly hurt my knee. This proved a blessing in disguise, for I spent a month in the hospital, and this probably saved me from being sent to the Russian front. When I had recovered and returned to active duty, I was dispatched to the front in France, for this was already after the Allied invasion.

Fighting the Americans was no picnic. One night my detachment was supposed to attack a village. A German sergeant and myself were doing some reconnaissance when we were pinned down in the middle of a stony field by heavy artillery bombardment. I got hold of a large piece of rock and placed it in front of me to protect my head from flying shrapnel. After two hours, taking advantage of a short lull in the fire, we made it to a barn. Inside it was warm and cozy, with four horses and twenty cows to keep us company. At dawn our situation was critical, so the sergeant suggested that we exchange our addresses in case one of us didn't make it. We talked about surrendering to the Americans: all German soldiers knew that it was the surest way to survive the madness of war. I jumped at the chance, but he felt honourbound and wouldn't go for it. In the end, he decided to hide deep in the bowels of the barn, while I raised my arms and slowly walked out. It was December 8, 1944. I was escorted to the prisoner registration offices, where the Americans recorded my personal data, and sent me to a temporary holding area, where I stayed for two weeks.

Despite my German-sounding name, I identified myself, without a moment's hesitation, as a Pole, and so did many others in my holding area. The Americans knew we had been forcibly conscripted and served in the German army under duress. They separated us from other German prisoners; they also set apart all prisoners from the units of General Vlasov.* For a while the Americans conducted debriefings and interrogations, and then they brought all Poles to Marseille, put us

---

* Andrej Andrejevich Vlasov (1900-1946), a Soviet general captured with his army by the Germans in 1942. He later commanded the Russian Liberation Army, formed by the Germans and composed of Soviet prisoners of war, which fought against the Red Army.

aboard a ship, and sent us to Taranto in Italy. There we became Polish soldiers and were assigned to various units of the 2nd Polish Corps. My group of twenty-five Wermacht ex-conscripts was incorporated into the Carpathian Lancers Regiment. We were duly registered and assigned various duties; I was sent to a communications training course.

The training lasted for six weeks, and, on its completion, I was sent into action on the so-called Gothic Line. Placed in the first squadron of heavy armoured vehicles, I rode as a radio operator. Our commanders were Captain Mentel and Lieutenant Mieczkowski; my platoon leader was 2nd Lieutenant Tomaszewski. I had no difficulty adjusting to Polish military discipline, for, in general, German discipline was stricter.

One episode from the last days of the war burned itself into my memory. We had just rounded up a group of German soldiers and taken them prisoner. Many of them carried excellent automatic guns—Schmeisers—so a friend of mine, Morawiec, asked for permission to get out of the armoured vehicle and collect their arms. The lieutenant reluctantly gave him permission, and Morawiec opened the hutch in the turret. No sooner had he stuck out his head than a single shot rang out and he slumped back into the vehicle, half his head blown off. The shot came from the group of prisoners, and our men, furious at the treachery, immediately trained their guns on them. They quickly picked out the one who killed Morawiec and, had it not been for Lieutenant Tomaszewski's firm orders, verging on threats, the perpetrator would have been riddled with bullets. But Tomaszewski held his ground, kept the flaring tempers in check, and sent the prisoners to the rear. And so my good friend Morawiec tragically lost his life a month before the end of the war, and we, thirsting for vengeance, were forced to remain on the moral high ground.

After the war we remained stationed in Italy for a while. To keep the troops occupied and to maintain the discipline, commanders placed a lot of emphasis on sports and sporting events. I took part in one divisional competition and even won the bronze in my race. The names of the winners were announced through the loudspeakers at the arena. It so happened that my uncle, who soon afterwards returned to Poland, was also there. He heard my name read out, and when he went back, he let my family know that I was alive. I contacted my family a few months later through the Red Cross. In 1946, when I arrived in Britain,

I got in touch with my brother, also through the Red Cross; he was stationed in Edinburgh and came to see me in Grimsby.

At the Hensley camp in Liverpool, where I spent some time, several commissions were accepting applications for emigration to various Commonwealth countries. I chose Canada. Before long, I was called before a commission, which enquired about my knowledge of farming and examined my physical condition to make sure I could work in the fields. Today we laugh at their questions—they asked us, for instance, if we could tell wheat from oats—but it did not seem funny then. I must have met all their criteria, for I got my two-year contract as a farm labourer and some time later arrived in Halifax with a group of 550 Polish ex-servicemen. Then we boarded a train for what we had been warned was going to be a very long ride. We knew we were going to Manitoba, but no one knew exactly where it was. Finally, we got off the train at the station in Winnipeg and transferred to the awaiting trams, which took us to the barracks. We were all still wearing our uniforms, and on June 1, we took part in the Decoration Day parade. They divided us into two companies, led by 2nd Lieutenant Baranowski and 2nd Lieutenant Panek. The Polish Gymnastic Association Sokół loaned us their colours, and we marched with them before the stand.

I remember our welcome in Winnipeg. Not all the locals were delighted that we had arrived; some openly asked, "What the hell did they come here for?" But the majority opened their hearts and their families to us. They invited us to dinners and introduced us to their friends in the parish of the Holy Spirit. I was most graciously received by the Rakowskis in Transcona. We have been close friends ever since.

After two weeks in the barracks, we were split into three groups: one destined for Emerson, one for Lettelier, and one for Roland. I found myself in the Lettelier group and went to work in the sugar beet fields. We were paid not by the hour but by a mile-long row. The more rows we thinned, the more we earned, but even the hardest working among us did not make much. When the sugar beet season was over, we were assigned to individual farmers; here I was lucky, for my farmer in La Salle, of French descent, turned out to be a very decent person and good to me. After the harvest, we returned to the sugar beet camps and worked on that contract until the first frost. In November, we were brought back to Winnipeg and told to look for farm work through the Employment Office. We were still bound by our two-year contracts. Some of my more enterprising colleagues found themselves farmers who signed formal declarations that they were working on their farms, while in fact they had gone to work in the forest as lumberjacks, making much more money. But I am straightforward by nature and prefer to stick to laws and regulations, so I went where I was sent, to a farm in Brandon. I arrived there in the evening, just in time for supper, and got up to work at 5:00 a.m. the following morning. Breakfast was at 6:00 a.m., and then we got a ride to the forest, where we cut lumber for the farmer. It was hard, cold work, and had nothing to do with farming, so I requested that the Employment Office change my assignment. A week later I was in Woodnorth. Here we got up at 8:00 a.m. during winter, and earlier when the day grew longer. The working conditions were much better, and the pay was decent ($60 per month in winter and $110 after April). In fact, I stayed on this farm for over a year and remember that time quite fondly, for I was treated as a member of the family.

When my contract was over, I returned to Winnipeg. I tried my luck as a lumberjack in Ontario, but the advent of winter forced us to look for work elsewhere. I applied for a job in a mine in Sudbury, but they had no positions available. I came back to Winnipeg, and took a cheap room (a dollar a day plus thirty-five cents for breakfast) and any work I could find. But that was not the life I wanted. So I conferred with several of my friends with whom I met regularly after work, and we decided to sign up as miners at a gold mine in Snow Lake in northern Manitoba. I lasted there for more than a year, from 1949 to 1950, working harder than I had ever worked in my life but also making more money than I had ever seen: $1100 a month, a fortune in those days. I needed all that money, for I wanted to sponsor the immigration of one of my brothers from Poland. Back in Winnipeg, I applied for a job at the Canadian Pacific Railway, in the meantime working for a construction company, Birth Construction. Jobs at the CPR were highly prized by Poles, for the work was permanent. The company, in its turn, appreciated the skills of Polish workers; assistant work manager Lenowski thought highly of Polish veterans and had no qualms about hiring them. I started at eighty-five cents per hour, climbing to $13.50 by the time I retired. I remained a loyal employee of the CPR, without interruption, from 1950 to 1985. For five years I also attended night school to raise my qualifications. That extra education helped me advance to the position of CPR inspector.

I married in 1953. My wife was an orphan. When she was nine, she was picked up by the Germans in the streets of Cracow; her parents were murdered at Oświęcim [Auschwitz]. It was a traumatic experience for her, and to this day films about Oświęcim deeply affect her, often causing depression. We have not had our own children, but we adopted a boy, Michael, and he has been our only son. Now we even have a granddaughter.

I had joined the Polish Combatants Association [PCA] already in 1946 while still in England. Here in Winnipeg, I helped organize the so-called Mutual Help Association. Every working member paid $5 a month to our common fund, which we then used to give inexpensive loans to those who needed them. Later, this association was replaced by the PCA Credit Union. Since 1962 I have also managed our PCA banquet hall, and even ran the beer parlour there for a couple of years. Our Saturday night dance parties have become a tradition. In the old days, we enforced a dress code, a jacket and a tie. Since we did not want to alienate any guests who may have been unaware of our dress code, we always kept several ties on hand and rented them to those less formally dressed. Times have changed, and today we pay less attention to formal attire. The new waves of Polish immigrants have been generally well dressed, and we see no reason to adhere to the old rules. Our establishment has always had a good reputation with the local law enforcement authorities and the Liquor Control Commission. Thanks to the income we generate, our Chapter #13 has been able to launch several social initiatives, such as financial help for invalids in Canada and in Poland.

I have stayed in touch with my family in Poland and visited them in 1968. After so many years, my return was very emotional. I spent many days and nights in the midst of my family, remembering the past and discussing the present. I was asked if Mother's signing the Volksdeutsch list had any negative consequences for me in Canada. Unfortunately, I had to admit that it did, for to this day some of my colleagues remind me about it, implicitly accusing me and my family of wartime opportunism, even though they have no idea under what circumstances Mother signed the list. I certainly do not feel even a shadow of guilt or shame. Saying goodbye after that visit was difficult and sad. Some sixty-three people came to see me off at the airport in Wrzeszcz near Gdańsk. We promised one another to stay in touch. We did and still do.

HELENA BATOR

My home town is Ostrów [Ostrov] in the Lwów [L'viv] region. I was living there when the war of 1939 broke out. My youngest sister was born that same year. In the early 1930s, my father worked in Canada. When he returned to Poland in 1936, we moved to Żółkiew [Zhovkva], closer to Lwów. Father bought some land, newly parcelled out, and put up new farm buildings. I suppose we were part of the general drive to Polonize those territories, populated mostly by Ukrainians, who were not allowed to purchase any subdivided land. In frustration, they often muttered threats that one day they would cut all our throats.

Shortly before the war, my brother, Józef, experienced a calling and joined the religious order in Niepokalanów. With a heavy heart, my mother said goodbye to her only son, who had decided to become a priest. But it never came to pass, for the war broke out, and Father Maksymilian Kolbe[*] blessed his brothers and sent them away, saying, "God be with you, maybe we'll meet after the storm." Józef returned home just as we were finishing the harvest. German planes were flying low over the fields, shooting at farm machinery and anything that moved. Then on September 17, the Bolsheviks invaded.

The Bolsheviks left us alone until February 10, 1940. On that day, at six in the morning, the Soviets banged on our doors, told us to gather

---

[*] Maksymilian Kolbe (1894-1941), a Franciscan friar who volunteered to die in place of another man at Oświęcim (Auschwitz), canonized by Pope John Paul II in 1982.

our things, and loaded us, eleven people in all, onto a sleigh. My father and brother were not home at the time, and we were frightened, for we remembered well the Ukrainian threats. They took us to the local train station, where we had to wait for a train for two whole weeks. In the meantime, Father and Józef rejoined us, and the family was united again. When the train finally began moving eastwards, we were already tired, cold, and hungry. The hardships of that journey are impossible to describe. Although the car had a small iron stove in the middle, we had so little coal that burning it made little difference. We were starving: the only food we had was what we had brought with us or what friends had given us along the way. And the journey was long, excruciatingly long, with freezing days turning into famished weeks. The train stopped often, but we were never allowed to get out.

After a month of suffering on the train, we arrived at Sverdlovsk, in the Ural Mountains. The Soviets transferred us onto sleighs and carried us deep into the forest, to a small settlement of about 400 people, mostly Germans and Ukrainians, who had been brought there before us. They showed us much compassion, for they understood our situation. Theirs had been even worse, they told us, for they had been dumped into deep snow and had to begin by digging earth shelters. We, at least, had houses waiting for us. Here, too, food was scarce. Once I lined up for bread from 4:00 p.m. till 7:00 a.m. I froze my feet only to find out that the bread would not be delivered that day. Some local people did open their hearts to us, though. A woman took pity on our little Zosia and gave half the milk from her only nanny-goat to her own child and the other half to my little sister. Sometimes she also shared an egg with us.

I was too young to work with the adults, so I was sent to school, to the fourth grade. The indoctrination was so blatant and so stupid—they tried to instil in us the sentiment that Stalin was God—that I stopped attending. Instead, I went to help my father and my brother in the forest. I collected loose branches and burned them. The pay was meagre, although it did not make much difference, for there was little to buy in the settlement anyway. Only those who worked qualified for rations of bread: 600 grams per person, later reduced to 400 grams.

Our houses were infested with bedbugs, so we had to burn resinous chips to get some relief from the bugs. We had no electricity, of course. In those primitive conditions, Christmas was not a joyous occasion. We were not allowed to pray or sing Christmas carols, and the Soviet children were often sent to spy on us and see if anyone was breaking the ban on religion. Sundays had nothing to do with the Lord but everything to do with communist propaganda. An officer responsible for political indoctrination, a *politruk*, would read a newspaper article and then sing the praises of Stalin and socialism. He told us that in Canada and the United States people were so hungry that they ate one another. He told us there was no Poland and never would be. He told us that Stalin was a protector of all working people. We, of course, knew that these were all lies, blatant, stupid lies.

When the amnesty was finally announced,* we packed our things and were sent south, to Qizil Ribat in Uzbekistan. There I worked on a collective farm, a *kolkhoz*, carting dirt in a wheelbarrow and gathering cotton. Those who worked got one corn pancake a day; others got nothing. We were starving so badly that some people bloated from hunger. We even ate dead cats and, once, a dead donkey. Sometimes I caught turtles for food; sometimes I stole. One had to steal; there was no other way to survive. People were dying in large numbers from hunger, from hardship, from disease. Four women from our room died. We wrapped them up in sheets and carried them to the graveyard on stretchers. One of my aunts died then, and one of my sisters, too. One funeral procession followed another. It was only when we moved to another *kolkhoz*, where they grew tomatoes, that our situation improved somewhat.

One day we got the news that my brother was seriously ill in the military hospital and had asked to see us before he died. Tearful, we went to Buzuluk, only to find both him and my father in perfect health. Józef's supposed illness turned out to be a ruse designed to get us out of the hopelessness of the *kolkhoz* and under the wings of the Polish army. With my father and my brother in the army, I decided to volunteer as well and signed up for the Youth Corps. I was fifteen at the time. We were issued new uniforms, but they did not help much against the lice and hunger that tormented us. We dealt with lice through weekly disinfections, but for the hunger we had no remedy. When General

---

* Polish political prisoners and deportees to Siberia were formally released from camps and prisons on the basis of an agreement, guaranteeing their amnesty, signed by the Polish and Soviet governments in 1941. The same agreement provided for the formation of the Polish army in the Soviet Union.

Sikorski* visited our camp, we tried to line up in front of him, but some girls were so weak they could barely stand. He told us to sit down and asked us about our families.

Finally the long-awaited moment arrived when we left Russia for Persia. From that period I remember mostly sickness and death ravaging our young army. Things got better the further we moved from Russia. We went first by trucks through the mountains to Tehrān, and later to Egypt. At one point in my peregrinations I met again with my brother and father. What a joyous occasion that was! In Palestine I attended a business school for a while but soon abandoned the idea and joined the Women's Auxiliary. I was dispatched to England and assigned to the air force. After a crash course in aviation mechanics, I served with the ground crew, servicing and maintaining the planes. Each of us had a narrow, precisely defined range of responsibilities: I checked the lines and clutches controlling the wings. We took our jobs very seriously, for we knew that an error on our part could cost the lives of the flight crew. Every time a plane did not return from a mission, we grieved for every member of its crew. I also experienced some personal grief when I learned that my brother had died in action near Loreto, Italy, in 1944.

By the time the war was over, I had served four years in the army. We did not rejoice as much as the British did at the news that Germany had capitulated because we knew we had no homes to go to. Our family began to reassemble in England: my father and I were already there, and my mother and two sisters came from a camp in Africa, but my brother and one sister would never rejoin us.

It was our old family ties that decided our future. Both my father and mother had siblings who had lived in Canada for many years. They sponsored us to Canada and guided our first steps here. Still the beginnings were difficult. I knew very little English, and jobs were hard to find. But eventually life settled into a rhythm. I began to work as a seamstress, met a Polish immigrant deported to Germany as a labourer, married him, and had a daughter. She, too, is married now, and I can boast of a beautiful granddaughter.

---

* Władysław Sikorski (1881-1943), premier of the Polish government-in-exile and commander-in-chief of the Polish forces fighting alongside the Allies in World War II.

I am an active member of the Polish Combatants Association, and for seven years served as president of the Emilia Plater Women's Auxiliary. I am also a member of the Polish Women's Federation, Cell #7. I am very fond of these Polish organizations. They give me an opportunity to get in touch with our small Poland in Winnipeg, where we can speak and feel Polish even though we are a part of Canada.

FELIKS BIŁOS

A trumpet has been my companion ever since the tender years of my childhood. Always by my side, it has helped me celebrate moments of joy, and survive times of hardship and even tragedy.

My first teacher was my father: he played the trumpet with passion and wanted his son to follow in his footsteps. Learning the basics was tedious and painful, for he had little patience and would pull my ears if the tones were not clear. To save my ears from this torture, my mother insisted that someone else give me trumpet lessons. That person was a member of the orchestra in Wiśnicz Dolny, in the region of Bochnia, who took his pedagogical duties so seriously that in a short time I became a competent trumpeter and was even invited to play with the orchestra. Wiśnicz Dolny had a long-standing musical tradition, and it fell to me to continue it.

My trumpeting skills came in handy when I was serving in the army, in the NCO School of the 10th Division in Radzymin, where I was recruited for the divisional light jazz orchestra. That musical side of the military life was partly responsible for my staying in the army beyond the usual prescribed term. Unfortunately, my budding musical career was interrupted by the war. I was serving in the army transport and supply columns and was responsible for 300 carts and 600 horses. In the very first days of the war, we became the prime target for German bombers, which effectively destroyed our unit. But it is September 17 that I remember most vividly, when the Soviets unexpectedly stabbed us in the back by invading Poland from the east. Worn out, surrounded, and confused, we had no other choice but to surrender to them. Knowing who we were dealing with, we had destroyed our identification papers and rank badges. The captors searched us and stole our watches and anything else of value we had on our bodies. I claimed to be a resident of Tarnopol [Ternopil'] and managed to make my way through Lwów [L'viv] to Przemyśl. But that's where my luck ran out: a Soviet officer recognized me there, and I ended up in jail and on trial. I was charged with illegally crossing the border and was sentenced to five years in a Siberian camp. From that point onward, I followed the well-trodden path of many Polish prisoners in Russia. I was shipped to the vicinity of Arkhangelsk to cut lumber in the forest, blistering my hands to meet the daily quota, which earned me the meagre, starving food rations. In a reflex of self-defence, I began to feign infirmity, limping whenever the guards were around. My deception worked, and I was admitted to the 40th Brigade, comprised entirely of invalids. Our bread rations were trimmed, but at least we did not have to work so hard. When they were looking for someone knowledgeable about horses, I volunteered and was sent to work as a water carrier. The job required that I got up earlier than the others, but it offered opportunities of winning additional food rations, which was the basis for survival in the camp.

Here again the trumpet wove itself into my fate. In Soviet and German camps, prisoners walked to and from work to the accompaniment of the camp band. When our bandmaster, a Greek, found out I could play the trumpet and read sheet music, he requested that I be assigned to his band. So once again I played the trumpet. My friends from other brigades swore at me for playing along with the Soviets, but not for long. They changed their tune when they discovered that, as an orchestra member, I could get additional rations of bread, which I then freely shared with them. The trumpet helped us survive the camp.

We began to hear rumours that someone somewhere was forming a Polish army, but nobody knew anything for certain. Then one night we were woken up for a roll call. A Soviet soldier read a list of fifty Polish names, mine among them, and announced that we would not have to go to work the following morning because we were leaving for the Polish army. It was a shock to us, a shock of joy. We could hardly believe our luck; people were crying and laughing and shouting in patriotic fervour. Those whose names had not been read out were also crying, but for being left out. We consoled them, saying that, if it was true that the Polish army was being resurrected, they would eventually join it as well. We left the camp the very next day at noon, and not in cattle trucks but in a real passenger train. Our sudden change of fortune was so unbelievable that we pinched ourselves to make sure we were not dreaming. Yesterday we had been starving prisoners, and today we were recruits and in the Polish army, to boot.

My passage to Tatishchevo was anything but dull. When we reached Yerchevo, in all that excitement and commotion, some scoundrel stole all my papers. I had to go to the NKVD office* for new travel documents, and in the meantime my train left. Eventually, after many more and even less pleasant adventures, I arrived in Tatishchevo and duly registered as a volunteer for the Polish army. Some time later, an officer came from Buzuluk to pick some soldiers for his lancers unit. I am not sure how, but I managed to get selected for his unit. We were a handsome bunch, some 150 men strong, and to our delight we were detached as the personal squadron of General Anders.† After many subsequent name changes, our squadron became the 2nd Podole Lancers Regiment.

And here I must again return to my trumpet. Since an army cannot exist without a band, the division command began to seek out soldiers with musical experience. The commander of my squadron, Captain Florkowski, knew about my fondness for the trumpet and knew I had bought one for fifty rubles and a piece of soap. I sometimes played it when I was off duty. So I, along with two other NCOs who also played musical instruments, was detached from the squadron to play in the band. We gave our first public performance on the occasion of General Sikorski's visit in Buzuluk. In the ringing cold, we tried to play a springy march, but the result was rather pitiful. General Sikorski only nodded with understanding, acknowledging that he was aware our fingers were stiff with cold and the instruments out of tune for the same reason.

When the decision was announced to evacuate from Russia, the

---

* People's Commissariat of Internal Affairs, or NKVD, was the Soviet political police and state security agency, which controlled the entire civilian population as well as the army.

† Władysław Anders (1892-1970), commander of the Polish army in the Soviet Union (later the 2nd Polish Corps).

band was also ready to go. But first, in the middle of a severe winter, we went to Yangi-Yul, where intensive military exercises were taking place. It was a cruel time, what with sickness, exhaustion, and starvation. We had our hands full playing funeral marches and paying last respects to dozens of friends. Finally, after months of painful waiting, we were ready to leave for Krasnovodsk. General Anders had received special permission from General Zhukov,* who was in charge of the evacuation, to take with him the band and a set of musical instruments. As we were about to board the ship, we learned that we were not allowed to take Soviet money abroad. At the same time, our conductor found out that Russian rubles were good money in Persia. Many of us decided to hide the rubles wherever possible, and our instruments seemed best suited for this purpose, so we stuffed their chambers full of banknotes. After showing our special permit, we boarded the ship without any difficulty, escorted by several NKVD officers. With the ship ready to sail, we were ordered to play the Soviet and Polish national anthems. The band members went pale with fright but did not lose their cool. The clarinets, saxophones, and other thin instruments led the way, supported by drums and percussion, while we, with our trumpets and trombones dumb with red rubles, tried to imitate their sounds with our own voices. We must have done quite well, for we certainly fooled them. Out on the high seas, we finally relieved our instruments of their unusual cargo, and after landfall, we blew them with full force, marching at the head of the long column of soldiers.

In Iran, we resumed the arduous and demanding work of a military band. I remember the day when General Sikorski visited our troops in Kirkuk. Our band played while he was having dinner. Only a few days later, the news struck us like a thunder from the cloudless sky that our Supreme Commander, General Sikorski, had died in a plane crash in Gibraltar. The orchestra fell silent, and the soldiers, so used to the harvest of death, were saddened and dispirited.

But the war and our training went on. When we reached Palestine, many Jews asked for short leaves, which were generally granted by the command. Half the orchestra was Jewish, and these musicians, too, went for leaves. Seventeen of them never returned, so for a while the

---

* Georgi Konstantinovich Zhukov (1896-1974), one of the key Soviet generals during World War II.

band practically ceased to exist. But since nothing under the sun is irreplaceable, we soon received reinforcements from other units, and after some readjustments, we were back in service. In the course of further reorganizations, the band became attached to the high command, and we, the NCOs assigned to it for the time being, returned to our units. I was back in the 3rd Squadron of the 2nd Podole Lancers Regiment. With this unit, I went through many battles in Italy, this time fighting with a rifle rather than a trumpet. I fought at Monte Cassino, Piedmont, Monte Cassaro, Arezzo, and other places. I was awarded several medals for my efforts, including the Cross of Bravery, which my colleagues who stayed with the band envied me the most.

After the war, I was transferred to England, and from there to the sugar beet fields of Manitoba. When my two-year contract as a farm labourer expired, I found a job at Dominion Bridge, and have worked for this company for the last twenty-nine years, the last eleven as a crane operator. I also started a family, and my son is now studying medicine in Scotland.

And my trumpet, the one I bought in Buzuluk? It stayed with me throughout my Italian campaign, and later crossed the seas and the ocean with me. It has accompanied me in the midst of battlefields and beet fields. I've played it in Winnipeg at various social events, and it is with me still, although both of us are now enjoying a well-deserved retirement.

KAZIMIERZ CHMIELOWICZ

I was born in 1918, in Krzemienna, district of Brzozów, near Sanok. After graduating from a classics high school,* I decided on a career in the military. In 1938, I signed up at the Artillery College for Officer Cadets in Włodzimierz [Vladimir]. After the first year, I requested— and was granted—permission to transfer to the Vocational Artillery College for Officer Cadets in Toruń. Unfortunately, I never reached my new school, for in September 1939 the war broke out.

With the rank of cadet corporal, I was assigned to the 33rd Light Artillery Division in Wilno [Vilnius]. Because of the tragic course of the September campaign, we were forced to withdraw to Lithuania. We crossed the border and surrendered our guns, minus the locks, to the Lithuanians. We were interned in Rokiskis, where several thousand soldiers were gathered, mostly artillerymen and lancers. The Lithuanians held us there until the Soviet invasion of Poland—that is, until September 17. Then the Russians moved in and took charge of the internees. They immediately began selecting officers and sending them to Kozel'sk, and from there—as we learned later—to their deaths in Katyn. Eventually, we, too, were taken by train to Kozel'sk. At one of the stops along the way, Soviet soldiers came to our car looking for Colonel Dąbrowski. When they found him, one of them said, "O, I pity you, Dąbrowski." But Dąbrowski retorted, "Have no pity for me. I had

---

* An old style of high school with an emphasis on the humanities, including the Greek and Latin languages.

none for you in 1918 and 1920."* They took him away, and we never saw him again.

At Kozel'sk, the Soviets began a campaign of propaganda and indoctrination. Every day after supper, *politruks* [propaganda officers] came for "serious" talks. They tried to convince us that the communist system was the best in the world and encouraged us to collaborate with them. No one believed them, of course, and no one was willing to engage in discussions with them. This continued until the outbreak of the war with Germany. Then they shipped us up north, to the Kola Peninsula, where we worked building roads. Later they transferred us even further north to Murmansk, where the sun never set during summer months, where the workday was sixteen hours long, and where food was scarce and starving prisoners many. There were some 2000 of us in that camp, mostly officer cadets, NCOs, soldiers, and policemen. Luckily, we did not stay in that cursed place for long.

The cruelty of the Soviet system indeed succeeded in changing our political sentiments, although not in the way the Soviets had intended. We cheered at the news of German victories on the Russian front. Who would have thought we would be pleased at the news of Hitler's progress! But his progress prompted the Soviets to sign the pact with Sikorski and to allow the rebuilding of the Polish army in the Soviet Union. Soon afterwards all Poles from our camp were put aboard a ship; only then were we told that we were going to join the Polish army. In Totskoye, tents were already waiting for us. We were registered and assigned to various services and units. I found myself in the 6th Light Artillery Regiment. We went through the basic training in Russia, then were transferred by ships to Iran. At long last we could breathe freely.

In Khānaqīn I was promoted to 2nd lieutenant and made a platoon leader. This promotion not only enhanced my standing in the army but also my wages: I was now getting £25 a month, nothing to sneer at. My platoon consisted of two guns and a crew; two platoons formed a battery. We finally got some British equipment, including 75 mm guns with a range of up to thirty kilometres, and resumed training full time. When we reached combat readiness, our regiment was transferred to

---

* A reference to the Polish-Russian wars after the Bolshevik Revolution.

southern Italy and went into action on the Sangro River. In May 1944, we dug in around Monte Cassino. Before the main assault, we tested our guns, which brought us under heavy fire from German artillery. On May 11, at 11:00 p.m., when the assault started, our 1500 guns roared in unison and hurled a hail of deadly shells on German positions. We kept firing throughout the night until early morning. When the gun barrels overheated, we cooled them with wet blankets. To reach the centre of the German positions, we experimented with firing the guns under a much wider angle than usual, imitating howitzers, and had some excellent results. The Germans stopped shelling us, so we had no casualties, but the Canadians, who were right beside us, did get hit a few times, and they lost a few good men.

After the victory at Monte Cassino, I got a month off, which I used to do some sightseeing, especially in Rome. In Castel Gandolfo we got new, heavier guns and were regrouped as the 9th Heavy Artillery Regiment. Two squadrons were equipped with seven-inch howitzers with the range of thirty to forty kilometres, while two others had 155 mm guns with the range in excess of fifty kilometres. The power of those guns became evident when we saw a little church collapse from the vibrations caused by firing them. We brought those heavy guns to bear in the battles for Ancona and Bologna. In the final stages of our Italian campaign, our ranks were reinforced by the Polish POWs from the German army and by some others who reached us from France and England. After Bologna I was promoted to lieutenant and appointed deputy company commander.

The war was over, and the time came to dismantle our heavy equipment. I received the order to take our guns to a collection point in Rimini. Moving with those large, heavy guns through the narrow streets was not easy. At a particularly difficult turn, we lost control of one gun, and it slammed into a lineman's booth, resting just beside the railway tracks. Just then we saw a passenger train approaching. We tried to pull the gun back but to no avail. The train went past us without slowing down, and the barrel of the gun smashed all the windows on that side of the train. The barrel, too, was smashed so badly that I could not fix it. As it turned out, fixing it was quite unnecessary, for after we surrendered the guns, all the barrels were cut off. It was hard to watch those powerful weapons being mutilated and turned into scrap metal, but not nearly as hard as giving up the guns after the defeat in 1939, when seasoned soldiers were literally in tears.

Although we had won the war, we continued training and were encouraged to play various sports. Healthy exertion and competition helped maintain army discipline and good morale. I played on a soccer team. We were also getting ready to move to England. To fortify ourselves against the anticipated seasickness, we drank quite a bit, and then filled five-gallon containers full of whisky and smuggled them aboard the ship. As far as I know, no one was seasick during that sea passage to Southampton, although some complained of hangovers.

From Southampton we went by train to Scotland and were quartered in barracks, the so-called "barrels of laughter." But the decisions we had to make were not laughable: should we go back to Poland or should we emigrate? Personally, I did not hesitate. I had lost all contact with my family there, and after my experiences in Russia, I had no illusions about socialist Poland. I went before the medical commission qualifying for emigration to Canada and was ready to go as soon as I received my acceptance papers.

I arrived in Canada in 1947 with a group of ex-servicemen; all of us had signed contracts obliging us to work on Canadian farms for two years. Three representatives of the old Polish community—Maria Panaro, Waleria Szczygielska, and Michał Szarzyński—came to meet us at the railway station in Kenora and greeted us warmly. In Winnipeg, we were placed in barracks, and three days later were sent out to various farms. I happened to be assigned to a farmer named Walker in Elva, near Melita. I worked for him for six months before my patience and forbearance gave out, mainly because of the long hours of milking cows by hand. I returned to Winnipeg and found a job as a house painter, first for a Pole and then for a larger construction company.

Around the same time, I started singing in the choir of the Polish Gymnastics Association Sokół, and there I met my future wife, Halina. Although we were very much in love, we had to postpone our marriage plans for almost a year while she was finishing a year-long nursing course. In the meantime, I was lucky to get a job with Inland Steel, thanks to Konstanty Jackiewicz, who had already been working for that company for a while. Many Polish veterans worked there, and they helped others get hired as well. I began as a welder and was soon promoted to foreman, supervising several other welders. It was a good job, and I thought I would stay there for good, but then an opportunity arose

46

to set up my own business, so I quit. Together with Junkierski (and later Wójcik), I opened and ran a Polish butcher shop called "Wawel."

My life soon became settled between my business and my family. We had children, five daughters. The oldest, Basia, moved to the United States after graduating from the university; the youngest, who finished her studies just recently, now lives in Calgary.

Through the Red Cross, I re-established contact with my family in Poland. I went to visit them for the first time in 1958. Later I began sending my daughters to Poland from time to time to ensure that they could speak their native tongue fluently. Over the years, we have also had visitors from Poland.

But not all family reunions ended on a pleasant note. I have a brother in Poland, five years my junior, who had chosen a military career in the communist army and even reached the rank of lieutenant colonel. He is retired now. During my first visit to Poland in 1958, I wanted to meet him, so I phoned the army but could not get his address, or even his telephone number. At last I received a message from Warsaw, from my brother, saying that his son would get in touch with me. He did, and through him we arranged to meet in my brother's flat in Gniezno. After so many years of separation, the hugs and greetings were warm and heartfelt. But then my brother began to excuse himself, saying that he had no idea why they would refuse to give me his address. This did not sound very sincere, and I did not quite believe him. The next day he had a phone call from someone in the army. "We must go to see my commander; he wants to meet you," he said. We went. There was a small office with a desk and a small table on the side. In the corner sat a nondescript person writing down everything that was said in the room. After the ritual introductions, the colonel—my brother's commander—apologized that he could not offer me any alcohol because they had closed their mess-room. He asked how I was doing in Canada and what I did for a living. I told him I was doing fine and that I was working as a butcher, making hams, sausages, and the like. "You had been an officer in the army, hadn't you?" he asked, not at all innocently. I knew he was insinuating that my current occupation brought disgrace on my former military rank, so I said, "Yes, I was, but now I am making an honest living as best I can, given the circumstances." His next question shocked me even more, "And which regiments, which services are stationed in Winnipeg?" This crude attempt at turning me into an informer infuriated me, and I told him that I had not come to Poland to bring them information about Canadian regiments. I did not know who was stationed in Winnipeg because I took no interest in it. If he wanted to know, he could come to Winnipeg and easily find out for himself. Unperturbed by my outburst, he said he could not go but my brother might. That was the end of our conversation. I was so upset by his brazenness and audacity that, on my return to Winnipeg, I went to the RCMP and told them exactly what had happened.

Lately, I have finally retired, but I continue to participate in various activities of the Polish organizations. My involvement with the Polish Combatants Association [PCA] began right after my arrival in Winnipeg. I was one of the thirteen founding members of the PCA Credit Union, which was later incorporated into the Holy Spirit Credit Union. I also supervised summer Scouting camps at our facilities in the Whiteshell Provincial Park. Not far from there I built my own summer home, which we called, rather romantically, "A Dream." Too far away from the city to be a retirement nest, it is nonetheless a place of peace and quiet, the attributes that I am beginning to appreciate after a lifetime of chaos and frantic pursuits.

BOLESŁAW CZUBAK

I was born in Wadowice, near Cracow. My grandfather, on my mother's side, was a very affluent man. He was a descendent of the Fidelus family, which had probably come to Poland from Spain. He bought a large estate in the Stanisławów [Ivano-Frankivs'k] region from one of the counts Jabłonowski. That's where my mother grew up. But I spent most of my teenage years at a boarding school in Cracow, not at home, which I visited only on major holidays. After passing the matriculation exam at a Cracow high school, I signed up for the Officer Cadet College attached to the 19th Infantry Regiment, stationed in Lwów [L'viv], and later served my apprenticeship in the 48th Regiment in Stanisławów. On graduation in 1938, I was promoted to 2nd lieutenant, which was rather unusual and clearly intended as an encouragement for me to pursue a professional military career. I did not stay in the army, though, but remained loosely associated with it until the war, working as an instructor at the Cadet Corps in Lwów.

When the war broke out, I was called up, in the second wave of mobilization, to the 48th Regiment in Stanisławów. By September 3, the company I commanded was on the move, withdrawing from Dębica all the way to Lwów. At times we had to fight our way through the attacking German lines. In Piaski, near Lwów, we tried to set up a line of defence, but the better-armed German forces soon broke through. Just then, like a bolt from the blue, the news came that the Soviets had invaded Poland and taken Lwów. At 2:00 a.m., we called a meeting of officers to decide what to do. The decision was made to disperse and try to make it to Lwów. I had some friends there who took me in. After a few days, they told me that the Soviet authorities had posted a proclamation, calling on all Polish officers to assemble near George's Hotel. A few thousand retired officers of the reserve, including myself, heeded the call and gathered at the appointed place. Few of us expected evil, but no sooner had we assembled there than we were surrounded by Soviet troops, taken to the train station, and loaded onto cars. Our train moved back and forth between Stanisławów and Podhajce [Podgaytsy] a few times, as if the Soviets did not quite know what to do with us. Finally we stopped beside a village and were allowed to go and get some food, but few officers were eager to venture out because of the Ukrainian bands marauding in that region.

As time went on, we grew more concerned about our destination and our fate. One of my friends, 2nd Lieutenant Nitka, decided to jump the train. His father, an engine driver, helped him escape. He brought his locomotive to the neighbouring tracks, let out a large cloud of white steam, and Nitka dove into that steam and onto his father's engine. Seconds later he was gone. I, too, grew concerned, especially after a Soviet soldier said to me—in a surge or honesty or malice, I'm not sure—"You'll regret that you're an officer. You'll go before the squad." I took his warning seriously and asked for permission to go to the station and bring some hot water for the sick. Out of the guards' sight, I managed to get some civilian clothes from the railwaymen and hid in a nearby bakery. This saved me from certain death, for all my friends from that train were later murdered in Katyn.

In a civilian disguise, I worked my way towards the Romanian border. When I finally got there, the border was sealed and guarded closely by the Soviets. Aware of others like myself, stuck on the Soviet-occupied side, I decided to organize an underground conduit to smuggle over the border those who needed to cross to Romania. To set up a front, I took a job as a teacher at a local school and taught there for two months. At the end of November, we celebrated St. Andrew's feast. One of the local girls read my future from molten wax—a custom common in many parts of Poland—and told me I would shortly travel to the Ural Mountains, then go south, and then to another continent. It sounded too fantastic to be true. I laughed and dismissed it, but soon discovered that her reading had indeed foreshadowed my future.

I put my plans to smuggle people across the border into action. I found a guide who knew all the paths, and he successfully led several groups across the mountains and into Romania. We paid him with clothing, for money had no value. Then I organized an underground cell and established contact with others in Lwów; they sent me more people to take across the border. Things were going well until I noticed strange characters lingering in the vicinity of my house, which I shared with a Ukrainian priest, a Nazi sympathizer. I concluded I must have been under surveillance. I heightened my precautions, went only to school and back, and decided it was time for me to follow the others to Romania. But before I had a chance to make the arrangements, one evening I found NKVD [state security police] officers waiting for me in my apartment. I was put under arrest but allowed to put on my fur coat and warm boots.

They did not interrogate me at the local police station in Nadwórna [Nadvornaya], but the officer who arrested me personally escorted me to Lwów, where I was locked up in the Zamarstynowo prison. The interrogations began. They asked me whom I knew in Nadwórna. "I knew all the teachers," I said, "no one else." I didn't know how much they knew until they accused me of collaboration with counter-revolutionaries in Lwów. Of course, I denied everything. It turned out that the border guards had caught two people from the last party I sent across the mountains. One of them, whom I had disguised as a lumberjack, took with him—despite my warnings—a wallet with pictures of his wife and child, and from these the NKVD found out his identity and his weak points. In the course of interrogations, he admitted I had organized the smuggling. I spent several months in the same cell with him and others caught crossing the mountains. They also threw into jail our guide, a highlander, who could not stand the imprisonment, broke down, and hanged himself.

Later they sent me to a camp in Targopol, a centre overseeing numerous concentration camps in the region, and made me work unloading freight cars. I found it peculiar that the Russian prisoners who were among us, despite the shared hardships, tried to bully us Poles and make our lives more difficult, for instance, by playing nasty tricks on those carrying heavy sacks. Quite understandably, we did not share with them what we managed to steal from the cargo. Even the Soviet soldiers seemed to have more compassion for us than our Russian fellow-prisoners. Once I swiped a few cookies from a package intended for the commander of the camp. A guard clearly saw me, but his face was impassive, and he turned to the side, pretending he had noticed nothing.

When the Soviet-German war broke out, I was still rotting in prison, over fifty of us in a single cell. It was an interesting group of people, Poles from Russia and Lithuania; I was probably thrown in with them because I was an officer. Almost daily, we could see from the window of our cell a firing squad executing prisoners. Then we learned about the agreement between Sikorski and Stalin. We waited in anticipation for our release, but all in vain. Finally, a friend of mine and I decided to see the prison's commanding officer and demand our release on the grounds of the Polish-Soviet agreement. In response, he threatened us with a firing squad, and in the end transferred me to another camp. There I met a prisoner who went by the name of Brandys, and who later became the prime minister of Israel as Menachem Begin. He was a clever man and never worked in the camp. Every morning, when all of us were taken to the forest to cut lumber, he stayed behind. Maybe, we speculated, it was because there were many Jews in the NKVD, and they protected Jewish prisoners. At any rate, I agreed with Brandys that we would demand immediate release from the camp, and that this time we would threaten them with a hunger strike of the entire camp. The commander must have liked the idea of a hunger strike, for we ended up in a dark cell without any food for three days. But we did not give in. An NKVD officer suggested that since we were now allied nations, they would drop us behind the German lines to join the Soviet guerilla units operating there. We refused, because we wanted to serve in the Polish army. We demanded they send a telegram to the Polish ambassador to confirm we were indeed to be set free. "We will continue our hunger strike," I said, "until we get his reply." That reply came three days later, and the following morning we were released. We took a train to Arkhangelsk and then to the south of Russia. After that I never saw Brandys again.

We went to Lugovoye, where a part of the Polish army was being organized, and from there to Krasnovodsk and on to Persia. I was assigned to the 26th Regiment, and moved with it to Palestine. In the camp in Palestine, I got sick. Doctors suspected typhoid fever, for I had red spots on my abdomen, but fortunately it turned out to be a false alarm. Shortly afterwards, I ran into Major Borkowski, my former commander from Stanisławów. He recognized me and arranged for my transfer as an instructor to the NCO school. They kept moving us from place to place, first in Syria, then in Iraq. In the meantime, I was put in charge of the program verifying military credentials and training of those NCOs who could produce no documents, for there were many who had joined the army with nothing but the shirts on their backs (and even those were often in tatters). The commander of the brigade, General Peszek, recognized me, too, and suggested I be sent to the Senior Officers College in England. Unfortunately, I was two days late, and the group of selected officers had already left for England. My battalion commander then assigned me to the Officer Cadets College in Kirkuk, where I taught topography and military tactics.

I recall from that time a major mishap. During a lecture on the use of grenades, some fifty young men gathered in a room around a table, on which the instructor had assembled some basic exhibits. He was handling a live, unsecured grenade, when, in a moment of carelessness, the grenade slipped from his hand and fell onto the table. The son of Colonel Gigiel, trying to save his colleagues, covered it with his hands. He lost them both in the explosion, and one eye, too. Fifteen others were also wounded. The colonel's son later got artificial hands. When I met him in London, he was teaching at a British military college; after that, he worked for the British Intelligence. He looked great when I last saw him, a brave man, whose courage doubtless saved many.

Once again I was transferred to Palestine, then to Egypt, and finally, as a deputy commander of the 3rd Company, to the Italian front. With little experience in the Italian mountains, we went out on our first patrol, heading towards the river. The day was grey and the sky was of no help in making our course. Soon we were lost. We needed to find someone who could guide us back. Fortunately, we spotted a German scout who seemed to know the terrain quite well. We set an ambush and captured him. We got back to our base camp without any difficulty and, thanks to our German guide, even got to know the vicinity of Monte Cassino.

Even before the storming of that mountain stronghold, we knew it would be a bloody battle. And yet, many youths could not wait to go into action. I remember two boys, Leszek and Tytus Kunc, who had just graduated from the Officer Cadets College. They were ordered to wait until after the battle and then join the company as reinforcements. But they did not obey that order and ran away from the college to take part in the assault on the stronghold. The first wave of attack suffered heavy losses; Tytus was killed and my company commander, Tarnowiecki, was wounded. Without waiting for the orders from the battalion headquarters, I had to take over the command.

At this point, I must correct the oft-repeated account of the first units entering the Monte Cassino monastery. It was not the 12th Regiment that first set foot in the German stronghold, but Major Paluch and I. Paluch, a very brave soldier, came to me at 8:00 a.m. and suggested we explore the monastery. We took two scouts with us. The major was of the opinion that, after so much bombardment, there should be no live mines left there. The place was empty and quiet, and we reached the monastery without any difficulty. Not a German was in sight. The place was so devastated that we could not find any objects worth taking as souvenirs.

I was firmly against plundering the captured towns or estates, no matter the potential for profit. One of my officer cadets was an engineer, and he tried to persuade me to take the platinum from a power plant we had just overrun. We'll be millionaires after the war, he argued. But I would have none of it and forbade him to mention it to anyone else. Stealing was one thing, but enjoying the wealth of the leaders of the pro-Nazi regime was quite another. At one point I set up my headquarters in a former governor's palace. It was beautifully equipped with porcelain and silverware. All that display of affluence stirred my ambition to show that my mother, too, had taught me how to receive guests in style. So I invited all the commanders, including the division commander, for an elegant dinner. One of my soldiers, Jasio Małolepszy from the Foreign Legion, found us some alcohol. When all was set, I proposed a toast with what I thought was cognac, but what turned out to be pure spirit. Everyone drank up and started choking and gasping for breath. Only the division commander remained composed and asked for more.

Ancona was one of my last major targets. It was well defended, and we needed a strategy to get in. We watched the German lines for several days, especially at lunchtime, and noticed that their soldiers were the least attentive when absorbed with their noontime meal. So I decided to attack at noon. I took several volunteers with me. We took out their forward positions without firing a shot and then surprised the rest with spoons still in their mouths. We took thirty-two prisoners without even once using our guns. Our surprise attack was the last thing they expected. Thanks to that coup, we were the first to break through into Ancona. That exploit won me the Cross of Virtuti Militari.*

The war was over, and we faced the prospect of demobilization. Still in Falconara, we set up the first chapter of the Polish Combatants Association, and I was chosen as its president. Now I had to think not only of my own future but of the future of many others as well. Since Canada was one of the first countries to open its door to Polish ex-servicemen, we decided to take advantage of it: almost half of my company decided to come with me. I made a request to the Canadian authorities that the entire board of the association be localized together in the centre of Canada, in Manitoba. But despite various agreeable noises, only I ended up here, while the rest were scattered across this wide country.

The local Polish community gave us a warm welcome. We were greeted by Brigadier General Morton and taken to the barracks. After the first few days, we had to start fending for ourselves, and at times we did fall victim to some unscrupulous salesmen. For instance, we wanted to buy some group insurance for the veterans. With our limited knowledge of English, we were relieved when a Ukrainian, a representative of the Metropolitan Insurance Company, offered us his services. He registered all 150 of us in his insurance company and collected the initial premiums. At first we thought we had made a good deal, but we soon found out, after a conference with Colonel Sznuk in Ottawa, that we had been taken in. The agent had had no right to collect any money up-front. It took several interventions of the editor-in-chief of *Czas*, Dr. Synowiecki, and Mr. Gruszka, an editor from the local *Free Press*, and several phone calls to the head offices of the Metropolitan Insurance Company in the United States to annul the agreement and recover the money.

My farm experience was rather short and painful: I was kicked by a cow when trying to milk it. Synowiecki tried to find a way to release me from the farm contract but without success. Shortly afterwards, I was formally transferred to a Polish farm owned by a certain Dudkowski,

---

* The highest Polish military distinction, comparable to the British Victoria Cross.

and he did not insist that I actually worked for him. So I rented a place in Winnipeg and devoted myself to organizing and attending the affairs of my fellow ex-servicemen scattered on various farms across the province.

When it was discovered that many of the veterans were infected with tuberculosis, the Canadian authorities wanted to send them back to where they had come from, that is, to Italy. We launched a series of protests and managed to ensure their placement in a sanatorium in Brandon. Resting and convalescing in a comfortable setting, all of them fully recovered. To help them financially, we organized a collection among the veterans and looked after them as best we could.

There were also cases that required our intervention with individual farmers, when, for instance, our boys were beaten up on their farms. We had requests for transfers to different farmers and heart-wrenching accounts of loneliness on isolated farmsteads, where men could not speak the language. We had complaints that both the farmers and the authorities treated our veterans like prisoners of war. At one point I even contemplated the possibility of organizing a strike to ensure better treatment, but Dr. Synowiecki persuaded me to abandon the idea, and he was probably right. Many of those matters had to be negotiated with a representative of the Canadian Ministry of Agriculture, Mr. Christianson. We also had to deal with the serious problem of delays in payments owed to our veterans by virtue of their demobilization. The money from England arrived in Canada, but the Canadian authorities were afraid that, once the veterans were paid, they would leave the farms and go to the cities. To make matters worse, the Dominion Bank, which was holding the money, refused to pay interest on it. We managed to resolve all these and many other problems thanks to close collaboration with Dr. Synowiecki and especially with Mr. Dubienski,* who had a good working relationship with Mr. Christianson.

In the midst of various veteran initiatives, I also ran into some personal financial difficulties. I dealt with them as simply and directly as I could. My only spoil of war, which I had brought with me to Canada, was Mussolini's photograph album. As I said before, I never took any valuables from the places we captured, but after a battle in which we

---

* Bernard Dubienski (1891-1981), a Winnipeg lawyer and one of the founders of the Polish Canadian Congress.

took Mussolini's castle, della Caminata, I thought I deserved a small memento of that victory. We did not plunder the place, but I did take with me a few small items, including Mussolini's sword and a photograph album. I was stupid then and dumped all the photographs. Pressed for money in Canada, I sold the album for $300. It was enough to live on for a few months and to go to Ottawa.

In Ottawa, I met several members of the Polish Canadian Congress and asked for their help. I also met Jan Ostrowski and Karol Rozmarek from the Polish American Congress. These were my first encounters with the central authorities of the Polish community in North America. We expressed the readiness of the Polish Combatants Association to join the congress. As one of our first initiatives, we proposed setting up our own credit unions. The congress promised to contribute $200,000 to the fund, but those promises never materialized. I gave my report to the association at a meeting in Toronto, which brought together representatives of various chapters. I also resigned my position as president. At the next general meeting, the Polish Combatants Association chose Ostrowski as my successor.

Since then my life has taken many turns. I spent some time in Vancouver, working in a sawmill with Antoni Barzycki. I went to school to improve my qualifications and took accounting and medical first aid courses. For a while, I worked on a ship as a steward. At one point I applied for an American passport and got it without much trouble, probably thanks to the support of a friendly senator from Seattle. I found myself in San Francisco, where my medical courses helped me get a job as an ambulance worker. Later I landed a good job as an accountant and was eventually promoted to superintendent of the planning department, with twelve people working for me. Now that hectic life is behind me. I am enjoying my retirement in good health and good humour, reminiscing about my past and making plans for the future.

IRENA EHRLICH

I was born in Mazovia, but when I was three, my parents moved to the Wilno [Vilnius] region. I grew up to the lilting music of Wilno Polish. My father's job required us to move a lot, so at various times I called home Wilno, Podbrodzie [Podbradė], Święciany [Švenčionys], Bezdany [Bezdonys], and Kinieliszki [Kiauneliškis]. In the spring of the fated year 1939, I passed the matriculation exam in Wilno and proudly accepted my first posting as a primary schoolteacher in Kinieliszki. But the red gold of September that year broke my heart and made me cry for my country, for my family, for myself. The following spring the winds of war swept us far away from home and from one another.

On the thirteenth of April 1940, at three in the morning—at the thief's hour, as they say—Soviet soldiers woke us up battering at the door with butts of their bayonetted rifles and demanding in Russian, "Odchiniaite!" [Open the door!]. Mother froze, as if paralyzed. The children, waking to this nightmare, began crying. Father had died a year earlier, and now Mother was alone with the six of us, five girls and a boy. My youngest sister was ten. I was the first to break the spell of terror. I grabbed a basket and shouted, "Start packing!" In the confusion of the half hour they gave us to gather our things, we found some clothes, and Mother took down the hangings from the walls, and a picture of Jesus in Gethsemane. We had no bread in the house, for the night before Mother had leavened new bread in a kneading-trough to be baked in the morning. So she pleaded with the soldiers at least to let her milk the cow, Lola. A sweet and tender beast, Lola took an instant dislike for the *boets* [soldier] who guarded Mother with a bayonet at the ready. She tried to put her horns to him—a beast, yet she sensed our feelings.

The soldiers herded us—half the town's people marked for deportation into the heartland of Russia—to Mr. Greulich's estate. We were a sight of misery and despair: some were sobbing, some praying, some arguing, some prophesying, and some sitting all too quiet, their eyes glazed with shock. Still in a state of confusion, we were taken to the railway station and loaded onto cattle cars for what we knew would be a cruel journey to an even crueller existence.

Our journey lasted for two weeks, and the stench of our bodies and miseries grew worse day after day. There was no toilet in the car, only a small hole bored in the floor, and no sanitation of any kind, only some straw thrown in from time to time to cover up the mess. At first people were embarrassed to squat over the hole and screened one another with coats or blankets. But as exhaustion and hunger set in, and as the first children began to die, the sense of shame faded away.

When the train finally stopped, we staggered out of the car in a small town called Bulayevo, not far from Sverdlovsk in Siberia. We were directed to a collective farm, a *kolkhoz*, called Oktyabrsk, a wretched, wretched place and a poor one as well. From its muddy common, when we finally reached it, Oktyabrsk looked as if had been abandoned by God. We dropped our bags and baskets and sat in their midst, waiting for further instructions from those who had sent us here. For two days none came. But local people did come: worn, exhausted, grey faces atop grey rags and shoes made of car tires. Our crumpled, sweaty clothes must have seemed like regal attire to them, as they regarded us with a mixture of surprise and respect. At the first sight of the NKVD, they scurried away. Finally the Soviet authorities deigned to inform us that we were to look for lodging and work on our own. Smaller families squeezed—for a fee—into *kolkhozhniks'** cottages, sometimes sleeping on stove benches in kitchens, sometimes in the only other chamber cramped with bunk beds. But the seven of us could find no place. We sobbed for a bit and stayed on the common until a

---

* Peasants working on a *kolkhoz*, or a collective farm.

good man showed us a half-ruined clay cottage a howl away from the cemetery and offered it to us for fifty thieving rubles a month. We had no choice but to accept his terms: the cottage reeked of starving ghosts, but it gave us a roof over our heads.

The next day my sister Jadwiga and I set out to the town of Bulayevo. I spoke some Belarussian, and we hoped to reach someone in the NKVD [state security police] and plead for help in finding work. On our way, by a rare stroke of luck, we met Mrs. Topolska, an old acquaintance, who told us about an orphanage in a nearby grange, its stable and barn turned into dining rooms. The director of the orphanage, a would-be Henry VIII, had just married for the sixth time; he drank for pleasure, on and off the job. Thanks to a good word from his latest wife, Mrs. Topolska managed to get us jobs in the orphanage: my mother and I working in the kitchen and Jadwiga scrubbing the floors.

The kitchen, a low, primitive lean-to, fed some 200 children, most of them the offspring of failed marriages. Their fare was below modest: milk, half-diluted with water, in the morning, potato soup with dumplings for lunch, and the same for dinner. Once a month they got a spoonful of meat, that was all. No wonder their eyes always shone with hunger, and with hatred of the director, "a thief and a bad man," they said, "not at all like Batiuszka [Stalin], who loves us so much." They would kill the director with their knives one day, they said. They were serious, I could see that, and on night shifts I was always afraid. One night, as I was dozing off on the table, I was woken by shouts, "Nanny, open up or we'll cut your throat!" Six boys aged ten to thirteen, knives in hands, clamoured at the door. Terrified, I let them in. They took the entire supply of bread and disappeared. I lay in shock by the open door, where Mrs. Topolska, the chief cook, found me in the morning. I told her what had happened. Minutes later the NKVD showed up and, in no time, picked out the six culprits; just in case they had missed someone, they took away all the ten- to thirteen-year-old boys, presumably to some jail for juveniles. After this incident, all the Poles were fired from their jobs at the orphanage.

When winter came, Russian winter, we trudged several kilometres through snow to a barracks construction site, where we worked as labourers. On Christmas Eve 1940 the snow was blowing hard. As my mother and I were struggling against the wind, a cart drawn by a horse, as miserable as we but apparently stronger, passed by us on the road.

Before the cart disappeared in the drifts, we saw a sack of wheat fall off its back. We rushed to it and immediately covered it with snow, rejoicing at the thought of the evening feasting, all the Poles together. Alas, the *kolkhozhnik* noticed his loss, turned back, and recovered the wheat. The Christmas star was to shine a cold and hungry light on us that night. We rushed on to get to work on time, for fifteen minutes of lateness could earn a year in a Soviet prison. That day Mother was assigned to pitch making, a good job by the fire (the stench notwithstanding). I was sent to clean snow from ditches where pipes ran. As long as the ditch was shallow, I could cope, but when it got deeper, the snow began to slide back from the shovel before I could throw it over the edge. I had to work against a quota to get a small daily ration of bread, about 200 grams; the other children at home were hungry, so I could not fail them. In frustration and close to despair, I started loading the snow into a sack, then climbing up on a ladder and emptying the sack on top. And yet, by the end of my shift, utterly exhausted, I failed to meet the quota. I was hungry and sad that Christmas Eve in Nyevyezkah*—yes, I remember the name of that place—near Bulayevo. Mother did get her ration of bread that day, the precious 200 grams. In the evening, she divided it into small pieces, and we shared it as if it were the Christmas wafer we used to share at Christmas Eve suppers in better years. Alinka, who was too young to work, had cooked us our main dish, some old flour, clawed from the corners of a pillowcase, boiled in water. The flour was the last of our supplies bartered for clothes in the *kolkhoz*. The evening was awash with sad memories. Later I desperately wanted to sleep, to forget, but my mind was flooded with images of past Christmas Eves, of the smell of baking and of freshly cut spruce trees, of the starry rides to the Midnight Mass, and of so much more.

In the spring we were moved again, to a different *kolkhoz*. We were quartered in small, filthy houses, with clay floors crawling with insects of all sorts. Before we could move in, we had to thoroughly clean and disinfect the house. We were assigned new jobs in the fields, growing cabbages, cucumbers, and other vegetables for the orphanage. But seeds were in short supply and often rotten, so the crops were very

---

* Possibly Medvezhka.

poor. There I became a water carrier, taking over from Fiedzia, a local man who had fallen ill with malaria and who spent most of his days lying on the grass, his face bluish grey, shivering uncontrollably. The water cart was drawn by a lame ox. It took some skill to get it going. The whip did not help much, but pulling hard at the bridle and cursing loudly in Russian did. Soon I also noticed that if I used a branch to chase away the horseflies that were biting my ox mercilessly, he would pick up the pace. And so I looked after the beast's comfort, and he hardly ever gave me grief during the month we worked together.

By then it was obvious to us that we were a cheap, mobile labour force to the Soviets. Once again they loaded us onto trucks, with all our belongings, and then into railway cars, and shipped us off to the city of Akmolinsk [Astana]. We were forced to work at the construction of a new railway line. The Soviets threw thousands of labourers at that project, apparently spurred by the recent outbreak of war with Germany. The work went on around the clock, seven days a week. We were assigned to the morning shift, from 2:00 a.m. till 10:00 a.m. Usually we shovelled sand from the railway cars or dumped crushed stones on the embankment. By six in the morning we were so tired that some would doze off standing up, leaning against a shovel. It happened to me once, but the foreman must have noticed, and screamed at me so loudly that, in fright, I lost balance with my shovel and fell down on a heap of stones.

In October it grew very cold. Few people had warmer clothes, and we feared we would soon freeze to death and so meet our end. The elders among us sent the youngsters to the NKVD to ask for warm boots and *kufaiki,** for we could not work in the cold much longer. I went with them. In the office sat a big man, stiff like a mannequin, his uniform tight, a slate of medals on his chest. He was smoking a good, scented cigarette, his nose flowering red and shining from behind a cloud of aromatic smoke. Shaking like half-set jelly, we came up to the table and explained our business. Much to our surprise, he did not scream us out of the room but told us not to worry about clothes, for soon we would be going to Alma-Ata [Almaty]. Of course we did not believe a word he said, suspecting another Soviet ruse, but for once the immediate future proved our pessimism wrong.

---

* Parka-like garments warmed with rough cotton.

A few days later they crammed us again into cattle trucks and brought us a few sacks of frozen potatoes, already rotting (we could tell by smelly wet spots on the sacks). By way of condiment, they threw in a few bags of musty flour. We were indeed on our way to Alma-Ata, but few of us had reasons to cheer. After several days on the train, children began to die, and, of the older women, many were sick. Mr. Pieńk, the only man in our car and one of the few in the whole transport, made no show of emotions as he held a dying child in his arms, his fourth to perish. But in the midst of that suffering we desperately wanted to live, and to live, we needed food. Someone had to get out at every station and brave the snow and cold to bring some *kipiatok* [boiling water] to the car. Mrs. Świętokrzyska offered her late husband's shoes to the person who would volunteer for that task. I did it. The left shoe had a hole in it, but the pair of them was a definite improvement over bare feet. For the most part, *kipiatok* was what sustained us. Some tried to make pancakes with the mouldy flour, but the pancakes stank so much that the rest of us in the car could hardly breathe. We kept consoling each other that this journey would not last forever, and that it was sunny and warm in Alma-Ata.

I was returning to the car with boiling water at Orskoye, one of the bigger train stops, when something I saw made me think I was hallucinating. It must be the stench in the car, I thought, or my head is getting sick. I doubted my senses because I had just seen a Polish soldier. He was wearing a short, three-quarter coat, pulled tight at the waist, and a large fur cap with a Polish ensign, an eagle with its wings outspread. "I must be losing my mind, it can't be true," I whispered, hoping with all my heart that it was. I walked up to him, a bucket of *kipiatok* in each hand, and, looking at him as if at some sacred figure, I asked, "Are you really Polish? That eagle on your cap, is it really ours?" He fixed his gaze on me for a while and then nodded slowly, saying nothing. He must have shared my own doubts about my sanity. But I needed more than a nod, I needed words, Polish words, so I asked him again if it was indeed our Polish eagle on his cap and how come it was spreading its wings in the heart of Russia. Still watching me, and now somewhat bemused, he asked, "So you haven't heard, Miss, that we already have our Polish army?" The two buckets of *kipiatok* fell from my hands. I knelt on the wet, hot snow and crossed myself and stared at him speechless, dumbstruck with happiness. My tongue refused even to thank him for the news. It must have been a minute before I could stammer out, "Could you enlist me and my sister? Could you take us with you?" "I'm sorry, I can't," he said. "I don't make such decisions. You'd have to talk to the chief, he's in charge of this transport, but, frankly, I doubt he'll take you, ladies. We're carrying food and English uniforms and are not allowed to take passengers. But he's in charge, so you talk to him, Miss. He's a good man, our chief. That's him over there." The chief was walking towards us, wearing a similar fur cap with a distinctly Polish eagle ensign. He looked fortyish and sported a large walrus moustache. Although I must have been quite a sight, he greeted me tactfully, with respect, and inquired about my business. But his response to my plea was "Categorically no." Perhaps trying to soften his emphatic refusal, he asked, "Where are you from?" "From the Wilno region," I said. Suddenly there was a glimmer, a spark in his eyes. "Whereabouts did you live lately?" "In Wilno itself," I said. His face broke into a smile, and I seized upon that smile as upon a ray of hope. "Very pleased to meet you. My name's Plawgo, Sergeant Plawgo," he said, my Wilno roots visibly thawing his military mien. He began to scratch his head, and puff, and I was praying that the Lord might inspire him how he might smuggle us in. I led him to where our train was and showed him a caterpillar of cars loaded with Polish exiles. With a tear in the corner of his eye, Sergeant Plawgo agreed to deliver us to the Polish army.

With the speed of lightning I ran to get my sister. When I announced what I had learned about the Polish army, a hurricane of joy swept through the car. Some began praying, "O Jesus Christ, thank you! Blessed are you, Virgin Mary!" Many were crying, singing, even dancing. A few, overwhelmed with emotion, sat in silence, too happy to talk. "Polish army! Polish army!" these words resounded like a powerful chant. My sister and I said goodbye to our mother and to everyone in the car, and, zigzagging among railway trucks and locomotives to avoid the NKVD, who were crawling all over the station, we sneaked away to the Polish military transport.

When we got inside the car, the sergeant made some room for us on one side, beside a pile of firewood, ordering all the men to the other. He encouraged us to make ourselves at home, to rest and enjoy the clean warmth. He and his family had also been forcibly removed by the Soviets and perhaps someone would help his children the way he was helping us. There was nothing to fear, for he would look after us as if we were his own daughters. Even in hardship and misery, Poles knew how to respect women, he said. He was thus cheering us up when someone banged on the door. The sergeant jumped, thinking it was the NKVD, and whispered to us to hide behind the pile of firewood. He pulled open the door and saw an old woman standing barefoot in the snow: our mother. She held out her toil-worn hands and pleaded with us, "My daughters, come back! It is not proper that you ride with men in the same car. Whatever is going to happen to us, let it be as God wills. But stay with me, come back! We'll lose touch if you join the army; how will we find each other afterwards? It's better if we stay all together as a family." Signs of impatience appeared on Sergeant Plawgo's countenance; he was afraid the NKVD henchmen could show up any moment. "If you want to go with your mother, young ladies," he said, "you must go now!" My sister yielded to Mother's pleas, grabbed her bundle, and jumped out of the car. I, too, was torn, balancing on the verge of indecision. But often, at such moments, one suddenly feels the force of deep, heartfelt conviction take over. It was that way with me. I believed, with every ounce of blood in my veins, that I would be safe with these men, these honest soldiers; that I would join the army and would help my family and all good families. I said my last goodbye to my mother, and the sergeant shut the door.

I was issued two English blankets and was treated to a royal supper. The transport had a generous supply of canned food, milk, jams, meat, and I could eat all I wanted. I even got a ration of tobacco, although at the time I did not smoke. I thought I was dreaming. I had read about such sudden changes of fortune in fairy tales, but this was my life, flesh and blood life. Yesterday my flesh was hungry, my blood cold; today I was full and warm. I lay down in my space behind the firewood and wrapped myself in new, fragrant blankets. But the moment I felt comfortable, my conscience began to stir. One moment I felt I had done the right thing; the next I felt disgusted with what I had done. How could I leave my mother, sisters, brother, and all those needy people on the train to Alma-Ata? I was still wearing Mrs. Świętokrzyska's husband's shoes, and there was no other decent pair in our car, so who would go out for *kipiatok*? My conscience was tearing at my will. I tried to pray, counting the beads of a rosary wound around my wrist, but the prayer faltered. Finally, worn out by this struggle, I fell asleep.

The ride lasted perhaps a week before the train screeched to its final stop near Totskoye. An order had come that the convoy should go no further, but I wanted to go to Buzuluk, where the Polish army was. I was distressed and did not know what to do next. The soldiers I travelled with had no time to worry about me; they had their own orders. Quietly I gathered myself and stealthily, to avoid detection by the NKVD, climbed out of the car. As I was leaving, Sergeant Plawgo gave me a last bit of advice: I should go to Totskoye, for there was a Polish army unit there, and there were women, too. I thanked him and hugged him, and we wished each other luck. I never met him again, but the memory of Sergeant Plawgo has stayed with me all my life.

It was the middle of the night, yet I would not wait until the morning. I had to go right away. The moonlight cast long shadows on the snow; contorted trees in dense thickets took on a menacing look. Shuffling through the snow, I suddenly heard a savage howl, not too far away, then another, much closer, and yet another. A pack of wolves, probably hungry. The wind began to blow, snow swirling in the air, muting the moonlight. I was on the verge of panic, not sure if I was walking in the right direction, but then the first lights appeared, and the howling grew distant. The lights turned out to be the military barracks. I reached a building with the word "Tock" painted on the roof, the Polish name for Totskoye. Once in the compound, I inquired about the quarters of female volunteers. The commanding officer, a woman dressed in beautiful English pajamas, was eating fried bread with sugar. It smelled heavenly. Standing in the doorway, I timidly said I wanted to enlist in the army. The commander, a slice of bread in her hand, swallowed, and her face grew red as if she had choked on that last bite. She was angry, angry with me because I should not have entered the quarters without going through quarantine, and because I must have been mad to walk through the woods at night. I clearly had no common sense and would not make a good soldier; and, besides, they already had a full contingent and did not need any more volunteers. I should go back to where I had come from, to the train station. I was shattered, my dreams dashed. Dejected, I left the compound and started back to the station. I had no other choice. The woods were quiet now; the wolves must have already made their kill.

At the station, I found a spot behind a stove and sat down to warm up. A major struck up a conversation, suggesting that I should forget the army. He had no family and travelled a lot. Soon he'd be going to Kuybyshev [Samara] for some musical instruments. But here in Totskoye he had a small room and could take care of me. Why should I bother with the army? It was even worse in Buzuluk, he told me. Finally, perhaps to show how much he cared, he looked at me and asked, "You're hungry, aren't you?" He got up and went to see if he could get something to eat at the station. I took that opportunity and ran away from the waiting room; he wouldn't go looking for me. Outside I ran into a military policeman. He was bubbling with joy because he had just found his wife and two children. I told him about my troubles and how much I wanted to get to Buzuluk, but there were no trains going in that direction. He took pity on me and suggested I spend the night with his wife, who indeed received me very warmly. Her name was Szmit, and years later I met her again in England, where she worked in a hospital.

The next day, the gendarme managed to get me on the train going to Buzuluk. The journey was, thankfully, uneventful. And Buzuluk was all I hoped it to be: no "Shyraka strana maia radnaia" [Great is our native land] blaring over loudspeakers, but a quieter buzz of Polish military activity. What a relief: so everything I had heard about the Polish army was true! The place was crowded with Polish soldiers and with volunteers hoping to enlist. They came tired, worn out, wrapped in blankets and tattered quilts, but with eager hearts and burning eyes. The army was taking in these exiles and turning them into soldiers. There was much suffering in Buzuluk, but there was also joy. I found out that I should report to the headquarters, located in an impressive imperial building, probably a former home of some aristocratic family, later taken over by the Komsomol.* The other buildings were typical Russian cottages. In front of the headquarters, a large Polish banner fluttered in the wind. I thought my heart would burst with happiness.

Inside I was greeted by the hum of voices, clatter of typewriters, and radio noise. And above all, Polish speech everywhere—it was exhilarating and immensely gratifying. I was told that female volunteers were quartered at Pervomaiskaia Street. When I got there, my enthusiasm was again nearly quashed by the commanding officer. She said

---

* A youth political organization affiliated with the Communist Party.

they had no space for more volunteers, and I might just as well return to the station. Fortunately, a military inspector appeared, Mrs. Puchawska, from Wilno. The name of that city worked another miracle: she gave an order that I be enlisted and then left. The commander complied but warned me that space was in such short supply that I might have no place to sit down. What she said was indeed true, the place was packed with women, and the only space available was just beside the door. That space was my bedroom for two weeks. People, pressed by nature, walked over me at night trying to get outside. Although nearly trampled every night, I was happy, so happy to have my little space behind the door. The choking cough from the draughts did not matter, I was happy. We had three meals a day and, at first, nothing to do. When a fellow volunteer from an upper bunk died from typhoid fever, I got her bed. It was warm and comfortable. But just as I settled down, my conscience spoke, "You fool, a human being, your friend, has died and you are happy!" I suppressed that voice; I had to.

Later, I was assigned to the education platoon in the company commanded by Jadwiga Domańska. I reported to her, a beautiful woman sitting on a cot, "Volunteer Irena Baranowska reports her assignment to the education platoon." I'll never forget her smile, warm and gentle and engaging. We all needed such a smile and a tender human touch. Years later, when Mrs. Domańska came to Winnipeg, I told her my story and how much I had appreciated her warmth. At first she only vaguely recalled certain episodes, but the images grew sharper as we talked. The sands of time have already begun to erase and cover up the past, so those of us who still remember should do our best to keep that past from oblivion.

We were sent to Koltubanka to run the military community centre. But our education section had little to do there. It was mid-winter, yet soldiers were living in tents so worn out that they could see moonlight through the canvas. Their bodies were numb with cold, and their minds were on survival, not culture. It was not the time or place for educational work. Then we were transferred to Kermine. The camp in Kermine is now remembered as the camp of death. Malaria was rampant there, and so were typhoid and spotted fevers. In the constant shadow of death, we organized excursions for the soldiers, gave lectures, and translated Russian radio news to keep the men informed. We worked there until the early spring of 1942.

When the snow began to melt, we were taken by train to a transition point in Krasnovodsk. We were to leave by boat for Pahlavi, but the NKVD decreed, "Zhenshchiny net" [Not women]. It took some intense negotiations before they let us embark, and not only us but also a whole contingent of civilian women and children. Our soldiers formed a lane and first the civilians, then we passed through it to board the boat. The men boarded last. For a while, I was stationed near Tehrān and assigned to the headquarters. Later we moved on to Baghdād. Wherever we went, I asked after my family. I left their names at all the contact points and gave them to all the emissaries. I was hoping, with the same stubbornness that had led me to the army, that eventually I would meet with them again. And eventually I did. As I discovered later, my sisters followed in my footsteps and enlisted. So did my brother, who joined the Youth Corps. He survived terrible bouts of spotted fever and was later recruited to the air force in Britain. My mother, with my youngest sister, went to a resettlement camp in Africa. I learned all of that when I met with my sister Jadwiga. This came about thanks to aide-de-camp Peski. We were enjoying a short period of rest in Palestine, and he, a gallant bachelor, introduced me as his fiancée—which I wasn't, really—to a good friend of his family, Mrs. Zieliński, who happened to be a nursing inspector. He told her the sad story of our separation and how much I wanted to reunite with my sister, a nurse in one of our military hospitals. Whether for the sake of a lifelong friendship or out of the goodness of her heart, she arranged for me to be transferred to Egypt and assigned to the same hospital as my sister. I was overjoyed. We flew into each other's arms, and hugged, and cried. We talked for days before we each had had our fill of news, gossip, and memories.

But the winds of war kept blowing, and soon they swept us apart, with the moving armies and relocating hospitals. I was shipped to Italy, and, through Barletto, eventually reached Ancona. Ancona, a city of the dead: empty streets, choking with ominous silence. There were only ourselves and a few brave chickens, walking along the path staked out by the sappers through a sea of mines. In the hall of the hospital, the chandelier kept ringing the accompaniment to nearby explosions. But Ancona was good to me. Working as a receptionist, I met a doctor who at first annoyed me with his show of attention, yet with whom I could not help but fall in love, my future husband. It was he who persuaded me to take a nursing course, and, thanks to him, I found a vocation that brought me a great deal of joy.

On November 25, 1945, we were married in the hospital chapel by our chaplain, Father Wróbel, in front of a small but appreciative audience. Our marital bliss was soon disrupted when my husband was transferred to Conegliano and I to Rimini. We had known it was inevitable—the army was for soldiers, not lovebirds—and we accepted the transfers with brave faces. In Rimini, I worked in an isolation ward, and we were seriously understaffed. Sometimes one nurse had to look after a hundred sick or injured so that even orderlies were sometimes called on to help with certain medical procedures.

On one of the greatly appreciated breaks from hospital duties, I drove with an English captain to Loreto to buy a little medallion of Our Lady of Loreto for my mother. On the way back, the captain lost control of the vehicle and it rolled over, landing on the roof. No one was hurt, just very uncomfortable from hanging upside down. Fortunately, a truck full of soldiers was driving not far behind us. When they saw the captain and me struggling to get out, they burst out in laughter. Apparently we were quite a sight. Still kidding around, they helped us right the car, which also escaped damage. The initial shock and the friendly jokes over, we climbed into the car and cautiously drove on to Rimini. In the meantime, word had reached the hospital that there had been an accident on the road. When I walked into the hall, I was greeted by a sad poster: "Sister Irena has died in a car crash!" Somewhat bemused, I put on my white coat and walked into my ward. Before I could say anything, one of the patients screamed in terror and covered his face. He took some convincing before he reluctantly accepted that I was not my own ghost.

Eventually, the 6th War Hospital was relocated to Britain. My husband requested a similar transfer, and when he joined me in England, we began to contemplate the return to civilian life. We thought about staying in Britain, or emigrating to Australia, but a friend of ours from Lwów University was so enthusiastic about Canada, and his enthusiasm was so infectious, that we, too, staked our future on Canada. The formalities, medical exams, work permits, and professional credentials all delayed our departure but did not dampen our spirits. Finally, by boat and by train, we arrived in North Battleford, Saskatchewan. My husband was offered a position in the psychiatric hospital: a new specialization and much work for him, but the position came with a furnished house for our growing family (our first daughter was born in England, and our second and third in North Battleford). The climate was harsh, the snow deep, and the temperatures freezing, but people seemed much warmer and more cordial than in England. Soon we had a good circle of friends, some from the hospital—immigrants, like ourselves—others from the community at large. With every passing year our roots grew deeper into the prairie soil. My husband worked in the hospital until he died, during the last few years as deputy superintendent. Besides his administrative duties, he maintained an active program of medical research and a wide range of interests, corresponding with writers like Czapski and Giedroyc* from the Polish Literary Institute in Paris. And myself? I assumed the role of a wife and mother, and, like most Polish women, doted on my daughters and husband. I have no regrets. If our early dreams of life in Canada were like outspread sails, the demands of daily life may have stolen some wind, but they never blew us off the course.

---

* Józef Czapski (1896-1993), a painter and writer; Jerzy Giedroyc (1906-2000), a writer and editor of the monthly *Kultura*, published in Paris. Both were active members of the Polish émigré community in France.

LECH FULMYK

I was born in 1925. My father was mayor of the town of Zambrów, some twenty kilometres from Łomża, and that's where I was living when the war broke out. I remember the first day. Airplanes were still a novelty in those days and stirred quite a bit of interest, especially among the youth. So while the adults were taking shelter in bunkers, I and my buddies climbed the rooftops to get a better view of the low-flying planes. That first day, the war seemed to me quite exciting and not at all tragic.

A few days after the outbreak of the war, my father, as the town's mayor, received a government order to evacuate towards the east. Following that order, around September 14, my whole family—that is, my parents, two sisters, and myself—left for Pińsk, in the company of a few other families. My brother was at an officer college at the time and, as we learned later, took part in the defence of Warsaw. Along the way, on September 17, we received information that the Soviets had already taken Pińsk. There was no point going further into the Soviet-occupied territory, so we decided to turn back.

Our first encounter with the Soviets was revealing. At one point we had to cross a bridge, but as we approached it, we saw a Red Army guard in front of it. We walked up to him and identified ourselves as refugees returning home; then we asked for his help in crossing the bridge. "You want me to help you?" he repeated our question, as if to make sure he understood it correctly. "I will help you, with a couple of rounds from my machine gun," he replied, swinging his gun to the front and aiming it at us. He couldn't be clearer as to what we might expect from the Soviets. We crossed the bridge without his help, but it became obvious that we were quite vulnerable. Father, as an important official, was dressed as was proper for his office, "like a human being," we used to say. But his clothes must have appeared quite "lordly" to the *kufaika*-clad* Soviet soldiers. It was our cab driver, whose services Father had requisitioned while still in Zambrów, who assessed the situation most soberly. He said to Father, "Mr. Mayor, to get through the Soviet checkpoints, you can't look like a lord; you must look like a churl." In one of the villages, he found my father an old cloak and forbade him to shave. The next time we met a Soviet patrol, Father looked like a regular country beggar.

We didn't return to Zambrów but to a farm in Kupiski, not far from Łomża, which Father had received for his service in the Polish Legions.[†] We hadn't lived there for years—it was leased and run by my uncle—but now, faced with wartime hardships, we came back to that old place of ours. We could expect few comforts there, but at least we had potatoes and some fat and could survive. Father didn't stay there with us for long, for, as an old POW[‡] conspirator, he knew that sooner or later they would be looking for him. So one day he simply disappeared, and nobody knew where he had gone. Eventually, he resurfaced in Białystok.

We lived in Kupiski until February 10, 1940. That day has carved itself into my memory like no other. Still before dawn, around 5:00 a.m., we were woken up with a loud banging on the door and an order in Russian: "Open the door!" Two Russian soldiers, with two Polish helpers, read our names from a piece of paper and announced, "Sabiraites' s veshchami! [Get your things and get out.] You're being deported in two hours." We packed everything we could think of, and at the last moment I crammed my pockets full of bread. Who knows, I thought, maybe I'll need it. We loaded the sleds and just as we were leaving, I took a long look at the buildings, the trees, the skyline of our farm as if to imprint all the details on my memory. I had a premonition I would never return. And I never have.

---

* Wearing parka-like garments warmed with rough cotton.

† A formation of the Polish army during World War I.

‡ Polish Underground Military Organization before and during World War I.

The Soviets had prepared well for these deportations and clearly must have been planning them for a long time. My sister did not live with us on the farm, but in Łomża, where she attended high school. They found her there, brought her to the railway station, and reunited her with the rest of us. The train ride lasted about three weeks. There were fifty people per cattle boxcar. In the middle of the car was a small stove, a *teplushka*, and around it were crude bunk beds. We didn't use those beds very long: within days we ran out of coal and had to break up the beds for firewood. We reached Arkhangelsk and went on, through the night, to a settlement, a *pasiolek*, identified only with what looked like the letter x.

The settlement consisted of several shacks scattered in the wilderness. The locals were prepared for our arrival, for I remember a fire blazing in a small stove in the shack assigned to us. Compared to what the Ukrainians deported to the same region six years earlier had gone through, our conditions were quite luxurious. They had simply been dumped from the railway cars into the snowbanks in the midst of a forest and left to fend for themselves. Only the young and the strong among them had had a chance to survive. By the time we arrived, they had buried many dead but had also adapted to the harsh environment and organized themselves. They were quite friendly towards us and helped us get settled; later, we often worked with them to our mutual satisfaction, I am pleased to say.

On the second day after our arrival, all the adults were assigned to work teams, some cutting down trees in the forest, others carting them away. Mother got a job as a cart driver. Her two horses looked as miserable as the people who worked them: you could easily count the ribs under their dull hides. To get them going you had to urge them, often with a whip. After a while, Mother got sick, and I had to replace her at that job. I don't remember receiving a single full reckoning for the work we did in the camp. We were forever getting advances towards the full pay but never the pay itself. But strangely enough, when we were leaving that godforsaken place a year and a half later, the authorities claimed that Mother owed them 400 rubles. With this kind of math, no wonder the Soviet Union was always in economic shambles.

On the evening of our second day in the settlement, we were brought some fish soup for supper. It smelled so foul that nobody wanted to touch it. When we began to grumble, the Russian who delivered it said,

"Calm down, it won't kill you. You'll soon learn to like it." He was right, in a way. A few weeks later, when our own supplies from Poland gave out, we did indeed get used to it, though to me it never smelled any better.

Life in the forest was harsh and joyless. Once, in the early days, my uncle, who had been deported with us, asked a Russian what it was like to live in that northern settlement in the long run. "You'll survive," was the answer, "but making love will be the last thing on your mind." I was too young to worry about love; what bothered me more was the cold, especially at night. But soon the authorities solved that problem for us as well. We were moved to the settlement of Kudryn, to larger shacks, each with ten beds and each housing ten families. There I was no longer cold at night, for I slept in the same bed with my mother and my two sisters.

Our first Christmas in the north was bittersweet. We were in exile, true, but we were not starving during the festive season. Our family in Poland did not forget us and sent us parcels with food and goodies. After the Christmas Eve supper, we sat with other families and sang traditional Christmas carols long into the night. I really don't know how we would have survived our northern ordeal, physically and mentally, if our relatives hadn't helped us. Even after many years, my feeling of gratitude has not diminished, and when I settled in the West, I in turn began sending parcels to Poland to help them, their children, and their grandchildren.

Finally the day came when we were officially informed that an amnesty had been declared and that we were free to leave the settlement. I was sixteen at the time, and for me it was a special day in more ways than one. A mark of manhood in the camp was being sent with a team to cut trees in the forest and meeting the daily norm of five cubic metres of wood. On that day, for the first time, I managed to accomplish that. When I came home in the evening, exhausted but proud of myself, all the Poles were gathered together by the NKVD [state security police] officer in charge of our settlement and told about the Polish-Soviet agreement, about the outbreak of war with Germany, and about the fact that we were now Soviet allies and should join the army and kick some German ass. I was apparently so excited that right after the speech I intoned the Polish anthem, "Poland is not yet defeated." I didn't remember doing that—the evening is a bit of a blur in my memory—but my mother reminded me about it here in Winnipeg.

Within a month of the announcement we managed to leave the settlement. Mr. Bieniecki, an elderly gentleman with vivid memories of World War I, encouraged us to go south, to the region of Kuybyshev [Samara], which flowed with milk and honey, he said. For lack of better advice, we went in search of his vision. The going was not easy. We were travelling by train on our own and had to look for food whenever and wherever we could, usually around railway stations. There was precious little that could be purchased, and one could more easily steal than buy, which we occasionally did. We kept an emergency sack of dry biscuits, "for the darkest hour," my mother would say. But when even those gave out, we started begging.

I must here confess that I have a special place in my heart and special sympathy for ordinary Russian people. Although stricken by poverty and unimaginable hardships, they always helped us out in our misery, sharing a few potatoes or half a slice of bread with us. A scene played out many times during our trip: I would knock on a door and plead with a woman or old man for help; she or he would disappear for a minute inside the hovel, and emerge with some crumbs of food.

Once, I remember, this familiar scene took an unusual turn. I knocked on a door that was just like any other, but when it opened, to my shock, I saw a room full of NKVD soldiers and officers holding some kind of a meeting. Half-frozen with fear, I blurted out what I always said: we were exiles from Poland, forcibly removed by the Soviet authorities from our homes. And to my even greater shock, those gathered pulled out their wallets, collected a few rubles each, and pressed a bundle of notes into my hand. It seems that, in that country described by [writer Józef] Czapski as the "inhuman land," human feelings survived in most unexpected places. I thank God for that.

After some weeks, we finally came to Ufa, where instead of the milk and honey promised by Mr. Bieniecki, we found only knee-deep mud. We couldn't find any work there—the place was dirt poor—so we settled on a *sovkhoz*, a state farm, near Melekes. I got a job tending a herd of horses. At first, when potatoes were plentiful, I was paid with a sack of potatoes a month, but later I was paid in cash, 200 rubles. I supplemented my pay in two ways. Since one of my jobs was taking potatoes to the distillery, I always managed to lose some in such a way that they found their way to our family pan or pot. We were living with a woman whose name was Voronikha—strange that I remember it after so many years—and who had a cow. When bringing alfalfa from the fields to the *sovkhoz* barn, I often dropped some from the cart near our house. The cow had something to eat and we could occasionally enjoy some milk.

In the spring of 1942, the *sovkhoz* director was a Mr. Kozlov, whose real name, as I later discovered, was Polish, Kozłowski. His father was a general in the Tsar's army. He called me up on Easter Sunday and told me to go to work. I pointed out to him that according to the Polish-Soviet agreement, we were free citizens and had the right to celebrate our religious holidays. This clearly angered him, for he shouted, "I set the rules here!" I was still young and stubborn, so I replied insolently, "Maybe for your own kind but not for me." Without another word, he caught me by the collar and literally threw me out of his office.

The next day he informed my mother that we had to leave the *sovkhoz*. Looking back at those events from the distance of years, I feel grateful that he reacted the way he did. He could have reported my refusal to work to the authorities, and I would probably have been sentenced to five years in a labour camp for my insolence. Still, at the time my mother was not happy. We packed our few belongings and went to another *sovkhoz*, which before the war had been run by German settlers. German collective farms were the envy of the countryside. They were very well managed and self-sufficient. In contrast to the Soviet farms, the labour among the Germans was divided: only men worked in the fields, while women looked after the farm buildings. No wonder their homes looked clean and affluent, and even sported polished hardwood floors, a luxury we hadn't seen anywhere else in Russia. To get rid of these settlers, suspected of pro-German sympathies, the Soviets used a provocation. They dressed a military unit in Wehrmacht uniforms and sent them to the region. The locals quickly established a friendly contact with the unit's German-speaking commander, and for that they were all immediately deported into the barren heart of Kazakhstan.

After their deportation, the farms were resettled by refugees from Moscow. Most of them had no idea about farming. I remember the superintendent of the barn, the wife of some NKVD officer, who did not know how to feed hay to a cow. In a matter of months the farms were devastated and the livestock wasted away. In the barns cows were starving to death, while huge stacks of alfalfa stood just half a kilometre away. But the superintendent from Moscow didn't know what they were for. In the spring, they let the cows out into the pasture, where many overate and died. In the midst of all that havoc, I learned a new skill. According to the *sovkhoz* regulations, every dead cow had to be skinned. Once I learned that basic task, I had more work than I could cope with. For every hide I was given five kilograms of flour, and sometimes I even managed to carve out some meat from a dead animal for a "dead-cow broth." Life was bearable in the *sovkhoz* of Nova Put', near Kuybyshev.

Our situation did have some disadvantages. Although we were free citizens of an allied country, the *sovkhoz* authorities took away our passports, making it practically impossible for us to leave the *sovkhoz*. Despite the dangers of travelling without documents, my mother went to Kuybyshev to the Polish embassy. She found a Polish church there, so she stayed for Mass, praying for the safety of our family. And, during the Mass, a miracle happened: she saw her older son, Kazio, walk into the church in the uniform of a sapper lieutenant.

At this point I must backtrack a little. My brother, as I mentioned, took part in the defence of Warsaw. After the fall of the capital, he went east, only to be captured by the Soviets, thrown into prison, and eventually sent to a labour camp not far from where we were. We learned of his whereabouts, and I recall Mother once readdressing to him a food parcel we had received from Poland, for he was probably much worse off than we were. After the amnesty, he joined the Polish army in Buzuluk, and we lost track of him. But suddenly there he was, in the Polish church in Kuybyshev.

The next day they both came to the *sovkhoz* in a horse-drawn cart, Kazio in his Polish uniform escorting Mother. To this day I have tears in my eyes when I recall that moment. He was six years older than I, and I always admired and tried to equal him. He, of course, gave me a beating at every turn. When I saw him, my first jubilant reaction was to try to throw him down to the ground, to show him that I had grown into a big boy. We started to wrestle, but as usual he got the upper hand and threw me around at will. When I shook the dust off my clothes, I took his cap and traced with my fingers the eagle ensign. The Polish eagle. For two years I had heard from the Soviet bureaucrats that "Pol'shy ne budet" [There will be no Poland], and there, as if in a dream, the Polish eagle spread out its wings. It moves me to think about it even today.

Kazio, a Polish officer, took us under his protection. We left the *sovkhoz* and without any incident made it to Dzalal'-Abad, where the 1st Infantry Division was stationed. My brother was in the 5th Sapper Battalion. I was almost seventeen and immediately volunteered for the service. Despite my age and inexperience, I was admitted. I suspect the Polish military command was getting ready to leave the Soviet Union and wanted to help as many people as possible to leave Russia. It was not known at the time whether military families would be allowed to leave with the army. Like my brother, I became a sapper, a fancy name for a military engineer. Sergeant Szykiel issued me a uniform and handed me a razor as part of my equipment. "Sir, I don't need it yet," I said. "You're a sapper now," he replied, "and all sappers shave in the morning. And so must you." I followed the order.

We arrived in Buzuluk shortly before the exodus to Iran. My registration took a while, but in the end I left with my brother's 5th Battalion. It was a happy ride to Krasnovodsk, despite the constant shortage of food. For lack of anything better, we were fed lots of rice. We weren't quite used to it, so everyone had to run to the latrine every few hours. And the latrines were quite a sight: we had no toilet paper but plenty of red rubles. We had been told we could not take them out of Russia, so we put them to good use in the latrines. By the end of our stay in Krasnovodsk, the shit holes were stuffed with Soviet banknotes. It was our revenge on the Soviet economic system that had starved us for so long.

The commander of the base in Krasnovodsk was Colonel Berling. He was always present when the ships, loaded with Polish soldiers, were leaving the Russian port. Standing at the end of the quay, he saluted the departing troops. And those troops were jubilant; after the abject poverty of Russia, Persia looked like a land from a fairy tale. Even beggars there seemed more human than the starved, emaciated peasants and workers of Russia. The abundance, the variety of things to buy was shocking to us all.

In Persia, we learned that our family had also managed to get out of Russia. We were quite a sight when we went to visit them for the first time. The British dressed us in shorts that made us look more like Boy Scouts than soldiers—especially me, who still had no trace of facial hair. Kazio, too, despite his twenty-three years of age, looked very youthful and could easily have been mistaken for a Scout team leader.

And yet the army uniform gave a tremendous sense of identity and a boost to the self-confidence of youths like myself. After a month in the army, I already thought I was something better than ordinary civilians. Pin a few bars or ribbons on a soldier's uniform, and he thinks that the world should turn upside down for him. The army held a great attraction for and a power over our young, impressionable minds. So it's no wonder that I was shattered when I got the news that my health was too poor to remain in the service. We had just been transported from Pahlavi over narrow, winding mountain roads to Khānaqīn, where new medical examinations were ordered. I knew I was rather slender, but the medics discovered that I also had a heart defect and a spinal curvature. I had no recourse against their decision and was discharged from the army on medical grounds. It was a terrible blow to me: I wanted to be a soldier, like my brother, so desperately. My brother: I have a nagging suspicion he may have had something to do with my dismissal, although he never admitted it. He may have been trying to protect me, or perhaps he reasoned that, since Father was a soldier and he was a soldier, two Fulmyks were enough to win the war. But be that as it may, that dismissal was a much harder blow than anything I had ever suffered at his hands.

My career in the army was thus short-lived, and I was back to civilian life before my seventeenth birthday. I hated my civilian clothes, and the civilian camp in Tehrān, where I had to stay for the time being. It turned out that my family had left for other refugee camps three weeks earlier. I followed them to Ahwāz only to find out that they had moved on to Karāchi two weeks prior. I kept following in their footsteps until I found them in Karāchi, three weeks before we boarded ships bound for eastern Africa. The destination of our convoy was Mombasa, Tanganyika [Tanzania]. It had previously been a German colony but now was administered by the British. We were sent on to a camp in Tangeru to wait out the war.

It must be part of our national character that when life gets easy, we tend to mess up, but when it squeezes us hard, we can accomplish miracles. At the camp in Tengeru, without waiting for any official instructions, we immediately organized a grammar school, a high school, and even a Boy Scout troop. Thanks to the interventions of Major Czapski, responsible for education and culture in the 2nd Corps, and to the forward thinking of General Anders, the 2nd Corps sent both teachers and Scouting instructors to the African camps. They were badly needed, for the majority of refugees in our camp were youths in their early teens, mostly children of military settlers deported by the Soviets from south-eastern Poland. There weren't more than two dozen seventeen-year-olds, like myself, in our camp of 2000 people.

I had finished the first grade of junior high in Poland before the war. Now I was starting the second grade under an old baobab tree because we still had no classrooms. At first we also had no textbooks, so our teachers had to rely on their own memories. Later some textbooks were printed on portable printing presses we got from the military, and school took off at full speed. I was also active in Boy Scouting, where I earned the rank of Eagle Scout and became a team leader. In our spare time, we organized camping trips in the African wilderness. The fearless, nomadic Masai warriors were frequent guests at our camps, firing our imaginations and our sense of adventure. During one of those camping trips, on the shores of Lake Victoria, we all learned that death was part of Africa's beauty. One of our friends, Jurek Międzyrzecki, was swimming in the lake when a crocodile attacked him. We never found his body. The tragedy dampened our spirits, although did not entirely extinguish our thirst for adventure.

The atmosphere in our refugee camp was charged with patriotism. When our men went against Monte Cassino, we were with them in all our hearts. We sang uplifting songs and wrote letters to Italy. The soldiers in Italy remembered about us, as well. Many gave up their rations of chocolate so that we could get them instead. The boys, or should I say, young men in our camp couldn't wait to join the ranks of Polish soldiers. When in 1944 the army began to recruit, I volunteered again. For two months we were quartered in a transition camp. One day the principal of our high school, Mrs. Dorosz, paid us a visit to inform us that she had intervened with the military command and that several of us, myself included, were ordered back to school to finish the fourth grade. It seemed to me that the army was determined to keep me out of its ranks. But eventually my perseverance paid off, and in April 1945, I put on a military uniform once again, although I never fought the Germans. As we were approaching Aden, we received the news that the war had ended. The Germans must have learned that the third Fulmyk had finally joined the Allied forces, and decided that they stood no chance against him. Shortly afterwards, we disembarked in Italy, and I was sent to the 3rd Corps for basic recruit training. My brother visited me there on his way to Lebanon and helped me get admitted to an officer school which trained sappers in Capua near Naples. On graduation, I was assigned to the 5th Sapper Company and granted two weeks leave to visit Rome. Unfortunately, the day before my departure, we received orders transferring us to Britain. My leave was immediately cancelled, and I saw neither Rome nor the Vatican.

We travelled to England by train. The Polish Resettlement Training Corps was already operational. Since I knew some English, which I learned in the refugee camp in Africa, I was often called upon to serve as an interpreter. I enjoyed that function but it wasn't always easy. Sometimes I was at a loss for English words when our soldiers spoke in their coarse vernacular. In my spare time, I honed my language skills and learned to be tactful by going out on dates—after all, I was twenty by then. After several weeks, both my pronunciation and my ability to translate the soldierly jargon into polite speech improved dramatically.

When I was finally discharged, I went to work in a cookie bakery. A while later I received a two-year scholarship from a fund established by the Polish government-in-exile. I think that the government's efforts to give the young men who had spent a good chunk of their lives on the front a decent start in life are still not fully appreciated. Thanks to my scholarships, I was able to graduate from a vocational school of leather fashions and specialize in designing ladies' handbags. This gave me a good job and excellent prospects for the future.

My mother and one of my sisters finally came to England in 1948. Like most Poles returning from the African camps, they came back with yellowish complexions, revealing that they had been through bouts of malaria. I was one of the few who never suffered from it, although later, in England, I simulated that illness to stay close to my sweetheart, who had come down with it and needed to be hospitalized.

I met my wife a few years later, in 1953. I was twenty-eight and seriously thinking of starting a family. After six months of courtship, we were married in 1954. In the fall of the same year, we immigrated to Canada and settled in Winnipeg. My mother and my two sisters—both married by then—also came with us. In England I had worked as a designer of ladies' handbags, and in Winnipeg I quickly found a similar job. Eventually, I bought my own equipment and started a shop of my own.

At first, we lived with my brother-in-law, Henryk Lorenc, who already had a house in Winnipeg. Within a week, he took me to a meeting of the Polish Combatants Association [PCA], where I met a few of the more active colleagues, including Tadeusz Gardziejewski and Antoni Malatyński. The question of combining the old Polish Chapter #34 of the Canadian Legion, "The Defenders of the Homeland," with our chapter was then being hotly debated. Equally heated were the disputes about the purchase of a house for the association. Wacław Kuzia was deeply involved in that latter venture. At first I was sceptical of those initiatives and kept my distance, but before long I found myself in the vortex of organizational activities.

A few years later, I even became president of the Winnipeg Chapter #13 of the PCA. It was during my tenure, in 1959, that General Sosnkowski* paid us a visit. I sat beside him at the banquet in his honour and confessed to him that I had a terrible case of stage fright and didn't know how I'd manage to give my welcoming speech. He turned to me and said, "Don't worry, son, I'm also nervous as hell." Somehow it made me feel better. Sosnkowski had a special gift of making people feel at ease in his presence; he treated us like his colleagues, without so much as a hint of aloofness. He bore himself just like the rest of us. When I first met him, he was wearing civilian clothes and a well-worn pair of shoes. I felt sorry that a person of his stature did not have a decent pair of shoes. But that was why he commanded so much respect: he had turned down the comfortable pension offered to him by the British and lived, like the rest of us, from his limited means. Today we may have assimilated into Canadian society, but in those days, we were still active, political émigrés from Poland. Sosnkowski was then for us a symbol of Poland still fighting, still not defeated by communism. I also remember meetings with generals Anders, Tokarzewski,† and Kopański,‡ but none of these visits made a comparable impression on me.

My presidency of Chapter #13 coincided with a stormy period in our organization. We were still young men with a clear vision of what

---

* Kazimierz Sosnkowski (1885-1969), commander-in-chief of the Polish Armed Forces, 1943-44.

† Michał Tokarzewski-Karaszewicz (1896-1964), deputy commander of the Polish army in the east (1943-44), commander of the 3rd Polish Corps (1944-45).

‡ Stanisław Kopański (1895-1976), commander of the 1st Carpathian Mountain Brigade (1940-42), chief of general staff (1943-47).

we wanted to accomplish, but with different notions of how to accomplish it. We had the faith of youth but also the inexperience that goes with it. Now I can see that at times our plans were too ambitious, too visionary to come to fruition within our lifetime.

At the same time my personal life began to bear fruit. My son, Witek, was born in 1955; three years later, my daughter, Hania. Like most combatants' children, they both finished university: Witek became a lawyer, and Hania a biologist. My own business flourished as well. Since my arrival in Canada in 1954, I have never asked for a cent of unemployment money. We always managed without it. And the same could be said of practically every Polish veteran of World War II: we were never a burden to Canada. Most of us came with little English but with eager hearts, sturdy backs, and plenty of determination to succeed in our adopted country. And most of us did indeed succeed.

They say that my soul must have horns. And I agree that I have always had a sense of justice and could never walk by glaring injustices without doing something about them. That's why I often spoke up on issues of public interest, wrote to the press, and gave interviews for TV. I have become a part of Canada and joined the mainstream of Canadian life, but in the midst of my involvement in Canadian affairs, I have always tried to smuggle in the Polish cause to show that "Poles are not geese and can speak, too."* Over the years I have also been active promoting Polish Scouting, organizing Polish Saturday schools, supporting the Canadian-Polish Congress, and presiding over *Czas*, a Polish weekly in Winnipeg. My involvement with *Czas* came about rather unexpectedly. A minor crisis was precipitated by the death of Józef Krajewski, the publisher of *Czas*, who was also, for a while, the paper's editor. The matter was discussed in Polish circles, but no one was willing to assume the vacant position with the attendant responsibilities. I was aware that *Czas* could not compete with the leading Polish weeklies but was convinced that it played a crucial role in the life of the Polish community in Winnipeg. That is why I decided to step forward and take up the challenge. I served as publisher of *Czas* for several years. Despite the ups and downs we went through, I remain convinced that it is our duty to support and maintain that publication for the sake of our Polish past, our present, and particularly our future.

---

* A famous quote from a Polish Renaissance writer, Mikołaj Rej (1514-69).

TADEUSZ GARDZIEJEWSKI

I was born in 1919 in the royal town of Kuty, the southernmost town in pre-World War II Poland, a sleepy town dozing since the reign of the Jagiellonians, until it collided with history in the tragic September of 1939. That autumn it became one of the border crossings for the Polish troops, civil servants, and members of government evacuating to Romania. Poles were the minority in Kuty. Armenians were the mayors of the town and were, after Ukrainians and Jews, the third largest ethnic group. The Poles were dead last.

My father was a judge in this town, and I was the youngest of four siblings. We grew up in a home full of love and strict etiquette. No one dared so much as to raise a spoon to his lips before Mother sat down with us at the table. Then we were expected to compliment her on her cooking or to keep our mouths shut.

I attended a high school located some forty-two kilometres away in Kołomyja [Kolomyya]. It was a boarding school, and I often felt homesick. But I could go home to Kuty only for major holidays. The discipline in the boarding school was draconian. Strapping and time out in a special detention room were the order of the day. And yet constant interactions with my peers, camping, Scouting, and cadet corps helped me understand the importance of comradery in a group, and in the army. This Spartan upbringing probably had a considerable influence on the way I weathered the later vicissitudes of my life.

Then came the matriculation exams. My class was the second-last to take the old-style exams, before Minister Wacław Jędrzejewicz introduced his school reforms, which created different kinds of high and secondary schools. Complying with my father's wishes, I went to Jan Kazimierz University in Lwów [L'viv] to study law, although my heart had always been set on medicine. I was hoping to take up medicine after I finished law, as my father suggested.

At the university, I became a member of the Academic Legion, a paramilitary organization. As a rule, the rank earned in the legion was later recognized in the army. Once a week we were confined to barracks and instead of going to classes and lectures, we went to roll call and military exercises. That day we had to wear special uniforms, which we normally kept at home.

In the summer of 1939, after I had finished the second year of my law program, I went home for the holidays. It was a restless summer. Every day we listened to the radio announcements in an atmosphere charged with tense expectation. There were rumours about partial mobilization. There was also much posturing: "Let them try," some would say, "and we'll dance the next waltz in Berlin." My father would often go to the courthouse after hours, expecting at any moment an order to open the sealed, top-secret document cache containing mobilization posters. Finally the order came, and I spotted a policeman hanging a poster on an old oak tree. My brother, four years older than I and an officer in the reserve, was called up for active duty. We listened intently to radio broadcasts, trying to separate the grains of truth from the chaff of speculation. I was convinced that the Academic Legion would also be mobilized any day, so I jumped on my motorcycle and rode to Lwów, only to find that my conviction was unfounded. As there was little I could do there, I had no choice but to face the southern winds and the ride back home. Only later did I realize how dangerous this escapade was, for some Ukrainian factions were already stirring up unrest. Fortunately, I spoke Ukrainian well enough and made it home without incident.

Around the 15th of September, the first small military convoys began to approach Kuty. The main convoys were moving in the direction of Zaleszczyki [Zaleshchiki], and some went towards Śniatyń [Snyatyn], both being border crossings. But the flood of convoys reached Kuty, too. An unbroken chain of vehicles roared and rattled over the bridge on the Prut, built by military engineers. First to cross the bridge was the air force, in highly organized and disciplined units.

86

In the midst of this general frantic activity, I was drafted into the National Defence. They gave us white and red arm bands and old Austrian rifles, almost museum pieces, for which, incidently, we had no ammunition. We were meant to reinforce the Frontier Guards, but to this day I don't have the foggiest idea what that was supposed to mean. If professional Frontier Guards could not control smugglers, how could we do it with our make-believe rifles? Besides, those smugglers later turned out to be valuable allies and helped guide many people over the border. Eventually, we were sent to regulate the traffic moving towards the border, and I was posted at the crossing of two roads, one from the north, from Kosów [Kosov], and the other from Śniatyń. At that post I could see both the drama and the folly of the fleeing crowds. There was much talk, later, about the frantic exodus of civilians, and sarcastic accounts of fashionable ladies with their pets and canary cages streaming along the roads towards the border crossings. True enough, I saw some carrying lapdogs, and I probably thought then that it was foolish vanity, but today, from the perspective of years and experience, I find it neither very surprising nor culpable.

One day a troop of soldiers arrived in Kuty, led by a captain of the reserve and maybe a company strong. They came with jeeps, trucks, a light anti-tank gun, and machine guns, and set up their command centre across the street from our house. The captain announced that he would stop the Bolsheviks, and that he would defend this bridgehead. He sent out soldiers to take positions on the roads leading to town. Word came from Kosów that the Russians had already arrived there. This meant imminent fighting, and people began to panic. The mayor asked my father to persuade the captain that he could not win this war. The captain's nerves had begun to show: he ordered people around and behaved with unbecoming arrogance. So my father confronted him and tried to talk some reason into him. In the meantime, the first columns of Russian tanks were spotted three kilometres away from the town. Whether his common sense waxed or his courage waned, the captain took down his posts and made towards the bridge. Not long afterwards a Soviet tank roared into town. At that moment, a jeep from the captain's unit appeared from the opposite direction. The driver must have spotted the tank and immediately veered in the direction of the bridge. But his reaction was too slow: two bursts from a machine gun reached him before he could make it to safety. Minutes later a Soviet soldier pulled out some documents from the pockets of the slain officer cadet. He was Tadeusz Dołęga Mostowicz, the well-known writer. Some later accounts of his death are clearly inaccurate: I was an eyewitness and saw the manner of his death. I saw his wallet and, in it, an uncashed cheque from ROJ-Publisher for his second-last novel, *The Memoirs of Mrs. Hanka.* Jerzy Horodyński helped organize a decent funeral, and the Armenian Manugiewicz family gave permission to bury him in their sepulchre, which had not yet been used.

That same day local communists, mostly Jews from the Bund [an extreme leftist organization] and some Ukrainians, officially welcomed the invading Red Army. They hastily erected a platform in the market square and decorated it with a tapestry of the Polish national emblem, an eagle displaying its wings, taken from the building of the Gymnastic Association Sokół. From that podium, Master of Laws Krumholz, son of a local innkeeper, greeted the Soviet soldiers. His father had begged him not to do it, and when all his pleas fell on deaf ears, he cast a ritual curse on him. He was so shaken by his son's betrayal that he was stricken with a heart attack and died. His funeral became a quiet manifestation of resistance to the Soviet occupation.

Two days after marching into Kuty, the Soviets arrested my father and took him to the court building. Within four hours the local people collected 4000 signatures requesting his release. The Soviets agreed but classified us into the passport category no. 111, which meant that they considered us a "socially dangerous element." As such, we were forbidden to live within the 100-kilometre border zone or in any provincial city. They gave us three days to pack up the house and leave. A friendly Ukrainian highlander took some of our things "for storage" and gave us a horse and a wagon. We loaded the suitcases onto the wagon and made our slow way to Trembowla [Terebovlya] in Podole [Podolia], to join my sister, who was a teacher there.

Ushered in by the tragic news, the autumn settled in all too quickly. Soon our provisions ran out, and Mother began to think twice about every potato she put into the pot. To help feed the family, one foggy morning I went potato-lifting with some of my high school friends. Out in the field, my lack of agricultural experience became so apparent that I was told to concentrate on collecting potatoes into sacks. Despite this demotion, I was proud that I earned a sack and a half of precious spuds. Later, when the weather got worse, we would go to the woods to cut branches for firewood. Since firewood was scarce in Podole, we began to barter: a cart of wood for half a piglet.

Eventually I found more permanent work, first in a quarry, then building a road to an airport. The labour was hard and paid by the job, but it paid well; so well, in fact, that I was making more than my brother-in-law, a civil engineer supervising the whole works. My ambition was that for the coming Christmas we should have everything that we used to have for Christmases past, before the war. But what inspired me most was the sight of my father, shocked and depressed by the events of 1939, regaining his health and zest for life. Together, we signed up for an accelerated legal course in Ukrainian, which we attended throughout the winter. Our morale was further boosted by word from my brother, who had joined the Polish army in September. He had been taken prisoner by the Germans in a battle near Zamość, but managed to jump the transport and make it back to Lwów.

In October 1940, rumours began to spread that the Soviets would be drafting those born in 1917 and 1918 for military service, and soon the first recruits were sent as workers' battalions, without uniforms, to reinforce defensive positions along the river San. I was conscripted in May 1941. Before I went, I had a serious talk with my father.

"You know, son," he said, "you have to choose between the Soviet prison and the Soviet army. I would rather see you in prison than in a uniform with a Soviet star. But it's your choice, and their prisons are as merciless as the front line."

With these words in mind, after a cursory medical examination, I presented myself to the Drafting Commission, twelve people, including three or four women, behind a long table handsomely wrapped in red flags. The chair of the commission asked me if I should like to have the honour of serving in the worker-peasant army.

"Absolutely not," I replied, "because I grew up in, and identify with, the bourgeois system. The Soviet state declared us a 'dangerous social element,' doesn't allow us to live in the frontier zone, and does not trust us. So how can you draft me into your army?"

General consternation followed. After this reply I was sure they wouldn't talk to me any further but, rather, would throw me in jail. But the chairman got up and said, "Vot, panravilsia mne maladets [I like this boy]. He is not one of those who first shouted 'long live Piłsudski'* and are now shouting 'long live the Red Army.' He says what he thinks, and that's what's important to us. You'll join our army, you'll see what it's all about. And once you're released from active duty, we'll change that unfortunate classification of you and your family."

His opinion was entered into my personal records, and with that I was drafted. I had done my best to evade the draft, but now that my honest efforts had failed, the prospect of serving in the Soviet army didn't worry me much. In fact, it smacked of adventure—well, I was young and fearless. My father, too, came to terms with it. He himself had been a soldier, an officer in the Austrian army, who later had joined the Hallerczyks.† He taught me that the most important thing for a soldier was to have a clean rifle. From a piece of wood he cut out small gadgets for cleaning the rifle, packed them into a cigar box, and added two strips of flannel for the same purpose. Later, when I reported for service and was turning over all my personal effects to be scrupulously recorded, the officer called his senior captain over and asked me what those wooden sticks were. I told him that those were the implements my father had given me so that I could clean my rifle well. The captain ordered the whole company to assemble and showed them the implements with which a father had equipped his son. I was commended, or rather my father was, and this was duly noted in my personal file. I was also awarded 300 rubles for being so well prepared for the duties of a soldier.

From Ukraine, we were taken to a training camp in the Caucasus, in Ordzhonikidze [Vladikavkaz] on the Terek River. Our units were classified as tropical, and we even got hats made of thick canvas, officially called "Panama hats." The daily training sessions in the camp were extremely exhausting. I was already tired after the twenty-minute morning stretching exercises, which were, alas, but a foretaste of what followed. Next was the morning inspection. The Red Army was probably the only army in the world that, in its book of regulations, had an entire chapter devoted just to lice. Regulations demanded that, every

---

* Józef Piłsudski (1867-1935), marshal, statesman, and the first president of independent Poland (1918-22).

† Soldiers serving in the Polish army organized in France during World War I by General Józef Haller (1873-1960).

day, after the morning exercises, we had to take off our cotton shirts and the unit leader had to check us for lice. If he found any, the entire unit had to go to *voshoboinitsa* [de-lousing baths]. We used the latrines almost on command and had to train our bodies to be regular. After a long day jammed with physical exertion, relieved only by singing lessons and singing contests with other units, everyone was completely drained. To ensure that we all got a good night's sleep, the leader took attendance in the evening.

Our training was aimed at developing automatic, reflexive reactions. For example, on command we had to detach the cartridge-belt, open the rifle lock, insert the magazine with ten bullets, set the hindsight, assume position, and pull the trigger. All this had to be done in three seconds. At first it seemed impossible, but after a while one became so practised that the assigned regulation time was enough not only to perform all these tasks but to scratch one's nose as well. It was the same with wrapping our feet in cloth (instead of socks). On the first few tries, our feet would get entangled or the cloth would not hold, but with practise we could wrap our feet perfectly in seconds.

The Red Army wholeheartedly adopted Suvarov's[*] principle that "the more sweat during exercises, the less blood in battle." They adhered to it strictly, so much so that the commander would ride out on horseback to check if the shirts of soldiers returning from exercises showed the dark contours of sweat. Hardly any other army in the world could so consistently squeeze out the last gasp from a soldier. If the repetitive, mindless exercises didn't do it, the marathons in gas masks certainly did. After the war with Germany broke out, Stalin ordered that a recruit should be trained into a front-line soldier in three months. This was achieved by training sixteen hours a day.

The scarcity of military supplies in the camp encouraged stealing as an effective method of assembling all the necessary equipment. I remember someone once stole my gas mask. When I reported this to my superior, he shrugged his shoulders and said, "It's your business to make sure you have everything you need." This ability to swipe what one didn't have but needed was called a "soldier's resourcefulness."

---

[*] Aleksander Vasilevich Suvarov (1729-1800), a Russian field marshal who took part in the French Revolutionary Wars.

Most units were ethnically mixed and comprised a variety of nationalities. As a Pole from western Ukraine, I was considered an exotic chap. Few of the soldiers in the camp had been to the West, but all were very curious about the way of life there. They kept asking questions, which I tried to answer as honestly as I could; needless to say, the information they got from me did not always mesh with the official Soviet version political officers tried to inculcate in them.

In fact, we had two kinds of training officers: some taught us military matters, others political. The political officers, or *politruks*, had to go through special ideological training after graduating from a military college. We had to attend classes with the *politruks* every day. One objective of their intensive propaganda was to discredit religion. At one such lecture, a *politruk* strived to prove to us that making a sign of the cross with a holy icon to turn away a hail cloud was pure superstition. Then he turned towards me and asked if I believed him. "Sure I agree with you," was my reply, "because you've repeated what every self-respecting *pop* [priest] worth his robes says." This last part of my answer caused him some consternation, but he was not ready to accept that such superstitions have nothing to do with true religion, which tries to eradicate them. He could not get over the fact that I, "an educated man, believed in God." I tried to remind him that the Soviet constitution guarantees every citizen freedom of religion, but he cut short my argument with a rather ominous "We'll discuss this again, later." On other occasions, *politruks* tried to convince us of the moral superiority of the Soviet soldiers. The Soviet soldier, the argument went, instinctively understood the need for discipline, whereas in the Western armies, discipline had to be implemented with clubs. In those armies "corporal" was a special rank whose duty was to club the soldier into carrying out orders. That's why, if caught and interrogated, a soldier should never admit to the rank of corporal. The tortuous logic behind this advice still escapes me.

When the war with Germany broke out, the soldiers' morale was propped up by reading the orders of comrade Stalin. At first, Moscow also sent us new patriotic songs, which were self-confident, even swaggering. But when the Soviet units began to surrender in large numbers, the tone of messages from Moscow changed: we were informed of death sentences in absentia for twenty-three Soviet generals, including General Vlasov, for high treason.

In this increasingly tense atmosphere, endurance and shooting exercises became even more intensive. I was not particularly affected by the pace of these exercises because the experience I had gained as a student in the cadet corps and in the Academic Legion had prepared me for it. I liked target shooting and shot well. My steady hand even earned me some additional income from testing the rifles, a well-paid function in the Red Army. I made quite a bit of money this way, well over 3000 rubles. In addition, I was excused from some other exercises. I also had good results in the so-called application shooting. We were using, among others, old Maxims [heavy machine guns], which I knew well from the cadet corps. The shooter did not know which targets would appear and at what distance. I quickly got a feel for this, and only took a few rounds to fell the last target. At that moment the colonel ordered us to stop shooting and assembled the battalion in a square, the officers in the front. He called me into the middle of the square and recited the regulation formula thanking me for good shooting. As per regulations, I was supposed to reply "Sluzhu Savetskamu Saiuzu" [I serve the Soviet Union]. But I felt my flesh creep at the very thought of saying that, so I decided to say nothing. A tense, uneasy moment of silence followed, all eyes on me. And suddenly an illumination came. I remembered one of the recently promoted slogans and roared from the top of my lungs, "I serve the common cause of crushing fascism!" The colonel saluted, smiled, and dismissed the soldiers. Later I tried to convince the *politruk* that stage fright had made me forget the regulation formula. He didn't believe me, but he understood.

In order to intensify the ideological indoctrination of soldiers, all freshly recruited units were assigned so-called *politboets*, young students not yet of conscription age but with special political training, whose task was to help raise the socio-political awareness of the soldiers. They used every spare moment to pull out a newspaper from their gas masks, or some even less savoury hiding place, and quote from it the words of wisdom or encouragement recently dispensed by comrade Stalin. They found little favour with the soldiers because they intruded into the few quiet moments that could have been spent more profitably smoking a joint of shag. Some called them names and hurled unflattering epithets at them or their mothers, even though, officially, this was forbidden in the Red Army. Often this was done in an indirect way, using slang expressions that on the surface seemed innocuous enough, but whose underlying meanings were apparent to everyone in the camp.

One day, during the grenade-throwing practice, a newly arrived *politboets* took some unfriendly interest in me, having heard my name bandied about in the unit. He learned I was a Pole from western Ukraine. "Why do they feed him here," I heard him saying to other soldiers; "at his first opportunity, at his first patrol, he'll desert to the Germans anyway." I heard all this from where I was sitting a short distance away, after hurling my six regulation grenades. It doesn't bode well for me if this *politboets* thinks and speaks this way about me, I thought. So I decided to deal with this in a Soviet manner. I went up to him and said, "Comrade, I am that Tadia you've just spoken about. When we're through with these exercises, you'll go to the *politruk* and report to him what you've just said about me to the other comrades." He began to explain that he didn't really mean it, but I was firm and threatened that if he didn't report this, I would have to do it myself. I also added that I would go with him to make sure that his report was accurate. And so we went to the *politruk*, who listened to his report and then dismissed us. When we returned from exercises to the barracks, we found that the *politboets*'s bed was folded up and his things packed. He had ceased to exist as far as the company was concerned. I never learned what happened to him or where he went. On some later occasion the *politruk* remarked that I did the right thing, but to this day I don't know if what I did was really right or not.

Five of us in the unit stuck together and formed a small yet effective team. Kazimierz Świerczyński, from Mińsk, was a Pole, though born in Russia; his mother was a teacher, but he didn't speak much Polish and knew only "Powrót Taty" ["Papa's Return"].* His attitude towards the communist system was negative in the extreme, but when his grating, sour comments gave way to song, his voice was melodious and as strong as his well-built body. Bohachenko, another from our team, was a Ukrainian. As a civilian, he had been the leader of a rescue team on the Kasbek Mountain in the Caucasus. The third, Kolosov, was a

---

* A well-known poem by the Polish Romantic poet Adam Mickiewicz (1798-1855).

teacher of Russian literature in a high school. I enjoyed going on patrols with him because he would recite Lermontov[*] for hours, and, later, when I had gained his trust, Esenin[†] as well. Those three I remember well. Then there was the fourth, Evert, from one of the German republics along the Volga River. I knew a bit of German from high school, and Evert spoke the same dialect I was taught at school. But he did not stay with us very long and did not go with us to the front line because the Red Army did not trust the Germans in its ranks. The rest of us managed to stay together through most of the training and, even later, on the front line. We used a simple but effective tactic: whenever we suspected that some soldiers were to be moved to another unit, we positioned ourselves, one beside another, in the middle of the same row. We were more or less the same height, looked good and professional together, and must have projected so confident an image that our superiors did not think it advisable to separate us.

Our first front-line assignment was to the 101st Infantry Regiment of Coastal Defence, which formed part of the navy. We were moved to Krasnodar, where they gave us completely new uniforms. They also began to feed us better, according to the front-line norms. We stuck together, our old team, all except Evert. We were allowed to build a dugout, and, thanks to Bohachenko, who was quite experienced at that sort of thing, we soon had relatively comfortable living quarters.

In Krasnodar I was still learning the ways of the Red Army. One day Bohachenko noticed several bales of white cotton fabric beside some railway cars being loaded with troops. Those bales of fabric were used at airfields as part of a signalling system. So he quickly picked them up and carried them on his back to the dugout. Later we bartered the cloth for food with the local people. On another occasion our team managed to obtain a whole bunch of leather insoles, for the same purpose, throwing them out of a railway car through an opening in the roof. I tried to question the ethics of this method of acquiring provisions, but Bohachenko made fun of me, saying that I behaved like a child and not

---

* Mikhail Lermontov (1814-41), a Russian Romantic poet.

† Sergey Esenin (1895-1925), a Russian nonconformist poet, founder of the imagist movement.

a morally superior soldier of the Red Army. So I decided to grow up and took my share of the loot and provisions.

Eventually we had to give up our comfortable living, though, and were sent to Voroshilovgrad [Luhans'k]. Our regiment was assigned to evacuate civilians from the city because the Soviet command discovered that the Ukrainian population was welcoming the Germans as liberators. They were hoping the Germans would allow them to set up an independent Ukraine. To stop any subversive activities, the Soviets decided to remove all people from the urban centres, turning them into ghost towns below the expanse of the sky.

With Bohachenko in charge, our patrol went to Krasnomaiskaia Street, where the *crème de la crème* of local communists used to live. I remembered well the expulsion and forced resettlement of Polish families from the territories occupied by the communist Soviet forces. Now I tasted the bitterness of revenge. We would walk into an apartment and issue an order, "Sobiratsa s veshchami!" [Take your things and get out]. We gave them three hours to pack and allowed them to take only what was most indispensable. Sometimes people tried to resist our orders, tried to impress on us their importance as members of the Communist Party, but to no avail; there could be no discussion about it. At first my buddies thought this revenge for my family's exile would give me real pleasure or satisfaction, but revenge never does: it opens old wounds and shatters peace. The fear and anxiety of brutally uprooted people were the same here as in my memories from Poland. No one knew if or when they would be back. After overseeing the evacuation, our unit withdrew, leaving behind only messengers who maintained communication with other troops.

The front line was getting closer and closer. With the advent of winter, we went into action on the 4th Ukrainian Front on the Donets steppes. We were well equipped for the cold: warm underwear, gloves, caps with earmuffs. The Soviets had been looking forward to this winter. After Napoleon's failed expedition against Moscow, there lived a saying that it was not General Kutuzov* but General "Moroz" [Frost] who defeated the French. And now the Germans were also poorly

---

* Mikhail Larionovich Kutuzov (1745-1813), a Russian field marshal during the Napoleonic Wars of 1812.

prepared for the oncoming winter, proving, it seems, that history, indeed, repeats itself.

I'll never forget my first contact with the Nazi enemy. We were being transported to the front line in railway cars and had stopped at a small station called Likhaya, crowded with military transports. Suddenly several German airplanes dove towards us from the sky. The solitary train stop in the middle of the open steppe was an ideal target for them. Bombs began to explode. One of the first hit a car with horses. The roar of diving planes mixed with the neighing of the terrified horses. We were ordered to stay inside or under the cars; instinctively, everyone was trying to push himself into the frozen ground. The bombs hit the cars carrying ammunition, and the explosions looked like a festival display of fireworks. I was both terrified and mesmerized. Then I heard Bohachenko call my name. He led me to one of the bombed cars, and as we approached, I could smell vodka. We pulled out an undamaged crate of vodka and carried it back to our car. Right away several of our buddies smelled it too, and in no time we were drinking between the tracks. Someone took out an accordion, and we spontaneously broke out in song. The mood became joyful, as if there was no war. Fortunately, other than some damaged cars and drunken heads, our transport did not suffer any serious losses.

When we reached the reorganization centre of the 4th Ukrainian Front, we were taken by trucks and on foot to reinforce the most seriously endangered positions. For the first few days, we engaged in positional warfare during daytime and in reconnaissance excursions at night. Then came the first battle. I was assigned to 82 mm mortars directly supporting the infantry attack. The Germans had a whole company of machine guns hidden in stacks of pressed straw. They had an excellent firing position. Despite less favourable positions, the Soviets used the so-called wave attack: first one wave of soldiers rushed forward, another right behind it, and then a third one. Our task was to pound the stacks of straw, where the deadly machine guns were located. At that moment I really cared about the Soviet soldiers and desperately wanted to blow up that straw. We fired a whole round of shells before we managed to ignite it. I think we saved some Soviet lives and received a citation for it.

Although we took the town, we couldn't keep it long and had to withdraw again. There were no civilians left in the town except for an ancient man in a bunk on top of a stove. He did not care who came, or who went, and he wouldn't budge from his hut. After we left, one of our caring nurses, active also in counter-intelligence, stayed behind with him. She posed as the old fellow's daughter, who had remained to look after him. Some time later she forced her way back to us and reported that the Germans were preparing something unusual and were already celebrating in an Orthodox church turned into a clubhouse. Our battalion commander decided to send out an independent reconnaissance party. Eighteen of us went on that mission. We got to the Orthodox church without incident. The church had three windows on each side, so six of us took clusters of grenades, crawled up to the walls, and tensely waited for the right moment. From inside we could hear the clinking of glasses, ribald laughter, jabbering German voices—a party in full swing. Suddenly the doors opened and several Germans staggered out. It was time to act. We sprang up and, straining every muscle, hurled thirty grenades through the windows, then jumped back. The roof of the church bounced up with the force of the explosions. We ran away like hell. Out of the door and straight into my path dashed a German soldier, gun in hand. I bumped into him. He fell down, but kept his eyes on me. My index finger tensed on the trigger. So did his. But neither of us pulled. He got to his feet and, with his eyes still on me, scampered away. So did I.

Under the confused, frantic fire of the surprised Germans, some of us managed to retrace our way back to our units. But fewer than half were so lucky. Eighteen set out, but only eight came back: the six grenade throwers and two from the back-up. We reported to the general. He knew I was a Pole from western Ukraine. He praised us for the job well done and offered us vodka accordingly. We were also supposed to get some medals, but for the time being we got three days off duty. Thanks to that furlough, I missed a German assault in which a good many soldiers from my unit were killed. Then, after yet another attack, the Germans blew us completely apart and began to encircle the shattered troops. I got out of their tightening grip by hitching a ride on a truck fender. From my entire regiment, only a handful of men survived. When we reassembled further away from the front line, our regimental commander stood before us and said—and I still remember his exact words—"All that's left of our regiment is eighteen men and the number." We used to be the 101st Regiment.

The regiment had to be completely reorganized. We were joined by three new battalions and hoped we would not be sent to the front line for a while. In the meantime, we reinforced the auxiliary services, some of us working as messengers.

At that time we had already heard about the agreement between General Sikorski and Stalin. So the regimental commissar—he had a Jewish name, Ginsburg—once asked me why I didn't request to be transferred to the Polish army. I said I doubted it would be possible. But he told me to write up a formal request and to report to the commander, who must have had some Polish blood in him, judging by his name, Orzechowski. The commander looked at me, then at Ginsburg, and decreed that if I wanted to fight, I could do so in my present unit; if I didn't, I'd be put before a firing squad. This pronouncement sent shivers down my spine, and the mention of the firing squad brought back unpleasant memories from an earlier period of my service in the Soviet army.

It was back when we were still at the training camp. After our last exercises before promotion to officers, as I recall, we were surprised by a storm and soaked through to the skin. When three starry rockets announced the end of the exercises, everyone, muddied and exhausted, had only one thing on his mind: rest. One of my buddies in the squad was a Georgian, Kariagin. Georgians considered themselves superior to Slavs, and their attitude towards the Russians was definitely supercilious. As I was busy putting up a tent, Kariagin took his shovel and mine and went down to wash them in a stream. When he came back, the tent was already standing. He lay down and rolled a shag smoke. Just then the *starshyna*, the company sergeant, walked up to him, dropped six more dirty shovels, and ordered the Georgian to wash them. Kariagin eyed him up and down and said, "Okay, but not now. After such an effort I deserve a smoke. I washed our shovels, our tent is up. I'll wash yours later." Again, this time more harshly, the *starshyna* repeated his order that the shovels be washed immediately. I wanted to take the shovels down to the stream, but he would not let me, insisting that the Georgian carry out the order. Meanwhile Kariagin was sitting unperturbed and smoking his shag. The day after we returned to the barracks, all exercises were cancelled, and a court martial was announced. As we soon discovered, our Kariagin was being charged with "refusing to carry out an order during wartime." Two soldiers from each platoon were chosen to participate in the court's proceedings. The battalion commissar was the council for the defence, the *politboets* was the prosecutor. Very quickly the court reached the verdict that the defendant had indeed refused to carry out an order. Kariagin relinquished his right to say any last words and defend himself. He only declared that even though he might have something to say because he did in fact have a witness, he was reluctant to call on that witness, knowing that the witness might then have to share his unenviable fate. This was a compassionate gesture in my direction. For my part, I could not intervene or contribute in any way to the proceedings without being called upon. And no one summoned or tried to interview me. The next day the sentence was announced: execution by a firing squad. Such was Soviet military justice.

Returning to the reorganization of our regiment after its near-total destruction, the *zviaznoi* [courier services] to which I was assigned in the interim set my military career and my life on a new course, although at the time I did not know that, of course. In December 1941, I received an order to deliver some letters to the Ministry of Defence, Draft Board, taking advantage of the first train that was being assembled in the recently recaptured Rostov-Moscow sector. In the distance, we could still hear the rumble of the battlefield. The train could not have been more than a few cars, occupied mostly by the military. I had enough food for three days, but even if the journey was to take longer, I did not worry: it was generally accepted that couriers could eat at any military or field kitchen. Similarly, they had the right to use any available means of transportation.

On the train, soldiers liked to talk, whether out of loneliness or anxiety, and striking up a conversation was quick and easy. I remember one such eager conversationalist, a captain whose clothes and manner instantly betrayed a reservist. We shared a compartment. He offered me a piece of pork fat, a rather rare token of hospitality in Russia and a sign that he took to me warmly. His name was Polish, Kowal, and he was probably of Polish descent, he said. He guessed from my accent that I was either a Ukrainian or a Pole. At one of the train stops, when the cars screeched to a halt, he asked me to bring some *kipiatok* [boiling water], used for making tea or porridge. A water container and a spoon were the two utensils indispensable for wartime travellers. But I was not a regular traveller, so the captain gave me his kettle and asked me to bring enough boiling water for both of us. In the lineups for the water, there was another generally observed rule, which required that every tenth civilian give up his spot to a soldier. So I got through the lineup relatively quickly and returned to the compartment. The captain, somewhat surprised, looked up at me and said, "I didn't think you'd be back." "Why?" I asked. He explained, "Do you see those soldiers in the lineup? Half of them are deserters." Not the obvious kind of deserters, mind you, but deserters nonetheless. They were a special breed of deserters, known already in the Tsar's Imperial Army. Their tactics had not changed much in the Red Army, but little could be done about them, it seemed. Everyone had the right to get some *kipiatok*. So an unwilling soldier would join the lineup and contentedly stay in it until his unit left. Since it was practically impossible to catch up with a unit, no one even tried. The soldier would go to the station headquarters and report that he had been left behind; he would be registered, along with many others like him. A new unit would be formed and sent to the front line, only to disperse accidentally on the way in the same manner. Thousands of such soldiers roamed the front-line zone. My good captain Kowal thought I was one of them. I did not elaborate on this subject because I hardly knew him, and one never knew who one was really talking to. He asked me if I belonged to the [Communist] Party. I said I didn't. He nodded his head, but his eyes told me that he gave little credence to what I said. Well, one cannot trust what people say these days, he probably thought.

At first there were only two of us in the compartment. But later a few others joined us, including a military nurse and a few youths. Someone pulled out a guitar from a sack, and the nurse began to sing. The atmosphere became friendly and warm. I was sitting beside the window and noticed that it had begun to snow, the snowflakes dense and heavy. Until that moment I had not realized that it was the 24th of December. Outside the train's windows, dusk was falling. I withdrew from the conversation and sank deep into my thoughts and memories. Russians are unusually sensitive to this state of mind. There is only one common word for it in Polish, *tęsknota* [longing], but in Russian there are several. A Russian woman asked me if I felt homesick, but another cut in, "Leave him alone. Today is Christmas Eve. He is probably remembering Christmas Eve suppers with his family at home. It's a

Polish tradition; I know, my aunt is Polish." The compartment grew quiet. Then the guitar strings gently broke the silence: a soft tune and a song describing an evening over a freezing river, the moonlit night, and the silence among the frosted branches where a nightingale used to sing; then, an appeal to a friend that he not forget his own, though fate may cast him in foreign lands. "Milyi drukh, nezhnyi drukh . . . " [My dear friend, tender friend . . .]. I broke down. Captain Kowal asked the girl to write down the words of the song for me. Just recently, looking through some old scraps of paper, I found that song. The girl's name was Maria Orly. That was my Christmas Eve, 1941. I ate a piece of herring and some army wholemeal bread. The snowstorm behind the windows grew more fierce, and the train could no longer move on. We stopped in the middle of open fields, no towns or stations in sight. We could not open the door because the train was almost snowed under, so we climbed onto the roof. Only the black vents peeped out of the snow. Inside it grew warm.

Next morning came the snowploughs, and we made it to a junction station outside Moscow. We were redirected eastward. The High Command I was going to had moved from Moscow to Kuybyshev [Samara], and, as I soon discovered, all the embassies were relocated there as well, including an agency of the Polish army, which was being organized just then. I was deeply moved when, at the station in Kuybyshev, I saw our national emblem, the Polish eagle, and a sign that read in Polish, "Information point for those travelling to join the Polish army." I could hear loud conversations in Polish. But when I approached those rough-looking, tired men in my Soviet military uniform, I sensed resentment, or at least reservation. At that moment I decided to shed my Soviet uniform and join the Polish army. I was uniformed as per the Soviet regulations, and carried a rifle with ninety rounds of ammunition and six grenades. I walked up to a wicket with a Polish sign; there was a staff sergeant in charge, who etched deeply into my memory. I asked if he could tell me how to reach the Polish army. He looked at me rather scornfully and said, "You're already in the army, isn't that enough?" And then, with more than a touch of sarcasm, "What other army do you need?" I walked away disappointed but soon joined another Polish group. They were more sympathetic to my plight, and I bought them dinner at a restaurant.

Later I returned to the uncooperative sergeant and again tried to explain my circumstances, but it was all in vain. Yet I did not give up. I located the Polish Embassy in Piervomaiskaia Street, in a hotel housing a number of diplomatic missions, and I went there the next day. It was a Sunday. In front of the hotel, fluttering in the wind, were the British, American, and Polish national flags. Outside the entrance stood Soviet guards. Pedestrians had to cross to the other side of the street. There, for the first time, I saw Polish pilots in British uniforms with badges reading "Poland" on their sleeves. The difficult part was getting inside. I chose a moment when several officers were walking in, and quickly slid in behind them. It worked. In the Polish embassy, I almost bumped into a waiter carrying a tray of rolls and fresh coffee. From too much excitement, it seemed, the world swirled around me. I steadied myself and asked to see the ambassador. They asked me if I knew his name. "Stanisław Kot," I said. When asked about the nature of my business, I decided to show them all my cards. "I'm a deserter from the Soviet army," I admitted, and then explained how I had been drafted by the Soviets. I added that there were many others, mostly from western Ukraine and Belarus, conscripted like myself into the Red Army. I had to wait until breakfast and then Mass were over. With Ambassador Kot I exchanged not more than a few words, but the upshot was that I was sent to see Captain Przewłocki. He knew the academic circles at Lwów University, so the names I mentioned convinced him that I was telling the truth. He instructed me to return to the railway station and report to the sergeant in charge. "But that sergeant would have nothing to do with me," I objected. Przewłocki smiled and said, "Tell him to come see me tonight." Realizing that fate, too, was beginning to smile on me, I asked if he could give me a pass and some civilian clothes so that I could safely leave the building. "I'm afraid we can't risk our relatively good relations with the Soviet authorities. Warrants for your arrest have probably already been sent out. You'd better change your name." His advice was good, but so much for smiling fate. Right there I decided that I would take my brother's name and the surname of my last girlfriend in Trembowla. Tadeusz Gardziejewski would become Adam Pawlik. But I had to somehow leave the embassy still as a Soviet soldier, and I knew what would happen if they discovered that I was a deserter. The guard did ask me for an ID. I showed him my courier papers, and he looked me up and down but let me go. I had done it again. As I was walking towards the railway station, I was so lighthearted I felt like singing.

For the third time I faced the sergeant in the wicket. I spoke somewhat hesitatingly, "I'm sent here by Captain Przewłocki. He said you'd help me arrange transport to the Polish army." "What else did he say?" asked the sergeant. "I told you already." "Did he say anything else?" he insisted. Suddenly, in a flash, I remembered that Przewłocki instructed me to request that the sergeant come see him in the evening. Only then did I realize that this invitation was a code of sorts. "You should have said that right away." The sergeant's face brightened with a big smile.

A few days later, on the New Year's Eve, the winter dusk was falling. I was supposed to join the transport to Totskoye, but did not know which platform it was waiting at. I asked around but no one seemed to know. It grew dark and cold. Pressed by nature, I sought out the latrines, which consisted simply of several slabs of concrete, each with a hole in the middle and two spots marked for feet. Having served only in all-male units, I did not realize that the Red Army latrines were used by women and men, and I was about to be educated in this regard. As I was squatting over a hole, in comes a lass in a uniform and squats over a hole next to me. I tried modestly to avert my eyes, but at that very moment the sirens announced the coming of the New Year. My latrine neighbour turned towards me and, despite the rather undignified position, she extended her New Year's greetings, "Z novom godom, maladoi chelavek" [Happy New Year, young man]. I do not remember what I replied, but every New Year's Eve I recall what I suppose were her heartfelt wishes.

Shortly after midnight, I went up on an overpass that ran a few feet above the roofs of the trains. At random I picked a transport train, climbed over the railing, lowered myself as far as I could with my hands, and jumped onto the roof of a car. Quickly I slid down, and then I thanked my luck: I could hear people speaking Polish inside. It was the same group I treated to soup at the station restaurant. A bottle of vodka appeared, a few drinks, and I don't even know when I fell asleep. They woke me up in Totskoye.

In Totskoye I gave my name as Adam Pawlik. Captain Przewłocki must have already passed on the information, and I had no difficulty getting registered. I was assigned to the 19th Regiment, the "Children of Lwów." In the meantime, some friends from the train helped me change my clothes. Rather foolishly, I got rid of my good army great-coat in exchange for some rags. A few days later, on January 6, 1942, we were loaded onto another train going no one knew where. The cars had previously been used for transporting cattle; now, long boards nailed across the width of the car had to do as bunks. In the middle a *teplushka*, or a small stove, had been installed. Finding fuel for it was the occupants' responsibility, which usually meant stealing it from other cars. We decided to be different: we bought three buckets of coal from the engine driver and carried it back to the car in our jackets. The train ride was long. We passed through Toshkent and Gorod Khlebny. Finally, we reached our destination, Guzar, past Samarkand. As we were leaving the train, we could see peach trees in full bloom. Here was our camp, and the recruitment commissions began their work.

Called before the recruitment commission, I faced an emaciated doctor staggering from exhaustion. I was 175 centimetres in height and weighed seventy-five kilograms. The doctor, hardly able to walk without holding onto the wall, asked me, "Where have they kept you?" "In Russia," I replied. "Interesting," he murmured, and straight from the scales I was placed under arrest. Fortunately, a short interview with a lieutenant cleared up the matter: I told him about my meeting with Captain Przcwłocki and suggested they check with him. His name was like a magic word, and I was released right away.

My good physical condition turned out to be crucial for my survival at the next stage, when all of us had to go through the quarantine. Coming from all over the Soviet Union, people brought diseases: typhoid fever, spotted fever, amoebic dysentery. A lack of drinkable water compounded the problem. Cotton plantations in the vicinity of Guzar were irrigated through a system of canals called *ariki*. They were our only source of water, brownish-yellow in colour from the clay particles suspended in it. People were dying like proverbial flies. There was a period when only three of us, Sawicki, Pokrowski, and myself, were strong enough to carry the cauldrons with soup, the only hot meal we received. I quickly advanced in rank because I knew how to put up the Soviet tents issued to us. My Soviet training officers would have been proud of me. Lieutenant Mazur once eyed me, more piercingly than usual, and asked why I was trying to hide my true rank. I tried to explain that I had never served in the Polish army, only in the

Academic Legion, but he didn't believe me. Again, I referred him to Captain Przewłocki, if he wanted to know more about me. The magic of Przewłocki's name worked another wonder. Lieutenant Mazur left me alone, but not before delegating to me some additional duties— those of a scribe.

Someone had to keep records of the burgeoning personnel in the camp. The task was not easy for a very prosaic reason: we had absolutely no paper. The only cellulose material we could find were the army-issue paper bags used for packaging biscuits. We cut those bags into sheets and turned them into personnel record cards. But once, in a local town, I walked into a bookstore boasting complete sets of Lenin's works, printed on high-quality paper. The volumes were full of photographic reproductions, with the reverse side always left blank. I immediately bought a set: the blank pages were much better for record keeping than biscuit bags.

Lieutenant Mazur ensured that I never sat idle. What passed for our military hospital was overflowing with people suffering without any medications. I remember one of them, Stanisław Tworek, lying mostly unconscious for a fortnight, crying only, "Oh, God! Someone help." Under those conditions, working as a nurse was not only one of my assignments, but also a basic Christian duty. As days went by, many suffered from night blindness caused by vitamin deficiency. They were afraid to go to the latrines on their own because there were cases of people falling into the foul pits, so the healthier among us had to take the weak there and back. I worked out a pretty efficient method whereby I could take with me, simultaneously, four fellows in need of relief. They had to hold onto my belt with one hand and could use the other to unbutton their pants. I was strong enough to support them all.

During the quarantine bread was transported on a cart drawn by those who could walk. The cart also had another use. For the morning roll call, all had to leave their tents. The company sergeant required that those who died during the night be carried out and placed on the left flank. I remember one morning when sixteen bodies, out of a company of 450, were laid out there. Several nights later, I shared a bunk with a colleague who had contracted typhoid fever. Turning from one side to the other, I suddenly felt that his body was already rigid. I looked at him: his eyes were looking somewhere beyond life, his jaw drooping. I got out of the tent and walked about till the morning. Those same carts that we used to carry bread one way were used to carry away the dead on the way back.

The winter of 1942 was almost over. I was given my own squad, and we were issued one blanket for every two men. I lined up my squad and warned them not to trade their blankets for food or drink, which was a common practice. I asked their names for my records. The first from the left in the front row said "Kot" [a cat], and the fellow right behind him shouted "Sikora" [a tomtit]. I told them to change their places in the line because I didn't want to have a cat and a bird under one blanket. The joke was rather lame, but the men laughed at it. Their mirth broke the ice and earned me the reputation for a good sense of humour.

After a surprise spring snowstorm, it was announced that the camp would be moving, but in which direction no one seemed to know. Expectation and hope were almost palpable in the air. We could feel that this time we'd be leaving the Soviet Union for good. It was then that Stanisław Tworek came back from the hospital. He was still so weak he could hardly walk on his own, and someone always had to go with him to the latrine. I felt sorry for him because I knew that the seriously ill and weak were not going to make the transport. Stanisław knew that, too, so he said to me, "Grandpa (that was my nickname), you wouldn't leave me behind, would you?" What could I say? I assured him he'd go with us. I sent him to the railway stop together with the others and told them to look after him. Then I entered his name in the transport register. But at the roll-taking, just before the departure, Stanisław was not there. The train began moving. At that moment Stanisław emerged from a ditch with another, healthier fellow. There was no chance he could jump onto the moving train, so I caught him by his arm and pulled him inside the car. Many years later, in Winnipeg, when Stanisław had attained the remarkable weight of 110 kilograms, my friends had many a good laugh remembering how I had single-handedly pulled him onto the moving train. It was not much of a feat then, but it would be a miracle now.

We soon realized we were moving in the direction of the sea. When we arrived at a harbour, they transferred us onto a coal ship. Now we knew we were leaving Stepmother Russia, and with no regrets. In the general excitement, an error in judgement landed me in an act of good will. I thought that wherever we would arrive, *chervontse* [red rubles] would be worthless. I still had quite a reserve of them from my days in the Soviet army, so I donated most of them to the Red Cross, keeping only a few banknotes. As it turned out later, this was mighty generous of me because all *chervontse* could, in fact, be exchanged in Persia. But we were so excited about leaving Russia behind that we gave little thought to our destination.

We landed in Pahlavi on April 1, 1943. Marching through the town, we wondered if the abundance we saw was real or just an April Fool's Day's joke. The stalls were crammed with breads, meats, dairy products, fruits. No lineups, no rations. This was our first glimpse of Persia, and we could hardly believe our eyes. But back in the temporary camp, reality caught up with us: disinfection, baths, the burning of uniforms issued in Russia. Hindu nurses—all male—applied Lysol to our bodies with brushes, then shaved our heads and all the rest with blunt razors. Now we knew we weren't dreaming.

It was also on the sandy beaches of Pahlavi that we first tasted British food rations. After gut-wrenching hunger in the Soviet Union, our new rations seemed almost wasteful. In Russia, bread was sliced in the presence of a committee, and the drawing of lots determined who got which slice. But here in Persia, the British issued food for an entire squad, and then its members divided it among themselves. We also got one hot meal a day from the field kitchen. A loaf of bread was shared by three soldiers. Later we also got rations of bacon, butter, sardines, jam, and marmalade, all in larger portions for six. While stuffing ourselves with these delicacies, some of us worried that at that rate of consumption, the supplies would run out fast. It took us more than a month to realize that there was enough food for everyone to have his fill. Soon after our arrival, some boys found it hard to resist an extra helping, as if trying to make up for all the months of hunger. It was no surprise that many of them suffered the consequences of too much, too fast: aching bellies and indigestion.

If the abundance of food was one shock, the burning of heaps of battledress issued in Russia was another. The old uniforms seemed to us perfectly good, usable stuff, and destroying them seemed a terrible waste, especially to those among us who had experienced first-hand the lack of good clothing in Russia. But of course there was a good reason for the burning: to prevent the spread of disease and vermin that infested our Russian uniforms.

From Pahlavi we were transported to a desert camp in Ahwāz. For that move, the British hired a private Persian company, which packed us into their trucks like herrings into a can. Persian drivers sped along the serpentine mountain roads with bravura and panache, and, apparently, without any fear of death. Indeed, it took a lot of courage not to jump off the truck. Driving uphill, the driver used a special kind of handbrake: a helper riding on the step of the truck, hanging onto the door with one hand and holding a big stone in the other. If the truck had to stop, the helper had to jump off and push the stone under a wheel to make sure the truck did not roll back and over a precipice. Despite such precautions, there were two serious accidents with trucks rolling down, and two or three people died.

Before reaching our final destination, we stopped at yet another transition camp. The British had set it up in beautiful apartment blocks beside a munitions factory, which the Germans had built for the Persians seven kilometres away from Tehrān. Our entire transport, which had landed in Persia on April 1, was quartered there. The camp was surrounded by fences, and British military police kept order during the official record-taking. We stayed there for Easter. I don't know how, but the Persians got wind of our Polish taste for hard-boiled eggs at Eastertide and were selling them all over the place. Everyone could buy as many eggs as his heart (or pocket) desired.

After Easter we were taken to the desert camp in Ahwāz. I had not seen a real desert before. Ahwāz has one of the highest average temperatures in the Middle East. Our bodies recoiled now from the 43°C heat as they had from the -37°C cold in Totskoye. Probably as a result of those drastic changes in temperature, I lost all my hair, although my superiors attributed the problem to the excessive amount of time I stubbornly spent in the showers. The most painful place in the camp was, indisputably, the latrines. For disinfection, all wooden seats were regularly smeared with crude oil; the rubber soles of our runners melted in contact with the heated oil; and the odours were almost overpowering. When not in the showers or latrines, we dressed for the weather as much as possible: we were issued tropical cork helmets, and we rolled up our shorts above our knees. Sunbathing under the fiery sky was, of course, out of the question. That desert sky was never azure: during the day it displayed various shades of opal, while at night it grew cold and black and scintillated with bright stars. With the setting of the sun, the desert quickly lost its heat, so that those who were on duty at night had to wear sheepskin coats, and hoarfrost covered the tents.

Here again I incurred the displeasure of the Polish military bureaucracy. They were recruiting for the various branches of service, but mostly for the air force. To join the air force, one had to be young (eighteen to twenty-one years of age), have completed at least a few grades of high school, and, most important, be in excellent physical condition. I was tempted by the prospect of flying and thought I met all the criteria. Unfortunately, my chances were dashed by someone who had entered in my records that I had been a volunteer in the Red Army and a draftee in the Polish army. I insisted that the records be changed, claiming that the reverse was true: I was a volunteer in the Polish army and a deserter from the Soviet. The row ended with my being put on report.

I ended up in a reconnaissance unit of the 7th Infantry Battalion of the Carpathian Brigade, some of whose instructors had fought in Tobruk. We trained in light carriers: open, lightly armoured, tracked vehicles with a crew of two. They were so manoeuvrable that one could turn around on a spot, thanks to the differential rotation of the tracks. They were used mainly for reconnaissance but could also carry ammunition boxes.

In the Carpathian Brigade, the atmosphere was friendly and congenial. All ranks were on a first-name basis, and there was none of the soulless discipline prevalent in other units; in fact, we resisted and fought it at every turn. We carried out orders because failing to do so might hurt our commander's feelings or put him in a bad light. We thought that war in general was senseless and that mindless killing of young people defied reason. But since we ourselves were players in it, we had no choice but to follow orders. We were fond of drawing an analogy between war and the game of soccer. Stripped of its game status, chasing a ball across a field to kick it between two poles is pointless. But impose on this chase a set of rules and a semblance of order, and right away it seems a worthwhile activity. It is similar with war. If you accept certain rules and then play by them, the senselessness of war appears almost rational and comprehensible. Our commander didn't speak much about patriotism or other lofty ideals. Instead, he used to tell us, "Don't be stupid, don't get killed."

Unfortunately, I was not allowed to enjoy the congenial atmosphere of the Carpathian Brigade for long. As fate would have it, I was reassigned to the Carpathian Lancers Regiment, which did not have a particularly good reputation in the Carpathian Brigade. The regiment consisted of three fighting squadrons and one training squadron. The once-famous cavalier style of lancers on horseback could hardly show in motorized units; what remained was a special kind of discipline and the tendency to be different. White stripes on the uniforms and shining brass buckles distinguished the lancers from the rest. But these marks of distinction, especially the polished brass, were not sufficiently appreciated by the other soldiers of the Carpathian Brigade and were a frequent object of ridicule.

My own introduction to the Carpathian Lancers seemed to justify their reputation. During yet another registration, a corporal asked me— I lost count for which time—about my education. I told him I had two years of university. The corporal duly noted that I had two years of education, the reference to the university slipping his attention. And so it was entered in my file that I only had two grades of primary school. When the time came for deciding who qualified for what additional training, I and eight others were assigned to digging latrine pits, while the rest were sent to specialist courses. The instructors flooded them with information about direct and alternating currents, magnetic fields, and the like, and some of the fellows were quickly lost in those subjects. I tried to help them as much as I could, patiently explaining to them the basics of physics and chemistry. An instructor noticed this and asked me how come I knew all this if my file indicated that I could barely read. So once again I was put on report for concealing my education and confusing the authorities. Luckily, the whole mess was soon cleared up, and I was ordered to take a communications course. Such was the beginning of my career in the Carpathian Lancers Regiment.

We went through intensive training and tactical exercises everywhere from Trans-Jordan to Egypt. After so many dislocations and transfers, we stopped speculating about our new destinations. Our base was where we dropped our backpacks, that's how most of us felt. In Cairo, we learned that we'd be boarding a ship for Italy. We were allowed to take with us only what could be fitted into our backpacks and army bags. Many of us had to burn a lot of accumulated stuff in a big bonfire. Then one day, as we were watching the ships riding at anchor in the offing, all painted steel grey with a camouflage pattern, we were struck by the silhouette of one of them that strongly resembled the pride of Polish passenger sea-lines, the *Stefan Batory*. Soon afterwards we received orders to embark on this very ship and, much to our delight, discovered that it was indeed the *Batory*. It was now completely adapted to the transport of military troops, but the grand halls were still kept intact, and we could peek inside from time to time. As we started to file on board, the supervising British officers watched us with surprised indulgence, no doubt remarking among themselves on our idiosyncrasies. They must have thought we still suffered the delayed effects of the desert sun, for besides our allowed baggage, we also carried four-gallon water cans. The explanation, of course, was quite rational: the cans contained almost pure alcohol, which we had purchased in Cairo. Thanks to this supply, we quickly established excellent relations with the crew of the *Batory*, who were going through a dry period ordered by the captain because of some excesses in Bombay. Deprived of their own daily rations, they came to rely on our supplies.

We landed in Taranto, in the midst of Italian winter: snow, slush, and dampness. We began to light fires to dry out and warm up, but wood was in very short supply. When an order came forbidding fires, some of us became nostalgic for the desert sun. Fortunately, we had too much else on our minds. Our corps was slowly being put into action. The Carpathian Lancers Regiment went through additional high-mountain exercises, climbing up and down the mountains in full gear. We soon stopped complaining about the cold. We also took sapper training courses and became acquainted with different kinds of mines.

Nowadays when I watch movies about World War II, with the action and scenery changing at a rapid pace, I wonder at how much more colourful fiction is than life. In my own experience, a soldier spent most of his time waiting. Waiting for orders, waiting for news, waiting for relief. Training helped to deal with the boredom of waiting, even if it was training in the proper strapping of a mule. Who knows, every bit of knowledge might prove life-saving some day.

Soon after landing in Italy, I met Andrzej Bocheński, or Adziu, as he was called. He cut a rather sorry figure, with his long legs, thin as shinbones. I wondered what exactly his uniform was hung on. His face was drawn, the profile sharp, and he pronounced "r" after the French fashion. He had graduated from the Sorbonne with a gold medal, but his French "r" was not really French: like his stuttering, it was a speech impediment. He had the rank of 2nd lieutenant, but he was already the stuff of Tobruk legends, where he had burned down a German observation tower. He was a leader of a twenty-four-man reconnaissance platoon, and usually drove a scoutcar. By the time I met him, he had already been decorated with the Cross of Virtuti Militari [the highest Polish military distinction] and several British medals. He was also a Knight of Malta. Born of Polish nobility, he never flaunted his aristocratic origin, but it was him and a few others (like Andrzej Tarnowski from Dzików and Marek Lubomirski) whom our regimental chant referred to as lords: "A few lords, a few churls, that's the Carpathian Lancers Regiment."

It was in Tobruk that his idiosyncratic approach to all things military first showed. He was clearly having a lot of fun in the army, and he used to admit it himself. He was a scientist as well as an adventurer. For example, he proved to the British that the most modern gyrostats, intended to replace a compass in the desert, could fail, and he developed for the British Army a new system of desert navigation. Very quickly he also worked out the mechanisms used in mines, and even wrote an instructional booklet on how to detect and disarm them. But fate is an ironic fellow, and in one of the later actions near Loreto, he was blown up by a mine when he disregarded the principle he himself had advocated, that only one man should approach a mine to disarm it.

Lieutenant Bocheński's platoon thrived on difficult assignments. Once, they received an order to explore the feasibility of moving armoured vehicles beyond Monte Cassino, through the valley of the Selva, and onto the road to Rome. The platoon was backed up by an entire squadron of armoured cars. Since Lieutenant Bocheński had just lost his driver, I was ordered to take the driver's place. We advanced steadily until we reached a village called Selva, completely destroyed yet still under German fire. Here, for the first time, we encountered the so-called "German circus"—a rather bizarre form of German propaganda. The performance always began with an overture by several self-propelled guns of enormous firepower. To draw attention to themselves, the Germans pulled them together into a small area and aimed their drumfire on one sector of the enemy positions. Then the fire stopped, and the homely sounds of "Kujawiak," a sentimental Polish dance tune, wafted through the countryside. After several beats, the pleasant voice of "Wanda," the female speaker of a German propaganda radio station, began to describe the traditional Eastertide preparations, how the chambers were swept and adorned with sweet rushes, how eggs were boiled and painted. After this prologue, special missiles exploded in the air, raining propaganda leaflets on Polish troops in the area. The text, in acceptable Polish, indicated that the leaflets were passes to go home: by showing them at German checkpoints, one could easily take the first train going home for Easter. There was a rumour, probably also planted by the Germans, that a first sergeant indeed managed to get back to Poland that way. But this vulgar circus grated on the soldiers' nerves, and several young braves in the platoon begged for a foray to destroy the vehicle with the loudspeakers.

Reconnaissance patrols with Bocheński usually took place at night. He always "invited" me to join him on those patrols, but I consistently preferred an order instead. I knew well that just recently ten men had died on those night patrols. Bocheński always brought them back, I'll give him that, but only to the base, never to life. Sensing my dilemma, Bocheński worded his invitation in such a way that I could not refuse. Thus I became his companion on his precarious nightly "strolls." Every night we ran into Germans. Bocheński liked to listen in on them talking and took real pleasure whenever he could hear the "beautiful Vienna accent." This romantic, irrational streak in him showed in other ways, too. One night we found ourselves seven kilometres behind the German lines and came to a crossroads with a warning sign. Adziu decided that the sign would be a good proof of how far we had gotten. It was scary, but he acted on the principle that "I may be scared, but so are they." I had to climb on his shoulders and pull down that miserable sign. It made no sense, yet seemed strangely fitting. Adziu liked to have fun in his game of war. But in the end, all those nightly patrols did serve a useful purpose: they convinced us that there was no way around Monte Cassino. To advance forward, we had to go over the top of the mountain.

The stress of the battlefield is unlike any other—it stretches the nerves and then ties them into Gordian knots. Each soldier reacts differently to that tension. Those who had distinguished themselves in combat, who were decorated for bravery, often thought they were expected to do more and greater things than regular soldiers, which only heightened their anxiety. I have seen Knights of Virtuti Militari sulking and shaking before a battle. Keeping cool during artillery barrages was particularly difficult for some. I remember one incident when a fellow couldn't cope with his fear of death any more. He fell to his knees and began to pray, loudly, almost maniacally. I was asleep despite the constant explosions, but his cries pierced the arrhythmic pounding and woke me up. I was so angry that I got up and swore at him until he shut up. He could never forgive me for that. The matter ended up with our chaplain, whose reaction was similar to mine. "When you're on the front line," he said, "it's too late to pray. Better to swear, if it helps you." Almost exactly my words.

More typically, under heavy combat stress, many soldiers found that just talking to others helped to take their minds off pain and death. If you stayed in a close-knit group for a while, you got to know every detail of their lives, every nook and cranny of their villages, what their moms used to cook and how it tasted. Passive, patient listeners were in high demand. I had a friend, Karol, for whom this kind of gut-spilling was a real help to deal with stress. We were on the front line for four days running, staffing a machine-gun site. At one point he asked me if I liked beetroots, finely grated, fried in butter, and served with sour cream. In the midst of heavy shelling, he kept talking about those beetroots his mother used to make. We kept our heads low, and wore British helmets, which looked somewhat like Polish Highlanders' hats. Suddenly the earth jumped around us as a shell exploded just metres away; its impact threw our gun from its site. I felt something sticky on my face. I looked at Karol, who was strangely missing his helmet, as I was wiping a red, sticky substance from my cheeks. My first association was with the beetroots—the consistency and colour resembled the creamy red dish Karol was talking about just minutes ago. Then the realization hit me like another shell. He was motionless, death written all over him. A minute ago he had been alive and reminiscing about his favourite food—now life had been brutally blown out of him. I must admit that, since then, I have not particularly cared for beetroots, no matter how they're prepared.

We knew that our next action would be against Monte Cassino. German leaflets and broadcasts from the German radio station "Wanda" kept us well informed. One of the leaflets pictured a Polish soldier, a blind on his eyes, walking along the edge of a precipice; a fat British soldier was prodding him from behind. The caption read: "From here you'll go to Monte Cassino, where hell is waiting for you."

Indeed, soon we were trucked to the assault positions. Beyond that point, we had to carry everything on our backs, so equipment was limited to the minimum. To supply ammunition, the sappers built a special road under camouflage nets. Then the waiting began. I repacked my backpack, then did it twice more, just for practise's sake. In the process, I found several pairs of woollen socks, which, when pressed and packed together, formed a small, relatively round ball, quite adequate for our version of baseball. We agreed on the rules, and a game was in full swing in no time. Our officers, equally bored, soon wanted in. So we played a game: officers against the lancers. I'm sure we won, although I don't remember the score. Most important, time seemed to pass more quickly.

I am often asked what my strongest memories are from the battle of Monte Cassino. The first memory that always floats back to me is that of potato pancakes. It was because of our Staff Sergeant Zygmunt Rowiński, who was very popular with the soldiers. He confided in me that he was afraid of getting another bout of jaundice, which he had first contracted on the front line at Tobruk. It was from too much stress, he said. They'd had to send him away to a hospital. Now he was convinced that some potato pancakes would certainly help him relax and would prevent him from getting the yellows again. I, too, liked him a lot and wanted to do him a favour. Getting the raw, fresh potatoes and all the other ingredients (milk powder, flour, eggs, fresh water) on the front line required a great deal of ingenuity. But after a few hours, my efforts and determination paid off as I managed to assemble all the necessary items. To grate the potatoes, we poked holes with the tip of a bayonet in an empty tin can and used the can as a grater. When the Germans began to shell us with mortar fire, our cooks ran away from the kitchen. We took advantage of their fortunate desertion and obtained a frying pan and a primus stove. We mixed the grated potatoes, flour, and eggs, and threw some of the mixture onto the pan. The aroma was so appetizing, so mouth-watering, that the commander came running to us, shouting, "Grandpa, what the hell are you doing? If the Germans get a whiff of your pancakes, they'll organize a sally in no time." Fortunately, the Germans were 300 metres away, and the winds were favourable, so we did not have to share with them. The first pancakes were served to Zygmunt, garnished with sour cream made from powdered milk. There was enough for the whole platoon, all of it free of charge, except for the officers, who had to pay a bottle of vodka for every couple of pancakes. Needless to say, Zygmunt did not get jaundice, and the pancakes definitely improved his and the other soldiers' morale.

Another thing I remember all too well is the minefields. They were everywhere: some laid by the French, some by the Americans, some by ourselves. Making detailed sketches of their locations was of crucial, life-saving importance. The ugliest and deadliest were the so-called "Jumping Jacks," and of those we took special note. When disturbed, they jumped up to the height of one metre and exploded. The Germans added to them rusted nails, screws, and nuts, which had an insidious way of biting deep into the body. Our surgeons had a lot of tedious work because of them, and I lost quite a few good friends on those mapping patrols.

After Monte Cassino, our Carpathian Lancers Regiment was sent for a well-deserved rest. We moved away from the front, to a picturesque mountain place called Montagnana. I went there ahead of the others as a quartermaster of the squadron. In addition to preparing the living quarters, I was also charged with finding a source of good wine. Above the countryside towered an old castle, still inhabited by the owners. That would be a good place to rest and convalesce, I thought, and for my platoon I chose a small dancing hall, with frescoes and cupids on the ceiling. When asked about good wine, the owner, an old fellow well over sixty, brought me a bottle to try. He also took that opportunity to tell me all about his own soldiering career during World War I. He poured me a glass of wine. I checked its colour against the light, took a small sip, tasted it. The man gave me an inquiring look and remarked that I must be no stranger to wine; "You don't drink it like a soldier." He meant this as a compliment. Then he offered to supply us with wine from his own cellar as long as we stayed in his castle. As if to ensure that I understood his generosity, he went back to the cellar and returned with a large basket crammed with sixteen bottles of exquisite wine. I received the bottles with the appropriate gratitude, and, lining them up in my tent, began to relax even before the rest of our men arrived. Later my buddies told me that, throughout our stay in Montagnana, I did not report at assembly even once. Eventually the commander's patience ran out, and he ordered the sergeant to bring me to the next roll call. But at the next call the sergeant went missing. Finally the squadron commander himself found his way to my tent, and he spent the whole night with us. All that time the owner remained good to his word, and the wine almost washed away our military discipline.

Before we departed from Montagnana, we left a material legacy there. Our kitchen attracted a lot of local boys, because kids and dogs are not afraid of soldiers and always follow the army. The British had a rule that the civilians should not get any food from their kitchens, but we always fed them when they were hungry, which was practically all the time. One day I had a drunken idea to make some cloaks for those kids. We had quite a few American blankets, woollen but thin. It wasn't difficult to find a tailor in town who would make nineteen of these cloaks. After that the boys always showed up for food in serried ranks, proudly wearing their cloaks.

We left Montagnana in armoured cars and went into combat in Porto San Giorgio and Porto Recanati, near Ancona. Our task was to engage and tie up the enemy forces, not to gain ground or move forward. Here our second squadron of the Carpathian Lancers Regiment was ambushed by the Germans and badly shaken. Our orders were to reach and explore a twenty-metre-wide ford on the river Mussone. What we didn't know was that the Germans had dug themselves in on the far bank. They let four of our cars through but destroyed the fifth just as it was in the middle of the ford. This effectively blocked the ford. Other cars were hit, as well. A German soldier jumped on the back of one of the armoured cars to throw a grenade inside, but the driver noticed him and instinctively went into reverse. The German lost his balance and fell backwards, straight under the rolling vehicle, which crushed him into the earth. My partner and I got the order to evacuate our injured, who were still moving under one of the shattered vehicles. We approached them in our armoured car, and I climbed out and opened the hatch of the destroyed scoutcar: a phosphorus shell had burned out the inside. Lieutenant Polkowski was lying underneath, his hands holding his stomach. He kept repeating, "Take Henryk, take Henryk." His own injuries were too severe, and he died before our eyes a short while later. We took Henryk, but the next shell hit our own car, and we had to crawl back under Polkowski's burned-out wreck. We put Henryk into a blanket and crawled towards the tall clover, pulling him between us. We found a German supply trench and slid down. In the meantime, our boys opened fire with machine guns so vehemently that the Germans began to pull back in their trenches. As we were walking along the German trench in the direction of our positions, carrying the injured Henryk, a group of Germans suddenly appeared at the other end, walking directly towards us. They noticed us, too, but did not stop. They saw we were carrying an injured soldier, and when we met in that trench, they all stepped aside to let us pass. We literally rubbed shoulders with them, but no one tried to fight. A few minutes later, we safely reached our side.

The day after our failed mission, 140 boys from the Youth Brigade were assigned to our regiment. The oldest was seventeen. When my whole unit went to get some coffee, we ordered one of the youths, Gąska, to stay with our gear. He asked what he should do if the Germans came. I told him that he should shout *Hände hoch!* and take them prisoner. Maybe half an hour later we came back from coffee to be greeted by an unusual sight. From behind a rampart walked twenty-three German soldiers with their hands up and behind them little Gąska with a rifle. He explained that, as he was leaning against a scoutcar, he saw a German climb up from under the bridge, about to answer the call of nature. He grabbed his rifle and shouted *Hände hoch!* just as I had instructed him. At that moment twenty-two other Germans emerged from underneath the bridge, somewhat dazed but eager to surrender. They had all become separated from their units and had evidently decided they'd had enough fighting. Gąska became a hero of the day. Sadly, he did not enjoy his heroic status for long, for six days later a bullet found him.

Through much of our Italian campaign, luck must have been on my side, for bullets seemed to avoid me. But eventually my luck looked away, and my turn came. In one of the engagements, we found ourselves in the scope of German fire. The Germans hit us with a burst from a well-adjusted mine thrower. One of the shells exploded just beside our car and several pieces of shrapnel bit into my leg through the door, which I had opened to get the machine gun into position. I didn't feel any pain from those eighteen fragments, only numbness. Weakness and uneasiness came later, when I saw blood dripping from my leg. I was taken to a field hospital by an ambulance. Later our chaplain visited me there. "So it finally got you, too, you rogue," he observed, and asked if he could be of any assistance. He had come to offer me some spiritual consolation, but my mind was still too much on this world, so I said, "Oh yes, could you pass me the cigarettes; they're in my backpack." For a long time afterwards he couldn't get over my choosing a smoke over spiritual comfort.

Our surgeon, Dr. Sokołowski, signed me up for a transport bound for Egypt, the home base of the 2nd Corps. I refused to go. He threatened that I'd never move my leg again. I wouldn't budge. The truth was that I didn't really believe his gloomy prognosis about my leg. Just in case, I always had my spit-and-polished boots right beside me on the stretcher, as was the British custom (even those whose legs were amputated kept them). I was hoping I would jump into them soon. In the end I convinced the good doctor and stayed in Italy. When I returned to the regiment, the squadron commander warned me, "Grandpa, your luck seems to have left you." And he was right. In a short period of time, I was blown up by a mine not once, but twice, fortunately with more damage to my nerves than to my body.

More or less at the same time, an order arrived from General Anders that all instructors be sent from the front line to the Training Centre for armoured units. Simultaneously, those instructors who had been at the Training Centre for a while were recalled to their original units so that they, too, could smell powder before the end of the war. On the basis of that order I was sent to the Training Centre in southern Italy. I was not overly enthusiastic about this move, but, good soldier that I was, I obeyed the order.

The end of the war? Yes, I remember it. I had just rejoined my unit near Bologna. The squadron commander was playing volleyball with the lancers. I was watching them from the sideline when an orderly came briskly from the other side of the field and shouted, "Captain, I report that the radio has announced the end of military operations in Italy." The ball kept flying over the net from side to side. They would not let the end of the war interfere with their game.

Shortly thereafter, twenty-four of us from the 2nd Corps were sent to Britain because General Anders wanted some of his instructors to be trained in British centres. We boarded a ship in Naples, and a cruise of several days brought us to England. There we were transported to Cathric Camp, one of the large training centres, which included a Polish wing. The commander of the Polish wing was Major Poliszewski. All training followed British regulations, beginning with the most basic drills and daily inspections; the teaching methods were probably more practical and to the point than in the Polish army. My long military experience helped me get through the entire course without any major upheavals. I didn't learn anything earth-shattering, although we did get exposed to quite a few technical novelties. After a year of intensive training, we were promoted to officers, with an annotation indicating which post each cadet was best suited for. I graduated with an "exemplary standing," which was (mis)translated into Polish to mean "eminent standing" (*z wynikiem wybitnym*). This expression does not sound like a military phrase in Polish, and my buddies did not miss this opportunity to tease me.

All that time my own unit remained stationed in Italy. But because there was talk of the entire 2nd Corps moving to Britain, the brass wanted to keep us in Britain at the rallying station until our units arrived. They also found us useful. The station was full of Silesians from the German army. The war, and especially the waiting, had demoralized many, and discipline had become too lax. So we were given the task of restoring discipline and reminding the soldiers that for as long as they received their pay and wore the uniform, they had to conduct themselves as per regulations. This task did not prove too difficult, what with our recent training and the traditions of the 2nd Corps. We dealt with the new recruits quickly, almost effortlessly. The more seasoned, German-trained soldiers were less tractable, but, with the right mixture of threats and flattery, they were made to toe the line as well. This cleaning up of the rallying station earned us considerable respect among the officers of the 2nd Corps.

Despite the delays, we insisted that we return to our units. Eventually our persistence paid off, and we sailed back to Italy. Not for long, though. After several weeks of blue and bluer skies, we left for Britain once again, as part of the 2nd Corps advance group charged with preparing the quarters for the troops. Thus we arrived at Grimsby, a former POW camp, complete with observation towers and barbed wire fences. We couldn't stand the prisoner-camp look so we toppled the wretched towers even before we received permission to do so.

When the rest of the corps arrived at Grimsby, preparations for transition to civilian life began in earnest. For all of us, it was a time of decision: should we stay in the West or should we go back to Poland? The camp was swamped with fliers encouraging us to return, but most of us had misgivings. Every soldier individually had to declare in the presence of a British superior officer whether he wanted to go back. Those who declared that they wanted to stay in the West were transferred to the Polish Resettlement Corps; those who decided to return were assembled at rallying points. But the British would have had it too easy if soldiers made up their minds so quickly. Some fellows refused to sign up for either the return to Poland or the Resettlement Corps. They required considerably more coaching and goading and severely tested British patience.

For those who chose to stay in the West, the British offered a host of vocational courses. I'm not sure why, but clockmaking seemed most popular. One could also learn bricklaying, tailoring, and almost every other conceivable vocation. There was even a course for fishermen, probably because Grimsby was, among other things, a fishing harbour. Fishing boats that belonged to a Pole whom World War II had surprised on the fisheries near Iceland often came to port here. That was the course I signed up for. A boy from the steppes, I did not seriously intend a career in the fishery, but two of my friends, Jakubowicz and Jankowski, ensured that I got a taste of it. They had sent an advertisement to all fishing harbours that three "experienced fishermen" were looking for work. They counted me as one of the three but without my knowledge or consent. When one of the companies responded that it was willing to hire us, I decided to give it a try. Although our demobilization papers were already prepared, I explained to the officer that this job of mine was a result of a whimsical practical joke by Jakubowicz and that I had never caught a fish in my life. I suggested that I could try this job, but only if I got an open-term leave from the army. If I liked it, I would become a fisherman; if I didn't, I would return to uniform. My condition was accepted, so I went with the other two to the recruitment depot, where each of us had to sign up on a different boat. Apparently they did not want to have us all together.

My first trawler was called *Ejbich*. I signed up as a "brassy," and one of my duties was polishing all brass fittings on board. When we reached the fishery, one of the deckhands was too reckless pulling a rope, and it slit off four of his fingers. They took him to the nearest port in Sweden, and since the skipper did not want to wait for a replacement, he reassigned me as a deckhand. Our catch was good, and we got a higher pay rate because there were fewer of us. Altogether I made £47 in a few weeks, almost a fortune. Unfortunately my buddies did not fare as well as I did. One was escorted back to land in Sweden, and the other kissed the land on coming ashore and vowed never to set foot on a trawler again.

Despite my relative success, I did not continue my career as a fisherman. From early on, I had set my eyes on Canada, and there I wanted to build a life for myself. I first applied at the time when group immigration for contract work was being organized, but I was rejected when a medical examination concluded that I was too nervous for a country as relaxed as Canada. I'm sure it must have been my expressive face. For the examination, we were all lined up in Adam's garb. First they examined our muscles: we were told to flex them, to bend our knees, and they watched us from the front and from the back. I did quite well in that part, I think. I must have buried my chances, though, when I reacted strongly, although involuntarily, at one doctor's lack of respect for the uniform. As we were standing before the commission, an officer inadvertently walked into the room, and the doctor unceremoniously shoved him out. After years in the army, respect for the uniform, for the insignia, was deeply ingrained in me, and that was no way to treat an officer. I said nothing, but my physiognomy is by nature on the expressive side. When something hits me, it immediately shows in my face. The doctor must have noticed how strongly I disapproved of his behaviour, moved me to the side, and ordered an additional battery of tests. His conclusion: I was too nervous for Canada.

But just as you can't keep a bear from honey, so I, too, found a way into that country "flowing with resin and honey." One of my friends, Franciszek Wawrzyńczyk, managed to arrange for me a personal invitation from a farmer in Braintree. The boat passage to Halifax was monotonous, and the train ride from Halifax to Winnipeg further dampened my enthusiasm. But Franciszek Wawrzyńczyk and Adam

Mossakowski, who met me at the station in Winnipeg, sounded genuinely pleased to see me and soon rekindled my optimism.

One of the first challenges after arriving in Winnipeg was finding a job. I was not interested in farm work, and jobs at the Canadian Pacific Railway did not hold much appeal for me, either. That left work in the forest, and I began my Canadian life as a lumberjack. We worked throughout the fall and winter, contending with black flies in the fall, with cold weather in winter. Spring brought us back to town. Working as a lumberjack could be dangerous and, worse, it could be addictive. One could make quite a bit of money in a season, but back in town, that money flowed much faster than the Red River. Hard come, easy go, and than back for more. Luckily, I did not fall victim to that addiction and spent only one season in the forest.

That first winter was memorable. We were cutting pulp trees near Flanders for the Minnesota Pulp and Paper Co. in Mando. The pay was decent and by the job: the more we cut, the more we got. The work was back-breaking. I had never imagined that one could work with only a shirt on his back at -30°C. We always threw off our parkas and sweated in flannel shirts, double-layered on the back. The second layer was crucial because it kept the sheets of ice away from our bodies. In the fall I had grown a beard and a moustache. The foreman advised me to shave them off, but I ignored him. I discovered the wisdom of his advice a few months later. Breathing hard in very cold weather caused a crust of ice to form between my moustache and beard, which made eating almost impossible. I admitted my mistake to him and was ready to correct it, but he warned me, "Don't you dare. You'll get frostbite in no time." He was right, of course, so I had to suffer my beard for the rest of that winter.

The only job I could find, having emerged from the woods, was as a plasterman. Urbanowicz, a local contractor, gave me the benefit of the doubt, and I did not disappoint him. The work was hard but not difficult, and the boss let me work on the side as well. But since plastering was also a seasonal job, I kept looking until, one day, in the library, I met Kazimierz Chmielowicz, who helped me get a job in a company called Inland Steel, which manufactured farm equipment. The owner of the company was a retired captain of the Canadian army, a veteran of World War I, with the scars to prove it. He had some Polish soldiers on his staff, and he appreciated their honesty, effectiveness, and dedication. Once he even said that he preferred to hire Polish veterans because they could be trusted to get the job done. And he was right: we had done it in Tobruk and in Monte Cassino. As it turned out, we still had one last battle to fight. The older crew of the factory were not used to our pace of work and saw no reason to sweat if it wasn't summer. They wanted to get rid of us, or, at least, slow us down, so much so that they even tried to sabotage the equipment we used. It took some cool nerves, some tactical manoeuvres, some imaginative thinking, but in three years we managed to contain the situation, without any personnel losses or the use of brute force. In fact, we made some gains as the number of Polish foremen increased.

I began my career at Inland Steel by assembling harrows for sixty-five cents per hour. After five years my virtues, or perhaps just skills, were so appreciated that I was called into the office and offered an evening course to learn draughting. Since taking courses was my specialty—I had taken so many of them in the army—I completed this course with ease. With a diploma in hand, I was promoted and transferred to the engineering department, where technical drawings were my chief responsibility. A few more years on the job, and I was given a monthly salary. As a draughtsman, I often met well-educated engineers from other large companies, such as John Deere. There were moments, I admit, when I felt ill at ease around them, not because I was shy but because I was then painfully aware that my own education fell short of my pre-war aspirations and ambitions. I stayed a loyal employee of my company for thirty-five years. When I finally retired, my old job, I was told, was to be taken over by a computer.

Once I had a steady job, my life acquired a semblance of stability. Since I had never been good at counting money, a friend of mine, Kazimierz Kowaliszyn, bought a house for me: he found it and negotiated the price. I had not even been inside before I became its owner. Another friend helped me buy a car. My future wife I found all on my own, in the Polish library. Gradually, my life's entanglements kept growing: first marriage, then one daughter, then another, then a puppy. The daughters are both grown up now, and both have a university education. My wife dotes on the dog, and I have time to reminisce.

My job and family set the course for my life in Canada, but my wartime past was never far away from me. The bonds of friendship forged under enemy fire proved strong and resilient. From my first day in Winnipeg, I became an active member of the Polish Combatants Association [PCA]. I have served on the board of the association in various capacities, including two terms as president of Chapter #13. My work in the association, among friends with whom I shared the hardships and dangers of war, was my real passion. I cherish the memories of our struggles, our flops, and our successes here in Winnipeg as I do those from that earlier, more painful, and less godly time.

On the very day of my arrival in Winnipeg, the PCA organized a social—in my honour, joked one of my buddies from the Carpathian Lancers. Nineteen of them had found a home here in Winnipeg, and all showed up for the social. At a general meeting of Chapter #13, which was called soon after, I was formally admitted to the local chapter on the basis of my PCA documents from England. Franciszek Wawrzyńczyk acted as secretary. Some seventeen members came to that meeting, a far cry from the 450 who had come to Winnipeg as contract workers. Many of them went their own ways, and some were even resentful of the PCA. "They want to have their registration all over again," complained someone over a beer, and someone else added a mordant comment about former officers acting like "Polish lords." Something of this attitude persists to this day, although time has considerably eroded the old grudges.

At the same meeting, one of the founders of Chapter #13, Stanisław Ilkow, argued that the chapter had outlived its usefulness and should be dissolved. I was shocked and, though new to Winnipeg, I spoke forcefully against the dissolution of the chapter. Several colleagues found my arguments convincing, and together we survived the crisis. I was co-opted for the Auditorial Committee to check the financial records of our organization. Given my lack of interest in money matters, this might have been a tall order for me. Fortunately, the records of yearly income and disbursements, at the time kept by our treasurer Adam Żurad, could be fitted on a single sheet of paper. The burden of auditing them was not particularly onerous.

With renewed enthusiasm we set to work. We put the library in order, adding the books we received as our allotment from London and wrapping all the books in dust jackets made of packing paper. We organized an amateur theatre. We soon discovered that there was a high degree of loyalty to particular organizations among the local Polish community, so that, for instance, members of St. John Cantius

Fraternal Aid Society did not attend functions organized by the Gymnastic Association Sokół, and vice versa. To overcome this internal division, we had to perform at several venues in turn. Our prices were affordable, and we put on a new play every three months. In-between the plays, we organized variety evenings, changing the program weekly. These cultural activities stirred considerable interest and attracted people to our library as well as to the socials we organized in the halls of various organizations. All these ventures began to pay off, not only in heightened ethnic awareness but in dollars and cents as well. Soon the chapter became so vibrant a focus of activities that we began to think of buying our own building.

The first, unofficial, meeting place of Chapter #13 was the restaurant in the Empire Hotel. Franciszek Wawrzyńczyk, along with Adam Mossakowski and two others, made the leasing arrangements. The owner let us hold our monthly information meetings there, provided he did not have any more lucrative offers. But as the chapter gained in self-confidence and stature among the Polish organizations, the need for our own building became apparent. When the subject was broached, we knew one thing: typical halls, like the ones owned by other Polish organizations, did not appeal to us. They were vast, lofty, with stages and paintings of waterfalls and deer on the walls. Someone suggested building a clubhouse and a hall similar to those in the Empire Hotel. We also considered the possibility of joining forces with other Polish groups, like St. John Cantius Society, the Gymnastic Association Sokół, or the Parish of the Holy Spirit. Those groups played a vital role in the pioneering period of Polish immigration to Manitoba, but their influence and membership were on the decline. We maintained good working relationships with those organizations, which proved beneficial several years later, when the Polish Canadian Congress was being organized. Unfortunately, discussions concerning a joint effort to build a Polish Cultural Centre strayed into the wilderness of ambitions, arguments, and antagonisms. In the end, we decided to act on our own. When the funds from theatrical productions and socials reached $2000, we began to look for a suitable location. Wacław Kuzia, who made his career in housebuilding, helped us a great deal. We found an old shop for sale at the corner of Inkster and Main, and paid a deposit on it. Adjacent to it was an empty building lot. But as we were leaving that shop after our first meeting there, we noticed a "for sale" sign on a nearby furniture store. This store must have had the biggest shop window in Winnipeg. It was much larger and in better condition than the rather modest building we intended to buy. Beside the furniture shop, there was also an empty lot. Kuzia climbed inside the store and surveyed the building. The next day, with the help of our lawyer, Bernard Dubienski, we withdrew our premature deposit and arranged to buy the furniture store.

Our $2000 was just about enough for the deposit, but to finalize the purchase and to begin the necessary renovations, we needed more cash. Thus we decided to organize an internal loan, free of interest, with everyone chipping in at least $100. The majority of our members—and we approached practically every one—was supportive, although some had to overcome domestic opposition. All in all, we managed to collect $22,000, purchased the property, and began the renovations. Construction work was supervised by Wacław Kuzia; the rest of us were the work force. Everyone who showed up was immediately given a job. Even Łodzia-Michalski, who was not particularly fond of tinkering, specialized in straightening out the nails. Today this may sound a touch ridiculous, but our enthusiasm was infectious and we made excellent progress. On one occasion, on a Saturday, we began to plaster the walls around 10:00 a.m., and by 4:00 p.m. the work was done. Even the experienced plastermen shook their heads and admired the pace of our work. We tried to do as much as we could ourselves, but for some jobs we needed external help. For example, we needed an architect. He was impressed with our enthusiasm—more impressed than some of us were with his interior design solutions, although in the end we all learned to live with them. While the paint was still drying, we obtained a licence to sell beer and opened a pub, which, at the time, was considered the best source of income. The sale of beer indeed proved profitable, although not as profitable as the banquet hall. Together they quickly helped us reduce our debt.

Soon after we opened the hall to the public, other Polish organizations began to refurbish their halls, using our building as a model. The money spent on those renovations could, of course, have financed the building of a large, elegant Polish Centre, but, for a host of reasons, this did not come to pass then or later.

We paid off our mortgage and other debts relatively quickly, and soon we had a surplus, which could be used for social and cultural initiatives not pursued by other organizations. Chapter #13 was coming of age, and moving with confidence to the forefront of PCA chapters in Canada.

One of the PCA's socio-cultural goals was continuing the traditions of Polish Scouting in Canada. In Winnipeg, those traditions were quite old, and our aspiration was to revive them. Dr. Andrzej Gutkowski gave us the necessary impetus: he gathered us, the old, experienced Scouts, and set us to work. There was, sadly, no unanimity among us as to the format of our activities. Some believed that since we were all in Canada, we should forego Polish traditions and embrace Canadian notions of Scouting. But for others, the Polish traditions represented values definitely worth preserving. What began as a difference of opinion grew into an ideological rift, which caused a split in our ranks and prompted several members to join the Canadian Legion #246. Today, from the perspective of many intervening years, those sore points are simply a part of history, and we maintain a close and friendly relationship with our colleagues in the Canadian Legion.

Thanks to our considerable financial resources and a gift of four acres of bush on Big Whiteshell Lake, which we soon transformed into a summer youth camp, Polish Scouting once again flourished in Winnipeg. Every year we organized summer camps, hosted all-Canadian jamborees, and invited youth from both the east and the west of Canada. Many of our former Scouts hold important positions in Winnipeg today.

We also patronized and financed Polish dance ensembles. We have always believed that active pastime and immersion in Polish traditions is both attractive to children and most likely to enhance their pride in their Polish heritage.

According to the statutes of the PCA, Toronto is the seat of our organization. However, many initiatives and social or cultural projects have come from outside Toronto. Today the PCA is not so much an association of Polish veterans, I think, as a social organization founded by them. The amendments to the statutes, opening the organization to non-veterans who agree with its ideological assumptions, testify to that. I realize that we can't expect a flood of new immigrants clamouring to sign up with the PCA, but I am hopeful that when they have settled down in their new country, they will discover in themselves that need to get involved in the life of our Polish community. Then they may join the currents of the PCA's social and cultural activities and fulfil their own goals and aspirations. That's why I don't worry about our future, firmly believing that though each of us is but a small drop, if enough drops flow together, they become a strong river.

KONSTANTY JACKIEWICZ

I was born in 1922 in Dołhinów [Dolginovo], county of Wilejka, Polish Wilno [Vilnius] region. I was still a kid when I joined the paramilitary organization Strzelec [Rifleman]. At fifteen, I took a summer course in field communications, organized by the Border Guard Corps [KOP]; at sixteen, I spent another summer learning similar things about radio communications; at seventeen, I rode to war . . . on a bicycle.

In September 1939, I belonged to a reserve company of KOP. We knew we were losing the war with the Germans, but around Dołhinów, close to the Russian border, things were quiet. Until September 17, that is, when at four o'clock in the morning I got word that the Red Army units were crossing the border. There were three watchtowers in our sector, but only two engaged in some minor skirmishes with the Soviet patrols wading through the border river. Soon the crews received orders to withdraw. We waited in Dołhinów until they arrived around 2:00 p.m. In the meantime, our reserve company had been joined by several of my teenage friends from Strzelec and by the local policemen. Later that afternoon, the company headed for the battalion headquarters in Bucław [Budslav], fourteen kilometres away.

By that time it was becoming clear that the Soviets had come not to help but to invade. All local telephone lines had been cut. Contact with Wilno was maintained by radio, but from the countryside around Dołhinów and Bucław, we had no information. And so I was assigned to a reconnaissance platoon. We were issued bicycles and sent afield to scout for the movements of the Soviet troops. After we had gathered some intelligence, we rode back along the Katerinski Trakt, an old highway almost thirty metres wide, with twenty-metre shoulders marked out by ancient birches planted in two rows on either side of the road. The weather was foul, with rain and clouds and wind. We were riding along a section that was being paved. In a moment of carelessness, I rode into a bed of newly crushed stone, somersaulting over the handlebar, blowing both tires, and bending the front wheel. Badly shaken but unhurt, I got up, picked up the busted bike, and started jogging after my team. By the time I reached the bridge, I was dripping with sweat and staggering from exertion. The guards stationed there laughed at me; they told me to dump the bike in the river and commandeer another one from a nearby farm. I needed little encouragement: I plunged the wreck into the currents with a light heart and an even lighter shoulder. But when I got to the farm and started to say, "In the name of the Polish army . . . ," the woman began to cry: her husband had gone to war, she needed the bike, she had children to feed, and so on. In the end, I didn't have the heart to take her bicycle and was eventually assigned to a small troop travelling on foot.

Later that night the whole company was on the move again. At one of the short stops, I fell into a ditch but felt too tired to get up. I closed my eyes for a moment to gather my strength, and woke up six hours later, the day already breaking and the company gone. On the verge of panic, I jumped into the middle of the road and trotted to where the horizon was the darkest, towards the west. Fifteen kilometres later, I caught up with the battalion and found my company, already quartered in a small village. But we had barely two hours to rest. We had received an order to cross the Lithuanian border, but all who wanted to go home were allowed to do so, the commander said. He released the supply wagons, and the supplies of canned meat and cigarettes were distributed among the men. In the early afternoon we would walk over a hill, through a grove, and across the border.

At noon, the bugler announced the last meal from the field kitchen. We lined up, tins in hand, and just as I was about to get my ladleful of chow, someone screamed "Take cover!" A Soviet reconnaissance plane swooped from above. The cook jumped, knocked the kitchen over, and hid behind it, spilling my dinner to the ground. And so I went into my first battle on an empty stomach. We dug in on both sides of the road, expecting a Soviet attack. And indeed, several tanks soon appeared. We

132

loaded anti-armour bullets and started shooting: it felt good but did no harm to the Soviets. When the tanks responded with machine-gun fire, the older soldiers couldn't stand the pressure and began to raise their hands. They knew we stood no chance against the tanks; we had no choice but to surrender.

The Soviets lined us up along the road and collected all arms and ammunition; more than that, they took all our razors, too. Then they marched us for three hours towards a forest, where we had our meal of canned meat and enjoyed a smoke. I happened to overhear a conversation among a few Soviet soldiers, complaining that we ate meat while they, for months, had been fed only dried fish. I felt sorry for them, took out a pack of cigarettes from my backpack, and threw it over to them. They picked it up, obviously pleased, and shook their heads in amazement that Poles enjoyed such good cigarettes. Their political teachers kept repeating that in Poland ordinary people were dying of hunger; how could they afford such luxury?

We stayed in the forest throughout the night. In the morning came the NKVD [state security police]. A *politruk* [propaganda officer] announced that comrade Stalin would let all ordinary soldiers go home. They let us go in groups of five, one group every five minutes. With four of my friends, we set out in the direction of Dołhinów. By nightfall, we reached a reeve's house. He gave us some dark bread and sour milk, and warned us to avoid open roads because the Soviets had changed their minds about the captured Polish soldiers; apparently they had received orders to recapture as many of them as possible. I don't know if there was any truth to that rumour, but we took his advice and walked along country roads and only after nightfall. It took us eleven days to return to Dołhinów.

There were as yet no Soviets in Dołhinów, but the local communists had seized control of the town. Most of them were Jewish, armed with rifles, red arm bands, and newly gained self-confidence. Jews made up the majority of townspeople in Dołhinów: some 5000 of them lived in five communities, five times the number of Poles. They were easy targets for our childish pranks—I can't say I wasn't guilty of some. But the pranks always had a sour aftertaste for me because my father made me go back to my victims, admit my guilt, and apologize. I hated that; it took all the fun from the sport, I thought. Of course, my father was right. After all, we prospered in the town only because of the Jews. When my father had retired from the army, the Jews had given him a plot of land in their quarters for a store. True, they believed the plot was cursed, and no one had wanted it. But they had also given him money to build a store. And they were among his best customers (he dealt in leather goods). So in general, my family was on friendly terms with the new rulers of the town.

Their reign ended two months later, when the Soviets took over the town's administration. They did not trust anyone, Poles or Jews. They wasted no time in rounding up all the young men who had had any association with the Polish army or police and locking us up in the prison in Stara Wilejka. Most of my friends were taken: Leszkowicz, Bilewicz, Odorski, Kuncewicz. We stood accused of stealing the explosives from the KOP armoury and of intending to blow up Soviet transports. Other allegations revolved around crossing a foreign border and belonging to hostile organizations. The investigation lasted exactly one year and consisted of daily—or, more exactly, nightly—interrogations. Around ten in the evening, the key rattled in the lock, and our names were called out. Sometimes the guards would not bother to read the names but would instead call all whose last names began with a particular letter. They no doubt thought it a good joke. In a small room we faced one of six interrogators; the highest in rank was a woman. The questions were tedious and monotonous, night in, night out. "How did you steal the explosives? Where did you hide them? Who helped you? We have witnesses, they've already confessed," and so on, throughout the night. The interrogator was always taking notes of his questions and translating my stubborn silences into admissions and confessions. At the end, he would say, "Sign this!" "No way," I'd answer, "it's in Russian, and I don't know your letters." So he would read it out loud and demand, "Sign!" "You've written it, you've read it, you sign it," I'd say insolently. And he'd smack me in the face with one hand, then with the other, and keep hitting until his fury or strength subsided. This was only a prelude to the more serious beatings that always followed in the bowels of the night. In the morning, they carried me to my cell in a blanket, all bruised and senseless. But I still refused to give them the satisfaction and wouldn't sign their damn reports.

Occasionally the interrogations verged on the bizarre. Once the NKVD officer did not ask me a single question, but kept singing "Lubimyi gorod, mozhet spat' spakoina" [Beloved town, you can sleep safe] throughout the night. At the time I thought he had gone crazy; it did not surprise me, for the whole communist system was insane to start with. My friends in the cell were surprised when I walked back on my own two legs, without a single new bruise. On another occasion, an interrogator tried to convince me that others from my group had already confessed. "They'll get eight years and go to a labour camp, and you'll get a bullet into your head. Will you sign this?" "No," was my answer. I demanded to see Bilewicz, who had supposedly broken down and signed the report, admitting his guilt. Well, he had, and I don't blame him; how long can you bear the beatings? But I could bear them a bit longer, so I still refused to sign. I lost consciousness an hour or so into the session and was thrown into the cell in a blanket.

The female officer was probably the meanest among the interrogators. She was arrogant, spiteful, and had a foul mouth. She swore at me like a butcher, or maybe worse. "You'll never see another whore in your life," she screamed. "That's okay," I said. "The one I'm looking at right now is more than I can take." "You're damn right," she was positively breathing fire, and she swung at me with the butt of her handgun. I took the hit on the temple and went crazy myself. I grabbed the two guards who were rushing towards me and threw one into the other. Then I jumped on the table and started kicking around so that none of them could approach me. "You son of a bitch, I'll shoot you," she yelled as she ran at me, waving her gun. "Go ahead, shoot, I'll still sign nothing!" She called a few more *boitsy* [guards] and soon they subdued me. I'm not sure what exactly they did to me, but it took me two days to come back to my senses.

After one year, the interrogations ceased. For two months we were left in peace, and then the travesty of court proceedings began. Despite the short respite, or maybe because of it, I lost my resolve not to sign anything. What the hell, I thought dimly, I'll be sent to Siberia anyway. Besides, I was physically exhausted and mentally fragile. I walked into a courtroom to an almost dizzying presence of red caps and jingling orders. The prosecutor showed me a report and asked, "Will you sign this?" "Sure, why not," I said. He almost jumped for joy, not expecting me to be so compliant, and he ran for a pen, and brought it to me to sign the paper. The original charges had by now been toned down somewhat; for instance, they changed "crossed the border" into "intended to cross the border," but that didn't make much difference. After the trial I was left alone for a month.

The prison where we were kept remembered the imperial times, except that nothing was left of its original luxuries. Thirty-five of us were crammed into a cell formerly intended for a single prisoner. The few bunk beds were so crowded that everyone had to roll over at the same time. I hated the squeeze on the bed, so I slept near the door on the *parashka*, a large box housing a bucket that served as a toilet. After a while, the smell did not bother me at all. Our prison fare was rudimentary. In the morning we were served a cup of *kipiatok* [boiling water], two slices of bread, and some salt. To avoid quarrels over the size of the slices, we drew lots for them. In the evening, a pail with watery soup was brought into the cell; on state holidays, a piece of broken meat was floating in it. On such holiday occasions, those who had money could also buy some perogi and tobacco in the prison canteen.

If there was one thing the prison authorities were afraid of, it was contagious disease. In my cell, one of the prisoners died from typhoid fever. Immediately we were moved to another cell (which happened to be larger and more comfortable than our own). The floor, bunk beds, *parashka*, and everything else in our original cell were disinfected with a thick coat of Kreosol. Since stench does not kill, we were soon crammed back in there.

When the war with Germany broke out, I learned about it through Morse code, which we used to communicate with prisoners in other cells. Once the guards caught me sending the signals, and I was given time in a cold isolation cell, adapted from a latrine. I did not stay there long because just then the Germans bombed Stara Wilejka. The lights went out, there were shouts and people running in the halls, and then all the doors were flung open. We were ordered into the halls and outside into the yard. Those with death sentences were taken away. We were formed into a marching column and led outside the prison gates. They were taking us in the direction of the old Polish-Russian border. I was very weak, and with every kilometre my knees grew less steady. When we reached the border, I collapsed. Anyone who fell or lingered behind was shot on the spot. But I was lucky. First a few stronger prisoners picked me up and carried me for some five kilometres; then they managed to put me onto a lorry assigned to our convoy. Eventually, a soldier brought me back with a splash of cold water, kicked me off the lorry, and ordered me to walk. I walked, stumbled, and walked again until morning. We were still walking along an asphalt road when a

Soviet reconnaissance plane appeared above our heads, giving us some signs. We realized what they meant when we heard the drone of several German bombers. Our escort told us to lie down on the road, while they ran away from it, searching for cover. The planes dove after them. We took advantage of the confusion and started running towards a nearby forest. But the pilot of the Soviet plane began shooting at us, and the guards realized what we were up to. They turned us back, gathered us on the road, and marched on. Out in the open, they made us run; in wooded areas, they let us rest. This went on for several days. Occasionally, the weakest of us were allowed to take rides in the lorry, and I took advantage of this a few times. The driver was apparently as hungry as we were. Once he drove ahead with a few of us and went to a *kolkhoz* [collective farm] to get some bread. But he returned empty-handed. "Give me your caps," he told us. He walked into the forest and gathered some edible weeds; "hare cabbage," we called it and stuffed our bellies with it during the march.

When we reached Borysów [Barysaw], they loaded us into railway cars. Suddenly anti-aircraft guns began to bark, and we noticed a German reconnaissance plane below the clouds. After a while, the sky was marked with a white smudge of smoke. The Soviets thought they had hit it, but nothing could be further from the truth. The white smoke was a visual signal for the German bombers, marking a target for them. They came a few minutes later and bombed the entire station, at the time crowded with Soviet troops and refugees. Our car jumped with every explosion. Outside, the Soviet soldiers were falling to their knees, raising their arms, praying for deliverance. What a sight: the Soviets praying in the midst of blood, death, and twisted metal!

We survived the air raid. By train we were taken first to Moscow, then on to Riazan, where they put us in a big prison. There we learned about the agreement between Sikorski and Stalin. And so, instead of a punishing sentence, I got an amnesty, a certificate of release, a loaf of bread, some onions, 100 grams of salt, and eighty rubles. We were let out of prison in groups of ten, and our certificates entitled us to ride by train to the Polish army headquarters in Buzuluk. Unfortunately, no one told us where it was and how to get there.

And yet, some weeks later, we arrived at Totskoye. I was assigned to the 21st Infantry Regiment, the "Children of Warsaw." In Guzar, in Asia, I found myself in the communications company of our division.

On April 1, we were transported by a boat with the grandiose name *Velikaia Partia Bolshevikov* [The Great Bolshevik Party] from Krasnovodsk to Pahlavi, Persia. There we sunbathed naked on the beaches, waiting for our turn before the disinfection teams and our new British uniforms. We also stuffed ourselves with hard-boiled eggs, which the enterprising local merchants supplied in great quantities; those who had not surrendered all their rubles could even enjoy the familiar Bison Vodka. After the numbing poverty of the Soviet Union, Persia looked to us like an oasis of comfort and plenty. I pinched myself several times to make sure that it was not a mirage.

The Easter of 1943, we spent in the vicinity of Tehrān. From there we went through Basra [Al-Başrah], the Persian Gulf, and the Red Sea, until we ended up in Palestine, in a large camp called Kastino. After some intensive training, I was assigned, together with twelve others, to a communications platoon, attached to an artillery battery.

We went into action for the first time on the river Sangro in Italy. My platoon was ordered to bring some intelligence, preferably a prisoner or two. I stayed at the observation point, while my buddies waded and swam across the river to check out a little house on the far bank. While still in the water, they dropped the radio, and we lost all contact with them. We had a back-up plan to use the flares, but—as they told us later—they fired them inside the little house. Hissing and sparkling, the flares flew circles inside, wounding one of two German sappers they surprised there, but we never caught a glimpse of them. We heard some shooting and thought our guys were being attacked by the Germans, so we opened fire, aiming some 500 metres beyond the house. It was a heavy barrage, shaking the earth, the river, and everything around with deafening explosions.

On May 3 we relieved the British units at Monte Cassino. We stayed on the front line until May 17 and were pulled back just before the decisive attack on the stronghold. Thousands of guns hurled tonnes of explosives at the hilltop. In the firing frenzy, the barrels of our big guns turned red-hot; we had to pour water on them and wrap them in wet blankets in order to keep firing. The paint on them burned into a coat of blackness. We did not go up the hill; when the assault began, we crouched in our trenches, while the infantry marched over our heads to death and victory. For surviving those two weeks and for the battles near Piedmont, which followed shortly afterward, I was awarded the *Krzyż Walecznych* [Cross for Bravery].

I was wounded twice during the Italian campaign. First, at Rimini, I got a piece of shrapnel in my buttock. I hurt and bled a bit, but my life was in no danger, and I did not even go to hospital. I got rid of the shrapnel only after I arrived in Winnipeg. The second time happened at Imola, at the very end of the war, when a fragment of steel lodged in my leg. That souvenir I carry inside me to this day.

After the war, I stayed in Italy for a while and did not leave for Britain until the last transport. In Britain we were supposed to adjust to civilian life. We could sign up for various vocational courses that would help us resume our normal lives. Probably through some mix-up, I was initially sent for a course in conversational English, but it was not the kind of English I heard in the streets. And no wonder, because there was no one there—except for myself, that is—below the rank of lieutenant. The instructor threw them some highbrow word, and they chattered for four hours while I sat there quietly, dumbfounded by what seemed to me a sermon in Turkish. The second day, I went to the instructor and said that I was in the wrong place, that I was a private while the rest of them were all generals, and that I did not understand a word. I finally managed to convince him, and he let me go looking for something more practical, like bricklaying. Unfortunately, brick-laying was a popular course, and there were no places left. So I took furniture refinishing and did quite well in it, though I never used the skills I learned there.

I decided to stay in the West and was considering emigrating to Australia or Argentina, but when the opportunity to go to Canada came along, my commander made me take that chance. I arrived in Halifax aboard *HMS Aquitania* on May 25, 1946. The train ride to Winnipeg was long but uneventful. They lodged us in the Osborne Barracks. On Dominion Day we proudly marched through the city. Then, with many others, I went to Emerson to work the beetroot fields, but instead of the fields, I was assigned to the kitchen to work as a cook's helper. At least I never went hungry and even saved some good money, since I was making $120 a month. At harvest time I worked for a farmer, but for a measly $45 a month. Still, by the autumn I felt rich, especially with the £80 I had brought with me from England. On November 13, I took my final farming job, in Souris, and I lasted in it one year to the day.

On that farm I learned that once in a while ignorance can be a blessed thing. In early July, my farmer went to Brandon, telling me to look after the farm. I was also supposed to plough a tract of land, twenty-one acres to be exact, that was to lie fallow till the following year. I did as I was told, but then I remembered some oats seed I had found when cleaning the grain bin. I did not want it to go to waste, so in my ignorance I sowed it on the newly ploughed field. A neighbour who saw me doing this showed me in no uncertain terms that I must be crazy to be sowing at that time of year. But the beginner's luck was with me, and the weather stayed warm and sunny well into November, and from that field I gathered a handsome crop. My farmer could hardly believe my luck.

After that year on the farm, I returned to Winnipeg and took residence in the Yale Hotel. The shrapnel in my buttock began to hurt again from all those tractor rides, so I picked up a newspaper and looked for a doctor with a Polish-sounding name. I soon found one, Dr. Rybak. I went to see him, and he took me to the hospital, where he ably removed the offending fragment. I missed only a few nightly card games with my buddies and one or two dances; soon my social life returned to normal. I settled down a bit after I met my wife, Józia. I chatted her up at a bus stop. She recognized my accent, and we were soon joking in Polish. She had been born in Canada, but her family was Polish through and through. She was still very young, barely eighteen when we met. She agreed to go with me to a dance at the Holy Ghost Hall. The tickets, twenty-five cents each, were on me, of course. Our courtship was short but sweet, and a few months later we were married.

In the spring of 1949, I began to work at Inland Steel. The director of the company, Buchanan, was himself a veteran of World War I, and he openly supported the World War II veterans. I knew that he was hiring Poles. When a friend of mine came from a farm and told me he was looking for a job, I took him to Inland Steel. I knew they still had openings. Superintendent Pearson gave him a job on the spot, then asked me if I wouldn't be interested in working for him. Frankly, at the time I was not looking for a job because I still had over $800 put aside from my year on the farm. But in a friendly chat, he asked me what I had been doing back in Poland, and I said I had been training to be a blacksmith. He got very excited and kept telling me that I would not find a better job than in his company. Just then Buchanan came out and offered me and my friend a ride home. On the way he, too, tried to convince me that my future was with Inland Steel. I can give it a try, I thought, and reported for work the next day. I was given a job sharpening teeth for mowers. By the end of the day, my hands were swollen and blistered, but I returned the next morning, not because I needed money but because I wanted to show Buchanan that I was as good as I seemed to be. In the end, I became so proficient at my job that I could sharpen 6300 teeth a day. Each tooth had to be turned on the grinder seven times, which meant that I had to repeat the operation over 44,000 times a day. I worked faster than the older Canadian smiths, and most of them resented me. But their hard feelings did not slow me down, and eventually I was made a foreman.

The number of Polish workers at Inland Steel kept growing, for vets helped their buddies get jobs there, and the management liked the way we worked. All in all, 862 Poles worked for that company at one time or another, and many of us reached retirement there. Inland Steel was a joint-stock company with non-circulating shares, but workers who excelled at their jobs were given the right to purchase some shares. I happened to be among those who benefitted handsomely from those purchases. In the old days, one share went for forty-seven cents, while today its market value is close to $75. A good company. No regrets after working for it for thirty-five years.

My family life, too, settled into a comfortable routine. I bought a house on Cathedral Avenue for $4500 and twelve years later sold it for $12,000. Then came the children and the pleasures of fatherhood. I am particularly proud of my daughter Teresa, who graduated from St. Mary's Academy. Now they are all grown up, living their own futures, while we, more and more, return to our memories.

JÓZEF JANKOWSKI

I was born in 1914 in the Polish Wilno [Vilnius] region. I was drafted into the Polish army in 1937 and served my full term in the 10th Lancers Regiment. At first I was sent to a training camp, which I completed with the rank of senior lancer. Our training was very intensive and demanding, for horseback riding is not natural for most people. We had to learn to control the horse—and stay in the saddle—at a walking pace, at a trot, at full gallop, and we trained under various topographical conditions, on grass, on sand, in the forest. Then we practised more advanced skills, such as jumping on horseback in full gallop, then jumping off and on again, all at full speed. Finally, the fighting skills. One of the routine exercises involved three willow rods, each one centimetre and a half thick, stuck into the ground every ten steps. Charging on horseback, we had to cut them all with a sabre at the height of one metre above the ground. For another exercise, we had to cut off a twisted sheaf of straw set up two metres above ground and representing the head of an enemy, again at full gallop. Leading the horse with one hand, you had to fight with the other.

The horses, too, had to be trained and had to learn the proper rhythms for trotting and galloping. Our daily tasks included a lot of work with the horses. We brushed them, and fed them, and practised for hours. In my second year of service, I became a horse trainer, breaking in new four-year-olds and getting them used to the saddle. It was difficult and responsible work, but I quite enjoyed it.

In the first days of the war, I received an order to break in new

142

horses as intensively as possible. Later I was assigned to a machine-gun detachment and went to the front, east of Wilno. We took our positions and dug in. Our units first confronted the Soviets near Mejszagola [Maišiagala] but were badly outnumbered and had to withdraw. Even as we were withdrawing, Colonel Dąbrowski began organizing guerilla units in the occupied territories. At one point we were attacked by Russian tanks. Fearless, we fired at them with our Maxims but caused no damage. Our guns were useless against the heavily armoured vehicles. We were soon surrounded by the Soviet armoured forces. Our commander saw no other option but to disband the units. Those from the nearby villages could try to make their way back home; others intended to make their way to Lithuania.

I found myself in the latter group. The Lithuanians were well prepared for our arrival: they were well organized and well dug in. We had to surrender all our weapons and horses. It was losing the horses that I regretted most, for so much work had gone into their training. Lithuanian guards marched us to a camp in Rokiszki [Rokiškis], about 150 kilometres from Kowno [Kaunas]. The food in the camp was very good, and we even got lots of meat. There was no barbed wire around the camp. Now and then some internees tried to escape, but most were caught, brought back to Rokiszki, and locked up for two weeks. I, too, kept thinking about how to escape. With the help of some colleagues, I drew a map of the region, which would help me stay on course. One night, I and four others walked away from the camp. We walked only at night, sleeping off the days in haystacks. Near one of the farms, a little girl spotted us in our hiding place. She told her father, who found us out, but he was an honest man and gave us food and wished us good luck. Unfortunately, good luck did not stay with us for long, for one night we walked straight into a Soviet patrol. The commanding officer interrogated us and took us to their barracks.

We were kept in a local jail for a month; then the Soviets put us onto trucks and drove us towards the Soviet border. As we crossed into the Soviet territory, the simple and modest villages of the Polish side gave way to scenes of almost unimaginable destitution. The poverty of Soviet peasants defies description. After a while, they transferred us onto trains, which took us to Kozel'sk. At the station, they ordered us out of the cars and marched us to the nearby old monastery, which had been turned into a concentration camp. Each of us was photographed and assigned to a unit. Mine was number 8. The camp was huge and must have housed some 20,000 prisoners. We spent the entire winter (1940-41) there, and in the spring we were transported to Hermanów, near Kamionka Strumiłowa [Kamenka Bugskaya], where we worked crushing stones used for building a road. As elsewhere, the daily quota was hard to meet, but for meeting it one could get an extra ration of food.

Next we were shipped to the vicinity of Lwów [L'viv] to work on the construction of a new air strip near Złoczów [Zolochev]. Here I was given a job as a carpenter; we had more freedom and even walked to work without guards. One day we noticed three German planes circling above the air field: it was a clear sign that something was afoot, that the long-awaited German-Soviet war had indeed broken out. In the evening, a Soviet *politruk* [propaganda officer] explained to us that the Germans were untrustworthy and that they had treacherously attacked the Soviet Union. We did not have to ask what trust the Germans had broken with the Soviets, for we knew it all too well.

The Soviets began to evacuate our camp—some 15,000 people—towards the east in groups of 200 to 300 prisoners. Frequently attacked by German planes, we made it to Złoczów. But the railway station had just been bombed out, so we marched further on in the direction of Kiev, where the guards finally shoved us into railway cars. We were taken to Starobel'sk and lodged in an old Eastern Orthodox church. It was there, in that church, that we got the news about the Polish army forming somewhere in Russia. Somewhat later, the Soviets gave us 500 rubles each and sent us to Buzuluk, where many had already registered and had been temporarily assigned to various units.

I received an assignment to the 12th Podole Lancers Regiment, to the headquarters security unit. As we began training, I quickly discovered that my familiarity with the commands from the pre-war Polish army came very handy. Eventually, they began sending us by ship to Persia. I was among the last to leave, for at the time I happened to be serving in a Social Services unit, and we had to close down the camps.

After leaving that cursed country, which caused us so much suffering, we could at last freely sing, "O God, curb that sword, which has slashed our home." The Podole Lancers were transformed into motorized units, and we began intensive training in carriers and armoured vehicles. In December 1943, the 2nd Corps, of which we formed a part, was shipped to the Italian front. It took thirty-six ships to carry all the men and equipment to Taranto in Italy.

We engaged the enemy for the first time in San Basilio. Our regiment assumed the reconnaissance duties for the corps, and I seem to have done more than my share of scouting. Once my regiment got the order to take a fortified hill. There were some guys in my platoon who had previously served in the German army and knew German well. I chose a couple of them, and with a group of six we climbed the slope. We got very close to the German lines, and then we surprised two German platoons with a rapid assault. Even though there were only six of us, we took twenty-two prisoners, searched them, and escorted them to our rear.

For the battle of Monte Cassino, our regiment was turned into infantry. We went into action in the second wave, under the commanding officers Dziewicki and Dziekoński. At first we stood on the plain at the foot of the mountain, while the Germans were well sheltered behind rocky outcrops. At hour "zero"—11:05 p.m.—the artillery bombardment became so intensive that German and Allied shells met and exploded in mid-air. My platoon took part in the fierce fighting for the so-called "Doctor's House," a strategic position on the slopes of Monte Cassino. It also continued its usual reconnaissance duties. On one such patrol, I was supposed to check out several concrete shelters abandoned by the enemy. I went alone, and, as luck would have it, I found myself under sniper fire. It took me two hours to cover fifty metres between the shelters. In one of them, I found a seriously wounded German soldier, who was later picked up by our medical team. The German medics had their hands full, and at one point they even asked us for extra stretchers for their wounded. When Monte Cassino finally fell, a platoon from our squadron was chosen to place our standard above the monastery. The losses we suffered in that bloody battle were heavy: of the fifty-five men in my platoon, only five survived.

After the war, we were stationed in Italy for a while. Some of our lancers fell in love with local girls, married, and stayed in Italy. But the majority were eventually transferred to England and joined the Resettlement Corps, which was supposed to help them adjust to civilian life. I also managed to get in touch with my family in Poland. I wrote to my sister, who replied that my parents had been murdered by the Soviets. I do not know the details, but I suspect that it was their support for KOP [Border Guard Corps] that cost them their lives. They were buried at the Jewish cemetery in Berezowka [Berëzovka]. My brother was arrested and taken to Moscow or somewhere; he was never heard from again. Under those circumstances, I saw no point in going back to Poland.

In England, we could apply for immigration to several countries, including Australia, Argentina, and Canada. With a group of friends from my unit, we applied everywhere and decided that we would go to the country that sent us the proper papers first. Canada won the contest, and so we signed the agricultural contracts and came here as a group. Working in the sugar beet fields, we made little money, enough for food and an occasional drink, but nothing else. Afterwards I worked for a good farmer, an Englishman, but I still earned only $120 for the whole summer.

When I moved to Winnipeg, I found a job in a sewing shop, making forty-five cents an hour. Afterwards, I moved to the tailor's shop of the Canadian Army. My work involved primarily making alterations to military uniforms.

I have stayed in close touch with my old buddies from the army. We meet every Friday to play cards and talk of past glory. I also look after old Jan Kaszuba, who remembers the First World War. He treats me like his oldest son.

I was introduced to the Polish Combatants Association by Adolf Wawrzyńczyk. They chose me as a member of the colour party, and I have carried the chapter's colours ever since. I am seventy-one years old now but am determined to hold our colours proudly and high for as long as my strength allows.

ANTONI JÓŹWIAK

My family comes from the Poznań region, from the vicinity of Gniezno. In the winter of 1938, at the age of twenty-two, I was called up for military service. I served in the 69th Infantry Regiment in Gniezno and was assigned to the 9th Company of the 3rd Battalion, commanded by Major Chudzikiewicz. Thus the outbreak of World War II found me in active service.

In late May 1939, we began intensive training, apparently in expectation of some hostilities. We practised long, forced marches. The first such march, covering a distance of about twenty kilometres, gave us lots of blisters and tired muscles. But the very next night we walked for thirty kilometres, and a day after that for thirty-five. During a march we were not allowed to rest but were urged on and on. As we were passing near my village, I asked the commander for permission to visit my parents. "Permission denied," was the answer. After the third day of marching, some reservists collapsed from exhaustion and had to be left by the roadside; we kept walking until we reached the town of Skoki. There I was so tired that I fell asleep almost instantly. I did not even go to dinner. All I wanted was to sleep, sleep, sleep.

When we were not marching, we were reinforcing the trenches and machine gun positions with fascine.* Each infantryman operating a light machine gun had to be a marksman, identified by three ribbons. I happened to be one of them, not that it helped me much when, one

---

* Long bundles of sticks used to line trenches.

Sunday at 4:30 p.m., we were put on alert and set out toward an unknown destination. At first the atmosphere was cheerful, with lots of singing. From the turns we took, we guessed we were moving in the direction of Poznań. But forty kilometres later, as we approached Łapuchów, the jokes and joviality subsided considerably. By the time we finally stopped for the night in the village of Junikowo, everyone was dead quiet and just as tired. We arranged to sleep in a local school. I, too, was exhausted and could barely drag my feet, but a soldier breathes to follow orders, and that night I was ordered to stay on duty. Tough luck. We remained in that general area for some time, building anti-tank ditches. How much good they did when the war actually started, I do not know.

When the army began to requisition more horses, we knew that the war could break out any day. On August 26, we were on the move again, heading for Skoki. Near Lednickie Lake, we were issued three-hour passes. I took a bicycle and rode to my village to visit some friends and family; then I cycled back.

A short time later, we got an order to move out towards the east. In Gniezno, they collected all our passes and regimental badges and burned them. The war had started. We got the news that the town of Września had already been bombed. It was September 5, and we were marching towards Konin. Beside the road, I saw an old woman sitting motionless under a tree. I walked up to her, and only then did I notice that she was dead. Not much further, we found a tall man with a bushy moustache lying beside the road, also dead. People told us that they had been killed by German airplanes. These were the first corpses I saw in that war. On September 6 we came to Koło, where we witnessed an air battle between Polish and German planes. A spectacular sight and two more dead, one on our side and one on theirs.

We took positions on the east side of the road to Łęczyca. The Germans began shelling but overshot us. Our artillery platoon must have had little ammunition, for it did not retaliate. It was now September 8; I remember that day because it was the last time we got our regular army dinner. The next morning we attacked Łęczyca, already in German hands. They placed heavy machine guns in the two church towers, and held us at bay. We moved on towards the muddy banks of the Bzura River and came under heavy machine gun fire. In one place, I got entangled in the roots and mud and began to panic: I thought this was the end. One of the soldiers noticed my desperation and pulled me out. Some time later, I reciprocated by pulling him out of a similar bog. When we reached surer ground, a messenger from the command headquarters came on a motorcycle and promised us that help was on the way. And indeed, three lines of infantry soon backed us up. In the meantime, the enemy began heavy shelling; apparently, they aimed more than 230 guns at us. My unit received an order to withdraw to the rear for damage assessment and reinforcements. On September 11, I saw a long column of German prisoners of war; they carried no equipment, except for a rifle and a small shovel.

On September 12, we were back on the front line, and I captured a German transmitter-receiver. But the enemy pushed hard, and in the chaos of that day Major Chudzikiewicz was wounded. His place was immediately taken by a tall lieutenant of the reserve. He skilfully organized our line of defence, just minutes before six large tanks roared up ahead of us. We let them come close, very close, and then, at his command, we fired at them with everything we had. Four of the tanks were destroyed, and two turned back. Half an hour later, another attack. This time nine tanks were moving in our direction. Our new commander had nerves of steel. Once again we let them come very close and then fired at them at close range. Seven tanks were dead, and two running. But we could not defend that spot much longer. We expected German bombers any minute. Half an hour later, from a safe distance, we watched them destroy the whole area. After the bombing raid came several minutes of dead silence, shattered at last by the roar of German tanks. We repulsed yet another onslaught, and were relieved by the 68th Infantry Regiment from Września. Then we were allowed to rest for a day.

We returned to the front line a bit stronger but not really rested. A round of fire from a small cottage pinned us to the ground, killing Lance-Corporal Spychała and my good friend Jan Chrzanowski. We carefully circled the cottage, approaching it from the sides and back; inside the small basement was nested a German machine gun. We shouted to whoever was inside to surrender. No response. So we threw in a bunch of grenades. When the dust from the explosion began to settle, we heard moaning from the rubble. We moved on; they would die on their own.

Over the next few days we managed to take more German prisoners, but on September 17-18 our Army "Poznań" suffered very heavy losses and was in disarray. We were ordered to withdraw towards Warsaw. The commander of the 61st Infantry Regiment "Gniezno" and Major Majdanowicz from the 68th Infantry Regiment tried to organize some units from the scattered army. They managed to assemble about 7000 men, mostly infantrymen and two squadrons of cavalry, with eleven 75 mm guns and over sixty machine guns. But ammunition was in very short supply, with only nine carts left. Marching through the forest, we walked straight into a German ambush. They placed air-cooled machine guns up in the trees and showered us with deadly fire. On September 19, we ate our last cooked meal, prepared from a cow killed by shrapnel. Swallowing the stew, I heard the moans of a wounded soldier whom nobody could help. Our ranks were thinning, with only 300 left in my unit. Once again we stumbled on Germans but tried to avoid the fight for lack of ammunition. Lieutenant Wydra was now leading the survivors, taking direction from the stars and heading for Warsaw. In a clearing in the forest, we came across German scouts. We approached them quietly and cut their throats, without firing a shot. We were now only thirty-eight, including Wydra. Another German reconnaissance appeared on a motorcycle. We ambushed them and cut them to pieces with bayonets; we had hardly any bullets left. Yet another skirmish. Ignacy Kuczyński, from Sławno, dug in with his machine gun some twenty metres away from me. Then a shell exploded right in his nest; all that was left of him was his helmet and the soles of his shoes. Hungry and exhausted, we kept pushing in the direction of Warsaw. We ate anything edible we found along the way. Finally we reached the vicinity of the capital but were stopped cold in our tracks by a thick ring of German forces encircling the city. We could not go any further. We barricaded ourselves in a little house, with Germans all around us, but a dog sniffed us out. We were captured on September 26, at 5:00 a.m., and taken prisoner. There were thirty-six of us, including Lieutenant Wydra.

The Germans arranged us in two columns and marched us all day to Pruszków. I thought we were among the first prisoners of war, but the engine-house-turned-prison was already packed with Polish prisoners. In fact, I had no place to sit down and had to stand throughout the night. In the morning, the guards gave us some bread and a cup of coffee, and then marched us all the day long to Żyrardów, where the whole stadium was already full of prisoners. They took away our belts, so I had to make do with a piece of string. At the stadium, I met an old friend of mine, Sergeant Wałaszyński, who had volunteered for service even though he had already retired. We noticed a couple of compassionate people outside the barricades, carrying some bread for the prisoners, so the two of us jumped the fence and brought back two big loaves. Starved, the whole company threw themselves at us; they tore the bread from our hands, and we did not even get a taste of it. But neither did they, for in the fighting the bread ended up in the mud. Some tried to build primitive shelters against the elements, but there was not enough material. The next day a rumour spread that all prisoners from the Pomerania and Poznań regions would get passes to go home. On September 30, they put us on trains; we thought they were taking us to Ostrów Wielkopolski, from where we could go home. But instead, we were taken first to Wrocław and then to Germany as prisoner labourers. During that train journey, six men died in my car from exhaustion and starvation. We got almost nothing to eat: a scrap of bread and 250 grams of margarine for nine men. On October 5, we reached Cologne on the Rhine. They led us through the streets, with crowds staring at us. The commander of the transport announced that anyone throwing stones at us would be punished. No one did. They placed us in an old exhibition building, with cement floors, and gave us a bunch of straw to sleep on. I was so weak I could barely walk, and two friends had to support me. Inside, I collapsed on the floor. A German officer walked in, the guards shouted *Achtung!* and we had to stand up at attention. I tried but my legs gave in, and I fell to the ground, hitting my head on the floor. The officer saw my condition and mercifully announced that those who could not get up were allowed to remain on the floor. I wonder what would have happened if he hadn't.

There were 9000 Polish POWs in that camp, all starving beyond what we thought was possible. In several incidents, desperate prisoners attacked the bread cart, even though it was guarded by two armed soldiers. The Germans exploited that situation in their propaganda to show how immoral and spineless Polish prisoners were. They took pictures of two prisoners who had supposedly stolen some bread, and turned them into posters with a caption: "I stole bread from my brother Pole." They published those posters in newspapers and showed them in movie theatres. And the fact was that several men died every day from exhaustion and lack of food. Our daily food rations consisted of one loaf of bread for a dozen prisoners and a bucket of black molasses for a company. I must admit that I survived only thanks to my friends, especially Stefan, who took care of me. Czesław Ciesielski, from Kiszków, worked for a while in the kitchen and tried to help his colleagues by smuggling out a potato or two. But the guards caught him and beat him up, and that was the end of it. The Germans also gave us some kind of protective injections, probably experimental, but they seemed to work to my advantage. I stayed alive.

From Cologne, we were taken to the town of Lechenich, from where we were to be scattered to smaller places. We were standing in the street watching passers-by. One of them was carrying a fresh, fragrant loaf of bread, and the starving prisoners could not help making comments about it. The passer-by must have felt our eyes on him and heard our comments, for he walked up to us, spoke to us in perfect Polish— he was a Pole!— gave us the bread, and disappeared in the blink of an eye. The bread was devoured just as fast.

A group of us was sent to Ginnick and placed in an old bowling alley. We were guarded by a policeman named Mroz, from Opole. After a while, they brought us food: a cauldron full of hot rice soup. Famished, I ate two canteenfuls and then another half. In the evening, German farmers came in, sizing us up and asking if we could, for instance, milk cows. I and a few others were assigned to the manager of an agricultural co-op, who had eighteen cows. He brought us some blankets and put us up for the night. At first we worked side by side with his other workers, harvesting sugar beets. The beginnings were difficult: my body was weak, my hands were unused to such work, and the wet, muddy soil held onto my clumsy feet. But after three weeks of a good diet, rich in milk and cream, I regained my strength. Soon the collar of my uniform became too tight for me, and once again I could move with speed and agility.

On February 22, after we finished our work for the farmer, the Germans moved us close to the Dutch border. They took away our good shoes and gave us clogs instead. Here the work was harder and the living conditions much worse. I tried to run away, but they caught me right on the Dutch border. I learned my lesson: if you want to run away, do it in the summer months, when you can find food in the fields. They locked me up for four weeks and then sent me to work in a factory.

The food was bad. In 1941 I signed the papers releasing me from prison. Now I could work as a civilian worker but still had to wear a sign with the letter "P" for "Pole."

At the end of October, I decided to run away to Poland. I took a train to Berlin, then another one going to Poznań. I bought some German newspapers, pretended to read and sleep. I overheard two Silesians, speaking in Polish, doubting the possibility of German victory in the east. I joined in their conversation and that proved my undoing. I did have a holiday pass from a farmer but no confirmation from the *Arbeitsamt* [Employment Office], which was required in such cases. One of the Silesians realized who I was and reported me at the station in Poznań. A fat gendarme guessed at once that I was a former soldier and ordered me to stand at attention for over an hour while he wrote up his report. At the central police station, they interrogated me again and made another report to compare it with the first. I was thrown into a cell with twenty-seven others. The next day, we were sent to unload bricks. It was very cold, and my hands got severely frostbitten. The only consolation was that I managed to write to my parents, and my father came to visit me in prison. At least they knew that I was alive.

After a while, we were transported to Wrocław, and then to Cottbus. At a few stations, I saw deserters from the German army, starved and brutalized. We were moved back to Cologne, where we witnessed a horrendous British air raid, which apparently killed over 40,000 people. It was there that we were liberated by the American troops on April 14, 1945.

I got my papers to go to France, but later returned to Poland via Switzerland. It was not until 1953 that my wife and I decided to emigrate to Canada; for our son's sake, we said, if not for our own. At first I worked loading coal, but eventually found a much better job at Inland Steel. Now my son, an accomplished athlete and a university graduate, sells sporting goods. As for myself, I retired a few years ago with a decent pension and the customary gold watch.

JAN KASZUBA

I was born on April 25, 1897, and my earliest memories of war reach back to the time of World War I. After the Japanese-Russian war of 1905-06, my father bought a tract of land from the owner of a large estate, who needed cash. In addition to my father, two other Poles purchased portions of that estate; the rest was bought up by the Ukrainians.

In 1918 Petlyura's* army swept through our region. They took the cart, the horses, and me, a twenty-one-year-old. I was forced to serve in the artillery, assigned to a cannon crew because our horses were large. They marched us towards Sielce, where the front line was. There we placed our cannon near the railway tracks and began shelling the approaching armoured train. I was fetching the shells. In the end, we had to fall back in a hurry and in the midst of chaos, for none of our shells caused any damage to the train. A friend of mine from the village, Terenty Mazurok, ran up to me and shouted, "Stachu, let's run, or the Poles will cut us up." I could not run with a cartful of ammunition, so Terenty started throwing boxes of shells into the bog. Petlyura himself stood on the road, trying to stop his scared troops, but few chose the road: the majority went straight through the marshes and bushes and disappeared for good. Terenty insisted that we go home, and so we did. We left the cart and the horses in the yard and continued on foot towards Łukaczew. An innkeeper who knew us gave us a loaf of bread

---

* Simon Petlyura (1879-1926), Commander-in-chief (Ataman) of the Ukrainian army fighting for independence after the Russian Revolution in 1917.

and a pot of cold sour milk. We filled our bellies and took a nap. When we woke up, we were surrounded by a Polish combat patrol from the detachments stationed in Włodzimierz [Vladimir]. Four fusiliers, with rifles at the ready, escorted us to the headquarters of the 4th Division commanded by Major Jaworski. We were placed under arrest in the barracks. I thought we would be executed, for they treated us like spies. But luckily, one of the people interrogating us was Lieutenant Zakrzywicki from our village, and he vouched for me before the major and confirmed that I was the son of a Polish patriot well known to him. Jaworski asked me who my companion was. I answered that he was one of the settlers, who accepted the Eastern Orthodox religion under the pressure of local authorities, but in his heart he felt truly Polish, and that his name was really Mazurek, even though the locals called him Mazurok. The major accepted my assurances and sent me to the 1st Platoon of the 1st Squadron; Mazurok went to the regimental orchestra because he had qualifications as a conductor from the former Cossack army. As a Polish soldier, I took part in several skirmishes with Petlyura's troops until Piłsudski signed an agreement with Petlyura at Białocerkiew [Bila Tserkva] to the solemn accompaniment of the Polish and Ukrainian orchestras.

Some of the Polish regiments went to Kiev, where they were received with much pomp and circumstance. We returned to Włodzimierz. From there, we were sent to the Wilno [Vilnius] front as reinforcements for the regiments smashed at Mołodeczno [Maladzyechna]. Our major must have been born under a lucky star, for we never took part in any bloody battles until Kolankowice. According to our scouts, there were four cannons in Kolankowice. I got the order to search the thickets beside the bridge, where two machine guns were supposed to be located. I found nothing, but fell into a swamp up to my waist. Then I was sent ahead to draw enemy fire, but the enemy did not want to shoot. Finally, we managed to capture a Bolshevik with a rifle and a bunch of grenades. As it turned out, the "Bolshevik" was a Pole and a good friend of Major Rybicki, with whom he had once served in the same unit. Those were crazy times, and Poles from various contending armies met in the most unusual circumstances. They sent the false "Bolshevik" to Warsaw, and he later became an officer in the Polish army.

But the fighting around Kolankowice did cost us some good men. Lieutenant Wróbel and Major Rybicki were killed in those battles, and so was Major Lis-Kula. It was then that I met Lieutenant Kopański, later General Kopański.* Decades later I met him again when he came to visit the combatants in Winnipeg, and I reminded him about our first encounter. I even got a picture with him.

We were constantly on the move. One day Lieutenant Kozłowski, in charge of a battery of guns, took position on the banks of the Prypeć [Pripyat'] River. His orders were to stop the enemy traffic on the river, and his men proved expert gunners: of the ten ships that ventured out, only two may have escaped. But just then we got the news that a band of Ukrainian marauders was on the rampage around Chernobyl, murdering the Poles and the Jews. Acting on a tip, we surrounded a village but caught neither the band nor its leader. At long last, we were granted three weeks of rest. Our lodgings were comfortable, the food plentiful, and the horses well-looked-after. A cavalryman's heaven.

After our rest, we went on to Kiev. Along the way, I was sent on patrol towards the town of Pechki. Near the market square, an old man warned me not to go any further because the Bolsheviks were just ahead. But I had my orders and went on. I checked out the market square and much of the town—no sign of any troops. I fired in the air three times, as arranged, to let my detachment know that the town was clear. This caused much panic among the people at the market square, who ran wildly in all directions. Soon afterwards, my detachment caught up with me.

Pechki was known for its tanneries, so our lieutenant requisitioned some of their leather, and every soldier got enough for a nice new pair of shoes. Not that we had time to wait for those shoes to be made. The situation on the Kiev front worsened daily, and we had to withdraw. In Barbarów [Barbarov], with a small unit of twenty-two, we captured two cannons and two machine guns. Moving on, we came under heavy machine gun fire. Our platoon commander was hit in the head and died on the spot. Since I was second in command, I had to take charge of the platoon. To give my men a good example, I never shirked reconnaissance missions; once or twice I even captured a Russian scout. Providence must have been watching over me, for men were dying all around, and I was never even wounded. Once we were passing by some buildings, but I had

---

* Stanisław Kopański (1895-1976), commander of the 1st Carpathian Mountain Brigade (1940-42), chief of general staff (1943-47).

a bad feeling, a premonition of sorts, and forbade anyone to move close to them. A few minutes later, the buildings were blown into pieces by an unexpected barrage of artillery fire. We kept withdrawing towards Brześć [Brest], through Janów [Ianovo] past Kowel [Kovel]. We did not make it to the safety of Brześć unscathed. Almost within the sight of the city, we were attacked by a much larger Bolshevik unit and lost thirty-six men.

Brześć was a rallying point for our forces, where units of young volunteers reinforced our ranks. Most of us were dead tired, but we had to move on, eating and sleeping on horseback. In Kock, we noticed some Bolsheviks taking a priest from the church, apparently to shoot him. We hid behind a fence, and when they got closer, we fired. We saved the priest. Later, when chasing a Bolshevik supply cart, my horse was wounded. It barely brought me to Radzyń, a town overflowing with horses and soldiers. I reported to my lieutenant that my horse was hurt. "That's good," he said, "you'll stay here." Then he put me in charge of our spoils of war. For seven weeks I stood in Radzyń, looking after the equipment taken from the enemy. That's why I did not take part in the battle of Warsaw in August 1920.

After that Polish-Soviet war, I had to decide what to do next. I did not want to go back home, for my stepmother always raised hell when I was around. I thought of going to America, where I had a sister, but I did not know her address. I even worked for other farmers to make some money for the trip. In the meantime, most of my friends from the squadron applied for plots of land in Wołyń [Volyn]. They tried to persuade me that I, too, should apply, and in the end they succeeded. I got my plot in Nadwołczek, from the estate of Countess Sobańska. Because I applied late, I got sixteen hectares of the poorest soil, and no buildings. When my brother paid off my share of the patrimony—sixty American dollars in all—I bought a horse. A Jew who used to know my father and who wanted to help me out gave me a cart and loaned me the money to buy another horse. And so I began to farm. I had to hurry, for a decree came out that if someone had not begun cultivating his land before the end of three years, the authorities would cancel the original donation and give it to a more enterprising settler. For the first three years I lived in an old shed. Then, thanks to the support of the lieutenant from my former unit, who had become a land commissioner, I managed to secure a loan in the amount of 400 zlotys. With that money I built a stable for the horses and a small cottage for myself. To be honest, there were times when I had nothing to eat. My horses grazed in the pasture, and I lay beside them chewing sorrel. Times were hard, at least for me. One of my horses died, and I had only one left to work with. Once again a Jewish horse trader helped me out. He allowed me to choose from his stable a horse that would best agree with my other horse. He told me the horse was worth ninety zlotys but did not ask for money. "You'll pay me when you have money, and in place of interest you'll give me a wagon of hay." That was the agreement. Then another Jew sold me a cow for ninety zlotys, on similar terms. Heavy step by heavy step, I became a farmer. When I married, my wife brought me a cow in her dowry. I wanted to return the money for the first cow, but the Jew did not want any of it. "You'll pay me back when you're richer," was all he said.

My land had not been cultivated for a long time and needed much work, but, with stubbornness and persistence, I got good harvests of wheat and hops. When the land commission came to examine my progress, they were impressed. In the years that followed, my farm and my family prospered.

I was over forty when the war with Germany broke out. The Polish authorities announced mobilization. Then on September 17, 1939, came the Bolsheviks. I was just returning from a short trip when a Bolshevik patrol stopped me on the road and placed me under arrest. They took my horse and wagon, and searched it thoroughly, but found nothing. The commander of the Bolshevik detachment turned out to be an old comrade of mine from the Polish army. He remembered me and so did his wife, who protested against my arrest. But he needed to feel important and powerful, I guess, so he locked us up in a warehouse. I shudder to think what they did—for no apparent reason—to an acquaintance of mine from the village whom they arrested together with me. They bound his hands and legs, tied him to a pole, and ordered him to walk around it. Local children spat and threw stones at him. When he was too tired to walk and collapsed beside the pole, they picked him up, took him a short distance away, and shot him. Pointless cruelty, pointless death. I pleaded with the Bolshevik officer to let me go, and in the end he agreed. More than that: he offered to give me a ride back home, fearing, he said, that Ukrainian peasants might cause me some harm. I was in no position to challenge his concern for my welfare.

In the middle of winter, the Soviets began forcibly to remove Polish intelligentsia and anyone associated with the police or the army into the heartland of Russia. They came for us on February 9, 1940. We were prepared to die—others had been murdered in the vicinity—but fortunately they were "only" removing us to Siberia. My wife was still weak from her last childbirth, and we had an infant with us. We were loaded into railway cars and taken east. The journey lasted sixteen days, in horrible conditions, with no latrine but a dirty hole in the floor. For the first five days, they kept the car doors locked and opened them only on the sixth, somewhere near Sverdlovsk, to let us get some snow for drinking water. Finally, at the end of the line, at some nameless place, they threw us out into the snow. A few weeks later, we were lodged with the local peasants and sent to work in the forest. I was assigned to a brigade, and we began by sharpening the axes. Then, tree by tree, we carved into the forest. The labour was brutal and back-breaking, but with five children at home, I had no choice. Without the meagre rations I got for my work, they would die. When the conditions grew even worse, we decided to run away from the forest outpost to a *kolkhoz* [collective farm], hoping it would be easier to eke out a living there. And indeed, our situation improved. In the *kolkhoz,* even children could work harvesting vegetables. While cutting cabbage, my clever son always buried a head or two in the sand, and we came back at night to collect them. My wife dug potatoes, and for every ten bucketfuls, she got one for herself. We sliced them, dried them over the fire, and put them into a sack for winter. During the winter months, we waded through the snow to gather rosehips; they could be bartered in the *kolkhoz* for various necessities, including tobacco, which was a trading commodity very much in demand.

In the *kolkhoz,* we learned about the formation of the Polish army. We left with the whole family and got as far as Toshkent, where the guards ordered us off the train. We had twelve pieces of baggage with us, which made it difficult to move around, but ensured we would not starve. We had plenty of flour, peas, and other foodstuffs. People envied us our riches, and no one would help. Somehow we made it to Samarkand, where we had to wait out in the open, in snow and rain, for eight days before the authorities assigned us to a *kolkhoz*. Seven weeks later, it was announced that all men of the draft age should report to the Polish army, while their families stayed in the *kolkhoz*. We said tearful goodbyes, and I left for Kermine. Once again we braved the elements, the frost, snow, and rain, because there were not enough tents for everybody. There was also no firewood, so we walked long miles to collect cotton stalks. Living in those stark conditions, I caught spotted fever. They isolated me in the corner of a room. We had no medical supplies, and I soon lost consciousness. They transferred me to a rudimentary hospital, but the medic who looked me over decided I was only good for the morgue. On the way out, one of the stretcher-bearers noticed I was still warm and took me to the ward. I know this story only from what others have told me, for I lay completely senseless. When I came to, they forced some food into me, biscuits soaked in water. They let my wife know of my condition, and she came with the children to visit me. She was not allowed inside, so I saw her only from a distance. She stayed in the camp for a while with our youngest daughter, sending the others to an orphanage, which soon left for India. Later she, too, had to leave the camp and found herself in terrible conditions. Our youngest daughter died. When I got my wife's letter describing her circumstances, I shed bitter tears, and all my friends with me. We did not reunite as a family until four years later, after the war, in England.

I completely recovered from that bout of spotted fever and went with the army to Iran, Iraq, and Palestine. I served as a messenger, then as a guardsman, and, finally, I was transferred to England. There we were incorporated into the British army, and I was sent to work in the kitchen. I was promoted to corporal even though I did not know much English.

After the war I wanted to emigrate to the United States, but I still did not have my sister's address. Canada did not admit families, so I signed up for another two and a half years in the British army. By that time, the Canadian immigration restrictions had changed, and we left for Canada aboard the ship called *Lincoln*.

The most precious document still in my possession is the land charter issued to me as a military settler. This Charter number 238 was drawn up in 1925, and on its basis I received as my property a plot of land from the subdivision of the grange Wołczków, in the parish of Chotiaczów [Khotyachov], district of Włodzimierz, region of Wołyń. I also cherish the portrait of Marshal Józef Piłsudski, which hangs in the place of honour in my house. I look at it every day and take pride in the fact that I served Poland as one of his soldiers, just as half a century earlier my grandfather had fought in the ranks of insurgents in 1863.*

---

* A reference to the January Uprising of 1863 against Tsarist Imperial Russia.

KAZIMIERZ KLIMASZEWSKI

I was born in 1914 in Warsaw, soon after World War I had broken out. I arrived when Germans were shelling the Kierbedź Bridge, or so I was told. Twenty-three years later, in 1937, I graduated from the Central School of Commerce in Warsaw and was called up for military service at the newly established Officer Cadet Artillery College in Zambrów. The college, located in the old barracks from the time of the Grand Duchy of Warsaw, housed two batteries of light artillery and two of heavy; I was assigned to one of the former. I graduated in the rank of cadet platoon leader and received a lucky assignment to the 32nd Light Artillery Regiment in Rembertów, near Warsaw, which allowed me— at least for a time—to live at home and commute to my regiment. Not long afterwards, I took part in large-scale military games in the environs of Czerwony Bór, where I earned a promotion to cadet sergeant. A year later I participated in my first military games for officers.

The games concluded on August 22, 1939, in an ominous atmosphere, as war was looming on the horizon. On August 25, I was already on the front line along the border with East Prussia as a reconnaissance officer, initially of a battery and then of a company of the 18th Artillery Division under General Młot-Fijałkowski. We were well prepared for the German attack: we could hit with precision every stone and every bush within our range. We were issued French artillery helmets. We also received our pay: as an officer, I was paid 2.80 zlotys and half a canteen of vodka for ten days. We did not have to wait long for the Germans. On September 1, at 6:00 a.m., I was called to the command headquarters, where I learned that the war had started. I returned to my observation point with an order to dig anti-aircraft shelters. We remained dug in until September 3, when we received an order to withdraw eastwards. Apparently, to the west of us, German armoured units had broken through our lines along the Pułtusk-Ostrołęka road and begun to encircle us. We were thus forced to relinquish our positions without firing a single shot.

For four days we moved east, much of the time under heavy attack from German bombers. Late at night on September 7, we reached the bridge on the Bug River near Wyszków. Germans had been bombing it all day, and by nighttime it was already burning. We crossed it, took defensive positions on the other side, and sat there, waiting. On the 9th, a tragedy struck: the enemy armoured units cut us off from our supply column, and we were left without any food or feed for the horses. During the night, some German tanks were reported in the vicinity.

The following day, still quite early, I was brushing my teeth in the river when I heard the whistling of shells high above my head and exploding beyond our lines. The Germans were adjusting their fire, focussing it on our positions. I reported this to Captain Konopka, who sent my report up the chain of command. Orders were issued, countermeasures taken. I did not participate in the battle that followed because I had been sent for the badly needed provisions, oats and bread. With four men and a horse-drawn wagon, we set out in the direction of Mińsk Mazowiecki. After five kilometres, we were spotted by a section of German bombers. We threw ourselves into ditches and along fences: they dove after us, causing a lot of noise but, fortunately, no damage. As we continued in search of food, some fifteen kilometres down the road, we heard heavy artillery fire and rumbling explosions coming from the direction of our defence lines; we could also see squadrons of German bombers on the horizon. The battle was raging.

Eight hours later we managed to buy some bread and hay and headed back. The road to Włodawa was now crowded with the remnants of various withdrawing units. I left the wagon and rode ahead, hoping to find our men. The soldiers I met told me that our regiment had suffered heavy casualties, that Colonel Tabiszewski and his adjutant were dead, and that we would never find the scattered survivors. So instead of chasing our splintered unit, we—I, my two corporals, and two privates—decided to join what was left of the 1st Artillery

Regiment from Wilno [Vilnius]. Its officers were delighted to see our wagonful of supplies. The reconnaissance officer of that regiment had been killed, so I was assigned his duties.

In the vicinity of Kałuszyn, we ran into German machine gun fire. The guns, nested on the roof of a local school, pinned down our infantry troops. My Wilno regiment had only one battery left, but that was all we needed. We set up observation points, located the target, and blew the school to pieces. Helmets and shoes went up in a cloud of smoke, red from the brick dust. The infantrymen muttered a collective sigh of relief and moved on, at least for a little while, until they ran into German tanks. A few moments later, before we had a chance to get our horses, we came under strong fire from the side. With six shells left, we managed to shatter that nest as well, but we did suffer casualties. I could hear our telephone operator moaning in a ditch. I tried to cross the road, but a hail of bullets pinned me in a rut; some brushed my shirt, and one hit my leg just below the knee. Rolling from one rut to another, I reached the wounded soldier and pulled him to the nearby infantry unit. By the time I returned to where the battery had been, the guns were gone. Where? No one knew. There was no time to feel frustrated. I sat under a tree, cut off the top of my boot, and put a rudimentary dressing on my wound. Miraculously, my own horse was still waiting for me; I mounted and rode away to look for either of my former artillery units.

I found some scattered troops on the road to Mińsk and continued with them. Near the city, we came across a convoy of five trains, four loaded with soldiers, state police, and the reserve, and the fifth with guns and ammunition. We reported to the commanding officer— Colonel Zieliński, if I remember correctly. He sent us to the artillery train, and I was named artillery platoon leader.

The command headquarters was expecting a German attack from the direction of Siedlce. We were ordered to pull down the big guns from the train platforms and instal them on the embankment beside the tracks. We laboured the whole day, but by the evening only two gun sites were ready. Fortunately, we consoled ourselves, our train was well armoured. It may have been a relic from the 1920s, but the engine was reinforced with steel plates, and anti-aircraft guns were mounted at intervals along its length.

As expected, the German tanks came from the vicinity of Siedlce.

They were charged by our cavalry, but the way it happened is often misrepresented in history books. Under the cover of the forest, two squadrons of cavalry moved up along the flanks to the idling tanks and waited, unnoticed, some 300 metres away from them. Once the tanks started moving, the horsemen rode up to them in a quick manoeuvre and showered them with grenades; then they took cover again. Three tanks were destroyed, and the others withdrew. For one night we could relax a little.

Despite the temporary respite, the Germans began to tighten their noose around us. We had to leave the security of the train convoy and withdraw south. What happened to those trains, whether they were blown up or captured by the enemy, I don't know. We walked all through the night and into the morning under the cover of dense, milky mist. We could not see the enemy until we literally bumped into them: that's how some lancers were taken prisoner when we walked into a village already swarming with Germans. At the last moment, I jumped back into the white stuff and disappeared. Later I met a cavalry troop riding to Garwolin, where we knew the storehouses of the Centre for Artillery Training were located. The Centre had been bombed, but no Germans were there yet. Much to my relief, the storehouses were still full of supplies, and I was able to change my underwear and my uniform, and even found a pair of binoculars and two excellent colts. Then I rode on to a forester's lodge in Izdebna, where I found Colonel Więckowski with some 2000 men, readying for the rescue of Warsaw. After checking that I was who I claimed to be, they made me a provisions officer. My duties involved reconnoitring for food and information. We would dress in German uniforms and, in a German staff car, drive towards Warsaw to find out the movements of the enemy. On September 27, in such a disguise, we learned that the Germans had already entered Warsaw. Our hopes of rescuing the capital were dashed.

That same sad evening, we heard for the first time General Sikorski's appeal, broadcast from Paris, calling on all Polish soldiers to make their way across the borders to the Polish units in France. His advice was to go through Romania and Hungary. It was quickly decided that those with families could stay in Poland; the rest would go. In the forest, we buried the arms of those who chose to stay. The rest of us split into small groups and went south, despite some objections that we should push through to Lithuania. I exchanged my two

164

colts for a good horse, for my leg was still hurting, and the saddle, though uncomfortable, caused it less strain than walking. We crossed the German lines before dawn on September 28. We had heard that Polish soldiers caught near the southern border were being shot on the spot by German patrols. So as we reached the foothills of the Carpathian Mountains, we left our uniforms to the local highlanders (Lemkos) in exchange for well-worn, lice-infested—but civilian—clothes. In our new outfits, we looked more like a band of gypsies than a military unit.

Our last guide led us to Uman, a small village near the Slovak border, and then, in the morning, we descended to a Ukrainian village. That proved to be a fatal mistake. The Ukrainians, hostile to Poles, must have guessed who we were and immediately reported us to the Germans. Suddenly we were surrounded by German patrols, their machine guns aimed straight at us. We, too, were heavily armed, but there were only twelve of us, and we were trapped. And so I was taken prisoner, scratching the louse bites through my rags.

The Germans took us to Komańcza, and from there to Sanok, where a Volksdeutsch [a Pole who declared himself German] read us the death sentence: all armed vagabonds wcrc to be shot. For two days and a night we waited for the execution. Then at sunrise, we were finally loaded onto a truck, all of us convinced that this was our last ride before a shot in the head. But the ride took us past a couple of graveyards to Mościce, where—much to our delight—we were offered coffee and attached to a large transport of prisoners of war. We realized then that our colonel must have worked out a deal with our captors or somehow convinced (most likely, bribed) them that we were indeed Polish soldiers in disguise.

Together with hundreds of others, we were forced into railway cars, but we had no intention of staying with the transport. We were planning an escape from the moment we arrived in Mościce. When the guards began to draw up lists of POWs in every car, we kept changing cars to get our names on several lists so they couldn't tell which car we were actually in. Unfortunately, our clever plan helped us little. We remained under heavy guard throughout the short trip to Cracow, where all senior officers were taken off the transport, and then all the way to Dortmund. No one escaped.

We arrived in Dortmund at night. We had to jump out of the cars into a circle of blinding light. On its perimeter stood old women from the local Polish community, weeping for Poland and for us. I was sent to Stalag 6D, but first the guards drove us to the "Sportpalast," surrounded with barbed wire and flooded with white light during daytime and red at night. In a gallery, all around us, machine guns watched our every move. We were herded into small enclosures, almost like cattle pens, with a hundred per enclosure; we got some food, which tasted like cattle feed. I pretended I was just a private, an ordinary labourer. Because I knew German quite well, the Germans tried to pressure me into collaborating with them. That I would never do, and I took the first opportunity to be sent to a *Bauer*, a German farmer, as a farm labourer. Unfortunately, some Stalag pen-pusher discovered in my papers that I was in fact an officer, and I was brought back to the camp. The situation called for more cunning: with two packs of tobacco, I bribed a Volksdeutsch to delete all references to my officer rank from the records. The scheme worked, and once again I found myself working for a *Bauer*. But alas, not for long. The Germans began a campaign to convince soldiers to sign up for the civilian list; they promised good work, the same pay as for German workers, even holidays in Poland. But I advised the soldiers, quite openly, not to do it, for as long as we were POWs, we had the protection of the Geneva Convention. Then one black sheep in our Polish fold betrayed me. He had fallen in love with a German girl and couldn't wait to jump the fence. I was taken—for agitating—to Stalag 6C, a harsh place, smelling of peat moss and misery. There I saw, for the first time, a group of British soldiers taken prisoner at Dunkirk. They were hungry and exhausted, many suffering from wounds, but still disciplined, unbroken, defiant. At night, we quickly organized some help for them. Since any direct contact with them was forbidden, we tied loaves of bread to pieces of string, swung them over our heads, and threw them, like hammers, to the Brits. It wasn't much, but we felt better, hoping that our British comrades did as well.

Another penal transfer took me to Oberlangen, barrack number 10. We worked building dikes, setting up targets, collecting duds, but all the time thinking of ways to escape. Some indeed managed to run away but were soon recaptured and thrown into an isolation cell. Later I was sent to Hofnungstal, a valley of hope, although hope I saw there none. It was a murderous boot camp for the German Africa Corps. During our day-long shifts spraying the tanks destined for Africa with camouflage paint, we witnessed the most brutal methods of military training. Breathless and exhausted soldiers were kicked and beaten and harassed at every turn. I recall graffiti scribbled on one of the walls, *Vanerheide, du mordest meine Jugend* [Vanerheide, you are killing my youth].

By that time, escapes had become a daily occurrence, although the success rate was not very high. We even had a special committee organizing and coordinating those escapes. I tried three times. Twice I was recaptured; after the first time, I was given twelve days of solitary confinement; after the second, twenty-eight. Like other recaptured escapees, I was forced to wear a blue uniform that remembered World War I, with target circles painted on the back. "Just try that one more time, and we'll know where to aim," the guards laughed.

After the second stint in the isolation cell, in early February, I had to be carried out and taken to the hospital in Hoppenheim. When I got out of intensive care, a Frenchman, Leclerque, came to me and whispered, "Listen, we have an organization here," and he told me the hospital was infiltrated by the Maquis, the French resistance fighters. When the Germans announced that all incurably sick French soldiers could return to France, the Maquis searched them out, even as far as Rawa Ruska, a town in eastern Poland, and helped them return. In the hospital, they doubled as orderlies and couriers for de Gaulle's and Churchill's intelligence people. I would be welcome to join them, Leclerque continued, if I could arrange the escape of Captain Bratkowski. For some reason, Captain Bratkowski, of the 36th Infantry Regiment, had incurred the wrath of the German guards and had been kept in the worst isolation bunker in Germersheim. He was transferred to Heppenheim when he began simulating madness. The fear was that Dr. Schmell, a local scoundrel whose preferred method for disposing of the enemies of Hitler was phenol, wanted to liquidate him. I was still weak but took up the challenge. With the help of many good people, we duplicated the keys, arranged a ticket, and got some money and good clothes. On the night of Maundy Thursday, I led Bratkowski to a wall in the hospital garden, where a rickety scaffolding of planks and tables was already in place. He was dressed as a German and spoke German well. The guards noticed his escape only the following Monday and quickly announced that he had been captured and shot. But two weeks later, I got the news from a friend in Bern that Bratkowski savoured his freedom and some Easter eggs in his house. A few years later I met him again in England.

Having proven myself, I was welcomed into the ranks of the Maquis and took part in many of their operations. Most often we placed pouches for downed airmen, usually under the right corners of tool houses in vineyards, according to specific instructions we received from England. Throughout that time I also maintained my contacts with the Polish Underground Organization. In 1944, soon after Christmas, a contact arrived, as usual simulating some illness. He warned me that our communication cell was exposed and that the Germans knew of my involvement. If I remained at the hospital, I would be in grave danger. So my French friends arranged for a quick discharge. As I was being escorted back to the camp, I managed to escape for the third, and lucky, time.

The war was entering its final phase. The battle of Ardennes had been won, and the Allied forces were on the offensive. I eventually came across some American troops in Frankfurt. I was debriefed, given new clothes, fed, and rested for a few days. Then once again I put on my blue prisoner uniform and went back to where I had come from. The Americans had received intelligence that the Germans intended to move all POWs eastwards. My task was to delay those transfers. My comrades in the camp needed little convincing, and we were soon freed by the Americans.

Back in Frankfurt, in the Allied command headquarters, the number of rescued Polish prisoners was growing into thousands. I served as an interpreter, since I could speak both German and English. Many of us lived in squalid conditions in one half of a twelve-storey building. We called it the Tower of Babel, because the first floor was occupied by the Russians, the second by the Poles, the third by the French, the fourth by the Belgians, the fifth by Serbs, and so on, all the way up, a different nationality on each floor. We had no water there, no sanitation. The stench was terrible, and after a few days the Americans sectored off five streets in Romerstadt for the Poles. They organized several armed units and sent us to remove any Germans we found there, forcibly if need be. We gave the Germans a few minutes to take as much as they could carry in their arms. None tried to resist, but some were crying. I would lie if I said I felt any sympathy for them. In the emptied houses and apartments, we lodged our countrymen: families in the two centre streets, single females on one side, males on the other. Unfortunately, any semblance of order, even decency, dissipated under the cover of darkness. Newly found wardrobes, wine cellars, and general malaise resulted in much drunkenness and demoralization. That was not the Polish army I knew.

Through Captain Zieliński, who was working in General Eisenhower's headquarters, I suggested to the Allied commanders that we organize a Polish unit and send it to General Anders. My proposal was accepted. Soon afterwards, 1300 Polish soldiers, plus 1200 Poles from Silesia who had deserted (or were freed from) the German army, boarded ships in Marseille. At first the two groups were far from friendly, but not without reasons. Once, for instance, the Poles were issued an allowance of cigarettes while the Silesians were not. This caused complaints, even some confrontations. I called up the sergeants from both sides and told them to find a solution. They did: one group shared with the other, and soon frictions diminished. Practically all the Silesians had managed to buy or barter some Allied uniforms and throw the German ones overboard by the time we reached Taranto in Italy.

I greeted Taranto with much relief. Not only could I finally transfer the command of the transport to Major Niemira, waiting for us ashore, but I could also turn over to him my backpack full of money, the pay for our soldiers. I was so afraid someone on the ship might steal it that I carried it with me wherever I went and whatever I did, no matter how private. Thus relieved of the command and the precious backpack, I helped divide the troops into groups of fifty and load them onto trucks. Then I climbed into a cab, looked at the driver, and—as we Poles say—"turned into an oak," I was so dumbfounded. The driver was a very attractive woman, dark hair cascading from under her black beret. When I finally regained some self-control, I introduced myself, "I am Klimaszewski." "So am I," she answered, smiling. I thought she was making fun of me and wasn't sure how to react. "But I am, really, that's my name, too," she tried to explain, seeing my confusion. As it later turned out, she had every right to my name (or I to hers), for we also shared some distant ancestry.

Soon after we arrived in the 2nd Corps, we were issued tropical uniforms. But when I went to report to General Przewłocki in what I was issued by the Americans, the general, a stickler for the proper uniform, as I soon found out, looked me up and down and asked in a sour voice, "Have you come here for a masquerade, Lieutenant Klimaszewski?" And he seconded me to Imola, where, after a few final volleys, the war came to an end. I returned to General Przewłocki. "You were in a real hurry, son," he quipped, "but you came a bit too late." He appointed me as an education officer and a liaison to the British Mission.

The war was over. Until 1946, my duties revolved around editing *The Bulletin of the Press and Culture Department of the 2nd Corps* and a Polish newspaper in Bari. In July of that year, the corps was transferred to England. I became involved in the discussions concerning the Polish Corps for Training and Resettlement, voicing my strong opposition to that misconceived—or so I thought at the time—initiative. To silence my irritating criticisms, the command sent me to a teacher-training program. There I was introduced to Barnard's visual method of teaching English, quite effective, I must say, helping a soldier to learn over 600 words and some basic grammar in six weeks.

Unfortunately, many of the soldiers who decided to go to Canada on agricultural contracts hadn't had an opportunity to study English that way, or any way, for that matter. General Anders had begun to receive reports of friction between Polish ex-soldiers and the local administrators on the prairies. There were even rumours of a revolt. What the Polish veterans in Canada needed was some people with a good command of English, who could articulate their concerns and promote their just causes. And so I was sent to Canada, together with Father Malak and Jan Ostrowski. Winnipeg was a friendly city and a home to many Poles who had opened their hearts and homes to Polish veterans. Here I met others concerned about the plight of our ex-servicemen, who had just been released from farm contracts and were working as bricklayers and painters.

As the beetroot harvest of 1947 ended, almost all the members of what was to become the board of Chapter #13—myself, Wawrzyńczyk, Mossakowski, and Kiryluk—found themselves in the vicinity of Winnipeg, working throughout the winter as lumberjacks in Indian Bay on the 94th mile. We stayed in close touch with Winnipeg through correspondence. Every Wednesday, our voluminous mail was thrown from a passing train into a snowbank. The following day, as the train was returning to Winnipeg, we held up the return mail on a specially constructed pole; the train engineers plucked the mailbag from the pole without so much as slowing down. The volume of mail that was dropped for us was so large that the RCMP took an interest in our activities. They paid us a visit and, in our absence, rummaged through our quarters, but they found nothing suspicious. We had nothing to hide.

I came back to Winnipeg in mid-winter of 1948 for the first National Convention of the Polish Combatants Association [PCA], which was held between January 21 and February 2 and which I had helped organize. At the convention, Jan Ostrowski, a lawyer, was elected president; I became the first vice-president. The other members of the national executive board were Józef Kaczmarek and Kazimierz Wielobob. (In subsequent years, I served as president of the national association twice, in 1950 and in 1959.)

In the spring of that year, we all found employment in the city. We worked days at various jobs, while in the evenings we met in the editorial offices of *Czas* to organize the Winnipeg chapter of the PCA. Those efforts were both socially satisfying and crowned with success: our chapter was the largest in Canada, with almost 300 members.

My life revolved around the PCA, its aspirations, its problems. One of the convention resolutions called for a PCA representative to be seconded to the federal government in Ottawa. That person would look after such issues as hospital care for the veterans, outstanding pay for military service, unjust farm contracts, and so on. The Ministry of Labour agreed to engage me for the position, which it classified as civil servant level 6, with a salary of $165 per month. At the time still unattached, I was invited to stay with General Sznuk, who introduced me to some key figures in the Polish community in Ottawa.

One of my first priorities in the new position was the preparation of a statute for the PCA, which would give us all the rights and privileges of a Canadian organization. As a branch of a British organization, we had no legal status in Canada. We drafted most of the clauses but engaged a legal firm to prepare the final version. The lawyers complained that there was too much "politics" in our draft, but we managed to retain the sections that expressed the ideals of the association: freedom, justice, and independence. The statute was ready in 1950. We sent it to all local chapters, which, from that moment, could become independent legal entities.

In Ottawa, my personal life became greatly enriched. In 1949 I met a Canadian woman, a secretary of Deputy Minister Heighthorn, and in

December of that year we were married. According to the civil service regulations, if both spouses worked for the government, one of them had to be moved to the lowest level of pay. Needless to say, we strongly objected to that rule and began to plan our future without the government's involvement. Besides, the PCA statute was ready, the farm contracts were already over, and the problem of Blue Cross insurance for the veterans had also been settled. Most of my work at the time concerned displaced persons and the immigration of Polish women for work as domestics or nurses. We thus decided to move to Port Arthur [now Thunder Bay]. I had been promised a well-paying job there, which, unfortunately, disappeared on my arrival. So I found work as an accountant in the dry-cleaning and fur-storage business of Mr. Malicki. Later, Wawrzyńczyk got a job at the paper mill in Marathon and, at his instigation, I moved there as well, starting as a lab assistant. I received an apartment and could finally bring my wife to join me. In 1951 we bought our first house. At that time, I was promoted to technician, and not long afterwards I was transferred to the supply department, where I assumed the duties of a deputy chief accountant. I worked at that position for several years. Unfortunately, in 1957, my wife fell ill, and since, in a small town, she could not receive the medical treatment she required, we had to go back to Ottawa. A succession of jobs followed: first with Northern Ontario Pipelines, building a gas pipeline from Alberta; then with Plateaus as a head of an accounting office; then with a construction company as a manager and superintendent. That last position was quite lucrative, but my wife's ill health required extensive consultations with medical authorities in Canada and the US, and in the end left us with considerable debts. To get back on my feet financially, I got into the real-estate business, which helped secure my retirement.

In 1984, I moved to Victoria and took residence across from the Polish House belonging to the Biały Orzeł Association, a Polish organization whose activity in preceding years had considerably declined. Its library was lingering in someone's garage, and the school had been closed. Many of their members were Polish veterans living in Victoria since 1950, but they had never set up their own chapter of the PCA. So I got down to work, made some contacts, woke up some slumbering souls. In no time the chapter was up and active. Thanks to Mr. Barankiewicz, we received $2000 from the Millennium Foundation for various social initiatives. We also collected some additional funds and purchased the colours for the chapter. And so it came to pass that one of the oldest PCA activists established the newest chapter of the PCA in Canada.

STANISŁAW KŁOCZKOWSKI

I was born in 1918. At eighteen, I signed up for the Youth Work Brigades, a paramilitary youth organization, and reported in Stryj [Stryy]. Most of the boys who arrived there with me were sixteen or seventeen years old. We were issued brigades uniforms and assigned to one of two companies, each some 200 youths strong. As in the army, the companies were subdivided into platoons and teams. The discipline was also military style.

The brigades were all about the rudiments of military training and the value of hard work. Our teaching staff was recruited from among former commissioned and non-commissioned officers. We spent the fall getting acquainted with guns and gas masks, and learning to march and to shoot. After the Christmas break, which I spent at home proudly parading my uniform, we studied the basics of physics, chemistry, and general science. Then, in the spring of 1937, our entire unit left for Cisna, a small village south of Ustrzyki Dolne and close to the Czechoslovakian border. Our task was to build a road from Cisna to Łupków, an even more remote village, whose only link to the world was a rickety old train.

We had little time to settle down in the temporary barracks, hastily constructed for our arrival, and soon after unpacking we went to work. Hard, back-breaking, hand-blistering work. Each youth was expected to load forty barrels with dirt, cart them over to a specified place, and unload them there—that was our daily norm. At first only the strongest among us could meet it, but as weeks went by, we gained experience and muscles, and rose to the challenge.

My stay at the camp was disrupted by some health problems. It may have been in June that I caught scarlet fever. I was immediately transported to the hospital in Stryj and was forced to spend the entire summer in bed. Even worse, as a result of the fever, I got an inflammation of the inner ear. The doctors were talking of surgery, but fortunately I recovered without it. I was eager to return to my buddies, so I took a train to Łupków, and, from there, walked twenty kilometres to the camp. The shovel never felt so good in my hands as after those months of immobility and sickness. All in all, I stayed with the brigades for two full years.

At the time, my dream was to fly glider planes. I applied to the Glider School in Polichno, in the picturesque, hilly part of the Kielce region, and, much to my delight, I was admitted to the program. Training began with theory, but it was the practical exercises that gave me a real thrill. The frame of the training glider was constructed of light wood. A rubber rope was attached to its tail. To make the glider airborn, the students pulled the rope until it stretched, and then, on command, they let it go. The glider rose up and stayed in the air for thirty seconds or so. The trick was to keep it level and then land it smoothly; later we practised turns, left and right. The first flying category was A, awarded for the basic skills; the pin that went with it had a single flying gull. Category B—two gulls—required more complicated manoeuvres as one had to fly along a slope to a designated spot. The most advanced was category C, done on a more sophisticated glider, with more sensitive steering; to get it, one had to be able to use the air currents and fly longer distances. During my stay at the school, I managed to qualify for all three categories.

After graduating from the glider school, I returned to the Youth Brigades in Cisna and, in the fall, volunteered for the air force, with the navy being my second choice. Soon I received a draft notice for the 6th Air Force Regiment in Kniuchów. When I went home for leave, I was sporting a handsome air force uniform. My sisters were delighted and proud of me, but my mother was less enthusiastic: she already had one soldier at home, my father.

My other passions, besides flying, were radio communication and, especially, radio telegraphy. In March 1939, I was promoted to private 1st class and assigned the duties of a wireless operator. My first posting was at the harbour radio station in Lwów [L'viv], and my main responsibility was providing meteorological service for military and civilian aviation. Technically, I belonged to the 65th Bomber Squadron in the 6th Bomber Division. Our pilots flew single-engine planes, PZL Karaś, powered by the British-made Pegaz engines. At the time, we thought our machines were technically quite advanced.

For me the war began with an alert on August 24. We immediately started loading equipment onto railway cars, and the following day our train convoy moved towards the northeast. Our destination was Biała Podlaska, or, more precisely, the temporary airstrip in nearby Nosowo. We set up our camp and radios there. It was simply a flat, unploughed piece of land, bordered on one side by a little grove, which we later used to camouflage the planes. The twelve planes of our squadron arrived on August 31, bringing along another dozen from a neighbouring unit. The war found us early in the morning on September 1. Shortly after breakfast, several German bombers appeared on the horizon, but by the time we spotted them, we could do little more than take shelter. They bombed the airfield, fortunately without causing any major damage to the equipment. We did suffer our first casualty, though. I could see, from where I was hiding, Corporal Borkowski running across the field, with both hands on his behind, shouting, "Help, help, I've been killed!" As it turned out, he was wounded in the butt, and his life was not in danger.

The very same day, our planes took off for their first reconnaissance flights. I took charge of the division radio station. My main responsibilities were to establish communication with headquarters and with the crews in the air. Getting through to headquarters proved a hopeless task: I tried for three days, and all my efforts failed. Looking at that failure from the perspective of years and experience, I am quite certain it was a result of a misunderstanding about the frequencies to be used. I had no such problems maintaining radio contact with our planes in the air. In fact, we even scored some hits, thanks to effective communications. Once, three planes on a reconnaissance mission in the vicinity of Ciechanów reported that a strong German armoured contingent was heading south. We immediately dispatched several bombers and destroyed most of them.

From Nosowo, we were instructed to move to Ząbkowice near Siedlce; that is, we moved to the west. We immediately drew optimistic but rash conclusions that we must be winning the war. We knew that our air force was not as strong as the Germans', but we did carry out a number of successful missions. But the situation was worsening quickly. Our division's goal was to prevent the German offensive against Warsaw. We tried but were outnumbered and outshot by the enemy. We were losing pilots. Józef Machalski, from 65th Division, was shot down south of Warsaw and had to crash-land. Our optimism evaporated.

We started retreating southwards, stopping at the airfields in Franopol and Falenice south of Włodzimierz Wołyński [Vladimir Volynskiy]. Finally, we arrived in Hutniki. On September 11, the planes had just landed, and we had not yet had time to camouflage them, when fifteen German fighters and bombers appeared above our heads. They climbed high up into the sky and then swooped down on us, their machine guns blazing and incendiary bombs showering our makeshift airstrip. All our staff managed to get out of harm's way, but the machines and equipment were completely destroyed right before our eyes. The Hutniki squadron ceased to exist as an operational unit. Dejected, we followed orders to keep moving south, eventually reaching Ponikwa [Ponikva], an estate of Count Bocheński. We were received there very warmly and treated to a sumptuous supper. Then on we went through Horodenka [Gorodënka] and towards the Romanian border, which we crossed at Kuty. At the time, I did not know, of course, that Tadeusz Gardziejewski, serving in the National Defence, which was then reinforcing the border guards, was on marshal duty at the bridge we were crossing.

We crossed the Romanian border in Wyżnica [Vizhnitsa], surrendered our arms, and went on to Rădăuți. We set up camp at the market square, waiting for the trains. When they arrived three days later, we boarded them, not really knowing where we were being taken. There was talk that the air force was to be the first wave transferred to France, but the details were fuzzy at best. We stopped some ninety kilometres west of Constanța, in the middle of a field. The train was immediately surrounded by Romanian soldiers, and we received orders to get off. We were being interned in violation of the pact Poland had earlier signed with Romania, allowing Polish soldiers free passage through Romanian territory. Unfortunately for us, a military coup d'etat in Romania had brought to power the Iron Guard, a rightist, pro-Nazi organization, which simply disregarded the agreement.

They took us from the train and billetted us with peasants in villages in the Danube delta. We were free to move within the villages but not outside. Throughout that period, we maintained our military organization and discipline. Only army chaplains were allowed complete freedom of movement and could travel among the various village-camps; they also served as couriers between the interned troops and the Polish embassy in Bucharest. Our location in the Danube delta was a cause of considerable concern to the Polish authorities. In the autumn, we were tormented by mosquitoes, and many of us fell ill with malaria. I, too, came down with a severe bout, which laid me out, unconscious, for almost three weeks. Despite a severe shortage of quinine, I got out of it unscathed. Our authorities pressed the Romanians to move us to higher grounds, and eventually they succeeded: we were transferred to the village of Korudzha, away from the swampy delta.

In early December, I was called to our headquarters and informed about the plans to escape. The command had somehow obtained blank passports and was organizing a large-scale evacuation of our troops, in spite of the internment. The flying personnel were to be among the first to leave. Each of us got 1800 lei to buy civilian clothes. With the help of our hosts, the Bulgarian peasants who lived in those parts of Romania, we saved a bit by dying our military pants black. I used the money to buy a jacket and a hat, and, with four others, readied myself for the escape. The whole operation was very well prepared. I was given a false Romanian passport in the name of Wielowiejski, a student going to study at the University of Beirut in Lebanon. One afternoon, I received word that we should leave that evening. I said goodbye to my hosts and friends and set out across the snow-covered fields towards a rallying point, where a horse-drawn cart was already waiting for us. In the distance, we heard the shouts of Romanian soldiers and some shots, but all this had been staged and the soldiers bribed. After a night's ride in the cart, we reached the gates of Constanţa, where the employees of the local Polish consulate were waiting for us. They put us up in an elegant hotel, and we began arranging refugee papers. But it was getting the exit visas that proved the most difficult, even though the official responsible for issuing them must have been bribed by the Polish consular authorities. He would stamp nine exit visas in a row and the tenth would get a "military" stamp, effectively barring the bearer from leaving. We had been instructed that should this happen to any of us, we were supposed to lick it off immediately. The officers in the Polish consulate then did the rest, removing all the traces of the unwanted stamp. After this procedure, one rejoined the queue, hoping for better luck next time. We were also told at the consulate that those who knew German should speak to the Romanian officials in that language, and those with Semitic features should admit to their Jewish ancestry. I got my visa without any difficulty and did not have to taste the stamp. As soon as I returned to the hotel, my military superiors took away my passport with the visa, for it was urgently needed for someone else. I was given another identity and another passport, and had to queue up for the visa again. This scenario played itself out three times, and every time I was lucky with the visa. I suppose I must have really looked like a student.

At Christmastime I was still in Constanţa. I went to the midnight mass, and then for supper with a group of friends. The following afternoon, we got word of our imminent departure. An employee of the consulate collected all our personal papers that might betray our Polish identity, and we left for the Constanţa harbour. We went aboard the Romanian liner *Dacia*, and left port for Beirut in the evening of Christmas Day.

On arrival, we were quartered in a French military installation (at the time Lebanon was a French protectorate). Soon after New Year's Day, we boarded another ship, a French troop carrier, which took us to Marseille. About 3000 Polish pilots were shipped there, and then transferred to Champ de Carpiegne, not far from the Mediterranean. After the initial verification, the first 500 pilots were taken to the camp in Septfonds, near Toulouse. I do not have fond memories of that place. The camp was fenced with barbed wire, for it had previously housed Spanish republicans interned in France. It was cold there, and hungry, and lousy, in the literal sense of the word. I volunteered there for the fighter pilots' list. Fighters were supposed to stay in France, while bombers were to be transferred to Britain. I opted for France because I had a distant relative there and was hoping to meet him some day. When we were moved to what was supposed to be a training camp in Matha, we had to lodge in an old mill. There were no other living quarters for us, so we had to begin by constructing the barracks from prefabricated elements.

We were still building those accommodations when the German

offensive against France—which was not much of an offensive, any-way—took place. The myth of the French military power in which we so fervently believed before the war was dispelled. Our unit had at its disposal only two trucks, and each of us had a one-shot rifle from the Franco-Prussian war. We withdrew before the advancing German forces in groups of twenty, for only that number could fit onto a truck. When we finally reached a military supply centre of mechanized equipment, we were issued seven additional vehicles. Now we could continue together as a unit in the direction of La Rochelle, looking for a place from which we might be evacuated to Britain. Finally we reached Bordeaux.

Polish authorities kept sending us from one rallying point to another, and, in the meantime, France surrendered to the Germans. Marshal Pétain issued an order that all military units should stay where they were, but we decided to move on even though we knew we might have to confront the French units loyal to Pétain.* And indeed, at one checkpoint, a French officer with a unit of soldiers from Senegal tried to stop us. As per instructions from our Polish superiors, the first vehi-cle roared at full throttle through the checkpoint with all the others right behind it. There was some shooting but, fortunately, no casualties, at least on our side, and we managed to escape. Eventually we reached the gathering point for Polish pilots from central and western France— St.-Jean-de-Luz, a small harbour on the Bay of Biscay. The pilots from other parts of France had a much harder time, for they were cut off by the Germans and had to force their way south to Marseille.

After a week of anxious waiting, two ships dropped anchor in the offing: a beautiful passenger liner, *Arandora Star*, and a nondescript *Patrick*. Local fishermen ferried some 6000 of us to the ships in groups of twenty. More used to the air than water, some pilots felt disoriented in small fishing boats bobbing up and down in the choppy water. As we were pulling up alongside the *Arandora Star,* my boat began to rock violently. Before I had time to grasp a line from the ship, the boat cap-sized, and I found myself struggling in the cold, hostile, wet environ-ment. Fortunately the crew of the *Arandora Star* managed to fish us

---

* Henri Philippe Pétain (1914-51), a military and political leader, France's great-est hero of World War I; head of state of the collaborationist French government dur-ing World War II.

out, one by one, from the green currents, but the accident did cost me my rifle and a nice collection of coins from different countries.

Two days later we arrived in Liverpool and found ourselves in a completely different world. The British were much better organized than the French. We were welcomed by Liverpool ladies who treated us to a decent meal and a nice cup of tea. Then comfortable sleeping cars were brought in, and we continued southeast by train to a camp near Gloucester. Another, more solemn, reception awaited us there, attended by a British RAF general and our own General Ujejski. We were issued new British uniforms; the French ones were thrown in a heap and burned. We liked our new quarters: the tents were very well equipped, with sturdy beds and sheets. The contrast between England and France was striking and rekindled our hope that all was not yet lost.

In the meantime, the Battle for Britain grew fierce. German air raids broke the usual buzz of the days and the silence of the nights. Not far from us was an airplane factory, a regular target for enemy bombers. One night, we heard an explosion in the vicinity of the camp, and then a strange whistling sound cut short our dreams and exploded a shelf in our tent, just above one of our friends' head. He suffered no harm and took this to be a good omen. Indeed, he later flew and survived ninety missions as a gunner aboard a plane. He joked that his luck must be coming from that piece of shrapnel that nearly killed him, and which he always carried in his pocket as a talisman against enemy bullets.

In late August, I was sent away to Blackpool for training as an airborne wireless operator. One of the main challenges there was mastering Morse code, commonly used by the military: to be proficient, one had to send and receive 120 letters per minute. Although I passed the course, I was not allowed to fly because a medical examination showed that I was colour-blind. As a result, I was assigned to ground services and sent to Bomber Squadron 300 in Swinderby, in Lincolnshire.

I began my service there in February 1941, working as a radio operator, responsible mostly for receiving meteorological forecasts for the air force. After a month I was reassigned to a radio station more directly involved in flying missions. It was a high-frequency direction-finding radio station, maintaining contact with plane crews in the air and providing them with flight coordinates. That radio station was part of a vast network covering the whole country, which made it possible to plot the exact location of an airborne plane. I was working at one of the nodes of the rescue net: we were an independent unit outside the airport, with lodging and food provided on location. There were six of us at the station, four of whom were trained radio operators; we worked eight-hour shifts. The work was interesting, challenging, and at times nerve-wracking, for the lives of entire crews were often in our hands as we guided them to safe landings in bad weather.

The ground personnel was very close with the flying crews, and we did not observe the strict hierarchy common in other services. We were all friends, regardless of rank. This comradery grew out of common war experiences and was reinforced by training. We spent lots of time together, both working and playing. Missions were usually flown at night, so the ground crews also worked nights. They depended on us for equipment inspections and navigational information, and we felt personally responsible for their safety.

My Squadron 300 flew Wellingtons, twin-engine bombers capable of carrying two tonnes of bombs and several members of the crew. We had twelve planes, with two flying crews for each. The pre-war Polish air force had never had so many pilots: at best, it could muster 1.5 crew per plane. The targets of Bomber Squadrons 300 and 301 were German and French harbours and their equipment; our bombing raids were intended to make it more difficult for the German fleet to launch an invasion of England. Early missions were relatively easy, but later, German fighter planes became the main source of danger. One night, I remember, they took positions right above our airfield and destroyed two of our planes that were trying to land. We could not shoot at them because we might hit one of ours. The situation grew critical, and the command scrambled to minimize the losses and find a solution. Eventually, all incoming crews were ordered to scatter and land at other airfields; one that could not make it elsewhere crash-landed and the entire crew was killed. These were the first casualties I experienced, the first of many that followed. But once our planes cleared the sector, we could finally get at the intruders and bring them down.

I spent a year at Swinderby and was then transferred to Hamswell. The focus of our bombing campaign had changed: our targets were no longer continental harbours. Instead, we started flying deep into the enemy territory. The flights had become even more dangerous, for pilots had to avoid not only the Luftwaffe but ground anti-aircraft defence as well. In 1943 we began to lose crews and machines. We waited long hours for latecomers, hoping for miracles, but those rarely happened. Because of the obligatory radio silence, we could not establish contact with them. We worried about their finding the way back, and the mechanics worried that something might go wrong that they had not anticipated or looked after. We all deeply grieved when a plane did not return. It was a custom that when this happened, those closest to the crew took the money from the lost friends' lockers and drank, remembering their virtues and lamenting their death. Other personal effects from the lockers were collected by a commission, which distributed them among family and friends. All in all, Squadron 300 lost about 1300 people.

In 1943 I was moved to Cammeringham (thirty kilometres from Hamswell), and in January 1944 was reassigned to special operations Squadron 301, based in Italy. I stayed with it till the end of the war. With twenty-four machines, my new squadron was twice as large as a typical British flying unit. We flew special supply missions behind the enemy lines from a base that kept moving from Italy to Algeria, to Tunisia, and back to Brindisi in Italy. Squadron 301 had four-engine Halifaxes adapted to long-distance flying, and four-engine American-made Liberators, used for supplying partisans on the German-occupied territories, especially in Poland. Some flights to Poland lasted up to eighteen hours: the boys took off at five in the evening, flew over Germany at night, and returned before noon the following day. Until the Warsaw Uprising, those long flights were relatively safe. We lost only one machine; its crew eventually found its way back to the squadron. Things changed dramatically in August 1944, when the Warsaw Uprising began. Our losses began to mount, but the Russians still did not allow us to land on their side of the front line. Many pilots who never returned were my close friends, yet in the frenzy of war, death was life's constant companion, and one had to get used to it. British Squadron 148 and two South African squadrons also flew over Warsaw, and they, too, were decimated. The South Africans refused to fly any more missions over Poland, but Squadron 301 continued their flights. We knew, from closely monitoring all broadcasts of the insurgents' radio station "Błyskawica" [Lightening], that the fighters in Warsaw needed us.

Sometimes I think that, had I been assigned to the flying personnel back in England, after the radio operator course, I would not be telling you my story now. From my class of thirty, only two are still alive; most of the others were killed in action. In a sense, my colour-blindness gave me a chance to survive; but that means, of course, that someone took my place on those missions, risked his life, and probably lost it. Life has always tasted bittersweet to me.

We not only supplied the underground fighters on those missions; sometimes we also brought cargo from them. One of our Dacota crews brought back parts of the German v2 missile and a few agents of the Special Operation Executive, called *Cichociemni,* * including Colonel Rudnicki. We later sat with them in the mess, and they told us some of their adventures. On another occasion, one of the crews could not establish contact with the resurgents and deliver their cargo. They did not know what they were carrying, so before landing they dumped the entire load into the sea. As it turned out, it was a load of gold. For weeks, special teams kept searching for it, but whether they recovered it, I do not know.

Eventually, Squadron 301 was returned to Britain and dissolved. The remaining crews, including myself, were reassigned to the transport command. I was sent to a radio station near Carlisle. Our task there was to retrain bomber crews for the needs of air-transport companies. I taught flight radio operators, who had to master Morse code with the speed of 120 signs per minute and an accuracy of maximum one error per minute. I also taught them the conventions of establishing radio contact and various civilian procedures. It was there, after the war, that I began to fly. After a transfer to Whitton, I even flew some long-distance missions with supplies for the liberated countries.

After the war, I signed up for a vocational program, organized by the Polish Resettlement Corps, that was training radio mechanics and, upon completion, got the papers of a certified electronics technician. For a while, I worked in that field, maintaining equipment at a training centre for Allied pilots. That was my last military post before I requested civilian papers.

All the while, I was thinking about my future. I ruled out returning

---

* *Cichociemni* were Polish soldiers trained in Great Britain during World War II and sent back to German-occupied Poland to fight in the underground Home Army (AK); their training and deployment were conducted in cooperation with the British Special Operations Executive.

to Poland, given my family history. My father had fought the Bolsheviks in 1920, and they had long memories. That's also why I did not try to contact my family, afraid that my letters from the West might draw unnecessary attention to them. England at the time seemed to have little to offer, so in 1951 I applied for immigration at the consulates of the United States and Canada. Some of my friends from the air force left for Argentina. They set up a transportation company there, and some—as I hear—even made lots of money. But the hot tempers of the Latinos did not appeal to me, and when I got the acceptance papers from Canada in 1952, I decided to go. On arrival, I had to report before a medical commission in Montreal, but they found nothing wrong with me: I was young and in good shape. Finding a job proved to be quite a challenge. I filled out dozens of applications but nothing came of them. Then a friend of mine, Czyżewski, sent me a clipping from a Winnipeg newspaper about McDonald Air looking for workers. I applied, was hired, and moved to Winnipeg. I started out with $1.25 per hour, but by the time I retired my wages had increased to $13.60.

As I soon discovered, I was not the only Polish World War II pilot to settle in Winnipeg. There were others, such as Maślanko, Czyżewski, Gandecki, and Pittner; and later we were joined by Garlicki, Gajdck, Kmieć, and Milejszo. Quite a company, and we all joined the Polish Combatants Association (PCA).

In 1957 the Canadian government, together with the universities, organized a scientific expedition to study the continental shelf beyond the polar circle, from Ellesmere Island to the Bering Strait. The Bristol company I was working for at the time seconded me to the research team, with whom I travelled to the Arctic. The expedition had at its disposal several helicopters, and my task was to maintain radio communications among them and the various groups of scientists operating within a 450-kilometre radius. The work was fascinating, despite the Arctic cold, and highly educational. I could see with my own eyes the sunny nights of the North, where the sea and land are ice-bound throughout the year. Others can only read about those wonders.

In 1963, after I returned from the expedition, I travelled to Poland. This was the first and perhaps most fruitful of my several trips because it was then that I met my wife, Halina. Now our daughter is nineteen years old and soon may be thinking of getting married herself.

I have been involved in the work of the PCA for years, helping mostly with the youth. In my view, it is important that they remember their Polish roots, that they continue building our community, and that they carry at least some of our dreams into the future. To that end, we need to help them organize independently of the PCA. We cannot impose on them our half-century-old ways of thinking but, rather, should encourage them to pursue their own ideas. We must provide them with the foundations, but they need to build the structures themselves, for themselves and for their own children. Their initiatives may not always appeal to us, but we are a passing generation, and the future is theirs.

STANISŁAW KMIEĆ

I was born in 1926 in Grodzisko near Rzeszów. In 1938 my family moved to Podole [Podolia] as part of a campaign to resettle those territories. Thus, a year later, we found ourselves in the social group most hated by the Soviets. On the third day after they invaded, on September 19, they arrested my father. They did not let us have any contact with him, but on February 9, 1940, at 8:00 p.m., he came home. Yet, our joy was short-lived: the same night at midnight, the Soviets came to arrest him again, and with him the entire family. They loaded us onto cattle trucks and drove us eastwards by rail. The journey, in terrible conditions, dragged on for sixteen days. They gave us no food whatsoever, so we had to rely on what we had managed to bring with us from home at the last minute. They threw us out of the cars at the station in Murashi in the republic of Komi, ordered us into a column, and marched us to a tiny village of Gerkashovo, some 100 kilometres away from the station. It was the middle of the Siberian winter, with temperatures reaching 60°C below zero. To this day I do not know how we survived that march.

Gerkashovo was little more than a lumber camp. My father, my mother, and I had to work all day cutting lumber in the forest; my younger brothers stayed at home. The daily quotas were very high and difficult to meet. With whatever little money we made from so much toil in the forest, we could buy our rations of bread and, very rarely, a ration of sugar as well.

We worked in that camp until we learned from a Polish passer-by that the Polish government had signed an agreement with the Soviets, which provided for the formation of the Polish army in the Soviet Union. My father and I decided to find and join that army; my mother and brothers were not allowed to leave until six months later, when they made their way to Kazakhstan.

Our journey to the Polish army began with the 100-kilometre trek to the station in Murashi. Along the way, other Poles joined us from nearby settlements. By train we went to Uzbekistan, about twenty kilometres from the Chinese border. There we were detained to work on cotton plantations. We worked hard, but the food was decent because we were already considered military personnel. We arrived at the Polish army camp in Kermine three months later.

We came at a bad time, when diseases such as spotted fever, typhoid fever, and amoebic dysentery were raging throughout the camp. We had no doctors and no medicine. People were dropping like flies: every morning I carried out the corpses of my friends whom fate would not grant to see the day when we finally left Russia. Entire divisions, such as the 11th, wasted away, with hundreds of dead every day. But somehow I survived that hell on earth, and in early August we were transported to Krasnovodsk and then by ship to Pahlavi, Persia.

Our first steps in Persia led through a disinfection unit, staffed mostly by Hindus. They disinfected us with concentrated Lysol in the armpits and crotch; then, with large razors, they shaved us there to bare skin. We were afraid they might cut us in one of those sensitive places, but we heard of no such accidents. The uniforms in which we arrived were piled up and burned, and we were issued new British ones. In one respect we were disappointed: the English food rations were too small for Polish appetites, being only a can of sardines and some marmalade.

From Pahlavi, we were transported to Iraq, where they assigned us to various services. The medical commission decided that I was fit for the air force, and Captain Słodkiewicz informed me that I was assigned to bombers. My group of prospective fliers was transferred to Egypt and located in Heliopolis, on the outskirts of Cairo. We were trained by British instructors for almost a year, mostly as radio operators, telegraph operators, and navigators. A great deal of emphasis was also placed on collegiality and friendship, so important for the flying crews. After about a year, we moved to a temporary camp on the Suez Canal near Ismailia, and from there boarded a ship in Port Said bound for Liverpool. In England, we were taken to the headquarters of the Polish air force and billetted with private families on the coast. Finally we were split into crews and assigned to Polish Squadron 300, named after Mazovia. I was to be a radio operator and took some special training in that area.

We did our first training flights on Wellingtons. A crew consisted of the pilot, mechanic, radio operator, bombardier, and three gunners. Training flights lasted for two to three weeks, up to ten hours in every twenty-four-hour period, with day and night flights alternating. My responsibility was to maintain contact with ground control, with the crew, and with other airplanes in the formation. Usually we relied on voice communication, but sometimes we had to resort to codes.

At last it was time for our first operational flight. We took off on a Wellington at 7:00 a.m. Our target was an industrial complex in the Ruhr Basin. Close to our target, we flew into heavy anti-aircraft fire. I had a queasy feeling in the pit of my stomach, but with time I got used to it. We usually flew at the elevation of 5000 metres, so essentially beyond the range of the artillery. The downside was that we had to use oxygen masks. To drop the bombs, we had to come down to about 3000 metres, which was within the range of guns on the ground. Our first mission turned out lucky as all eighteen planes safely returned to the base. But it was not always like that. There were days when two or three crews failed to return, and once only three out of eighteen made it safely back. We celebrated when all came back, grieved when we lost colleagues and friends. It was a custom that if a crew did not return, the contents of their lockers were divided among those who were still alive and could make use of them.

Each flight was preceded by a briefing. We were told where we were flying, at what altitude, and what our targets were. When we returned, we had to go for another briefing to discuss the details of the aerial photographs taken during the bombing. There was little time left between the flights, for we flew daily. After flying three rounds—that is, thirty flights—we could get thirty days off. On those occasions we could go wherever we wanted as long as we stayed in Britain.

Polish squadrons were always equipped with the newest machines, so we were among the first to fly the Lancasters. They were larger than Wellingtons, had four engines, and required nine-person crews.

Regardless of rank, the pilot was always the commander. We usually spoke Polish over the intercom, which was always on during the flights. Our targets were typically the Ruhr Basin and Berlin, both of enormous strategic importance and both strongly defended. We could often see through the windows the many air-defence positions. When the fire barrage was too intense, and we could not make it all the way to our target areas, we had to drop the bombs anywhere on the enemy territory. That was no laughing matter, for a Lancaster could carry 7500 kilograms of bombs. The crew, flying under those conditions of constant danger, developed strong ties of comradery and friendship, which they maintain to this day.

Our base was not far from Nottingham, and we cultivated close and friendly relationships with the local civilian population. When off duty, we could go outside the barracks, to pubs frequented by the locals, for instance. This greatly helped us in learning the language. We also kept in touch with the Polish women who served in the Women's Auxiliary Air Force Services. We playfully called them *łafki** to distinguish them from the English girls, for whom we coined a rhyming nonsense term *wafki*. Many of our colleagues married *łafki*, including Milejszo and Gandecki.

During the stormy years of the war, we could not maintain regular contacts with our families. I met with my father in Iraq and in Palestine. Mother was left behind in Kuybyshev [Samara], and only later made it to a refugee camp in India with my brothers. I met with them again in 1947, during the action of reuniting families in Britain, five years after our separation.

My wife also came through the camps in India. Those camps were full of youths, and to keep them focussed and occupied, schools and Scouting were organized, with teachers and instructors recruited from the 2nd Corps. My wife met my mother while in India, but I met her in January 1948, two years after her arrival in England. I was heartbroken when she left with her family for Canada later the same year.

After the war, I tried to go to university, but the competition was too strong, and I did not make it. When I got my demobilization papers in 1949, I listened to the voice of my heart and went to where my future wife was calling me, to Canada. I arrived at Halifax aboard the liner *Aquitania*, and from there went by train to Winnipeg.

---

* A bilingual pun based on the Polish pronunciation of the acronym for Women's Auxiliary Air Force Services.

I found my first, poorly paid, job at a post office on Portage Avenue, but I quit after six months. Finding a new job proved quite a challenge, because wherever I applied, Canadians were hired before immigrants. Finally I was hired by Inland Steel, a company very friendly to Polish veterans. My friends joked that I was the best-dressed labourer in the company, always in a freshly pressed shirt, but I could not help the habits I got from the air force. We were always taught that those who fly must be well dressed, and dressing well became my second nature. I began at Inland Steel in 1950 and stayed with the same company until retirement, first as a labourer and later as a personnel relations assistant.

My wife and I were married one month after my arrival in Canada, and soon we started a family: first a daughter was born, and then two boys. My daughter finished university and married a Greek man. She now lives in Greece, which means high telephone bills for us and occasional vacations in southern Europe. My younger son—now over thirty—is also married and has a daughter. My middle son is still a bachelor.

I have been a member of the Polish Combatants Association, Chapter #13, since 1952. I served three terms as president of our local chapter, and afterwards as treasurer and secretary. Most recently, I have been elected to the national board of the association as vice-president for central Canada.

STANISŁAW KOCIOŁEK

I was twenty-four years old in 1939, when the war broke out, and on active military service. I was serving in the 1st Regiment of Air-Defence Heavy Artillery, stationed in Warsaw on Rakowiecka Street. In the months before the war, our regiment was moved to Katowice. The war broke out exactly two weeks before my scheduled return to civilian life.

In the first days of the war, we had few opportunities to defend our skies because German planes were flying either too high or too low. Nevertheless, we managed to shoot down at least one plane returning from a bombing raid somewhere in Poland to its base in Germany. Our 75 mm guns were mounted on lorries; they could be turned around within fifty degrees. To cover the entire circumference of 360 degrees, four guns had to be arranged at proper angles to one another. Those four guns formed a battery.

We were thus a fully motorized unit, so we could move with relative ease. Almost from the beginning, we had to withdraw in the direction of Cracow before the quickly advancing enemy. When we arrived in Cracow, there was not a German plane in sight; when the planes did appear, they began dropping bombs on our ammunition depot from a high altitude. They missed their target, and so did we. We heard rumours that we were going to help in the defence of Warsaw, but on September 12 we found ourselves in Brześć [Brest] on the Bug River. Four days later we were taking up positions in Stanisławów [Ivano-Frankivs'k], far in the southeast. Once again we sat there idle because no German planes came after us. We could see and hear Soviet planes but were ordered not to shoot at them, although technically they were in violation of our airspace. Even when they bombed a nearby railway station, we were not allowed to fire at them. Our guns posed no real threat to them anyway, as they were dropping bombs from an altitude beyond the range of our guns, but at least we might have felt better. Shortly afterwards, the news reached us that the Soviet armies had crossed the Polish border. Our only route of escape was through Hungary, and we set out immediately. We drove straight south, with all our equipment and with orders to surrender it after crossing the border. Hand weapons, with bullets and locks removed, we discarded into ditches; all heavier guns, we had to hand over at the military camp. For many it was a sad and emotional moment: hardened soldiers had tears in their eyes when they saw their weapons in foreign hands. Without them, they felt lost and useless.

Sad also was the Christmas season in the internment camp. We did put up a Christmas tree in the central square, sang Christmas carols, and even went to a Hungarian church to celebrate the birth of Christ. But we could not forget that Poland was defeated on two fronts and that we were powerless in our position as internees. We were determined to change that last unfortunate condition. Our command identified a possible route of escape through the Hungarian-Yugoslavian border and established a series of transit points. I was scheduled to run on New Year's Day. On New Year's Eve, I got a pass to go with a friend of mine to a nearby town; there we danced with Hungarians and celebrated the coming of another year. On the way back, my friend went straight to the camp, while I, documents already in my pocket, went to the pre-arranged transit point. I was extremely cautious, forewarned about some shady characters who were probably spies. I was one of several who gathered at the appointed place; we changed into civilian clothes and moved on.

The final obstacle on our way was the border on the Drava River. Our progress towards the river was slower than expected because of a heavy snowfall, which made walking difficult. By the time we reached the river, the boats that were to take us across had already left. We had to return to our last transit point and wait there for almost a week until the river froze. The ice was still thin, so we spread out and gently walked to the other side. We were highly visible on the river, and the

Yugoslav border guards were waiting for us in force. They wanted to turn us back to Hungary. After long negotiations, they took pity on us, took us to their station, and put us up for the night. In the morning, they even gave us a sleigh ride to the nearest railway station. From there we easily found our way to the French camp, where we were anxiously awaited. We rested there for a week before continuing to Split, on the coast, where we boarded a ship to Marseille.

I remained in France for about five months, until June. The Germans were on the offensive, and bombs were exploding in the harbour as we were boarding a coal ship bound for Southampton. The British welcomed us with tea, biscuits, and chocolates. After the frantic Channel crossing and the warm reception, I was reassigned to the air defence. We got new eight-pound cannons and started intensive training.

From England we were transferred to the Middle East, arriving in Chabbaniya on May 8, 1943. At the same time, Polish units from Russia began to arrive. There were lots of jokes about the "lords" from England coming to teach the "Buzuluks" from Russia,* but most of them were good-natured and meant no harm. Later we were moved to Kirkuk, where the units of the 2nd Corps were concentrated. In the vicinity was also a large oil refinery, and my unit formed part of its air defence.

In Iraq the weather was so hot that we could train only two hours in the morning and two in the evening. The rest of the time, we sweated in our tents, drinking up a sea of tea; alcohol was banned, but it was the heat rather than the ban that made it unappealing. In the fall, we left Iraq for Palestine, and later Egypt, where we celebrated the New Year with quite a bit of booze and wild cannonades.

Eventually, we were shipped to the Italian front. At Monte Cassino, we installed ourselves near Acquafondata as anti-aircraft artillery, but few planes flew our way. After the offensive started, late at night on May 12, our unit had orders to fire at German ground positions. We shelled them throughout the night, using timed anti-aircraft shells, exploding ten metres above ground.

I went through the entire Italian campaign and stayed in Italy until 1946, when we were transferred to Britain. I did not agonize over the decision to remain in the West: Poland was not free so there was no

---

* Buzuluk was one of the rallying points for Polish soldiers in the Soviet Union.

point going back. The last time I had heard from my family was when I was in Hungary; later, all contacts were severed until I re-established them after my arrival in Canada. At first I thought I would settle down in England and even registered to work in a coal mine. I changed my plans after Canada began accepting agricultural workers. Like many others, I signed a two-year contract. I worked tending sugar beets, then harvesting wheat, then harvesting the beets. Despite the hard work, we were making so little money that one of my friends suggested we go to work in the bush, cutting lumber. That was a well-paid job. Unfortunately, someone reported to the authorities that those who should be slaving on the farms were working in the bush, and the Employment Office demanded that we return to our contracted farms. I resigned myself to that idea and indeed spent most of my two years on a farm, making $45 a month. I skipped only the last few months, when my friend Świrski helped me get hired at a more modern plantation of sugar beets, where we could make $6 to $7 a day, and, if the beets were of high quality, even ten or twelve.

When the contract expired, we were allowed—in fact, forced—to look for jobs on our own. Friends from the army helped one another, if they could. At first, I worked for a contractor who did some work for the Canadian Pacific Railway, and later I was hired at CPR itself. I signed up for the Sokół choir under the direction of Mr. Radian. At one of the rehearsals, in the fall of 1949, I met my future wife. We were married in 1950. At first my wife worked as a waitress, but as the children arrived, she worked at home. We have two children, Róża and Kazimierz. They are both university graduates. Róża works for Air Canada and is a member of the Polish Professionals Club. Kazimierz works for Eaton's. Both our children speak Polish well and are not ashamed of their Polish roots. Róża was quite active in Polish Scouting and even today helps to organize the Polish pavilion during the Folklorama Festival.

I retired three years ago, and I am proud that for all those years I was never a burden to Canada. In fact, I feel that myself and others like me have helped create the Canadian prosperity. Thanks to our hard work, we were able to buy a house and a summer cottage on Lake Winnipeg. Life has been good to me in the last half-century.

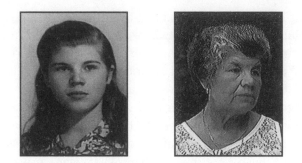

STEFANIA KOCIOŁEK

My family's homestead was in the Kopeczyńce [Kopychintsy] county, in the province of Tarnopol [Ternopil']. That is where the wars of 1939—with the Germans and the Soviets—surprised us. The Soviets left us alone until February 10, 1940. It was Saturday morning when I noticed some Russian soldiers riding on a horse-drawn wagon towards our house. They told us to pack only the essentials because we would get everything else we needed. Anyway, we were only going to another village, they told us. They put the four of us—my parents, my five-year-old brother, and myself, ten years old at the time—on a sleigh and drove us to Husiatyń [Gusyatin]. Along the way, friends and acquaintances from the village, seeing that we had but a few possessions with us, threw onto the sleigh whatever they could: a loaf of bread, a side of bacon. In spite of what the soldiers had told us, they knew we had a long way ahead of us. The soldiers took us to the railway station, where they had already assembled hundreds of others from neighbouring villages. They announced to us that we were *kulaks* [wealthy peasants] and were being resettled.

With guards all around, we were herded into freight cars. Ours was so overcrowded that there was not enough sitting space for everyone on the hastily erected bunk beds; some had standing space only. In those conditions, in the midst of winter, we were shipped to Siberia. Looking at high snowbanks and feeling the bone-freezing cold, my father cried. He might survive, he said, but, where we were going, the children would surely die.

They took us to the province of Arkhangelsk and put us in a shack. Throughout the winter, Father worked in a sawmill and Mother stayed at home with us; but when the snow melted, Father had to cut lumber in the forest and Mother had to shave the bark. My younger brother and I gathered wild strawberries and mushrooms in the forest. Schooling was, of course, out of the question. We only learned some Russian by talking to the local children. The locals lived in constant fear. Our shacks stood apart from the village, in the forest. They did not know who we were and were discouraged from having any contacts with us. Fortunately, my father knew some Russian and was on friendly terms with the foreman, who turned out to be a very decent man and helped us a lot. At first, we also had help from Poland in the form of food parcels with cereals and flour, and these enabled us to survive the most difficult initial period.

Our first Christmas was hungry and sad. Our only dish for Christmas Eve supper was bread. We broke and ate it with little joy. We all remembered the Polish tradition of tables groaning under the weight of sumptuous foods, and the lights, and the smells, and the cheerful noises of Christmas. Those memories did little to elevate our spirits.

We remained in those forests until my parents found out about the amnesty on the basis of an agreement signed by the Polish and Soviet governments. The Russians came to our shacks and told us we were free to go. We quickly packed what little we had and, with many others, boarded a southbound train. As usual, the ride took days, and we had nothing to eat. At one of the stations, my father got off the car with several other men and walked to a nearby settlement in search of bread. In the meantime, the train started moving again, and they were left behind, disappearing without a trace. My father had all our documents on him, so Mother was left with two children, no money, and no papers.

Going God-knew-where, we ended up on a cotton plantation in Piskent in Uzbekistan. In the summer, we gathered cotton; in the fall, we gathered peanuts and fed silkworms. We were paid not with money but with flour bran, which we used to bake a kind of pancake, our only food. To survive, we had to steal potatoes from the plantation storehouse from time to time: we used a long, thin stick to roll potatoes towards us through a hole in the loft's wall, one potato at a time.

None of us spoke the language of the local Uzbek people, and they had no idea who we were. We were strangers to them, too numerous to be welcome, and they showed us no sympathy. After a while, we were sent to another *kolkhoz* [collective farm], where my brother caught measles and a cold at the same time. There were no medical doctors available, and after a few days he died. He was six. We buried him at the local cemetery.

When we heard from some men that an outpost of the Polish army was being organized in Yangi-Yul, we decided to run away from the *kolkhoz*. We were six families, only women with children. Everyone collected their sparse belongings, and we set out in the direction of the railway station. To get there, we had to cross a rolling river, which we did riding atop five camels hired for that purpose. We reached the station, and went the rest of the way to the Polish outpost in Vresk by train. The army took care of us: their food rations were small, but they still shared them with us, unfortunate civilians adrift in the war. We asked about my father, then asked again and again, but no one had heard of him. He and all who were with him had simply vanished.

In Vresk, my mother placed me in an orphanage because the living conditions were apparently better there. At first she could not prove that I was indeed Polish because all our documents had vanished with my father. But two women from our colony spoke for me, as did a priest who knew us. They issued me temporary papers and admitted me to the orphanage. I stayed there for a few months, and during that time I was confirmed in the Christian faith by Father Gawlina.

The orphanage was transferred first to Krasnovodsk and later to Pahlavi in Persia. After we got off the ship, we were led to the baths, where the attendants shaved all our hair and disinfected us with soap. Then, in smaller groups, we were driven by trucks to Tehrān. I came down with malaria and was placed in a hospital. My mother, who stayed behind in Krasnovodsk and crossed to Pahlavi with a later transport, found me in that hospital, and we were reunited.

From Tehrān, we went to a refugee camp in Karāchi, India. What I remember most from that period is heat, burning and suffocating heat. We could not go outside without special protective helmets. When the authorities began to register for more permanent camps in Africa and Mexico, we decided on Mexico. We boarded an American ship in Bombay and set out for San Francisco. The transport consisted mostly of women and children, with only a few older men. Since safety was a major consideration, the ship took the long route—six weeks long—with stops in New Zealand and Australia for refuelling. In an Australian harbour, we also got lots of clothes collected by the Polish community there. Despite the precautions, the passage was not free of danger, and on a few occasions we were put on high alert, probably on account of Japanese submarines. We had to stay on deck, wearing safety jackets and worrying about the unseen danger. Luckily, we were never actually attacked.

After docking in San Francisco, we went by train to Mexico. We were greeted by a Mexican orchestra, which brought tears to our eyes, and by the Polish-American Council, which later looked after us. They put us up in a school in Guanajuato but after two weeks found us a place in a colony called Santa Rosa, in a villa of some rich Mexican. Children began schooling right away, although in the early days it consisted of reading a newspaper on the grass under some trees. Later, a lay sister arrived and began to hold regular classes. An old mill was refurbished as a school, and more staff was brought in: seven lay sisters, several Polish teachers, Professor Sobota, and Father Jarzembowski, the last two straight from England. They organized for us Scouting, a choir, and lots of activities, keeping the youth occupied and content.

We remained in Mexico until the colony was dissolved in 1946. We liked that place: it was safe, well provided, warm, and friendly. Many refugees from the colony went to the United States; others reunited with their husbands or fathers in England. My mother and I stayed on in Mexico nine months longer, working for the American consul, Mother as a cook and I as a babysitter.

In 1947 we were contacted by my aunt from Canada, and we went to a farm in Saskatchewan. I spent three months there and then moved to Winnipeg, where I have lived ever since. I found a job in a sewing shop and signed up for the Sokół choir. There I met a handsome Polish veteran, and we were married in 1950. The beginnings were difficult. He had one suitcase and I another, a wooden box-like thing from Russia: all our worldly possessions fit into those two. But things got better and more plentiful, with both of us working and my mother, whom I brought from the farm to Winnipeg, looking after the house. I gave birth to a daughter, and we bought our own house; I bore a son, and we bought another, bigger home—our family and our standard of living kept growing. Both our children finished university, and both have settled into their careers. After the many tragic events of my youth, the summer and autumn of my life have been normal and quiet and happy.

KAZIMIERZ KOWALISZYN

I was born in the village of Lasowa, not far from Lwów [L'viv]. In September of 1939, after they overran our part of the country, the Bolsheviks accused me and twenty others of murdering a Soviet officer. We were arrested in the middle of the night and tried the very next day. Our guilt was self-evident, we were told, so there was no need for any defenders; an NKVD [state security police] prosecutor was quite enough. Each of us was sentenced to twenty years in a labour camp. Without further ado, we were dispatched beyond the Ural Mountains, to Siberia. For a time we worked in sawmills, supplying lumber for *zemlianki*, or sunken huts, which were being constructed for potential refugees from Moscow, should it become necessary to evacuate the Soviet capital. Later we worked on the construction of various airfields, and it was at one of those that we learned about the pact between Sikorski and Stalin.

As soon as the news of the amnesty filtered through the layers of Soviet bureaucracy, we were released from the labour camp and allowed to travel to Totskoye. There we joined the ranks of the Polish soldiers and put on new uniforms sent by the British. My unit was assigned to the railway station: our task was to assist volunteers for the Polish army, arriving from all corners of the Soviet Union. Sometimes it was difficult to recognize them in the wretched crowds of Soviet travellers, but they never failed to recognize us by our uniforms and caps with the Polish eagle ensign. We had at our disposal a horse-drawn wagon and a sleigh to bring the volunteers to the military camp. We stayed at that post for two months.

When our troops began to leave for Persia, we were assigned to Transport no. 113, consisting of about 13,000 people. The journey took days and the conditions were typically Soviet, with people starving and freezing on the train. Our supplies were so meagre that we could scarcely keep people alive. So at one of the stations, my friend and I decided to walk to a nearby village and buy some camel milk for the children. By the time we returned to the station, our train was no longer there. Catching up with it by using a passenger train was quite impossible; our only chance, the station master advised us, was to get on a military train carrying wounded from the front. And, indeed, such a train pulled into the station later that night. We asked its commander to take us in and, much to our surprise, he agreed. More than that, the Russian soldiers who were in the car gave us bread, sausage, and vodka, and then told us to lie down and have a good rest. They woke us up when we were coming to a stop almost next to our Polish train convoy. We thanked them and wanted to run over to our people, but they stopped us, asked us back into their car, and gave us a sack of biscuits, some sausage, and two bottles of vodka. We thanked them again, even more profusely, and, after a few soldierly hugs, made it over to our transport. People were as delighted to see us as they were to see the food we brought for the women and children.

When we reached Krasnovodsk, we were ordered to surrender all Soviet money. We threw it into a large wooden box while the officer duly noted how much each of us gave up. Not that it mattered to anyone; we never saw that money again. Then we were ushered onto a Soviet ship, which took us to Persia.

Later my path led through Persia, India, Palestine, and South Africa. We were supposed to stay at that last destination for six months to recover from months of malnutrition, but after two months they asked for volunteers to serve on sea convoys. Most of us volunteered, and we spent three and a half months crossing the seas to Argentina, Australia, and the United States. On the trip to New York, we were guarding 2000 German POWs. I must admit that we had little compassion for them, and they complained that we were too rough with them. In New York, Canadian troops came aboard and took over the unloading of the prisoners. They insisted on welcoming each prisoner individually with a kick in the ass. This consistency of procedure considerably prolonged the process of unloading, but it also greatly endeared the Canadian soldiers to us.

From New York we went to Halifax and then aboard a ship that formed part of a large convoy ferrying American and Canadian troops to Britain in preparation for the invasion of Europe. We were escorted by several submarines and reached Glasgow without any incident. In Glasgow, they reassigned us to various services. Many of my friends volunteered for the armoured units of the 2nd Corps, but I signed up for the paratroopers, who seemed to promise a more daring career. They trained us in the so-called "monkey grove," equipped with all kinds of training gear. The first two jumps from the tower were scary, but after a while we got used to the sensation of falling. Later we practised jumping from a balloon tied at 300 metres, which could be reached in a special gondola. Our first real jumps were made from American Douglases, of the old type.

By a wretched twist of luck, I found myself in the 10th—penal— Company of the Polish Airborne Brigade, but later, with luck turning once again, our company won various honours and commendations. We made the largest number of jumps, for we were often called upon to demonstrate jumping to various visiting inspectors. All in all, I jumped twenty-three times, sometimes in full gear, sometimes in just my uniform. Jumping with the ballast of the gear was, of course, much more difficult. The set-up on the planes was rather primitive: you simply had to dive into a hole in the floor. The impact of the initial falling speed—seven to nine metres per second—was such that on diving from the plane, you momentarily lost all your senses. Only when the parachute opened up and jerked you back into consciousness could you regain some degree of control over the jump. After landing, the main thing was to avoid getting entangled in the parachute lines and free yourself as soon as possible. Our training lasted throughout 1943, and we were moved from place to place. There was talk of airborne landings in Norway, and we were even issued maps, but nothing came out of it; there were drops over Normandy, but we remained uncommitted, until Arnhem.

Our mission started with a red alert in the barracks; no one was allowed to leave. The weather was bad, so we stayed at the ready for quite a while. Once, we were already on the planes, waiting for take-off, but it was cancelled. On September 21, we were finally airborne in American Dakotas and flying over Europe. As the first squadrons were approaching the landing targets, orders were issued to abort the action.

Unfortunately, the advance squadrons had already turned off their radios and never received the message; those flying behind did and returned to England. As a result, only half of our brigade jumped that day, including General Sosabowski; the other half was dropped in the American sector two days later.

I was in the first group. We were jumping straight down onto the enemy's heads. They seemed well prepared for our reception and welcomed us with a hail of machine gun fire, picking us out as if it were a target practice. We took heavy loses. Under deadly fire and gathering darkness, those who landed safely cut themselves free of the parachutes and left them at the landing site. We were ready for combat, but the orders were to wait, so we waited till late at night, when the Dutch resistance got in touch with us and supplied us with horses and wagons to transport our equipment. We loaded the ammunition onto the wagons and marched behind them. (Later we got more equipment, including some jeeps, brought over by the glider landing forces. The gliders were hauled by planes, two to a plane, and each glider carried, besides the crew, a howitzer and a jeep. After landing, the gliders were blown up.) It was still dark when we reached a small village, where we dug in and waited till the morning. The terrain was wet, and soon we were lying in water, soaked to the skin. At dawn, my team was sent out on patrol. We did not have to walk far before we encountered a strong German detachment. Their firepower was far superior to what we could muster, so we were lucky to make it back to our unit without any casualties.

Our main objective was to capture a bridge on the Rhine, to be used by the troops of General Montgomery. Obviously, the Germans were aware of our intentions, and they put up fierce resistance. We got the order to cross the Rhine to Arnhem in the middle of the night, but once again the enemy seemed to be waiting for us. The river and the town turned into hell. Our boats were pounded by German artillery; we fought for every street and every house, but we were losing. We got an ultimatum from the commander of the German forces that unless we withdrew by 5:00 a.m., we would be "liquidated." We had fourteen boats, which took the wounded; the rest of us had to make it across the river on our own.

During that hasty retreat, I was wounded in the leg. Hurt and exhausted, with Germans closing in, we stood no chance. We received the order to save our lives and surrender. The Germans rounded us up and dispatched us to Brussels. We did not stay in the POW camp for long before being liberated by the Allied forces. I was immediately transferred to a British hospital. It was crowded with the wounded from various sectors of the front, and the preferred method of treatment was amputation. This made the work of the hospital much easier because two weeks after the amputation, the amputee was sent back home, freeing the bed and relieving the strain on the hospital. I was in the care of a good English doctor, a Catholic, who took me with him to church every Sunday, but it was clear that I, too, was heading for amputation. My wound was from an incendiary shell, and the leg was all red and would not heal. Fortunately, I was given some good advice by Major Sabaciński, my first battalion commander. He learned that the medics wanted to cut off my leg, so he paid me a visit in the hospital. "Don't be stupid," he said, "don't agree to it." And I did not. I did not sign the permission papers and, instead, demanded a transfer to a Polish hospital. The very next day they sent me by train to Aberfelde, for consultation with an excellent Polish surgeon, Colonel Dr. Mazanek. He took a good look at my wound and told me not to worry, in three weeks I would be fine. To my delight, three weeks later I indeed recovered. I was discharged from the hospital and got six weeks' holiday. And to this day I walk on the leg the British wanted to amputate.

By the time the war was over, both my mind and my heart were set on the West. My mind told me that Poland was not free, and my heart had been set afire by a *wafka*, an English girl from the Air Force Auxiliary Services, who specialized in the inspection of aircraft dials. I met her in 1944 while I was still in the hospital, where she came to visit her cousin, a nurse. We were married two years later in a Scottish church in Glasgow. Walking up the aisle in our military uniforms, we were quite a rare sight: it was much more typical for Polish servicemen to marry civilian Scottish girls. The unfortunate thing was that, after the ceremony, both of us had to return to our respective military units.

After demobilization, finding a job was quite a feat. My wife and I were eventually sent to work on farms. As a married couple, we wanted to live together, but suitable accommodation was simply not available, and the authorities sent us from one office to another but always to no effect. In the end, I found a job in the forest, thinning out the trees, where I was paid by the amount of work I did. I was making £15 a week, almost three times a typical wage. We also got a good apartment, which cost us only twelve shillings a month. I stayed at that job until 1952, when we were lured by the prospects of an even better life in Canada.

Our immigration to Canada was made possible by Mrs. Józefa Sebastianka, very active in the Polish parish of the Holy Spirit, whose efforts brought many veterans to Winnipeg. We were received with much warmth and enthusiasm, but, despite the generous welcome, our beginnings in Canada were not easy. At first we lived in a single room, with our two children; we had no jobs, and it was difficult to find a decent apartment if you had children. Eventually my wife found work in a sewing shop for thirty-two cents per hour. I was growing desperate and even considered going back to England, where we had been living much better. Finally, I was hired by Inland Steel, where I sharpened steel teeth for harrows. Since we were still struggling to find suitable accommodation, Mrs. Sebastianka suggested that we buy a house. We followed her advice, and our first home cost us $6500.

I worked for Inland Steel for eight years, spending most of my salary to pay off the house. When I lost that job, I spent one winter looking for work until, come spring, I found a temporary job with a building contractor. At last, I found a permanent position with the City, first as a labourer and then as a driver, and kept it for a number of years.

During that time, we raised our two sons, both of whom got university education. I augmented our income by buying several houses, remodelling and refurbishing them, and selling them for a profit. For the last eighteen years, we have lived on Henderson Highway in Winnipeg. We own eight and a half acres of land, and on much of it we plant garlic. The demand is good, and we have no problem selling it. After working at various industrial and city jobs, I find the work in the fields both relaxing and satisfying.

I have been a member of the Polish Combatants Association since my arrival in Winnipeg in 1952. Over the years, I have found many a good friend among its members, with whom I like to reminisce about the past and chat about the present.

HENRYK KOZUBSKI

I was born on the 17th of February, 1922, in Białozórka [Byalozurka], Krzemieniec [Kremenets] county, in Wołyń [Volyn], and attended elementary school there. In 1938 I started attending the Agricultural School in Białokrynica [Belaya Krinitsa]. Like many of my friends, I belonged to the local chapter of Strzelec [Rifleman], a youth paramilitary organization. In August 1939, Strzelec worked hand in hand with the so-called Citizens' Guard. Our collaboration involved going on patrols together with the uniformed police and the military settlers.

In the middle of September 1939, Marian Pawlicki, a local settler, and I were returning from one such patrol. We had been out most of the night, the shift uneventful. Around 5:30 a.m., the morning on the outskirts of Białozórka was still dark, drizzle coming from the grey clouds. Suddenly, out of the greyness, a mounted Soviet patrol appeared. Instinctively, Pawlicki swung his rifle, but before he could aim, the Soviet commander fired at him with a handgun. Pawlicki slumped to the ground, shot dead on the spot. I raised my hands, and they wrestled the rifle from my back. They took me prisoner and led me to Moskalówka [Moskalyuvka], a village ten kilometres away from Białozórka. There I joined a group of interned Polish policemen and soldiers from the Border Guard Corps [KOP]. Under whips and guns, the Soviets forced us to walk to Wiśniowiec [Vishnevets]. Along the way, Ukrainian popes [Eastern Orthodox priests] welcomed the Soviets with bread and salt; village after village played out the same ritual. We were given no food or drink, and those who were thirsty had to sip from puddles. In Wiśniowiec, they set us in the shadow of the castle walls and surrounded us, with machine guns at the ready. We sat there until sunset; then our captors loaded us onto trucks and drove us to a village on the Soviet side of the border. There they locked us up, some thirty men, in a stable, still refusing to give us anything to eat or drink. Next day, on September 18, they finally fed us some breadcrumbs and water, and forced us to march on foot to Yampol', fifty kilometres north of Shibena. After a night in the open, they herded us into the railway station and merged us with the previously interned 4th Battalion of the Border Guards. By train we travelled to Shepetovka. Another night under the cool skies; then in the morning a slice of bread and a can of fish for two. Later that day, they gave us some nondescript soup, but nothing to eat it in or with. It took us a few days before we managed to barter some spoons and tin canteens from the Soviet soldiers. Around September 23, the Soviets brought a group of civilians to our camp, but separated them from us with a wire fence. I recognized two of them, Marian Polański, an old acquaintance of mine, and Gustaw Czerniecki, a settler from the Niza settlement in Białozórka. A week or so later, Polański passed on to me a rumour he had heard that all military prisoners were to be deported to Russia, while all civilians were to be returned to Ostróg, on the Polish side. He and Czerniecki convinced me I should sneak into the civilian camp. So one dark night I jumped the fence. My friends were waiting for me with some civilian clothes. Afterwards, I used parts of my uniform as bedding.

In late October, the Soviets indeed told us to gather our things and led us eighty kilometres from Shepetovka to Ostróg and packed us into the barracks of the 19th Lancers Regiment. The next day, they told us that those who lived in the vicinity could go home. Polański and Czerniecki went north to Zdołbunów [Zdolbunov]; I worked my way south, through the woods, to Białozórka. The roads and woods crawled with gangs of armed Ukrainians, hunting down Polish policemen and soldiers of the Border Guards. Fortunately, I could speak Ukrainian and, pretending that I was a farmhand, I managed to reach Białozórka without harm.

In town, I ran into Mitka Krysa, the local commander of the Ukrainian police. He had served in the Polish army and retired to the reserve at the rank of platoon leader. He asked me—nay, interrogated me—about my weapons, and I had to explain that the Soviets had taken them away. I don't think he believed me. To intimidate me further, he boasted, "Your rule is over, now we're the rulers here." But he let me go home, adding only, "I know where to find you."

He did. Our estate was located three kilometres east of Białozórka, in a small place called Futor Bukowskiego, which had belonged to my mother's family for several generations. Most of the lands once belonging to my father's family lay beyond the Polish-Soviet border, which ran about a kilometre away from our house. Both families had lived in the region for over two centuries, and the moss-covered graves could prove it. My father was a respected farmer, on good terms—or so it seemed at the time—with his neighbours, the local Ukrainians, who made up close to eighty percent of the population. In the spring, when they ran out of wheat or potatoes, he often helped them out, and he even loaned them horses when it was time to break the soil.

I returned home on the 29th of October. I remember the date so well because it was my father's birthday. There was much joy, especially since it was rumoured that I had been killed with Marian Pawlicki. After the tearful welcome, I learned the sad news: the Ukrainians had taken most of my father's land, leaving us only six hectares, a horse-drawn wagon, a cow, and a pig. The rest had been stolen away by the local rabble. They laid an additional tax on us, 6000 rubles, as on any *kulak* [wealthy peasant]. To get the money for the tax, my cousin and I loaded the wagon with white flour, hulled barley, and millet, all in high demand among the Soviets, and drove across the border. We were selling the cereals to the local people for three days, avoiding the ubiquitous patrols. We ran into them on the way back. They stopped us, asked questions, and searched the wagon. Fortunately for us, the search was sloppy and did not uncover the money hidden under some boards. With that money, my father could pay the tax, but he did not pay it all at once lest they asked him where he got the money from. Instead, he paid it in small chunks, pretending he had to scrape the money together by selling more and more of his produce.

On December 10, in the morning, the local Ukrainian police came. They searched the entire house and the farm buildings, looking for weapons. My father had two rifles, a double-barrelled gun, and a fowling-piece, but soon after the Bolsheviks had invaded, he oiled them, wrapped them in rags, and buried them in the orchard. He told the policemen that he had given up his weapons to the Soviets when they marched in. The search proved futile, but the policemen told my mother to ready for me a change of clothes, a towel, some soap, and a blanket. They took me to Białozórka and locked me up in the communal jail. That same evening, I got a parcel of food from my parents, because it was the family's responsibility to feed the prisoner. In the parcel, I also found a box of 200 cigarettes. My father must have found out that I smoked. I had started in Shepetovka: we had next to no food, and when the soldiers offered me a drag to dull the hunger, I could not refuse. My mother knew about my habit, but I thought I had managed to keep it from my father. Obviously I had not. I stayed in that jail for two days, before they drove me to Lanowiec [Lanovtsy], and then to Krzemieniec. All interrogations revolved around my weapons: did I have any, had I hidden any, who had told me to lie. Ten days later, I was back at Białozórka. At the police station I met my father; he, too, was being questioned about his guns. Finally, the commanding officer said to my father, "You I believe, but not your son, that mad dog. I'll let him go but you'll be responsible for him." The irony was, of course, that I was telling the truth, and my father was lying.

And so they let me go again. Our family still enjoyed enough local respect that we were left alone by the Soviets and not immediately deported to Siberia. But life was getting harder, its small joys over-shadowed by ever-growing fear. Social contacts were difficult, some-times dangerous to maintain. Still I managed to meet quite often with my cousin Antoni Juchkiewicz, and my school buddy Stanisław Sieńczak, later an airman in Britain. We were not conspirators, really, just a group of friends trapped by a cruel time, trying to weather that cruelty. We also met with our former math teacher, Stanisław Walkusz, who had constructed a simple radio receiver. Its only drawback was that the battery had to be secretly taken to the power plant in Lanowiec for charging. With this radio, we were able to get some reliable news from the outside world; we did not believe the newspapers, Ukrainian or Polish, for both were full of lies and propaganda.

Our parish priest, Father Jałocho, had to flee the Bolsheviks. He also feared the local Ukrainian populace because, before the war, he had tried to convert them from Eastern Orthodoxy to Catholicism with the help of Captain Przybylski, commander of the 4th Company of KOP in Białozórka. They wanted to turn them into Poles, they used to say. But the Ukrainians would not be turned into anything and strongly resented any manipulators. So Father Jałocho left rather hastily, and Father Terlikowski took over the care of souls in our parish. And a vast parish it was, including six towns and five military settlements.

Christmas that year was subdued yet peaceful, and we eased into the new year with a growing sense of security. Nobody had foreseen the turn of events that shook our lives to the core: on February 10, 1940, the Bolsheviks began mass deportations. The first to be forcibly removed into Russia's heartland and beyond were military settlers and their families, policemen, and a few categories of wealthier Poles, Jews, and Ukrainians. At first our family was spared, both on my mother's and my father's sides. But my mother preferred to be prepared for the worst, so she baked breads and biscuits, and packed our sacks and suitcases.

The second wave of deportations crested in early April, but once again our extended family was hardly touched. Only one of my mother's distant cousins, Cyprian Rutkowski, and his family were taken. Eventually, he managed to join the Polish army and served in the 4th Armoured Regiment, the "Scorpions," and his family managed to escape from Russia to India, and then to Britain.

On Monday, April 12, I was out in the fields, getting them ready for sowing. In the distance, I could see our homestead: grey buildings with red rooftops, a wisp of smoke against the blue sky. A cart drawn by two grey horses drove up to the house. I turned around and looked at the fields stretching out to the horizon. When I faced the homestead again, a man was walking towards me along the balk, an ordinary civilian. He came up close and asked, in Russian, how far it was to the border. "About a kilometre," I said, somewhat disturbed by his sudden appearance and his rather nonchalant manner. Have I got matches, he asked, putting a cigarette in his mouth. I did, so I reached into my pocket. At that moment he pulled out a gun, aimed it at me, and barked, "Ruki v verkh!" [Hands up!]. I raised my hands; now I knew who he was. He pointed me in the direction of the house and ordered, "Go!" But I could not leave the horses in the middle of the field. They were harnessed to the harrow, and could get spooked and injure themselves. I must have sounded convincing, for he let me unhitch them and take them home with me. He walked behind me, gun in hand. I tied the horses to a post in front of the house. Inside was a mess. Mother and Father were backed against the wall as the NKVD [state security police] and some

211

soldiers were wrecking the house, tearing up the floors in every room, knocking on walls, searching for a cache of weapons. "Where did you hide them?" they kept asking, deaf to my parents' answers. I tried to explain again. When the Red Army crossed the border into Poland, a cavalry unit stopped here to water their horses. They had asked us about weapons. Frightened, my father had given them two rifles, a double-barrelled gun, and a fowling-piece. They asked about my service revolver. Again I explained patiently that my revolver was confiscated when I was taken prisoner. No, they still did not believe me. "Sabiraisia s vieshchami!" [Get your things and out], said the civilian-dressed NKVD who had brought me from the fields. They ordered my mother to ready for me a sack with underwear, towels, soap. We all knew it: Siberia. "Don't take that jacket, here is a sheepskin. It gets really cold there," Father was trying to check a sob. Mother was crying openly. Luckily, my brother and sister were at school, so they were spared this tearful sight.

They drove me to Białozórka to the police station. Apparently the NKVD had been busy since early morning, for the station was already full. I found there Antoni Juchkiewicz, Stanisław Sieńczak, Father Terlikowski, Ignacy Walkusz (my math teacher's brother), a former policeman Ryżakowski, Julek Morawski (a platoon leader in the KOP), and Kazik Niwiński. Others I knew only by sight. They put us on two horse-drawn carts and drove to the jail in Lanowiec. That same evening interrogations started. "Where is the gun? Where is the radio? Who was your leader?" We kept our mouths shut, but the NKVD clearly had some inside information. Sieńczak, Juchkiewicz, Niwiński, and myself, we all belonged to the Strzelec, and Morawski was indeed our instructor.

On the second day in Lanowiec, during an interrogation, I found out who the snitches were: two Jewish would-be communists, Gdański and Sotnik. They had squealed to the NKVD that we had arms, a radio, and an organization. We had gone to school together, played soccer, volleyball, and basketball together, often on the same team. They were our buddies, good friends. Little did we know.

After three days in Lanowiec, we were transferred by train to Tarnopol [Ternopil']. They took us to the railway station on foot, guarded by the NKVD and several vicious dogs. Along the way I saw my parents and my siblings for the last time. They waved to me, their faces streaked with tears. On August 5, 1943, just before dawn, my parents and my sister were murdered by the Ukrainians. My fourteen-year-old brother managed to wrench himself out of their hands and ran away. He hid himself in the nearby bushes and survived.

In the Tarnopol jail, the guards took away my sheepskin "for safe-keeping." Others, too, had to surrender their warm clothing. Then, one by one, the guards shoved us into cells. I found myself in a dungeon with some eighty-five men, mostly Ukrainian nationalists. There were only seven Poles: myself; professor Górski from the Agricultural School in Białokrynica; Furdyna, a former police commissioner in Tarnopol; Dola, a policeman from Trembowla [Terembovla]; and three others whose names I no longer remember.

Our cell was so overcrowded that there was not enough space on the floor for everyone to lie down. The least fortunate was the prisoner who came in last: with no more space left inside, he had no choice but to sleep beside the *parasha*, a hundred-litre steel barrel used as a big bucket for urine and faeces. There were no other sanitary facilities in the cell, and since we were let out to the lavatory only once a day, the barrel stank beyond our worst nightmares. We prayed that the guards would take away a few prisoners so that we could move away from the suffocating stench. No one even noticed the mild odour of our unwashed, sweating, frightened bodies.

Nights were thick with stench and fear. The NKVD started interrogations after midnight. Each session lasted at least half an hour. At first, the interrogator would offer a cigarette and a chair to build up a false sense of security. Then the questions would hit like a series of blows: what did you do with your weapons? with your radio? to whom did you pass the information? "You're too comfortable in this chair," he once told me, "sit on the edge," he ordered. When I did, with a kick he knocked the chair from under me. As I fell sprawling on the floor, he hit me with a rubber club and counted my ribs with his boots. "You, an educated man, can't even sit on a chair." His vicious sense of humour did little to cheer me up. I soon found out that it was dangerous not to answer his questions: all too often we could hear screams at night, and prisoners, usually Ukrainians, returned to our cell with swollen, blood-ied faces and broken ribs. So when asked whom I knew or contacted, besides those I was arrested with, I gave them the names of people I knew had escaped to the West or had already been deported to Siberia. My admissions could not harm them, but they could save my life.

Days in the cell offered little variety. We took turns emptying the *parasha* and washing the floor. There was no lying down during the daytime, and the guards watching us through a spy hole made sure of that. They also had at least one snitch inside the cell, who informed them who said what and to whom, and reported anyone who had a sewing needle. Why owning a needle was so dangerous as to be categorically forbidden, I don't know. To pass the time, the Ukrainians practised marching drills; their leader was one Sediaga. We Poles watched them from as far a distance as the cell allowed, leaning against the walls. The guards fed us twice a day. At lunchtime, we got a loaf of bread for eight and lukewarm liquid the colour of weak tea. The challenge was to divide the bread into eight equal portions. We did not have knives, of course, so we used a strong thread instead. Each day a different person was entitled to choose the first slice and to eat the crumbs. Evening meals usually consisted of soup made of barley or buckwheat.

I don't know why they kept us in the Tarnopol jail for so long, until the end of June 1941. Two weeks earlier, and a week before the outbreak of the Soviet-German war on June 22, 1941, a guard had walked into our cell, called out by name all Poles, Belarussians, and Jews, and herded us to another cell. Suddenly I was surrounded by familiar faces of friends from Białozórka I had not seen for fourteen months. We wondered about the reason for this unexpected reunion, for the NKVD was not in the habit of reuniting long-lost friends. An answer— whether true or not I cannot say—came some time later, from another guard. Apparently some Russian informants found out that a militant faction among the Ukrainians was planning to kill all non-Ukrainians as soon as the Germans walked into Tarnopol. As unbelievable as it sounds, the prison authorities were trying to protect us.

On the first of July, we were still in our cell, listening to the bombardment of the airfield in Tarnopol. We had no information from the outside, but we understood that the Germans must have attacked the Soviets. We were waiting for liberation, even by the Germans. It did not come to pass. The day the German army crossed the river Horyń near Ostróg, we were assembled outside the prison. It was early in the morning, and the sun was strangely reddish. The guards gave us a herring each for breakfast and then took us, on foot, towards Podwołoczyska [Podvolochisk], a little town straddling the river Zbrucz [Zbruch], on the former Polish-Soviet border. The salty breakfast soon began to take its toll: we were all thirsty, throats parched and bellies burning, but we had nothing to drink. Some tried to drink from the puddles along the way, but this urge to drink could have cost them their lives: the guards showed no mercy and hit anyone who slowed the pace with the butts of their rifles. In front of my eyes, they clubbed to death an old Greek-Catholic priest, a Ukrainian. His name was Dziadov. He was well past seventy and could not move his legs fast enough to keep up. A few strokes to the head slowed him down to a corpse.

We were not the only company fleeing east before the Germans: all Soviet military services were in retreat. Sometimes we could see them in the distance, armoured units, infantry columns, strings of trucks. After a long day's march, we finally reached Podwołoczyska. The guards drove us into deep pits where clay had been dug for bricks. There we waited for the dawn, surrounded by machine guns. Just after sunrise, the guards chased us across the bridge to Wołoczyska [Volochisk], a town on the other side of the river Zbrucz. At the railway station, they shoved us into freight cars, forty to a car, and the train pulled out heading eastward. Tending our bleeding feet, we kept wondering why the Soviets, in their retreat, insisted on taking us with them, why they spared the railway cars they sorely needed for the withdrawing troops.

Many years later, during my visit in Poland in 1960, I learned that my mother, together with Stanisław Sieńczak's mother, had gone on foot forty-five kilometres to Tarnopol to look for me in the piles of bodies of dead prisoners, whom the Soviets had not had the time or the wish to take with them. Whatever twisted war-logic made them take us as war booty, it apparently saved our lives.

Along the way the train passed scores of small railway stops and stations; when we halted in the open fields, the guards would draw us some water from stagnant pools. We had no cups to drink it with, so we used our caps or shoes. At times we had to wait long hours for military transports to pass, which always had the right of way. We had not eaten for days, our faces grew even longer and our bodies thinner. Seeing us so famished, local Russian people at the train stops tried to throw us some food, but the guards kept them away from the cars. They told them we were Germans. People believed them and spat at the cars instead and threw stones at us. After about a week on that nightmarish train, we finally got our first meal: a small fish, somewhat like a sardine, and some water from a puddle. After this feast—diarrhoea. Forty men in the car and only one shithole in the middle of the floor. Barely able to hold it, men fought for a moment over this stinking hole. This pressure to void already empty stomachs was probably worse than hunger.

Towards the end of August, we arrived at Magnitogorsk. They placed us in a transition camp, where we enjoyed a short respite from the suffering that had become our way of life. We were assigned to barracks with real beds in them. There were even mattresses. We ate bread and soup, and drank tea. Slowly we recovered from the bouts of diarrhoea. A week, or maybe two, later, we got the first snippets of information from the outside world. One of the prisoners read, on a scrap of newsprint used as toilet paper in the latrine, a few sentences about an agreement between General Sikorski and the Soviet government. The rest of the newspaper had already been put to unsavoury use and was past retrieval. For days we speculated what that agreement might have been and what consequences it might have for us.

At the end of September, the Soviets moved us once again, this time to a prison in Verkhneural'sk, some 120 kilometres south of Magnitogorsk. We set out in the morning and got our first meal from a field kitchen, right on the banks of the Ural River. They served us hulled barley, but as usual no utensils, so we were forced to eat with fingers from our caps. But we no longer cared how we ate as long as there was food to eat. We spent the night in the open, sleeping on the wet ground. The air grew stinging cold. Stanisław Sieńczak had lost his blanket, so I offered to share mine with him. Together, we managed to stay warm on the frozen grass till the sun rose above the horizon. After another long day's march, with shadows turning into darkness, we reached the prison. We ate our food rations in silence: 400 grams of mouldy bread, heavy with moisture. They checked off our names and assigned us to cells. My cell was smaller than the one in Tarnopol, and yet they crammed sixty men inside. We slept on the dirty cement floor. We, too, were dirty and smelly. We stayed in that prison for three and a half months, but washed only once. Only once a day did they let us out to the lavatory, where we could rinse our hands. No soap, of course.

Lice were a real plague. Those with a lot of body hair suffered the worst. I was not a hairy type; in fact, in spite of my twenty years of age, all I could boast was some fluff under my nose and not even a hint of a beard. It stung when others called me "a beardless wonder" or asked if they could wipe the milk off my upper lip, but not nearly as much as vermin bites in the thickets of beards or moustaches. When we finally got wooden spoons and metal plates, some prisoners broke off strips of metal and sharpened them on the cement floor. Then they used these primitive razors to shave themselves. But their relief was short-lived: when the guards saw their shaven faces, they drove us outside in our underwear and searched the cell. They confiscated all metal objects and gave us clay dishes instead.

Throughout the fall of 1941, the NKVD continued with their pointless interrogations, always following the same predictable pattern. The only cruel innovation was a small, dark, cage-like cell, with water on the stone floor, used to "inspire" those who thought they had nothing to say. Shortly before Christmas the interrogations ceased. We thought this was a sign that we were about to be sentenced and sent to labour camps. In the midst of such speculations, on January 12, 1942, well after midday, a guard called out my name and ordered me to get all my things. He led me to the office of the chief warden, where, to my surprise, Ignacy Walkusz was already waiting. In a tone of indifferent matter-of-factness, the warden informed us that by virtue of an agreement between General Sikorski and the Soviet government, we were being discharged from prison in order to join the Polish armed forces to fight for the fatherland. Ignacy and I were completely dismayed by this declaration, shocked and suspicious. We kept silent: a wrong word could earn us grave punishment, or even a grave. We had been questioned by the interrogators if we knew General Sikorski and how we maintained contacts with him. But the warden's words soon found confirmation in his actions. He picked up from his Spartan desk two certificates of release from prison and handed them to us, together with twenty rubles each for railway tickets and another fifteen for food. The slight matter of reaching the railway station, some 120 kilometres away, must have slipped his mind, for he made no mention of it. They led us outside the prison gate and smashed it closed.

We breathed in deeply our freedom, so unexpectedly gained, and it almost froze our lungs: it was -30° Celsius. We were wearing the only clothes we had, light pants, tattered jackets, and half a blanket each. Fortunately, we could see a settlement in the distance. Three kilometres later, as we were passing one of the first huts, a woman emerged from it and called out to us: "Come here. My husband and sons are in the Red Army, and I need someone to chop some wood for me." We followed her to the smoky hut; once inside, she turned to me and said, "*Golubchyk* [Dove], I know you have no strength for such work, but I had to say that outside. Walls have ears nowadays." She gestured us to sit beside a rough, stained table and fed us some goat milk and bread. She did not have much of it, only her own ration, which we devoured in minutes. She was watching us as we ate, nodding her head from time to time. "My boys, you'll freeze outside like that," she finally said, looking at our meagre garments. She went to another room and came back with two quilted *kufaikas.** "These are my sons', but God knows if they'll ever be back." She handed us the warm jackets. We thanked her with all our hearts, for she strengthened us in body and in spirit. Walking through the snow under the darkening skies, we reflected on the compassion, generosity, and hospitality of the Russian people.

Before we left the prison, we had been instructed that wherever we wanted to stay, we had to report to the police station. We did so and were sent to lodge in a nearby farmer's house. "House" is, perhaps, too big a word for it: one chamber with a stove and a mud floor, but no table, or chairs, or beds. We warmed up and went looking for an eatery. The place we found was crowded with Russian soldiers. We ordered cabbage soup for thirty kopecks a bowl and lapped it up with much pleasure. The soldiers at the next table must have enjoyed the sight of us, for they invited us to join them and offered some tobacco rolled in newsprint. They were waiting for boiled dumplings, which were to be ready in an hour. So we joined their wait and later their feast. When we came back to the farmer's house, late at night, our bowels began to twist and turn, and the pain was agonizing. Only then did we recall the warning of a Ukrainian doctor, a fellow prisoner, who had told everybody not to eat much for the first few days if we ever left the prison. We had not heeded his advice. Now we were writhing in acute pain, Ignacy even more than I. My cramps subsided by the morning, but his got even worse. He also began to swell. Three days later he died in terrible agony. I could do nothing to help. I dug his grave in the rock-hard ground, and placed my friend under a mound of frozen earth and marked the place with a simple wooden cross.

I did not mourn Ignacy alone. Every day the prison authorities let out

---

* Parka-like jackets warmed with rough cotton.

more people whom their records identified as Polish citizens. Ukrainian nationalists, who had it entered in their personal records that they were citizens of western Ukraine, were not released. Soon there was no more space in the farmer's house. With our numbers grew our self-confidence until we felt secure enough to approach the local military replenishment command with a request that they convey us to the Polish army. The reply was prompt and polite: as soon as the numbers of volunteers are sufficient, they will arrange a transport to Magnitogorsk. In the meantime, they assigned us accommodation with local people. I was sent to stay with an old couple whose three sons and one daughter were all serving in the Red Army. The couple were in their forties, but to me, a twenty-year-old, they looked ancient, especially their faces, creased with years of hardship. The husband walked with a stiff leg, so I asked him why. It turned out that a Polish bullet had shattered his knee in the Polish-Russian war of 1920. I wished I hadn't asked. I was sure they would make me, a Pole, pay for that unfortunate turn of fate, but, as I discovered, I could not have hoped for more generous hosts. They treated me like one of their own sons, feeding and clothing and looking after me. When we said goodbye, they pressed some money into my hand—I knew they did not have much—and could not hold back their tears.

On January 30, we left Verkhneural'sk by sleigh, all 300 of us. At first we enjoyed the sledging cavalcade, but after a few hours it grew so cold that we could not continue. We stopped in a village and arranged the lodging with the locals. Although I wore a quilted *kufaika*, I kept thinking of that sheepskin they were keeping safe for me in the Tarnopol jail. Ha! But it was my feet that bothered me the most, as I was beginning to lose my toes to frostbite. Once again a Russian peasant who took me in for the night turned out to have a heart of gold. Looking at my boots, he shook his head and mumbled something about the stupidity of Westerners. Then he picked them up, matted them up with straw, wrapped them with a rag, took them outside, and poured some water over them. By morning the boots were frozen solid, but my feet inside stayed surprisingly warm all the way to Magnitogorsk, where our train odyssey was about to begin.

In Magnitogorsk they loaded us into a passenger train, which included a restaurant car. Although we were malnourished, we were no longer in any danger of the food shock that had killed Ignacy Walkusz, so we enjoyed a decent dinner. When we arrived in Chelyabinsk, we reported to the Polish consular station. I don't savour the memory of that first encounter with the Polish authorities. The officer who interviewed us gave us the distinct impression that he was doing us a favour. After what we had gone through, his behaviour was like a slap in the face. But, in the end, there were 300 of us, and under our collective pressure, he gave us food vouchers, three railway cars, and a pass to Lugovoye, where the 10th Infantry Division was being formed. We had to wait for those cars at the railway station until February 5, with no place to warm up or to lie down. My legs began to swell and walking grew more painful. When the cars finally arrived, they were cold like freezers. We had no fuel of any kind, so to warm them up, the healthier and more adventurous among us ventured to the railyard and stole whatever coal they could from the locomotives. When the fires lightened up the cars and melted the hoarfrost from our faces, we finally took heart: we knew we were on the way to the Polish army.

Unfortunately, that way turned out to be neither quick nor straightforward. On the train, several men fell sick with spotted fever, so in Ariza, Tajikistan, they quarantined us. Our cars were rerouted to a sidetrack, and guards were posted around them. Our rations of 100 grams of macaroni a day left us hungry and angry. For the second time, I was forced to barter my boots. The first time was during the long wait in Chelyabinsk, when I exchanged my good boots for the boots of a Soviet officer, plus 100 rubles, plus a loaf of bread and a smoked fish. Now, for the officer's boots, I could get only a loaf of bread, a glass of shag, fifty rubles, and a pair of old felt boots. For a few days, I shared my gains with two of my closest friends, Antoni Juchkiewicz and Stanisław Sieńczak. When even the crumbs were gone, we decided we had no choice but to run away from the hapless transport. At the last minute, Sieńczak changed his mind, so Witek Kaźków, from Nowogródek [Navahrudak], went with us instead. In the evening, we sneaked into a passenger train and hid under the seats. As soon as the train pulled out from the station, we emerged from our hiding places. In this we miscalculated, for soon a conductor appeared, checking the tickets. We told her—the entire train crew was female, including the train-driver and her helper—that we were on our way to join the Polish army and that our commander had all the tickets. When she went looking for him, we moved to another car. We played this game of cat and mouse all the way to Lugovoye. We arrived there in the morning, and straightaway we went searching for the recruitment station.

The station was not difficult to find, but getting before the recruitment commission proved quite a challenge. We were told that, first, we needed a certificate from the baths, and second, that all our hair had to be shaved. We asked the directions to the baths. We spotted it easily from a distance but gasped in exasperation: the lineup looked a kilometre long. The waiting time was almost two days. We felt too exhausted, physically and mentally, simply to take our place in the line. The circumstances were extraordinary, and they called for some ingenuity. We returned to the recruitment station and took a good look around the place. We noticed some baths certificates lying around in the office: apparently the duty officer had forgotten to collect them all. Thanks to a lucky break and a good sleight of hand, we managed to "acquire" one of those certificates. We felt reassured: they could be "acquired" outside the baths after all. Now the hair. We pooled our financial resources and had enough for three haircuts and two shaves—I still did not need a shave. Thus sporting the bald look, we spent the last ruble on accommodation, nothing fancy, just a bunch of hay in a sty pleasantly warmed and scented by the presence of some goats. In the evening, in the privacy of the sty, we used a piece of broken glass from the window to shave the hair in our armpits and elsewhere. We were almost ready for the commission.

On March 5, in the morning, I bartered my *kufaika* for another bath certificate and a few rubles. The money was enough for a tasteless soup in a crowded eating place and for the third certificate. As we had anticipated, they were not all that difficult to get. The last one cost us five rubles. Finally, we were ready to face the recruitment commission. The medical exam was the worst. After so many months in prison, we were in pitiful physical condition: 181 centimetres tall, my bones—for muscles I had almost none—weighed only forty-nine kilograms. I prayed that the doctor did not reject me. He tapped and prodded and finally nodded his approval. Thank you, Lord! I was elated. At the next desk, I was assigned to the 10th Artillery Regiment. My father had served in a similar unit, first in the Tsar's army, and later in the Legions, under Dowbór-Muśnicki. Antoni Juchkiewicz was assigned to the sappers, and Witek Kaźków to the Signal Corps.

We went to collect our new uniforms, overjoyed that our tribulations were finally over. The uniforms were English; we were also issued two pairs of winter underwear and two pairs of summer, a coat, a rubber groundsheet, a backpack, a haversack, a mess kit including a spoon, a fork, and a knife, two towels, shaving accessories but without razors, and a pair of boots. We took off our old clothes with relief, and the warehouse attendant picked them up with a fork and threw into a blazing fire. We watched with satisfaction as the flames consumed the vermin-infested rags. I put on my new uniform and tried on the boots. They were much too tight. I went back to exchange them, but, sorry, no bigger sizes were available. Well, they had to do. I put them on and, all dressed up, I started in the direction of my new headquarters. I had not walked half a kilometre when my feet began to hurt so much that I had to kick off the boots and put on an extra pair of socks instead. I tied the boots with the shoelaces and hung them on my neck. When the chief, Staff Sergeant Chojnacki of the 2nd Battery, saw me walking like that into the office, he burst out laughing. "What are you saving your shoes for, son?" he chuckled. I explained my predicament, and he soon found me some worn felt boots. On account of my blistered feet, I was exempted from the daily expeditions to the railway station for supplies. Our regiment experienced an acute shortage of vehicles, and soldiers—myself excepted—had to lend their backs to the cause.

Food was also scarce because we had to share it with the civilians; for Polish women, children, and older men, the Soviets issued no food rations. In the evening, I ate my bowl of soup, but hunger kept gnawing at my entrails. Finally, I gave in to the temptation and went for another helping. Unfortunately, the cook recognized me and took a swing at me with his ladle. The provisions officer saw it all, scolded the cook, and took me aside to his tent. "I know you are hungry, son," he said in a fatherly way, "but there are many like you here. If you take a second helping, someone else will get none." Despite my twenty years of age, tears began to roll down my cheeks, and soon I was crying like a child. "I know, son, that you did not think about it. You don't mean to eat someone else's supper. But in the future, remember: if you are hungry, come to me. When everyone has been fed, and we have some leftovers, I'll give them to you." I stayed in the tent for a few more minutes to dry my face. And I was never that hungry again.

March 26, 1942. Our regiment was loaded into freight cars, and soon we were moving in the direction of Krasnovodsk, a harbour on the southeastern coast of the Caspian Sea. We stopped briefly in Toshkent, where we visited the baths, my first true ablutions since November 11, 1941. The baths were run by women, exclusively by women. When we pulled off our smelly uniforms and even smellier underwear, we had to hand them in to the attendants for washing and disinfection. Some guys tried to hide their shame—or pride—with one hand, scrambling to hold all the pieces of clothing with the other. The women collecting our clothes were not shocked, not even flustered. In fact, they watched us mock-critically and reminded us to take good care of our guns. After the bath, we felt newly born, and newly born we lined up before the women to claim our uniforms.

A few days later, we arrived in Krasnovodsk. Before we boarded an empty tanker, bound for Pahlavi in Iran, we had to unload a car packed with unused foodstuffs. For a good while we were furious: we had gone half-hungry for weeks, and now this food was going to waste because we could not take it with us to Iran. At that point, I had been a soldier for about two months. It took me much longer to get used to the paradoxes and absurdities of life in the military.

As we were disembarking in Pahlavi, after a day's passage, I had a sinking feeling we had gotten out of the rain and straight under the gushing water spout. Waiting on the wharf and watching us closely were the NKVD. But they did not touch anyone, and our commanding officer assured us that from that moment onward we were under British command, and we could piss on them. One soldier took this too literally, but he was quickly whisked away and, I presume, reprimanded.

The British were not quite ready to receive such large numbers of soldiers. No quarters had been arranged, and again food was in short supply. We thought back on that car full of supplies we had unloaded and left behind in Krasnovodsk and shook our collective head. Luckily, the British paid us our military wages, so we could make up for the shortages by buying bread, eggs, and sausages—probably made from an ass, we joked, but we were hungry enough to like them. We savoured fresh dates and halva.* We lived like nomads on the beaches, with groundsheets set up into primitive tents to protect us from rain and heavy dew. We had another bath, and our clothes were disinfected again.

---

* A confection consisting of crushed sesame seed in a binder of honey.

Life was beginning to settle into a routine, a bit rough around the edges but, after the hardships in the Soviet Union, quite pleasant nonetheless.

In the second half of April, we were uprooted again. Loaded onto trucks, we left Pahlavi and travelled towards Iraq, then through Jordan to Palestine. That was the end of April. On May 2, we were organized into the 3rd Carpathian Riflemen Division, with General Stanisław Kopański as commander. The Division included the 3rd Brigade of Carpathian Riflemen and the 10th Artillery Division from Lugovoye. I was assigned to the 1st Light Artillery Regiment, commanded by Colonel Domiczek, and, more specifically, to the 1st Battery, under First Lieutenant Jakub Lubowiecki. From that one unit, fifteen of us eventually came to Winnipeg, although only two made their permanent home here.

In Palestine, we went through an intensive recruit and field training. It was hot and tedious but necessary. The highlights of that summer were short sightseeing trips to Jerusalem, Tel Aviv, Bethlehem, the Dead Sea, and other places of historical and biblical interest. In September, we were on the road again. The 3rd Carpathian Division was being moved to Iraq to be merged with the 2nd Polish Corps under Władysław Anders. First we drove to Egypt, then by boat from Suez through the Red Sea, Indian Ocean, Persian Bay to Basra [Al Başrah]. From there, we reached Qizil Ribat [As Sa'dīyah] by trucks. It was already December when the 1st Light Artillery Regiment was quartered in Quajara, fifty kilometres from Mosul and close to the Turkish border. We trained there together with the units of the 2nd Corps; I also attended a special artillery program at the NCO school. Learning and training kept me occupied throughout winter. Compared to what we remembered from Russia, the Iraq winter was almost pleasant: no snow and only occasional ground frost. In early spring, the frost-dulled vegetation burst out in verdant frenzy, but by late April it was dulled again by heat, drought, and sandstorms. Days became painfully hot. We rose at daybreak to complete our training tasks by 10:00 a.m. Dismissed from duty, we drove to the riverside, where the air was cooler. The Arabs floated watermelons in big nets down the river, and we bought them cheaper than dirt. Some we ate raw, but the rest we asked the cook to boil with rice. We were craving some variety from the military staple of rice and greasy mutton.

In late spring 1943, we were inspected by Prime Minister and

Supreme Commander Władysław Sikorski. We marched past him with genuine enthusiasm: we were all ready to die for the cause he represented. But we did not get a chance to prove our sincerity for a few more months. The 3rd Division was sent to Lebanon for some high-altitude training and manoeuvres. It was a breathtaking country, steeped in history and sheer beauty, with a mild climate and even milder people. Its charms were particularly apparent to those of us who knew French, but others, too, seemed to have been affected by the congeniality of the people. Our stay in Lebanon was not nearly long enough. But the orders were for Palestine. More waiting—the soldier's lot. Then one morning we woke up to find several of our colleagues missing. We started searching and discovered even more empty, unslept-in beds. A rumour spread through the camps like wildfire: the Jews had deserted. In my battery all but one soldier of Jewish descent disappeared. The one who stayed behind was Ryszard Rubin, who fought with us in the Italian campaign, and came to Canada in the same transport as I. One of the Jewish deserters that night was Menachem Begin, later Prime Minister of Israel. In his autobiography, Begin claims that General Anders himself discharged him from the Polish army. No such claims have been made for dozens of others who vanished the same night, so I remain sceptical of Begin's account.

Our division returned to Egypt in November 1943. Shortly afterwards, we boarded troop ships in Port Said and left for Italy. After months of training, we were impatient for some real action. And indeed we got that action barely a few hours after leaving port, although not the way we had anticipated. Our convoy was hit by a powerful storm. Many soldiers became violently seasick and spent most of the passage hanging over the railings or toilet bowls. We were no match for the superior forces of nature. We disembarked in Taranto and moved into position, with all our equipment, in the vicinity of the Sangro River, relieving a British artillery regiment. We did not engage the enemy in any significant way, apart from the usual infantry patrols and the routine shelling of the main points of Nazi resistance.

By mid-April we took our position near Monte Cassino, once a famous monastery, now an infamous German stronghold. Our main responsibility was to store the ammunition and to shell the Nazi line of defence. Our barrages also created an artillery cover for the advancing infantry troops. The first assault started on May 10. Hundreds of foot soldiers went up the deadly hill with nothing but disdain for the Nazi bullets. Not that they were unafraid of death; we all were, but as the song says, "their anger was stronger than death." Many died in that assault, too many, for the little advance we made. But the second attack was even angrier, and it succeeded where the first one failed: a patrol of the 12th Podole Lancers Regiment raised the Polish flag on the ruins of the monastery.

Afterwards, our 2nd Corps was moved to the Adriatic coast, where we captured the port city of Ancona. From there we went to Osimo, where I lost a close friend of mine, Zbigniew Okulicki. He was the son of General Leopold Okulicki, one of the leaders of the underground resistance in Poland, who was treacherously executed by the Soviets. After taking Rimini and Bologna, our corps was taken out of action. I was relieved from my duties as a gunner in the 1st Battery and detailed to the training centre in Matera for a gunnery course. The course included both a theoretical part and a practicum in the Corps Armament Shops. I graduated from this course shortly before Christmas with a diploma of an independent gunsmith and returned to my home regiment to resume the duties in the 1st Battery. As it turned out, I never had an opportunity to put my newly acquired skills to the test in battle.

Our regiment was stationed in Ofido, about twenty kilometres west of the Adriatic coast. The challenge there was to avoid the demoralizing boredom, for we had more than enough free time on our hands. So we haunted the beaches and luxuriated in the Italian sun; so we explored the cities and the ancient sights of Rome, Naples, Venice; so we admired the art and the history and the beauty of the country. It was a relatively happy time for me—insofar as wartime could at all be happy. But for many of us, that time of war was also the time of our youth, of intense friendships, of comradery under enemy fire and over the graves of our friends. We rejoiced that the murderous war was over, but when we thought about the future, our thoughts were laced with anxiety. That is why we had mixed feelings when, in June 1945, we surrendered our guns and ammunition. My artilleryman's heart sank at the sight of the polished barrels of our new heavy guns being cut into pieces with blowtorches.

We stayed in Italy for another year. In 1946 it was announced that Canada was accepting applications for farm labourers. They were looking for healthy bachelors, no dependents and no attachments, except for two strong arms and a sturdy back. I was healthy and a bachelor, and I knew enough about farming to tell wheat from barley grain. After all, I used to help my father on the farm and often worked with basic farming equipment. So I applied and thereby sealed my fate.

I arrived in Halifax aboard the first immigration ship from Italy, the *Sea Robin,* on November 11, 1946. The ship was crowded: there must have been more than 2000 of us. We had been assigned to individual provinces while still in Italy. All I knew about Manitoba, and Winnipeg, was that they were somewhere in Canada's heartland. I guess I had imagined a city in the midst of tall stands of spruce, redolent of resin and wet vegetation. Had I known about its landscape, its cold winters, and its mosquitoes, I suspect I would have settled in Toronto. But I had not known, and four days after disembarking in Halifax, I arrived, by rail, in Winnipeg. I have lived here ever since.

When we pulled in at the CPR station, we heard Polish voices and saw some Polish welcome signs. Lots of people from the Polish community in Winnipeg turned up to greet us. They took us by tram to the military barracks, our temporary lodging. I was tired after four days on the train but also too excited to sleep. I washed, shaved, changed my clothes. In the evening, our Polish hosts picked us up again and drove us to a gathering of St. John Cantius Fraternal Aid Society to meet more people from the Polish community. The first person I ran into was Piotr Polański's brother's wife. When I introduced myself, she exclaimed that she knew my family and that my parents had been at her wedding. There must be some truth to that cliché about the small world. That evening I met so many people that their names became a blur, but since most of them invited me later for dinner, I got to know them quite well. All the while we were staying in the barracks, completing a long series of medical examinations and X-rays. The latter were prompted by a number of cases of tuberculosis. Those infected were sent to a sanatorium in Brandon to recuperate, while the healthy rest of us was soon dispersed to various Manitoba farms.

I went to a farm in Petersfield, about ninety kilometres north of Winnipeg. The farmer, an Italian, had had six German prisoners of war working for him, whom we replaced. My Italian was far from perfect, but it was enough to communicate about farming matters. What bothered me was that spending my days in the fields or in the barn offered little opportunity for learning English. Besides, the pay was a measly

$45 a month, and the living and working conditions on the farm were wretched. I was so frustrated that I wrote a complaint to the deputy minister of agriculture. The ministry sent out a special inspector, who confirmed the substandard conditions. He also promised that we would be transferred to another farm. Needless to say, the Italian farmer was not pleased with the outcome of the inspection. For several days, he hovered over us like a hail cloud, until, finally, lightning struck, and I was fired.

It was a cold February day in 1947. I took a bus to Winnipeg to the Ministry of Agriculture. I could not yet argue my case in English, so I was assigned an interpreter, a young, attractive woman who was very concerned about my plight. Eventually, we found a common, even intimate, language as several months later she became my wife. But in the meantime, I was sent to a milk farm, in the same region as before. There I was making $60 a month plus room and board. I stayed on that farm for ten months, saving as much as I could.

Both my heart and my temperament drew me to Winnipeg, where I returned in December 1947. But city jobs were scarce at the time. A friend of mine, who had worked with me on the farm, took a job cutting lumber for a paper mill in Ontario. The work was tough, but the wages were high, $20 a day, he said. He almost had me convinced to leave Winnipeg again. I was already packing up my things when I met some guys who promised to get me a job at CPR. They proved true to their word, and in January I was already loading large blocks of ice used for cooling railway cars. We worked ten-hour shifts, six days a week, making sixty-three cents an hour. Most of us ice-loaders were new immigrants; born Canadians were not interested in this back-breaking labour. I lasted there till May. Then my friends told me about Vulkan Iron and Engineering, a company specializing in building water tanks, lifts, and even shells for exactly the kinds of guns we had in our artillery regiment. They coached me how I should answer questions at the interview. "If they ask you if you can rivet, say yes," they advised me, "and if they ask if you are not afraid of heights, say no. You can always learn on the job and get used to the heights." I did as they told me and got the job. I stayed with it for twenty-five years.

I took my work very seriously. Since it required good comprehension of English, I went to night school to learn more English. I also signed up for a draughting course, but my job often took me away from

Winnipeg, and I never completed it. After two years with the company, I became a foreman, and after four, I was promoted to superintendent. I was responsible for hiring people—from ten to 120, depending on the job—and assigning various tasks to them. I did not mind the responsibility that went with my job and enjoyed the independence. I worked for hourly wages rather than a salary and for the most part was my own boss.

When I drive around Winnipeg today, I can easily find the sites I worked on. Some of them, like the Disraeli Bridge or the Norquay Building, have now become landmarks; and rightly so, for we made them to last. We built well, and not infrequently for less than the preliminary cost estimates, a thing unheard of nowadays. I cut the costs—but not the quality of workmanship—when building the power station in Selkirk, and again when installing steam boilers at a gas refinery in British Columbia. I worked in BC for half a year and could have stayed there longer, but my family was back in Winnipeg, so here I returned. When the company was dissolved in 1975, I continued to work in the same field as a freelance contractor. I retired twelve years later, in 1985, at age sixty-five.

My family life has gone through some ups and downs. My first marriage ended in a divorce, the second in a separation. But my children were—and still are—my pride and joy. We spared no effort to ensure that they had every opportunity to further their education. There was nothing unusual in this: most Polish veterans, whom World War II forced out of schools and universities and onto the battlefields, had a tremendous respect for education. Since the war denied it to them, they wanted to make sure their children could take advantage of it.

Over the years, whenever my work allowed, I remained an active member of the Polish Combatants Association [PCA]. I joined the association when still in Falconara, Italy. Here in Winnipeg, I sang in the Sokół choir, at the time led by Peter Andre and later by Mr. Radian. In 1960-61, I was elected member of the board of the PCA for the first time; in the years that followed, I served two terms as president of Chapter #13. After retirement, I was also co-opted to the board of the PCA Credit Union and worked there until our small fund was taken over by the much larger Holy Spirit Credit Union.

It has been my dream that, as we grow older, the board of our association might attract some members from the younger generation.

Unfortunately, so far the association is growing old with us. I should like to remain an optimist, yet thoughts about uncertain future weigh heavily on me: unless we manage to reach and appeal to our Polish youth, be it even the middle-aged youth, our organization may become a mere footnote in a history book within a decade or so.

EDMUND KUFFEL

I was born in a Pomeranian town of Przysiersk in 1924, and grew up as one of many siblings. My mother was a teacher, and my father ran a farm. I began attending high school in Chełm on the Vistula River in 1938, but in September of the following year, the war interrupted my education. I returned home for a forced practicum in agriculture—I had no choice in the matter—helping my father on the farm. In January 1942, the Nazis evicted us from our farm and gave it to some German settlers from Besarabia. Soon afterwards, they began forced resettlement of the dispossessed farmers from our region. My family was taken to Jasieniec, a small village near Koronowo. I was seventeen at the time and, according to the local German regulations, I was obliged to report to the Employment Office, the *Arbeitsamt*. The office assigned me to one of the itinerant labour teams specializing in maintaining the infrastructure. This forced employment eventually took me to Italy, where my team was sent to build and repair roads, railway tracks, and even airstrips.

In 1944 the war had entered its final phase, and German troops, with all their support units, were already withdrawing from Italy. My work team, comprised of youths from the countries conquered by the Nazis, was also supposed to withdraw. It was then that three of us, the only Poles on the team, decided to make a run for freedom, although a "run" may be too big a word for what we actually did. We managed to stray from the unit and find a hiding place in an olive grove. There we waited for the approaching Allied troops. When, a few days later, we ventured outside, we easily located a rallying point for marauders and volunteers who wanted to join the Allied forces. We were registered and dispatched to a transition camp, where we signed up for the Polish army.

It was spring 1944, and I was wearing a uniform with Polish insignia. I had always dreamed of joining the air force, but there were already too many candidates for that service, which was so attractive to young men. I was assigned to infantry, more specifically to the 15th Rifle Battalion of the 5th Brigade in the 5th Division of the 2nd Polish Corps. During the initial screening of the new recruits, Colonel Gnatowski asked me, rather unexpectedly, if I could read and write. When I answered in the affirmative, he delegated me to information services in the command headquarters. I was surprised that all that was required of the personnel in the so-called *Dwojka* was basic literacy, but I soon discovered that it was indeed quite sufficient for a courier in the command headquarters. Because of this assignment, I was not among the troops storming the Monte Cassino stronghold and thus did not partake of glory—and perhaps death—on the poppy-covered slopes.

Later I was reassigned to a regular unit and saw action in the last phase of the Italian campaign, fighting at Ancona, Monte Rippe, and Rimini. I must admit that I had more luck than wisdom at my age: although on numerous occasions I heard bullets whistling past my ears on the front line, I never suffered an injury. In one of those actions, we were crawling up a hill, staying close to the ground and hiding in the foliage. Suddenly earth and shrapnel exploded all around us: we had crawled straight into the sights of German mine throwers. One of the ugly-looking shells landed right under my feet. I froze for a split second, waiting for a deafening explosion and a brilliant flash of redness to extinguish my life. But neither came. The shell spun and stopped, its murderous force unspent. A dud. My legs were soft and my knees were shaking, but I exhaled a sigh of relief. At that moment, it occurred to me that Providence must have had some other plans for me.

That fleeting thought seemed to have been confirmed by another episode that left me badly shaken but physically unharmed. Near Monte Rippe, I had received an order to take my squad for a pre-dawn reconnaissance, shortly before a planned attack. At the last minute, as the squad was about to leave, I was reassigned to another duty, and my closest friend was ordered to take my place. His name was Stefan Polak, from Silesia, and we had been together in the Information

Services. Less than two minutes later, before they had a chance to move further away, we fell under heavy artillery fire. One of the first shells exploded beside his head, severing it from his neck. I froze in body and mind, looking at his mutilated corpse, and thinking the severed head could just as well have been mine. And in the midst of that horror and shock, once again the thought of Providence flashed though my mind.

When we passed Forli, the front stabilized for the rest of the winter. Our engagement was limited to regular patrols and occasional skirmishes. In the spring of 1945, in the last stages of the war, our units followed the withdrawing Germans without any major battles.

The war officially ended in May. The news, when it reached us, stirred mixed feelings. Some welcomed it with relief, with enthusiasm, with cheering. But in our unit the mood was rather subdued and cheerless. Many of us had nothing to go back to, and we all knew that, for us Poles, the end of war only meant a change of the occupying force. Tragically shortchanged by history, Poland held no future for us. We tried to drown the feelings of sorrow, bitterness, and resignation in alcohol, and must have drunk up a sea of vermouth. The sparse news from our homeland did little to encourage us to return. We had known earlier about the Yalta Pact and about the Allied nations' betrayal of Poland, but as long as the war raged on, we lived in hope that somehow things would change and we would go home. And as long as there was hope, the thought of permanent emigration did not even cross my mind.

During that crucial period of transition from war to peace, the leadership of the Polish Armed Forces showed unusual wisdom and farsightedness. A tremendous effort was expended to educate the masses of youngsters who had spent their school years on the battlefields and, on the cessation of hostilities, faced the difficult task of adjusting to life in peacetime. Immediately after the war's end, while still in Italy, each division began to organize junior and senior high schools. The 5th Division, in which I served, organized its high school in Modena. Former high school teachers, who had joined the army as officers of the reserve, were now returned to their vocation as educators. Their ranks were reinforced by the teachers who had been shipped by the Nazis to the Reich to work as free labour. It was relatively easy to get admitted to that high school: all one had to do was show that one had started high school before the war or to take an entrance test. With many others, I signed up for high school, but before long, in 1946, the Modena school was transferred to southern England. In the summer of that year, I, too, was sent to England to prepare the quarters for the thousands of soldiers about to be moved from Italy to England. After the schools were reorganized in Britain, I had an opportunity to continue my schooling near Norwich, in East Anglia, and there I completed the four years of high school.

In the meantime, a concerted campaign was underway to encourage soldiers to go back to Poland. Yet opinions on the question of return were divided, and this created much confusion and disorientation among ordinary soldiers. The topic, so relevant and so emotional, was frequently and hotly debated. I remember one of the captains agitating in favour of remaining in the West. "We'll go back later, as true heroes, when Poland is free of the Soviets," he argued (soon afterwards he changed his mind and went back himself). He was answered by a young lieutenant, a Silesian, who said, "Listen, boys. In the past, political emigrants had never returned home, and not because they lacked good intentions. If you do want to go back, you must decide now." The future confirmed the wisdom of his words.

I did not agonize over my own personal decision to stay. I had maintained contact with my family in Poland and listened to the Polish radio broadcasts, so I had a fairly good grasp of the political situation there. I had no illusions and knew I would not return to live under the communists. Instead, I arranged for my demobilization and, disregarding British efforts to lure ex-servicemen into farming or mining jobs, I went to London to look for work on my own.

I began by washing dishes in restaurants but soon moved up to the position of stoker, tending furnaces and killing rats in basements. Climbing to the next level in the hierarchy of jobs then available, I became a "hotel engineer," meaning I repaired locks, unplugged sinks, changed carpets, and so on. The owner promised me further advancement, trying to dissuade me from my intention to pursue education. He could not understand why I wanted to waste so much time in school if I could earn decent pay working in his hotel. In the end, he assured me that if I ever needed a job, he would gladly take me back.

Needless to say, I did not give in to the temptations of decent pay but instead applied and was admitted to Joseph Conrad Korzeniowski

Senior High School in Hayden Park. About 200 students attended the school, all of whom were admitted through the same rigorous selection process and expected to excel in all their academic endeavours. Courses were all taught in English. I was in a hurry so I chose the most intensive program, which covered two grades in one year. I took my matriculation exam at London University. I was twenty-five then. Successful graduation from Joseph Conrad Senior High ensured a scholarship funded by the British government on the basis of an agreement with the Polish government-in-exile. I applied to several universities, but because my applications were late, I was politely turned down and invited to reapply in the following year. The only positive answer came from the University College, Dublin, and so to Dublin I went.

Under the influence of Professor Łojowski, one of my teachers in London, I decided to study physics. While a student, I was a frequent visitor at the Dublin School of Medicine. The reason for these visits was not my failing health but an attractive Polish female student, Alicja Gromnicka, who soon became my wife. Together with her parents, Alicja had been expelled from the Polish territory taken over by the Soviets. Her mother, who had Italian citizenship, was allowed to emigrate with her children to Italy. Her father had to remain in Russia and only later managed to rejoin them. Alicja began her medical studies in Bologna, but did her final years in Dublin, where she had moved with her family. And there we met. Our wedding took place in Manchester in 1952.

The Polish community in Dublin, though not numerous, was very well organized, partly because, for quite some time, a consulate of the Polish government-in-exile was located there. I belonged to an organization of about 100 Polish students in Dublin. After graduating from the Department of Physics, I found a job in a large company, Metropolitan Vickers, making electrical equipment and employing some 30,000 people. Since my Master's thesis was concerned with ionization of air, I was hired by the research department specializing in high voltage currents. At the same time, thanks to the generous support of Professor P. Nolan, my MA supervisor at the University College, I was also admitted to an extra-mural doctoral program, so I could both study and work to support my family. I received my doctorate (PhD) in 1959.

Working at Metropolitan Vickers, I often met Polish engineers who came to England for training provided under equipment licence agreements purchased in England by Polish companies. One of my responsibilities was taking care of them and preparing Polish translations of user manuals. My other responsibilities related to research on high voltage currents. From time to time, I presented the results of that work at the University of Manchester, and in the spring of 1960 the university offered me—and I accepted—the position of lecturer. Seven years later, I received the degree of Doctor of Science and was appointed to a professorship at the same university. While pursuing my academic career in Manchester, I did not lose sight of the Polish community and tried, to the extent allowed by my research and teaching, to contribute to and participate in its life. For instance, I organized and helped prepare our youth for the matriculation exams in Polish at the University of London.

In the late sixties, after many rainy years in England, we decided to seek a drier climate, and I accepted an invitation from the University of Manitoba to assume professorship in its Department of Electrical Engineering. My wife, Alicja, soon found work in the veterans' hospital, Deer Lodge. Unfortunately, our enthusiasm about Winnipeg was dampened and cooled by the first two winters, which were exceptionally cold and cruel. So once again we began to contemplate changing the climate. When the University of Windsor invited me to head their newly formed Department of Electrical Engineering, I accepted the invitation and, for the next eight years, steered that department towards its future. In 1977 I accepted a position at the University of Manitoba as head of Electrical Engineering, a much larger department than the one at Windsor. This challenge brought us back to the Prairies, this time for good. Two years later, in 1979, the university appointed me Dean of the Faculty of Engineering. In this position, my responsibilities extended to a whole group of engineering departments, such as Electrical, Mechanical, Civil, Geological, and Agricultural. I served two terms in that office, until 1989.

During my tenure as Dean, I strongly encouraged didactic and scientific initiatives and oversaw a considerable increase in academic activity in the Faculty of Engineering. I managed to convince the provincial government about the need to strengthen the engineering departments in Manitoba. Especially receptive to my arguments and helpful in my endeavours was Muriel Smith, at the time Minister of Economic Development. As a result, in the space of one year, we saw a thirty percent increase in funding for science and were able to establish two additional departments, Industrial and Computer Engineering. Finally, with the assistance of the Manitoba government, I was able to set up a special engineering program for members of the First Nations, the first such initiative in Canada.

During my academic career I wrote about 200 scientific publications, including several textbooks on high voltages and related phenomena. Those textbooks have been translated into many languages and have reached a wide audience at universities around the world. So wherever my academic travels take me, I meet people who studied or taught from them, and their familiarity with my name definitely helps in establishing new scientific contacts. Staying in touch with my former students, many of whom are now established scientists in positions of influence in various countries, has also proven beneficial, for they frequently invite me to give guest lectures or act as a consultant at their home institutions.

My scientific activities often took me to foreign countries, and I used those travels to promote international cooperation in scientific research on high voltage engineering and in development of engineering programs for the future. I participated in research initiatives sponsored by the Canadian International Development Agency and the International Development and Research Centre (IDRC). On behalf of those institutions, I organized scientific projects and training programs in Thailand, Malaysia, and China. My contacts with Chinese scientists have been particularly fruitful. Xian University awarded me the title of professor, and I continue to collaborate with its scientists to this day. With their assistance and with the financial support of the IDRC, we launched a four-year research plan, primarily in the area of discharges in gases. Although my contacts with China were perhaps most extensive, I also collaborated—during my sabbatical leaves—with universities in Japan, Australia, New Zealand, and Switzerland.

My lifelong contributions to science have been recognized also in Canada. In 1984 the Institute of Electrical and Electronic Engineering (IEEE) awarded me the Centennial Medal for "exceptional contributions in the area of engineering of high voltage currents isolation." Other honours followed. In 1988 I was elected member of the Canadian Academy of Engineering on the basis of my "exceptional contribution to the training of engineers and economic development of Canada";

and a year later, I was elected member of the IEEE on the grounds of my "exceptional contribution to the training of engineers and research on isolation of high voltage currents and on ionization phenomena."

Time flows swiftly yet imperceptibly, so it was with some surprise that I learned about the retirement of one of my first doctoral students. I, too, retired almost a decade ago but continue my professional activities by planning future collaborative projects with China.

Although my academic and scientific responsibilities prevented me from active participation in the work of the Polish Combatants Association, I did not lose touch with my old comrades in arms. I had become a member of the association while still in England, and, after arriving in Winnipeg, I joined Chapter #13. Here I found the spirit of old comradery very much alive, and here I revived some old friendships, among others with Kazimierz Smoliński, with whom I had not only served in the 15th Infantry Battalion but also shared a school bench in the division high school in Modena.

Summing up, I can say that I am quite pleased with what I have accomplished. Fate has been kind to me, has presented me with an opportunity, and I have tried to take full advantage of it. If I were to formulate a recipe for success in life on the basis of my experiences, I would have to say that one needs some talent, some luck, lots of hard work and persistence, and lots of confidence that one can do as well as others and maybe even a bit better.

Here I must add that a crucial ingredient of my professional success was the full support and understanding of my family: my wife Alicja and our four children, daughter Anna, born in Dublin, and sons Jan, Ryszard, and Piotr, all born in England. Anna followed in Alicja's footsteps and became a physician; the boys followed my example and are now engineers. It is to them, in large measure, that I owe my success in life and work.

WACŁAW KUZIA

I got my first glimpse of the world on the 15th of November, 1913, in Mały Płock near Łomża, on the river Narew. This region is known for having been swept over by the contending armies in both world wars. I was a tot of two when, during World War I, the Russians deported my parents to Siberia. For about six months the front line ran through our parts, and when the Russians finally began to withdraw, they ordered the evacuation—or, more precisely, the deportation—of the civilian population. My parents loaded their possessions and me on a large, open farm wagon (one wagon was all we were allowed to take), and we set out eastward. Eventually we reached Irkuck in Siberia, but the guards marched us right through it to a place seventy kilometres to the north. There they showed us a spot where we could settle down. We had to begin by constructing dugouts, the best type of dwelling for the Siberian climate. But ours never got completed, for my father, a very enterprising man, got us a permit to move back to Irkuck in exchange for his gold watch.

Soon my father was doing quite well in Siberia. From an estate which belonged to the Zamojskis, he bought a pair of large Belgian horses and began to make his living in the transportation business. In a short time he saved enough to buy a hectare and a half of land on the outskirts of Irkuck and started a vegetable farm. Our family was large, and there were enough hands to work the fields. Father decided to grow primarily cabbage, a good choice, for already in the first year the results were excellent: part of his produce he sold right away in Irkuck, and the other part he sent by railway to Tomsk.

The communist revolution, when it reached Irkuck, woke us up in the middle of the night with bursts of rapid gunfire. In the morning we learned that a colonel of the Tsar's army had been killed. I remember looking at his body sprawled out in the snow. The warm blood from his wounds had melted the snow around his body into small red craters. I was not yet five at the time, but that image burned itself into my memory for the rest of my life.

When the Soviets announced an amnesty in 1918, some Poles immediately decided to go back to Poland. But my father, well established by then, was in no hurry. Only when his parents began to press him that they wanted to lay down their bones in the Polish soil did he arrange to leave Irkuck. To take his horses with him on the train, he needed special permits, but with his resourcefulness, this did not pose a serious obstacle. The first train did not take us very far: in Omsk we were forced to get off and wait, out in the open, for the next one. Three weeks later it came, and this time we got as far as Sverdlovsk. Eventually we reached Mińsk, and from there travelled on horse-drawn wagons to Łomża, and on to Mały Płock. We were back at home. The house was still standing, but the barns had been burned to the ground. My father had brought lots of rubles from Siberia, and that money helped him restart the farm. He also sold one of the Belgian horses and bought a lesser horse and a cow.

Life was returning to normal, which for me meant school. When I finished primary school, I intended to sign up for junior high, but Father decided that his son would be a farmer, not a scribbler. Farming was not a bad way of life, and we were doing quite well. But despite our growing affluence, I felt something was missing from my life. So at first in private, and then more openly with the help of Stefan Wojtowicz, superintendent of the local extramural education program, I began to study junior high subjects, and eventually passed all the requisite exams as an external candidate.

In 1933 I was called in for military duty and assigned to the Gendarmerie Training Centre in Grudziądz. Later I served in the 1st Gendarmerie Division in Warsaw, located on Szucha Avenue, which looked after all military establishments in the capital, including the Ministry of Defence, Belvedere, and the villa of Marshal Piłsudski's wife. When Marshal Piłsudski died, a gendarmerie squadron was recruited to take part in the funeral cortege. It must have been soon afterwards that I stood guard at the villa. An elderly lady walked up to me, dressed all in black. As per instructions, I asked to see her identity card. She began to rummage through her bag but found nothing. "If you please let me go inside, I'll bring it for you," she said, somewhat disconcerted. At that moment I belatedly realized it was Marshal Piłsudski's wife herself. I clicked my heels together and apologized. She smiled faintly, nodded her head, and walked towards the house. Later, I reported this incident in my squadron to avoid any unnecessary hassle.

Having fulfilled my military obligation, I returned to the farm. In 1937 I was called up again for additional training but was given a two-years' reprieve, until 1939. In the meantime, I ran the farm and studied for two years at the agricultural school in Marianów.

In 1939, in the expectation of hostilities, the authorities ordered general mobilization. I reported to Łomża, to the same officer from whom I had received my training. His name was Adam Altkirche-Kirchmeier; later he discarded the first part of his name and remained Captain Kirchmeier. I was sent to Nowogród, where we stood guard on the bridge over the Narew. The civilian population was fleeing eastward en masse, pouring over the bridge we were guarding. In the chaos, I managed to convince one of the refugees, Wiśniewski, an acquaintance of our family, to go back and look after his farm. "If you just leave it like that," I said, "your farm will get pillaged." He thought about it for a minute and then turned back; the other refugees followed his example. He remembered this incident and years later, before his death, thanked my parents—for I did not meet him again—for my counsel.

Nowogród burned in front of my eyes. Łomża was in flames, too. On September 10, the Germans broke through the Narew line; soon, shattered and decimated, the 18th and 23rd divisions surrendered. Together with a few friends, we managed to break through the encirclement. We reached Grodno [Hrodna] and took part in its defence against the Soviets, but we were crushed. Hiding from the Soviet troops, we made our way to Lithuania. We knew the war was lost. With tears in our eyes, we threw away our weapons in such a way that no one could use them again. Some could not cope with the overpowering sense of despair. In Lithuania we were immediately interned, and thus in early November, I found myself in the camp in Wiłkomierz [Ukmergė]. The Lithuanians prohibited any celebration of Poland's

Independence Day on November 11, but, despite the ban, small banners and a flag appeared above the crowd of the internees. In response, the Lithuanian commanding officer ordered his men to shoot. Three unarmed Polish soldiers fell dead, and several were wounded.

Later the Lithuanians handed us over to the NKVD. An NKVD [state security police] major, standing in front of a line of internees, ordered, "Priests, engineers, doctors, gendarmerie, and Border Guard Corps, step to the right!" He also had a list of names, and from it he called out others who were members of the Polish intelligentsia. All of us were loaded onto railway cars and taken eastward. Rumours began circulating that we were being taken back to Poland. But I grew suspicious, even convinced, that we were going elsewhere after I saw a Soviet soldier breaking the thread on the window bars to prevent them from being unscrewed—a pointless precaution if we were being sent home. We soon discovered that we were going in a southeasterly direction, but exactly where, we could not figure out. Eventually they unloaded us at a small station and ordered us to march towards some camp, its towers visible on the horizon. We were stopped before the gate. It was hot, and several people lay down on the ground from fatigue. One of my buddies, Antoni Ruchała, sat on a stone; he moved it to the side a little and discovered a scrap of a newsprint, torn from the margin. On it, a hastily written note in Polish: "The last group was led out, as usual, in an unknown direction." We didn't know why they kept us so long in front of the gate. Towards evening, a team of Russian workers left the camp with buckets, brooms, rags, and such. It was obvious that they were erasing all traces of those who had been in the camp before us. Finally, we were led through two sets of gates in barbed wire fences. On one of the Eastern Orthodox churches in the distance, we noticed a metre-high inscription: Kozel'sk. As it turned out later, this was the camp from which Polish officers were taken to Katyn and murdered by the Soviets. But at the time we did not know this; we also did not know that we were the first group that lived through Kozel'sk, except for seven men who were led out one day and never returned. They disappeared without a trace.

At Kozel'sk we were sentenced, for crimes unknown, to various terms. I did not know the length of my sentence. Only later, when I was sent to the Kol'skiy [Kola] Peninsula and sentenced again for some minor infraction of the camp rules, I discovered that in the first instance I had received eight years. They took us to the Kol'skiy Peninsula by boats across the White Sea, then further inland by barges. At this latitude, the tundra consisted only of dwarf willows; the whole area was within the range of permafrost. We were brought to that frigid landscape to build roads and airfields, but we did not labour there for very long. When the German attacked the Soviets, we were again taken south. Our Polish government-in-exile knew about our group of interned soldiers, and it is possible that it was on its intervention that the Soviets released us relatively quickly. So once again we found ourselves on the train heading southeast. We got off at a place called Suzdal' and were quartered in the buildings of a monastery. After three days we were gathered in the courtyard, where a NKVD major announced our amnesty. The Soviet authorities had already known for some time that we would be released but treated us cruelly almost until the last day. I remember on a hot day, towards the end of our internment, we ran up to a well in the middle of the road to cool ourselves off. At that moment several shots rang out—the guards had given us no permission to drink. Two prisoners fell dead, and seven were wounded.

From Suzdal', we went to Tatishchevo. On arrival, I reported to the registry office, where recruits were assigned to various services. I did not want to go back to the gendarmerie; instead, I was considering the cavalry, artillery, even infantry. But as I walked in, I saw my former commanding officer, Captain Kirchmeier. He ran up to me exclaiming, "Wacław, the gods must have sent you here. You are my first true gendarme!"

And so I sank again into the military police. He placed me in the 5th Company of Gendarmerie, which was soon transferred to Kirgiz. One of our responsibilities there was to keep watch over the transports going to Krasnovodsk. One day, Kalbowiak and I were patrolling the tracks. We were walking along a branch line when suddenly the door of a nearby latrine swung open and out stepped an NKVD soldier, the same who, on the Kol'skiy Peninsula, had hit Antoni Ruchała so hard with his rifle that blood had burst from Antoni's mouth. We remembered the soldier's face well: marked by smallpox, with an L-shaped scar on the left cheek. The rifles rose automatically in our hands and pointed at him. He, too, recognized us, turned pale, and stood nailed to the ground. Back on the Kol'skiy Peninsula, he had told us that hair would grow on the palms of his hands before there was a Poland. We had sharp and painful memories of him. "Let's waste the son of a bitch," said Kalbowiak in his usual pointed manner. I was very tempted to press the trigger, but after a few seconds relaxed somewhat and replied, "Let him go in fear." I looked the Soviet soldier in the eye and said, "You may go but never forget this day!" Thinking about that incident now, half a century later, I think I did the right thing.

The first transports of Polish soldiers to Persia were a dirty and crowded affair: we had to cram the men into blackened coal barges like sardines into tin cans. The passage was most uncomfortable, but it took us to a land of plenty, or at least it seemed so to many of us at the time. Not surprisingly, many could not withstand the temptation of plentiful food, and there were many cases of sickness from overeating. Stanisław Iwanowski, a good buddy of mine, began to devour such quantities of hard-boiled eggs that I knew he would soon regret it. I knocked some eggs out of his hand and stamped them to the sand. Enraged, Stanisław jumped at me with his fists, although he didn't stand much chance. But we stayed friends, and he soon realized the folly of his compulsion when he saw several starvelings, like himself, almost at the verge of death because they could not resist the temptation to eat. We managed to rescue them, but only just.

In Iraq we had to contend not only with unruly soldiers but also with the much more powerful forces of nature. Soldiers we could control; nature occasionally wrought havoc upon us. One violent *hamsyn*, or desert hurricane, blew across our camp with so much force that in our 5th Company not a single tent was left standing.

Ordinary soldiers did not always appreciate the gendarmerie, but I enjoyed a rather playful, even flattering, nickname: "the righteous Wacuś."* True, I tried to be a gendarme with a heart. At the time we had some problems with the Women's Auxiliary Corps, and I had the dubious pleasure of being on duty in the 317th Transport Company staffed by women volunteers, nicknamed *Pestki*. It was not an easy posting. One hot day, a female volunteer had an accident: her truck flipped over to the side. The vehicle was slightly damaged, but she managed to get out of it with only minor scratches. I just happened to be driving by, and what did I see but a shaking, crying volunteer, her

---

* "Wacuś" is a diminutive form of "Wacław."

eyes watering the desert sand. But her tears had less to do with the driving mishap than the fact that she saw that I saw that she had her boyfriend, a cadet officer, with her in the cab, which was strictly forbidden by regulations. To make matters worse, her boyfriend lost his cool and turned on me with some harsh words. I was aware of the quandary they found themselves in and of the potential consequences. So despite the gallant's angry words, I showed them some heart and wrote a lenient report, which allowed them to get out of that mess.

From Iraq, I was sent to Palestine to find quarters for the 5th Company of Gendarmerie. In Rehovot lodging was scarce, so it was decided that the unit would be based in Gedera. There was lots of work for us there, hard work. The soldiers had little to do: the main reason for their stay in Gedera was to help them recover from malnutrition and return to good physical condition. From all that eating and little work, the whole company ran loose like the proverbial beggar's whip. Our hands were full most of the time. I recall how, once, soldiers from the Carpathian Brigade smashed a restaurant run by a Jew from Poland. As I walked into the building, I encountered a soldier, flushed and not entirely steady on his feet, waving a bottle in my direction. And yet I managed to convince him to get out of there before the military police from Rehovot arrived: the Rehovot guys would have little sympathy for the youthful, alcohol-induced over-exuberance.

In Egypt, we patrolled Ismailia and the surrounding area, the road to Cairo, and especially Zagāzig [Az Zaqāziq]. The city was forbidden to our soldiers, but the prohibition posed no great obstacle for them: we found them in the city almost nightly. The New Year celebrations in Cassasin, which I remember very well, were another example of the cavalier spirit with which the camps were bursting. As midnight neared, soldiers began shooting into the air, first with blanks, then with live ammunition, finally with anti-aircraft guns. There were several accidents—fortunately none fatal—and it took some effort to restrain this explosive enthusiasm. During the cannonade, we received a phone call that one of our jeeps had collided with an Egyptian truck. I was sent to investigate and so did not witness the conclusion of the noisy festivities.

While still in Egypt, I was sent for a special training course for traffic-control instructors. This kept me busy for quite some time, and I was given a few days off only shortly before my unit's departure from

Egypt. I joined a group of soldier-tourists and travelled with them across southern Egypt, ending the trip in Port Said. Soon afterwards our 5th Company boarded a ship and was ready to cross the Mediterranean. At the last minute, another gendarme and I were called off the ship and sent back to train the new cadre. These orders were not much to our liking, but orders were orders; we grumbled but carried them out.

I continued training new personnel almost until the end of the war. Thus I did not have a chance to settle my personal score with the Germans. I missed a chance to repay them, not only for the buddies I had lost at the beginning of the war, but also for what they put my mother through. The Germans were taking her before a firing squad for hiding a young Jewish woman in a cowshed when she was rescued, at the last minute, by a regional administrator, an old, retired Prussian general by the name of Grabowsky, a Mazurian by birth.

In the middle of June 1944, I went to Naples, where I was promoted to platoon leader. The black market was flourishing there, but fighting it was like ploughing the sand. It was there that the end of the war found us, and there we began to think of our futures. But to some of us it was not given to enjoy the fruits of freedom. A friend of mine, deeply in love, was making arrangements to bring his fiancée to Naples. Having dodged hundreds of enemy bullets, he died one night of a heart attack. We had to send word to his fiancée not to come.

From Naples I went to England. I re-established contact with my family, and in their first letter they encouraged me to go back to Poland. But the second letter seemed to suggest that it would be safer for me to remain abroad because of my political involvement before the war. Ten of my buddies decided to return to Poland, but only one of them survived. The rest simply disappeared. I never had any doubts that my decision to stay in the West was the right one.

I came to Manitoba in May 1947 to do contract work on a sugar beet farm. I was not afraid of farmwork, for I had known it since childhood. From the train windows, we could see the fields still covered by snow: for a fleeting moment we thought we were back in Siberia. But finally, many days after we left Halifax, we arrived in Winnipeg. At first we were lodged in the Osborne Barracks, but later many of us found individual quarters. I proudly took part in that first, now famous, parade, with all of us marching in our uniforms. We were no longer in the army, but we still took pride in our group identity. And we spared no effort to take care of our own: I, for instance, was sent right away by Kazimierz Klimaszewski to Emerson to prepare quarters and to collect ice necessary to preserve food for our group. That first season I worked in the fields. For the second, a farmer signed my contract although, in truth, he didn't need a helper. Eventually I started looking for work in the city, but good jobs were very scarce. Once I applied for a job in a coal yard. The owner looked at my decent clothes and said the job was not for me. In the end I got that job, but the owner was right: I lasted there only two weeks. Then I worked for the Canadian Furniture Factory on Main Street. For fifty-two cents an hour, we made frames for furniture. I was doing quite well, so well, in fact, that the owner gave me a two-dollar bonus, which at the time was a considerable amount. And yet, one Saturday afternoon, I found an even better job as a carpenter at a construction company called Haag Construction Ltd. I stayed with that company for the next six years; during that time I learned how important hard work and dependability were. My hands became scarred, but my workmanship was appreciated: I was promoted first to gang leader and later, in 1948, to foreman.

In 1949 I started building my own house, and as soon as it was ready, I married. My wife, Genowefa, is also Polish and, like myself, had been deported to Russia by the Soviets. Her father joined the 2nd Corps, while she, with the rest of the family, made her way through Asia to Mexico and finally to Winnipeg. Although we had plenty of wartime memories to share, we preferred to look towards the future: in 1951 our son, Henryk, was born and three years later Krystyna, our daughter.

By that time, I had learned enough of the construction business that I decided to set up my own company and be my own boss. To this day, I remain the owner of K. and K. Construction Company Ltd., and although I retired a few years ago, the company still prospers.

In my time, I built hundreds of homes, but the one I remember best is that first one, my own. I remain deeply attached to it. The flood of 1953 almost broke my heart: water reached forty centimetres above the floor level, devastating the first floor, so meticulously finished in specially selected oak boards. With the fury of a Polish soldier, I swore at the waters that turned my hard work into mud; then I tore up the wasted flooring and started building my house again.

I built my home on Canadian soil, but it has always been a Polish home. I am proud that both my children finished university and speak Polish fluently. So does my little grandson. My son-in-law is a major in the Canadian army. I was once invited by his unit as one of several guests of honour on the occasion of some regimental festivities. As each guest was being introduced, the band played some bars from the march of his regiment. But since no one there knew the march of my regiment, they played for me an excerpt from Chopin's "Revolutionary Étude." It was a touching gesture, and I was so proud of my Polish roots, and of my children, and my son-in-law.

Living in the Canadian present, I did not lose touch with the people from my military past. One of them was Dr. Wiktor Turek,* whom I met in the Middle East and who made a big impression on me. A few years later, I helped him immigrate from Lebanon to Winnipeg; here he and his family stayed in our home until the flood of 1953. Wiktor was a demon for work, pouring over books with a stamina I had not suspected he had. I often found him in the kitchen in the wee hours of the morning, still engrossed in his papers after a night of heavy reading. Three months after his arrival in Winnipeg, he was already giving a lecture on international law for local lawyers in one of the halls of the courthouse.

I have also stayed in touch with my comrades in arms. I have been a member of the Polish Combatants Association, Chapter #13, since its inception and for two years served as president. Things have changed greatly since the early years when we were struggling to keep our chapter from disintegrating while looking for a suitable home for it. Some saw no need for the chapter after the expiry of the farm labour contracts; but others, bold spirits, thumped the tables and strained their throats to convince the doubters that we could and should build a hall of our own. We had considered building jointly with Polish Gymnastic Association Sokół, a more established Polish organization in Winnipeg, but they were $32,000 rich and we had barely $1700. We did not seem strong-enough partners for them. And so we decided to build without their help. Three of us signed the mortgage papers; several more came to work on the site. Not everyone believed in the project: it was a time of turmoil and heated arguments. But in the end we proved wrong all

---

* Wiktor Turek (1910-63), lawyer, bibliographer, and historian of Polish immigration to Canada.

those who thought that we dreamed too wildly. We realized that dream, for ourselves and for those who will succeed us.

Now that I hear talk of building a common Polish House in Winnipeg, I fear that history might repeat itself, that short-sighted interests of individual organizations might thwart a wonderful initiative. I think we should all support that project, we should all dare to dream. I certainly will, for as long as I breathe.

MARIAN LISOWSKI

I was born on April 5, 1919, in Obuchowicze [Obukhovichi], district Grodno [Hrodna], province Białystok. I did not serve in the army before the war, nor did I take part in the September campaign. World War II came to our town in late September, hand-in-hand with the Soviets. Their planes circled above the town, dropping leaflets that explained they were freeing us from the yoke of Polish "lords." Many Belarussians, who made up half the town's population—the other half being Polish—began forming committees to welcome the "liberators." My aunt was coerced into picking flowers in her garden and throwing them under the feet of the marching Soviet soldiers. But this enthusiasm was short-lived, and scarcely two weeks later, the same Belarussians complained that "it was much better under Poland."

The announcement of conscription to the Red Army was perhaps the worst of the harsh measures introduced by the new Soviet authorities. Everyone was crying, Poles and Belarussians alike. They put us into freight cars and sent us southeast, to Baku in the Caucasus. In a single building in the barracks, there were eighty-six of us Poles from the province of Białystok. The barracks were part of a Soviet anti-aircraft artillery officer college. Of course, it was not us who were being trained as officers there; our duty was to maintain the compound, although some of us did receive rudimentary training. I was sent for six months to a driving school. Since I did not know enough Russian, I had to take notes and write down all instructions in Polish. Despite that handicap, I passed the course with the score of ninety-five percent!

Other Poles also passed their exams with much better scores than the locals. I am not sure why, although I suspect that it may have been our national pride that pushed us to excel.

On the day Germany attacked the Soviet Union, all the Poles were gathered and sent to a transition camp in Georgia. There were rumours that the Soviets wanted to organize a Polish army to fight the Germans, but apparently the first attempts were not successful because many Poles deserted and ran to the Germans. I did not know if there was any truth to those rumours; if so, the Russians must have changed their minds about the Polish army, for they sent us to labour battalions and not to the front. And yet, some time later, we learned that the Polish army was forming somewhere in the south of Russia. Our requests for permission to join it were consistently denied.

The Soviets moved our brigade from place to place. At one point, a group of drivers, including myself, was sent back to Baku, and then by boats to a small island south of that city, where the Soviets were building some special fortifications and cisterns for fresh water. Starvation and atrocious working conditions took the lives of many Polish conscripts. There were even cases of suicides; death seemed preferable to that nightmarish life.

After six months, they transferred us to Armenia, near the Turkish border. With six others, I planned to escape to Turkey, but at the last minute we were warned that the Turks returned all escapees to the Soviets. Under such circumstances, an escape looked too risky. Instead, we kept insisting that we wanted to join the Polish army. The Soviets tried to persuade us to declare ourselves as Belarussians, which would qualify us for the Soviet army, and to join the ranks of *komsomoltsy*, or young communists. Some gave in to those pressures, but I was determined to resist them at all cost.

The issue of the Polish army could not be ignored for ever. In the end, the Soviets relented and compiled a register of all Polish citizens who wanted to join their national forces. Then those who had let themselves be deluded by the propaganda and signed the Belarussian lists pulled their hair in frustration. Those who persevered were shipped to Guzar in central Asia, one of several gathering points of the Polish army, and were handed over to the Polish military authorities. And yet, for many of us this was not a happy ending. Not only was the climate in Guzar intolerable, but soon all kinds of infectious diseases began to reap a grim harvest of death. Spotted fever, typhoid fever, and dysentery were raging throughout the camp. Soldiers were dying like flies, so much so that, at times, there were not enough healthy hands to dig the graves for the dead.

In the midst of these lethal epidemics, I was assigned to a communications battalion. With that battalion, I left the Soviet Union for Pahlavi in Persia. Immediately upon arrival, we went through intensive delousing, burning of our old uniforms, and reassignments to various services. I was attached to a lancers regiment. The food was also different from what we had known in Russia. They fed us mutton, lots of fat mutton, which caused many a stomach cramp and sometimes even a more serious condition. Our bodies could not tolerate such a sudden change from starvation to an abundance of rich food.

To drive us from Pahlavi to Iraq, the army hired local trucks and drivers. The ride along the steep, winding mountain trails was as breathtaking as it was dangerous. There were many accidents, and competent drivers were always in short supply. With my driving credentials from the Soviets, I had my hands on the wheel most of the time. The army was urgently training new young drivers, but the supply never quite met the demand. When we were moved to Qizil Ribat [As Sa'dīyah], we met the women's units there, the so-called *Pestki*. They served in communications and transport.

From Iraq, we were relocated, again by trucks, to Palestine. The road was long and monotonous, and you had to make a conscious effort to stay alert. The Palestinian camps continued the program of physical rehabilitation, gradually restoring our bodies, wasted in the wilderness of Russia, to a combat-ready condition. As the intensity of our training increased, we also received plenty of brand new equipment, compliments of General Anders, who was particularly fond of our Podole Lancers Regiment. In due course, we boarded ships bound for Alexandria, taking all our weapons and vehicles with us. Each ship carried personnel from all types of services: this was the British system, designed to ensure that even if a ship were sunk by the enemy, no military unit would be wiped out completely.

Our ultimate destination was the Italian front. We went into action almost immediately upon unloading in Taranto, going out on patrols and never shying away from a fight. During the assault on Monte Cassino, I was assigned to the command troop and often drove our regimental commander, Colonel Fudakowski. He was extremely popular with the soldiers, as was Colonel Florkowski, who made sure that his lancers never went to battle on an empty stomach. When Monte Cassino finally fell, our 12th Regiment of the Podole Lancers was allowed to hoist its guidon on the ruins of the stronghold. After Monte Cassino, we were repositioned near Piedmont, but as an infantry unit; so many of our drivers had been killed or wounded in action that those who remained unharmed had to make several trips to move all the vehicles. Later we pushed the front to the Adriatic coast, fording mined rivers, taking town after small town, and finally launching a major assault on Bologna.

And then the war ended. In spite of that, we continued to train new drivers to maintain combat-readiness. It was by no means rare to see a lancer teaching his superior officer how to manoeuvre a military vehicle. We savoured—but did not abuse—those moments when we could polish the military skills of the brass.

Some of my saddest memories from that period are of our disarmament in Tingoli. Over the years, we had grown attached to our equipment: it had protected our lives, and we had kept it clean and in perfect working order. So no wonder that when we had to part with it, when we saw giant bulldozers crush our sparkling vehicles, we had tears in our eyes. But such was the harsh logic of war. Deprived of their equipment, the soldiers felt confused and cast adrift; but it was not long before they, too, became surplus personnel and were cut loose.

We left Tingoli for Britain. I had no qualms about not returning to Poland. Those who made it through the camps of Russia lost all illusions about the Soviet system. I did not meet a single person who had escaped its claws and still wanted to go back into its grip. In England, I decided to appear before a commission qualifying for emigration to Canada. The commission paid special attention to the marital status (those who were married were rejected outright), physical condition, and rudimentary knowledge of agriculture (the ability to milk cows was a plus). I was directed to Winnipeg, Manitoba, while still in England, and a little note was pinned to my army coat with that assignment. Frankly, it did not matter much to me where I was sent; as a soldier, I was quite used to being moved from place to place and had developed a special ability to adapt to new conditions.

We sailed forth from Southampton, and on May 25, 1947, arrived in

Halifax, Canada. There we transferred onto a train; from its windows we caught our first glimpses of this country: open fields covered by snow, glittering in the sunlight. It was the end of May, but we were shivering with cold. Luckily, the reception in Winnipeg was much warmer: we were welcomed by the local Polish community and the Canadian military, who transported us to the Osborne Barracks. Soon after our arrival in Winnipeg, we took part in a military parade down Portage Avenue: I remember showers of applause as we marched by the gathered crowds.

A week later, we left for the sugar beet plantations of Emerson, where we took over the barracks vacated by German POWs. Our leader was Kazimierz Klimaszewski, who knew the language well and served as an interpreter. With rain every other day, the weather was lousy, and so was the pay. We earned next to nothing for those weeks of hard work. On payday, I was called to the clerk, who said to me, "You're a good labourer; you owe me only a dollar. Others are deep in debt." When we finished thinning out the beets, farmers came and hired us for the harvest. I and two of my friends happened to be chosen by a very decent family. Their farm was well run, and they treated us like human beings. Driving a tractor, I was making $7 per day. Despite the blood-sucking plague of mosquitoes, I quite enjoyed that work. In the fall, we returned to the sugar beet fields to help with harvesting the beets. This time we were paid by the ton of lifted beets, so if you worked hard, you could make much more than in the spring.

Afterwards, I was sent to work on a farm in McGregor, Manitoba. The farmer refused to pay a cent more than the minimal rate set by the government—$40 a month. For one month I worked fourteen hours a day driving a tractor, and then I quit. The work was brutal and the benefits minimal. The Employment Office in Winnipeg reassigned me to work in the grain elevators of the Grain Company. Here, too, the work was hard, but at least we were being paid sixty cents an hour. I probably would have stayed at that job till the end of my two-year contract if my health had not started to deteriorate: I became quite sick from all the dust in the elevator. At that point I decided to take charge of my own future and signed up for a hairstyling course, hoping for a clean and relatively well-paying job. I got it in 1954 and continued in that line of work for two decades. When the establishment I was working for closed down, I was ready to try something else, so with two friends of mine, I applied for a job—and got it—with a company called Maintenance and Engineering. For the last twelve years before my retirement, I worked as a cleaner at the University of Manitoba, and that's where I secured a pension.

It just so happened that the year I retired was the fortieth anniversary of the Battle at Monte Cassino. With lots of time on my hands, I decided to go back to Italy and revisit the places I had once known. The changes were, of course, dramatic, and the country was completely rebuilt after the wartime devastation: I saw beautiful highways, modern hotels, and elegant shops. The town of Monte Cassino has also been transformed, and I could no longer find the spots once familiar to me. Only the red poppies are still the same. I brought a bunch of dried poppies with me back to Canada.

I joined the Polish Combatants Association [PCA] while still in Tingoli and was an active member both in England and Canada. The PCA looked after our interests while we were working on the farms and, together with the weekly *Czas*, helped us stay in touch with the world and one another. After a short lapse caused by illness, I renewed my membership in 1956. For many years now, I have served in the organization's colour guard, both on happy occasions and on sad ones, such as when we pay our last respects to colleagues who have passed away. I am quite satisfied with my life, financially secure, and optimistic about the future.

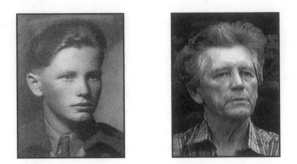

HENRYK LORENC

I was born in 1928 in the province of Stanisławów [Ivano-Frankivs'k], in Podole [Podolia]. We lived in a village we called Polska Wola. My father was a veteran of the Polish-Soviet war of 1920: he had served in the army of General Haller, been wounded, and finished his military career in the 49th Infantry Regiment in Stanisławów.

I was eleven years old when the war broke out in 1939, but I remember well the tense atmosphere of those days. In late September we knew the war with Germany was not going well: columns of Polish armoured units could be seen withdrawing towards Kołomyja [Kolomyya], and further to Romania. Transports were rolling day and night, all in the same southerly direction. When the war finally reached us, the enemy came not from the west but from the east: the Soviets invaded on September 17, and within days had overrun the entire region. At first, the rural, mostly Ukrainian, population greeted them with enthusiasm, deluded as much by their own wishful thinking as by the Soviet propaganda. But our village was settled mostly by Poles. Before the war my father had been a tax collector and later had become a secretary in our rural district office. We were not rich, so it was not wealth but our nationality that visited upon us the evils of Soviet repression.

The Soviets began to deport those known to be Polish patriots into the heartland of Russia immediately after the invasion; mass deportations started only in 1940, with the first wave on February 10 and the second on April 19. The last massive uprooting of the Polish population took place in June 1941, just before the outbreak of the German-Soviet war. We were among the first to be taken, on February 10, 1940. I remember that day very well—bitterly cold and frightful. Before dawn, someone started banging on the door. My father got up and opened it. In a blast of freezing air, a Soviet soldier walked in, followed by an officer. "Get your things and get out," the officer said. Father had been prepared for the arrest, had been expecting it, so he started to dress. "All of you," the officer raised his voice. They had come for the whole family. He gave us half an hour to pack but did not let us take any clothes except what we wore. Then we were ordered onto a sleigh and driven to Tłumacz [Tlumach], the closest train station. Our entire village was in that transport, with only a few families missing. They packed us into freight cars, those used for moving cattle, and slammed the doors shut, without as much as telling us our destination. "You'll be better off there than here," was all we heard from them. At Kotlas, they transferred us onto large barges drawn by tractors. Several days later, and six weeks after leaving Polska Wola, we finally arrived "there"—one of three camps north of Kotlas and east of Arkhangelsk, in Komi. Our camp, number 3, had been previously occupied by the resettled Ukrainians, but most of them had died of hunger and exhaustion. The closest human abode was a small town of Chasovo on the river Vychegda, a tributary of the Severnaya Dvina. We were placed in a large shanty made of logs, and assigned one bunk bed in a communal dormitory. One bunk bed per family. There was one common kitchen but nothing to cook. Our main meal, provided courtesy of the Soviet authorities, was fish soup, often cooked from rotten fish with some bones thrown in. It stank to high heaven. At first no one wanted to touch it, but hunger, gut-wrenching hunger, dulls the senses and whets the appetite. The life I experienced there was exactly what Solzhenitsyn described in *One Day in the Life of Ivan Denisovich*.

I was a sixth-grader then, so the authorities sent me to a *komsomol* [communist youth] high school in Chasovo. It was attended mostly by Russian youth and by the Komi locals, with whom we were billetted. I felt like a complete stranger there; the entire surroundings were alien to me. To make matters worse, the teachers wanted to turn us into instant communists. I strongly resented their zeal and, together with a friend, made a statement by scratching out the eyes on the portraits of Lenin and Marx. All hell broke loose when this was discovered. The staff began looking for the culprits. Sensing danger, we decided to run. We struggled through thirty kilometres of dangerous wilderness before reaching our settlement, luckily for us, just as the amnesty was being announced. That saved our skins.

The news of the amnesty, giving us back our freedom, reached our camp in October 1941. Some did not want to believe the news and smelled in it another Soviet provocation. But the camp commander confirmed that we were free to go. The immediate problem was how to get out. My father, one of the most energetic and venturesome people in the camp, immediately gathered our belongings and prepared back-packs for all of us, that is, himself, Mother, my two younger sisters, one younger brother, and me. My youngest brother was not with us: born on the way to the north, he had not survived the hardships of the camp. We set out on foot to Chasovo. My father's friend, Mr. Leśniak, came with us. We did not have any papers confirming our official release from the camp, but Father did have some passes, although I do not recall what exactly they were for. We had to hurry to catch some transport down the river before it froze. In Chasovo, we caught a ride on a coal barge returning empty to Kotlas. The passage took several days in hunger and cold and choking coal dust. At the train station in Kotlas, we met, quite by chance, my aunt, returning from another camp in the region. From Kotlas, we aimed south, but trains never moved in a straight line. Our train rides lasted from October till the end of December and took us across the Ural Mountains not once, but twice.

I am not sure I can describe the emotions that swirled in me at the first sight of Polish soldiers at the train station in Sverdlovsk. The feelings were beyond words. I swelled with national pride and was buoyed with a mixture of hope and faith. "Go to Bukhara," we were told. "Polish units are forming; they'll look after you." And so we did. From Bukhara, we were sent further south, to Kasan. Finally, we knew we were free—hungry and dirty but free.

From that long train journey, I remember an event that might have ended in tragedy. At one of the stations, Father left the train to go look for bread. Finding food was our constant preoccupation. People shared every crumb with one another, which meant, of course, that all went hungry all the time. Having money did not help much, for basic staples were in such a short supply that the most effective method of getting food was stealing it. I did it, too, and I feel no shame admitting it. We wanted to live. At that small station, our train was supposed to wait for two hours, but for some reason it pulled out, leaving Father behind. Fortunately, he realized the danger, chased the train, and was lucky to catch up with us.

In Kasan, the diplomatic mission of the Polish government-in-exile took all Polish refugees under its protection. It sent us to a *kolkhoz* [collective farm], running mostly cotton plantations on the Amu Darya River. The intentions of the Polish bureaucrats may have been good, but it was a God-forsaken place, and eventually our government forsook it as well. Father realized that sooner than others and arranged for us a passage back to Kasan, first by barge down the Amu Darya River to Tûrtkûl and from there by train. Back at the diplomatic mission headquarters, we met Mr. Zakrzewski, who found us a place in a nearby *kolkhoz* located between Kasan and Kermine. The location was better than on the Amu Darya, but in those days there was no hiding from death.

Assured that the government would now look after us, Father joined the Polish army in Kermine and was assigned to the 22nd Infantry Regiment of the 5th Division. To make doubly sure someone took care of us in his absence, he made a pair of officer boots for the commander of the *sovkhoz* [state farm]. Any Russian would sell his soul for such boots. The commander, an NKVD [state security police] officer, supplied the leather, and Father made the boots in exchange for a promise of assistance for his family. And I must admit that the commander stayed true to his word.

With Father in the army, we had to fend for ourselves. It was not easy, for we had no money and no food. We ate anything edible. Once the two Machniak brothers, now also Winnipeggers, killed a *sovkhoz* dog. They brought it to our shack, and we had some meat. We also caught turtles in the Uzbec desert, gathered edible grasses, anything to fill our bellies. But there was never enough: from starvation and dysentery and scarlet and typhoid fevers died my younger sister, Jasia, and my younger brother, Alojzy. My little brother suffered terribly from dysentery, and to this day I remember his cries. Soon after his death, Mother fell sick with typhoid fever. I immediately ran to the *sovkhoz* commander and begged him to let Mother be admitted to the *sovkhoz* hospital. He agreed. The commander's wife once confessed to us that she was a Catholic, although her husband, of course, knew nothing about it. While Mother was in the hospital, she always found for us a piece of bread or cheese, and thanks to her the rest of us managed to stay alive. One day, when I came to see Mother, I found the commander's wife sad and somehow changed. She told me Mother was dying and would not let me see her. After much pleading, she relented, and I discovered that Mother, not quite dead yet but already unconscious, had been moved to the morgue and covered with a white sheet. I was so shaken by that sight that, back in our shack, I became violently ill. I developed a high fever and went into a coma. I recovered my senses only seventeen days later—a miracle, no doubt. When I opened my eyes in the evening, still only half conscious, I saw Mother standing above me. I did not know whether I was asleep or awake. I asked her— so they told me later—if I could whistle. "Of course you can whistle," she said. And I whistled with all my might. The next morning my fever was gone, and I discovered that the commander's wife had managed to convince the doctor to take my mother back into the hospital. He did, and she survived. And thanks to God, she is still alive today.

Not much later, my grandma died. Still reeling from all those tragedies, we suffered another blow: we were informed that Father had died in the army, not from an enemy bullet but from disease. At the time, at least thirty corpses were carried away from the tents every morning. It was a true harvest of death.

By then we were already registered as a military family. Lieutenant Wnęka, a wonderful man who helped hundreds of refugee families, promised us we would not be left to perish in Russia. He also ensured that we were transferred to a more prosperous *kolkhoz*, where we even received some food supplies from the American relief effort. Slowly, we regained some vestiges of hope and recovered from severe malnutrition. Life even became so tolerable that I bothered to learn some Uzbec.

Finally, after months of waiting, we received word that we should report to the convoy leaving Kermine on August 15. In Kermine, we were plunged into crowds, chaos, and noise. Joy mixed with despair as some were departing while others had to stay behind. The three of us survivors—my mother, my sister, and myself—boarded a train bound for Krasnovodsk. I remember our arrival there: the sun was just rising, the morning still fresh. We got off onto the dirty, oil-stained seashore, and from there were soon led aboard a ship. It was only after disembarking in Persia that we dared to believe that we were truly free.

At first we were quartered in tents. After compulsory disinfection, our old clothes were all burned, and we got new ones from a Catholic refugee relief foundation. Then buses took us to Tehrān, where a week later we were selected for a transfer to an African camp. The transfer was slow: first by train to Ahvāz, two weeks later by boat to a transition camp in Karāchi, Pakistan, and after another month by boat to Tanganyika [Tanzania]. In Karāchi, my mother suffered a return of her sickness, but we pleaded with the authorities that she be allowed to travel with the rest of us. But eventually she got so sick that she had to be left in the hospital in Mombasa, while my sister and I went on to the camp in Tengeru.

Immediately after our arrival, we went to school. We had to make up for the years wasted in Russia, so we covered two grades in one year. I also joined Scouting, which was superbly organized and charged with patriotic fervour. But I desperately wanted to be in the air force. Unfortunately, I was only fifteen, and they would not take me without my mother's permission. She was dead set against my high-flying dreams because it was soon after the tragic death of General Sikorski.[*] It was not until the following year, at the ripe age of sixteen, that I managed to convince Mother to allow me to sign up for the Youth Corps. In April 1945, I was officially admitted to the Polish Armed Forces, and a month later Germany capitulated. The war ended without my help.

I have heard accusations directed against the Polish refugee authorities that they pushed youth to join the army. But nothing could be further from the truth: the youth, growing up in the patriotic atmosphere of the camps, needed no encouragement. We were bright kids, wise beyond our age, and we knew quite well what freedom meant. We were eager to fight for it and, if need be, die for it.

I was assigned to the 56th Independent Communications Platoon in Al Qassasin, engaged by the security forces to guard various military objects against Arab attacks. We left Egypt, bound for England, in 1947. Shortly after arriving there, I arranged for Mother and my sister to join me. Unlike some of my friends, I had no qualms about staying

---

[*] General Władysław Sikorski, premier of the Polish government-in-exile and the commander-in-chief of the Polish armed forces, died in a plane crash near Gibraltar in 1943.

in the West: our home was now on the Soviet territory, and one stint in Siberia was quite enough for me. I was formally discharged from the army and joined the Resettlement Corps. After working for a year at a civilian job, I realized that my prospects in England looked rather bleak and decided to emigrate. I set my heart on Canada, since some of our relatives were already there. I applied at the Canadian embassy in London, and, without much ado, in 1949 set my foot on Canadian soil.

I became a member of the Polish Combatants Association [PCA] while still in the Middle East. The association was the idea of General Anders,* who strongly encouraged joining the organization while we were still in our regular units. My membership card was numbered 46. In England I had few contacts with the association, but I renewed my membership after settling down in Winnipeg. I re-entered the PCA at the time when it was experiencing a serious identity crisis. One of the first meetings I attended in 1949 was the general assembly in the Polish House of the Parish of the Holy Spirit that debated whether the PCA should continue as an independent organization or whether we should forget our Polish roots and join the Canadian Legion. Many of our former colleagues at arms left the ranks of the PCA, which shrank down to twenty-five or thirty members. At that crucial meeting, Mr. Zybała, editor of *Głos Polski* (*Polish Voice*), suggested that I take charge of the cultural section of our organization. I accepted the challenge and began by organizing variety shows—we called them "tea-time with a mike"—every Sunday in the Holy Spirit Parish hall. Most Polish ex-servicemen were still bachelors, so the shows were popular with them, especially since they also attracted many young women, immigrants from labour and refugee camps in Germany and elsewhere. Not surprisingly, the shows ended with ever-popular dances. In a more ambitious vein, we organized an amateur theatre and staged several plays, including N. Sadek's *The Quarters on the Adriatic* and *Sutler Girls,* and T. Dołega-Mostowicz's *The Third Gender.* I acted as both director and choreographer. In 1966, when Poland was celebrating a millennium of Christianity, we staged I. Kraszewski's *The Old Legend,* one of our final productions.

---

* Władysław Anders (1892-1970), commander of the Polish army in the Soviet Union (later the 2nd Polish Corps).

We complemented our artistic ventures with a series of politically invigorating talks by such guest speakers as General Tokarzewski, former ambassador and minister Tadeusz Romer, generals Duch, Kopański, Anders, Sosnkowski, and many others.

Thanks to those cultural initiatives, our chapter of the PCA earned new respect in the Polish community, and it earned new members, too. In fact, by 1963 we had grown sufficiently self-confident, not to say prosperous, that we decided to expand and refurbish our club. We purchased it in 1955—an old furniture store on Main Street—and renovated it with our own hands. Now I was given the responsibility of chairing the committee in charge of its expansion. At the risk of sounding self-congratulatory, I think the expanded facilities have served us well over the years.

Shortly after our arrival in Winnipeg, both my wife and I joined the choir of the Polish Gymnastics Association Sokół. Eventually I became the artistic director of that choir, serving until 1966. At the same time, I founded a dance ensemble under the patronage of Sokół, which marked the beginning of my lifelong involvement with our Polish youth in Canada. In 1967 I founded a similar ensemble for the PCA and led it for seventeen years. At first, my new troupe called itself Młodzi Kombatanci [Young Combatants], but later we changed the name to Iskry [Sparks]. Hundreds of young people, many of them—though not all—children of the veterans, passed through my rehearsals. Our doors were open to anybody curious about Polish culture, and we did our best to keep our traditions alive in Canada. Ours was no small task: to inspire young imaginations with our memories of Polish glory required much ingenuity and patience; to deal with the parents, not always appreciative of our efforts, required even more patience and perseverance. But in the end, our dance ensemble was both a cultural and social success: our Polish dances dazzled audiences from Vancouver to Montreal and in the process infused the love of art and culture in generations of young Polish Canadians.

In addition to my various artistic engagements, I also served two terms as president of the PCA Chapter #13, in Winnipeg. Initially my professional responsibilities conflicted somewhat with the demands of the presidency, but that changed during my second year. I always took my responsibilities very seriously, so I tried to set the tone and direction for the organization, demanding a lot from myself but also from our membership. I am aware that I was not very popular as president, but I take comfort in the knowledge that many of my organizational reforms have stayed in place to this very day.

The highest honour I received in my cultural, social, and political career was being named a representative of the Polish government in London for the province of Manitoba.

I must emphasize here that in all my endeavours, my wife was always by my side. We met in the Wheaton-Ashton camp in Britain, where she was staying with her mother. We got engaged in 1949, before I left for Canada, and were married after she joined me on this side of the ocean. We have two children, son Krzysiu and daughter Bożenka. They have both finished university—Krzysiu in law and Bożenka in education—and both actively participate in the life of Winnipeg. Krzysiu, in particular, joined the currents of Canadian political life as a member of the Liberal Party and a city councillor. At one time, he even chaired the important Environment Commission, planning the expansion of the city of Winnipeg.

I am convinced that Canada has benefitted greatly from the arrival of the Polish military immigrants. Statistics show that ninety percent of Polish veterans ensured that their children finished university. Today that second generation of Polish Canadians holds many key positions in Canadian industry, commerce, and education. They have prospered in their parents' adoptive homeland and are now making it prosperous, drawing inspiration from their Polish roots and the Canadian soil.

JANINA LORENC

I was born in 1929 near Łomża, in the district of Warsaw. My father was mayor of Zambrów, a small town twenty-five kilometres from Łomża. Both my parents, whom I remember with great pride and affection, are dead now.

The atmosphere in my childhood home, as I recall it, was always charged with patriotism, and we as children breathed it like air. I was not yet ten when I first heard talk of the approaching war. In June of 1939, my mother went for a tour of Denmark; two weeks later she came back convinced that war was just round the corner. In the Gdynia harbour, she saw German warships on high alert, their guns aimed at Gdańsk. As soon as she returned home, Mother began to stockpile provisions. I, a brave fourth-grader, helped her in the frantic gathering of supplies, all of which were eventually packed into a large wooden crate. We then taped the windows with paper strips to prevent them from shattering in case a bomb exploded nearby.

On September 1, bombs did indeed begin to explode. We were forewarned of the bombing raids because Father knew the radio codes and had access to current information. After a few days he was ordered to secure the city documents and evacuate. He had the papers deposited in a metal box and buried it in the ground. It is probably still lying there today. At the same time, we began to prepare for evacuation into the heart of Polesie. To keep the family together, Father sent to Łomża for my brother Lech and to Sokół Podlaski for my sister. Then we set out towards Kobryń.

After about a week on the road, around September 17, we ran into a detachment of the Red Army and realized that further escape was pointless: we had been attacked from the east as well. We turned back. The roads were very dangerous. Armed bands of locals often attacked the refugees. We, too, were stopped at one point, and rough-looking men pulled Father from the wagon. I started crying, and my sobbing must have thawed the ringleader's heart, for he let him go, and we escaped unscathed.

We returned to Kupiski, an estate my parents had leased out to my uncle. We had spent many summer holidays there. Since, by then, the Soviets were searching for my father, he made himself a hiding place under the floor of the house and hid there whenever a stranger approached the grange. But over time this grew tedious and dangerous, so he moved to Białystok, assuming the fictitious name of Domalewski.

On February 10, early in the morning, we were woken by a banging on the door. The Soviets. This came to us as a complete shock. They told us to pack. The first thing that came to my mind was to find my favourite doll, which, by the way, I have—and cherish—to this very day. Outside the weather was so cold I could almost hear the crackling of my breath as it froze into clouds of ice crystals. The Soviets loaded us, with some forty other people, into a railway cattle car; at Mother's request, they allowed my sister, taken in Łomża, to join us. The train sat at the station for a whole freezing day; it started to move on the second day and after two weeks reached Arkhangelsk. We survived that journey on the provisions Mother had prepared just before the war started.

The Soviets took us to a settlement—a labour camp, really—where everyone worked cutting lumber in the forest. Eventually, they assigned us to a large shanty, divided into two parts, each housing fifteen families. Each family had a single bed. Only Mother was sent to work because we were too young; we simply stayed "at home." Later, a local forester helped my sister get a job in the kitchen, and my brother went to work with the men. In the spring and summer, I gathered blueberries and mushrooms and sold them to the local people. The Russians and Ukrainians from the neighbouring settlements were quite friendly towards us, for they, too, had been forcibly resettled in the midst of that forest. I also remember a period of time when Mother was sent to another settlement to raft timber—it was a lonely time for me.

In the fall, the Soviet authorities decided to open a school for the children of the camp families. Mother was aware that we should be attending school. We would get three meals a day and learn some Russian, which would definitely be an asset to us, but she dreaded the Soviet propaganda. She warned us about it and hardened us against it. She impregnated my mind with Polish patriotism, with Polish Catholicism. So when I went to school, I was immune to the communist lies. The majority of children at school were Polish, but each class had a few Russian kids as well, little spies who told on us when we spoke Polish or prayed. When caught, we were reprimanded, but that did not stop us: if we could not kneel, we prayed lying in our beds. After the outbreak of war with Germany, the same little kids were used to spy on the camps. The Soviets were obsessed with the idea of German spies torching the camp. A crazy idea, for what in the world was there to torch?

Finally the news reached us of the agreement between Sikorski and Mayski,* and the amnesty was announced. At last we were free, and Mother wanted to leave that place as quickly as possible. So first we went to Ufa, and from there southwards, to Melekes. In one of the *kolkhozes* [collective farm], near Kuybyshev [Samara], all our documents were confiscated—I do not remember why. This made it almost impossible for us to travel. Searching for help, Mother went to the Polish embassy in Kuybyshev, hoping it would intervene on our behalf. While there, she quite unexpectedly ran into her eldest son—our eldest brother—who had not been in the labour camp with us. He had already joined the Polish army and was himself looking for us. We had tried to keep him informed of our whereabouts, but in the chaos of war, letters often went astray. Mother brought him back with her to the *kolkhoz*, him and lots of tinned meat from the American supplies for the Polish army, which greatly improved our lean diet.

On June 22, 1942, we left the *kolkhoz* and followed the Polish army to Dzalal'-Abad in Uzbekistan. From there, on the night of August 6, we left by train for Krasnovodsk. We were instructed not to display excessive joy at this long-awaited departure, presumably to avoid provoking the NKVD [state security police]. We slept two nights out in the open

---

* Ivan M. Mayski (1884-1975), a Soviet diplomat who, on behalf of Stalin, signed the 1941 agreement between the Polish government-in-exile and the Soviet Union.

while waiting for the boat. We had few belongings with us: whatever we had brought from home had long been exchanged for food. Finally we were led aboard a coal boat, the *Zhdanov,* and taken across the Caspian Sea to Pahlavi.

We were free—the omnipotent NKVD could no longer threaten us—but freedom was a dirty business, quite literally. We had to go through the so-called "dirty camp," with its compulsory delousing and burning of clothes brought from Russia. From the "clean camp," we used to go the harbour to welcome the incoming contingents of troops and refugees from Russia. Much to our joy, in one of them we spotted our two brothers, Kazio and Lech. Later we, the civilians, were relocated across the mountains to Tehrān, and from there to Akhvāz. Wherever we went, we saw Polish graves; this was still the legacy of Russia—the typhoid fever, dysentery, and other killers—ravaging the wretched bodies of those who thought they had escaped that cruel land. We were among the lucky ones.

Our next destination was Karāchi in India (now Pakistan), which I remember as a sprawling city of tents, complete with its own temporary schools, where we practised singing, among other things. Once we were asked to give a concert for the American army, which supplied us with food. The concert was going quite well until the intermission, when the Americans began to holler and whistle. Thinking they hated our singing, we started crying. Fortunately, someone soon explained to us that this raucous behaviour was a sign of highest appreciation, and not of derision. So with cheeks still glistening, we sang again to the appreciative crowd.

The next stage of our wanderings was Africa. The person who made sure we reached it without any incident was our superintendent, Mr. Rarogiewicz. Under his watchful eyes, we and the many orphans travelling with us landed safely in Tanga, in eastern Africa. I was shocked at the sight of so many black people, and my surprise must have shown in my face. But no one took offence, and the Africans were very friendly towards us and treated us with compassion.

On the way to Tengeru, we saw many wonders: white-capped Mount Kilimanjaro towering above the horizon, wild giraffes, elephants, lions—and all for real. The camp was located at the foot of Mount Meru, bald on top but with slopes overgrown with thickets of banana trees. There was also a volcanic lake nearby. Our contingent was the third to reach the camp, and we were greeted by the local Masai tribesmen, by the Catholic Women's League, and by tables spread with dainties and delicacies. Each family was assigned a round clay hut, complete with windows and shutters, which was characteristic of Tengeru. That camp was my home for six years.

Life in Africa quickly settled into a routine, despite the various maladies we had brought with us from Russia. I suffered from vitamin deficiency, which manifested itself as a tendency to cry. I was advised to eat lots of lemons, oranges, bananas, and onions, and after some time the strange symptoms indeed disappeared. The local pests also posed a constant threat, especially spiders, snakes, and lions. And we were plagued by tiny fleas, which laid their eggs deep under the nails of fingers and toes; and by the Mango flies, which laid their eggs under the skin of our backs; and above all by malaria-spreading mosquitoes. There were even cases of people dying from the "black malaria."

And yet in the midst of those alien dangers, life seemed pretty normal to us. We went to school immediately after our arrival and were assigned to our respective grades on the basis of an improvised exam. All the courses we took were accelerated, or condensed, to make it possible for us to cover the material of two grades—in my case, fifth and sixth—in one year. Besides the grade schools, the camp also organized vocational schools, teaching commerce, practical mechanics, and agriculture. After all, the camp in Tengeru housed over 4000 refugees, and half of them were still under eighteen.

Outside school, our lives were organized around families, real or adopted, around church, and around Scouting. The adults in the camp, the generation of our mothers, teachers, priests, and Scouting instructors, sought to imbue us with the same patriotism that shaped their lives in the aftermath of World War I and the resurrection of independent Poland. We used to gather in the central square to hear the latest news from the fronts. We wrote letters to unknown soldiers and waited for letters from our fathers and brothers in the army. The air of expectation was always tinged with apprehension and anxiety, for all too often the letters from the front brought news of death or injury. From one of them we learned that my brother was wounded at the battle of Ancona. To keep our young spirits up, the adults organized for us sightseeing tours and camping trips, appealing to our youthful sense of adventure and turning the sad reality of exile into a unique learning experience.

The end of the war was received with mixed feelings. Those whose families survived unscathed were jubilant, but those who had left behind shallow graves scattered across the emptiness of Russia did little more than acknowledge the news. My family was among the lucky ones, but the war scarred us, too. Those of us who escaped Russia reunited in the Wheaton-Ashton camp in England in 1948. All but my father. He was hiding from the Soviets under the assumed name of Domalewski, but he was eventually found out. Sentenced to fifteen years, he went through Lubyanka, Kozel'sk, and Ostaszkovo, before he was sent to Siberia. He returned to Poland a broken man, unable to take the bold decision to emigrate. Our family remained splintered by war.

It was at Wheaton-Ashton that I also met my future husband, Henryk. An adventurous soul, he left for Canada in 1949, while I stayed in England and finished a two-year course in millinery. Two years later, I joined Henryk in Canada, where our life took the usual course through marriage, children (Krzysztof and Bożena), children's education (both are university graduates), and grandchildren. Canada has treated us well, and we look forward to our golden years with optimism and peace.

ADAM MOSSAKOWSKI

I was born on December 24, 1912. My parents, both from the old landed gentry stock, had an estate called Pomaski, in the vicinity of Pułtusk. Mother came from the manor of Kliszewo.

My childhood was profoundly touched by the events of the First World War and by the rebirth of Poland that followed. In 1920 I was eight and the oldest child in the family. I was still only vaguely aware of national politics, but I knew enough to be very proud of my father, who had volunteered for the Polish army and was serving in the 203rd Lancers Regiment. When the Bolsheviks invaded our region, Mother kept reminding me not to mention to anyone where Father was. But a young boy can't resist a good boast, and eventually, despite repeated warnings, I let the secret out. This caused Mother plenty of trouble. Fortunately, the Bolsheviks were soon chased away, and two months later I finally had my father back, hale and sound.

My first school year was marked by similar patriotic upheavals. Many eighth graders had served in the armed forces, and their return to school was a moving experience. For us youngsters, they were true heroes. The school organized for them special classes and smoking rooms near the latrines. We worshipped their courage and their panache. Once Sergeant Major Sokołowski, a popular eighth grader, put me up on top of a huge stove in the classroom and said, "When the teacher comes in, I'll raise my finger, and you'll say 'Peek-a-boo.'" The prank may have been silly, but I delighted in it. I played my part and "peek-a-booed" the teacher, as instructed. The class exploded with laughter. When the merriment subsided, the teacher had to call for the school janitor and a ladder to take me down from my perch.

After graduating from high school in Pułtusk, I wanted to sign up for the army. Military service was part of our family tradition. One of the Mossakowskis was an Olympian and a lecturer at a cavalry college. (Among our other traditions were membership in Roman Dmowski's National Party, unqualified support for his ideology, and addiction to cigarette smoking—that last tradition I cultivated for over fifty years.) But my uncle despaired that everyone wanted to be in the military, and soon there would be no one to run the estate. So the family decided that I should become a clod-breaker, and I signed up for the Szkola Główna Gospodarstwa Wiejskiego [Central Agricultural University] in Warsaw. Shortly afterwards, I was called up for obligatory military service and sent off to the Officer Cadet College in Grudziądz. There we were put through the mill by Sergeant Major Król, whose motto was "the army doesn't need wise guys." He consistently did his best to root out anyone who might even vaguely fit the description. I served for two years, from 1933 to 1935, before returning to the Central Agricultural University. Later I transferred to the Agricultural College in Cieszyn, where I completed my residency in 1939. The outbreak of war prevented me from finishing my dissertation.

I was not much perturbed by the news of the impending war, thinking it would be like the military manoeuvres I knew (in 1938 I had gone to Zaolzie with the Academic Legion), only grander in scale. But this war turned out to be quite different. I was called up to the 5th Lancers Regiment in Ostrołęka and experienced my first German air raid near Maków. My regiment was assigned to the independent operation group Narew, under the command of General Młot Fijałkowski. Our campaign was mostly retreat. I was in the last unit that withdrew across the bridge on the Narew River near Wyszków. Right after we crossed it, the bridge was blown up. On the Narew we managed to hold our positions for only one day. The Germans threw at us a whole brigade of dismounted cavalrymen, reinforced by heavy armoured units. They had a clear advantage, and we had no choice but to fall back towards Siedlce. Near Węgrowo, we witnessed five German planes swoop down on a village, shred it with machine gun fire, and set it ablaze. I survived the attack by hiding with my horse in a potato field. I remember feeling completely helpless, like a hunted rabbit.

When the hunters were not looking, we pushed eastwards, around Siedlce, and in the direction of Brześć. Fewer than thirty horses were left in my squadron. We passed through Biała Podlaska and tried to defend Włodawa, but in vain. Near Chełm Lubelski, we were regrouped as the 12th Pioneer Squadron and dispatched towards Zamość. When we reached it, the battle was almost over, and we got an order to disperse and get out of there. About a hundred of us reassembled into a squadron, most with good horses and well armed. We started moving southwards.

Somewhere along the way, in late September, a friend of mine and I were sent ahead as scouts. We were trotting along a forest path when suddenly we froze in our tracks: from round the path's bend emerged a detachment of armed men with red stars on their caps. We knew who they were: the Bolsheviks. We stared at them, and they stared at us; then they turned around and galloped away, and so did we. We immediately reported the sighting to the commander, and it was decided that we should abandon the beaten track and move across the fields. Cutting across fields and forests, we came to a forester's lodge and took some well-deserved rest. To make sure the horses stayed quiet— a horse always neighs when it senses another nearby—we used an old cavalry trick of tying stones to the horses' tails: a horse will not neigh if it cannot lash its tail. Finally we could get some sleep and think through our situation.

After some discussion, the majority of the men decided to disperse and return to their homes. Only twelve of us were determined to push south. We travelled only at night, mostly through wooded areas. We would take a local guide, usually a Ukrainian, put him on horseback, and ride behind him with our revolvers drawn. If he led us to the Bolsheviks, we told him, we would still have time to blow his head off. On September 28, we stopped before a triumphal gate adorned with a red sickle, leading to a village where a rally of some sort was in progress. We were still wearing our Polish uniforms and were quite conspicuous. Suddenly two men jumped out of the bushes and tried to snatch the reins of my friend's horse. Acting on instinct, he slashed at their hands with his sabre. We started at full gallop down the narrow path, with swamps on either side. Unluckily for us, that path also led to the village. As soon as we emerged from the bush, we were surrounded by the Bolsheviks. They jumped at us from all directions, pulled us down, and tied us up. The next morning they brought us some coffee and began their investigation. They had information, they told us, that travelling with us was a government minister carrying sheaves of money. Since we knew nothing about it, we were deemed uncooperative, loaded onto a truck, and sent off to Lwów [L'viv]. The whole city was draped in red, and was swarming with Bolsheviks, most of them Jews. They drove us to an old tobacco factory in Winniki [Vinniki], where the tedious, ridiculous, and often painful interrogations began. They asked me how I was captured, and where my family was, and how many cows and horses we had, how much money we were carrying, and other similarly absurd questions.

From Lwów, the Bolsheviks shipped us to Stanisławów [Ivano-Frankivs'k]; it was there that I ate real Polish sausage for the last time. Next we went to Volochisk, where thousands of Polish POWs had been assembled before being exiled to various labour camps. All, that is, except officers, policemen, corporals, and gamekeepers, who were singled out and taken to Kozel'sk; shortly afterwards, they were murdered in cold blood. Corporals found themselves in that fateful group because the Soviets believed they enforced military discipline in a capitalist army by bashing worker-soldiers' heads; gamekeepers, through some twisted logic, were blamed for similar mistreatment of forest workers.

I was sent—with hundreds of others—to a manganese mine in Dnipropetrovs'k, in the Donets Basin. At first the Soviets did not call us prisoners; rather, they told us they had liberated us from the yoke of capitalism. To ensure that we expressed our proper gratitude, they divided us into two camps, surrounded us with armed guards, and sent us to sweat in the mines. Later the camp commander must have received new instructions, for one day we learned that we were, after all, prisoners. I was assigned to mine number 16, to a team that tore down the rock face and carted it away. The team leader, or *zaboishchyk*, had two helpers who loaded the cart and a cart driver. I was made a driver. My leader was Czajkowski, a foul-mouthed man but, as it turned out, a good Pole. He swore like a sailor, or, as a Pole would say, like a shoemaker. He showed me the cart and how to drive it, then he went about his own business. But when I pushed it, the cart derailed. He turned around, swore at me, and said "What, you a Polish nobleman?" "Yes," I said, pretending not to catch his sarcasm. "So am

I," he replied quietly, and helped me right the cart. He was a good man, and I did well working with him.

There was much discontent in the camp, what with hard labour, meagre food rations, and the guards' brutality. Eventually all the Poles refused to go to the mines. The Soviets responded by locking us up in a penal camp. They also announced that those from western Poland would be shipped elsewhere. Indeed, in May the NKVD [state security police] conducted detailed verification of our personal files, then loaded us into cargo cars and shipped us by rail via Moscow to Kotlas. From there they sent us by barges to the Komi Republic. There we found out that we were considered particularly dangerous because we had been to the West and been infected by capitalism. That was the Soviet diagnosis of our audacity in demanding decent treatment.

In Komi, we were supposed to build roads and railway tracks, which ended in a small place called Knyazhpogost. It was June, the time of the longest days in the north, so our shifts were excruciatingly long. Most of the time, we tore up moss and dirt and wheeled it away in primitive wheelbarrows. We had to watch our step—literally—because we had been forewarned that any deviation to the left or to the right would be treated as an attempt to escape and dealt with accordingly. Our guards were partly regular NKVD troops and partly disciplinary units from the army. Things got better when they assigned me to a Belarussian brigade that was cutting down the forest. I was given the job of collecting branches and burning them. My new colleagues quickly taught me how to meet the required quota: by cheating, of course.

Our food rations depended on whether or not we met the quota. The least we could get was the so-called "twelfth cauldron"; that is, some soup in the morning and 120 grams of bread. For carrying out seventy-five percent of the norm, one could get 300 grams of bread and some porridge; for 100 percent of the norm, one got 600 grams of bread, better porridge, and a small fish. The bread was heavy, sodden, and even 600 grams was not much. I survived thanks to extra helpings smuggled out for me by Józef Jankowski, now a Winnipeger, who was a cook there and a good friend of mine.

On July 15, 1941, we were brought back to the camp from the forest, loaded onto a train, and sent back to Kotlas. No one bothered to tell us where we were being taken. In Kotlas, we were ordered off the train, tossed some biscuits, and marched throughout the night to a new camp,

Tatyana. By then many men were suffering from exhaustion and vita-min deficiency, and almost half of us were afflicted with the so-called night blindness. Those suffering from it had to be escorted if they wanted to use the latrines after dark; the situation was both awkward and taxing to the good will of tired men. After the outbreak of the Soviet-German war, rumours started about an agreement between Sikorski* and the Soviets. Then one day, Polish and Czech flags appeared on the flagpole, and we learned that Colonel Wiśniewski from the Polish army had begun to register the soldiers and compile their records. There were also no Soviet guards in sight. We were again Polish soldiers!

I left the camp with the first transport heading for Tatishchevo, with 500 rubles in my pocket, a token compensation for months of slave labour. Through some confusion, our convoy ended up in Totskoye on September 8. The day after we arrived, General Anders† came to Totskoye, and we marched past him, barefoot, famished, and in tatters. We must have been quite a sight. I was assigned to the 12th Reconnaissance Squadron of the 6th Infantry Division; my commander was Lieutenant Barcicki.

Living conditions in the army camp were beyond primitive. We had to begin by constructing our own dugouts and by fashioning stoves out of clay. The weather got so cold that we had to keep the stoves burn-ing all day. We obtained wood mostly by stealing it. Food was also in short supply, especially since we had to share it with the civilians. To remedy the situation, we organized special "raids" on the neighbouring kolkhozes [collective farms]. Those "raids" usually involved a couple of adventurous fellows collecting various pieces of clothing from the refugees and venturing into the countryside to barter them for food. I went on one such "raid" with a guy from the Poznań region. We left at night, made it safely past the testing range, heavily guarded by the Soviet police, and made our first call in the kolkhoz named after Lenin. As we moved on, it began to snow and the temperature dropped. After an hour in the blinding snowstorm, we lost our way. Fortunately, we

---

* Władysław Sikorski (1881-1943), premier of the Polish government-in-exile and commander-in-chief of the Polish forces fighting alongside the Allies in World War II.

† Władysław Anders (1892-1970), commander of the Polish army in the Soviet Union (later the 2nd Polish Corps).

ran into some people stealing wood. We helped them load it onto a cart, and they showed us the way to the village we had planned to visit. By now the snowstorm was so bad that going back was out of question. We found shelter in an old hut crawling with lice. For four days we were forced to suffer those bloodsuckers, until on the fifth the storm subsided and we could return to the camp with the precious supply of food.

In January we were transferred to Otar, near Alma-Ata [Almaty], where I was assigned to the 2nd squadron of the 1st Krechowiecki Lancers Regiment. On May 25, on the feast of the Annunciation, we were ordered to leave for Krasnovodsk. We surrendered all Russian money—only to regret it later when we discovered that it had value in Persia—and boarded a ship. On June 1, we arrived in Pahlavi and set up camp on the beaches outside the town. At mealtime, we were served white bread, a delicacy we had not seen for months, and fig jam and sardines. Unfortunately, our emaciated bodies could not eat as much as our minds craved, and we had been forewarned about the dangers of overeating. When the first civilian convoys arrived, we were ordered to collect all their belongings and burn them to prevent the spread of vermin and diseases. I happened to lead the patrol charged with that unenviable duty: did I get an earful from the people whose most cherished possessions I had to confiscate!

From Pahlavi, we went by trucks to Palestine. Our Persian drivers navigated the rickety trucks through narrow mountain roads with gusto and daredevilry, but they delivered us to Palestine without a major tragedy. We settled on the shores of a lake and soon gave in to the temptation of diving into its cool waves. But while we were frolicking in the water, a whirlwind struck and scattered our camp in all directions.

Later our path led through Jordan to Bashyd, near Gedera, where our troops were fed back to health and strength after starvation in Russia. By then we were no longer very keen on sardines with jam or simple porridge, so we supplemented our fare with things we bought from local shopkeepers.

[Adam Mossakowski passed away before completing his memoirs.]

STEFAN OLBRECHT

I was born on November 27, 1926, in the village of Sobiesko, near the town of Podhajce [Podgaytsy], where Jan III Sobieski* defeated the Turks in 1667. (My real family name was "Olbrycht," but people often mispronounced and misspelled it even before the war. When I was in the Polish army, in Palestine, my name was registered as "Olbrecht," and I let it stay that way.) My family had its roots in the Lwów [L'viv] district, in the area around Jarosław and Przeworsk. Today my Polish has lost its characteristic Lwów accent, but when I was younger, serving as a cadet in Russia, I often said *ta yoy*, just as I had heard it at home. I finished the first five grades in Podhajce, in an elementary school named after—who else—Jan III Sobieski. We had no high school in Podhajce: the closest one was in Brzeżany [Berezhany].

There was much talk at school about the impending war: we sewed our own gas masks, gathered scrap metal for war purposes, and collected money to purchase more equipment for our army. At home, we listened eagerly to Father's stories of World War I: he had served in the Austrian army, in the artillery. The first harbingers of World War II, in early September 1939, were the refugees who came to our village from Silesia. Their kids made fun of our accent, saying that we sang instead of speaking. Their own speech was not unlike my mother's, who had apparently come from the same general region. Despite this taunting, we liked to play with them for they knew boys' stuff we did not.

---

* Jan III Sobieski (1624-96), king of Poland 1674-96.

In our region, the war arrived with the Soviet cavalry—*cherkesy,* people called them, remembering the name from World War I. They stopped at our village, and Mother immediately pulled us all indoors and forbade us to go out into the street. We were so excited we peeked through the windows and cracks in the walls, but what we saw did not impress us. The cavalrymen wore characteristic pointed caps, but their uniforms were dirty and in tatters. Their overcoats looked the worst, all different styles and frayed at the bottom. They had rifles tied with pieces of string. The horses they rode looked as bad, all starved and infected with glanders. The Soviets took our good horses and left us their sick jades. With other boys, I chased after them in the pastures, their hooves unshod, their noses dripping.

After the cavalry, Soviet tanks rolled in, and then we knew the Soviets had come here to stay. The new administrators were mostly Ukrainians and Jews. One of their first reforms was to introduce coeducational schooling (in our Polish school, girls and boys attended separate classes) and two new languages, Ukrainian and German. But I did not attend that new school for long because Poles became targets of vicious Ukrainian attacks. They called us "Mazury," threw stones at us, and beat us up. Our village was settled by Poles from other regions who bought the land from the estates parcelled out by aristocratic landowners, such as the Poniatowskis. Father had come to these parts from Raczyń near Jarosław and had used his savings to buy fourteen *morgi* [about seven hectares] of land, a decent-sized parcel. Our farm was not as big as the farms of settlers who had made their money in America. They bought larger tracts of land and put their American experience to good use on their farms. Our village thus had become a Polish island, surrounded by the ever more stormy sea of Ukrainians. The situation grew so dangerous that our authorities asked the Russians for protection from our neighbours-turned-enemies. The Russians acknowledged the problem and issued us four rifles and a quantity of ammunition. We then stationed two guards at each end of the village; armed with the rifles, they were supposed to protect us in case of a Ukrainian assault. Just in case, Mother prepared for each of us a little package with clothing and provisions to take with us if we had to run for our lives.

During the first winter of the war, we were hearing rumours that Poles would be deported to the West. Shortly before Christmas, the

Russians took away our guns, so many of us thought that the deportations were imminent. And indeed they were, though not to the West. On Saturday, February 10, 1940, Soviet and Ukrainian militiamen came to our house and ordered us to get out. We threw what we could onto the sleigh, and the militiamen drove us to the railway station, three kilometres outside Podhajce, where thirty-five-tonne cargo cars had already been readied for us. We were herded into a car with several other families, and the doors were slammed and bolted shut. Inside the car were some primitive bunks knocked together from rough boards; in the middle of the floor, a hole was cut out and plugged with a bundle of straw—that was our privy. Other cars had more private latrines, but not ours. Performing physiological necessities in the middle of the car and in plain sight was most embarrassing. Girls screened one another with sheets; boys did it through the cracks in the doors; and things that required squatting, we tried to attend to at night, when the others were asleep. My sister's children were so ashamed that they did not go to this "bathroom" for three days, until my mother got so worried that she ferreted out some castor oil. Needless to say, the treatment proved most effective.

The train did not move for three days, and no one bothered to tell us where we were not going. We realized we were heading east only when they transferred the cars onto the wide tracks. After a week of intermittent progress, we reached Yurla in the Omskaya Republic, in the Ural Mountains. Throughout that journey, we were issued no food. We lived on what we had had the presence of mind to take with us from home. Our bread ran out quickly because the custom was to bake fresh bread for Sunday, and we were forced out when new bread had barely been started. Mother did take some flour, though, so at least we could bake some simple cakes on an improvised stove.

In Yurla, we were loaded onto trucks, stinking of crude oil, for three more days of excruciating journey. The stink combined with the bumpy road caused people to vomit, which further worsened the sickening atmosphere in the truck. I really do not know how we managed to survive that ordeal. When we reached our destination—wherever that was—we spent a night in a school building; the following morning we were put onto sleighs for three more days. Our entire trip lasted about two weeks.

Our final destination turned out to be two shanties erected for woodcutters in the middle of the forest, some eight kilometres from the nearest village, or *pasiolek*. A week earlier, another group of Polish deportees had arrived there and had already started to work. I was thirteen at the time but too weak for the back-breaking labour in the forest. That labour involved felling trees, cutting them up, and stacking the wood along the banks of the Berozka River. Berozka is a tributary of Kama, which flows into Pechora. In the spring, when the ice broke, the wood was floated down the rivers.

Come summer, life in the forest became miserable. Adding to the daily struggle for survival was the plague of mosquitoes. They swarmed around our sweating bodies and bit us mercilessly. We scratched the bites till they bled and got infected, but even that did not stop the itching. Our bodies were covered with scabs.

Fortunately, after a while, we were moved to the *pasiolek*, which had a bakery and public baths. Finally we could steam and wash away months of dirt and scabs. We still lived in communal shanties, heated by two ovens. The same ovens were used for cooking, although most of the time there was nothing to cook. Our food rations consisted solely of bread: a working person was entitled to buy up to two kilograms, while those who did not work, only one kilogram. If you had some other provisions, you could survive, but living on the rations of bread alone meant going to bed hungry. Besides, many people could not afford to buy their basic rations, let alone supplement them: my sister, for example, was paid less than a ruble a day, which was not enough for her entitlement. Other women, who could not work cutting down large trees, suffered the same lot. When we complained about our wretched living conditions to the local NKVD [state security police] commander, he replied, "Pryvykniesh, a ne pryvykniesh to padokhniesh" [You'll get used to it, and if you don't, you'll drop dead].

Why did we not run away if life was so miserable? Well, where could we run? We were so far away from any human settlement, right in the midst of a wilderness stretching for hundreds of kilometres, that the thought of escape did not cross many minds; and if it did, no one acted on it. Any escape would have been discovered the very next morning, when attendance was taken before leaving for work. How far could one walk through the night?

As we saw it, we had no choice but to suffer the small cruelties and hardships and idiocies of the labour camp. One of the pointless exercises was the monthly pep talks, intended to "enlighten" us politically. The NKVD officer in charge of the *pasiolek* extolled the benefits of the communist system in a futile attempt to make us accept Soviet citizenship. We were not forced to accept it, as sometimes happened in the camps, but his talks were tedious in the extreme. Despite this monthly mental torture, no Pole from our *pasiolek* took advantage of the Soviet "generosity."

In late 1940, a wave of arrests swept through the *pasiolek*. Apparently not all people were aware of the danger of speaking their minds freely. We had always suspected that several local Russians who mingled with us were in fact NKVD spies and reported on us to the commander. In December, four men were arrested; they were forced to admit to various "crimes" against the Soviet Union and sentenced to eight to fifteen years. Soon afterwards, another six were taken. Our family was spared, probably because we kept our mouths shut tight, but Mr. Łanuch, whose family shared a shanty with us, got eight years in a penal labour camp. The quota in that camp was so high—he was making wooden boxes—that he could never meet it, and, consequently, his food rations were systematically cut. He slowly starved to death.

At the time, my father and I worked sawing birch trunks into rings, which were then dried and used as fuel for tractors. Many of our coworkers were Belarussians, among them a soft-spoken man who admitted to my father that he had been a priest. He also told us that when they had been brought to that place, the Soviets had simply dumped them in the forest and said, "You'll live here." They had no houses, no shanties waiting for them. Most of their children and elders died from hunger and exposure. Listening to his stories, we counted ourselves fortunate.

The Belarussians seemed to know more than we did. It was they who told us about the war brewing with Germany. When that war actually broke out, the commander announced that we were free citizens and could go wherever we wished. We were issued proper papers and given leave to go. Father decided that we should go to a *kolkhoz* [collective farm] forty-five kilometres away. It was the season for picking potatoes, so food was plentiful, if you could steal it. We were not allowed to gather potatoes from the fields that had already been picked, because whatever was left belonged to the state. The leftovers would simply rot, but we were forbidden to touch them. After the season of plenty came some very lean months. The bread rations were much skimpier than in the *pasiolek:* a labourer was entitled to one kilogram of bread, while those who could not work, to half a kilogram. Sometimes they also gave us coarsely ground hulled barley; the hulls were so rough they wedged into our gums and caused bleeding. God knows why I still remember the name of that place: Yum.

That winter Father got sick with flu and became so weak that we feared for his life. My brother bribed a local cart driver with shag, and they took Father by sleigh to the hospital in the nearest town, about fifty kilometres away. The nurses in the hospital asked about Father's age. "He's sixty," my brother replied. "Then why don't you throw him out into the fields. Come spring, things will grow better," they advised. After such a reception, my brother stayed by Father's side through the night and brought him home the next day. After a painful week, without any medicine or medical help, Father died from exhaustion. We dug his grave for three days in the frozen Siberian ground, with temperatures hovering around -40°C. When we buried him in this shallow grave, with rock-hard lumps of earth barely covering his flimsy coffin, tears froze on my cheeks.

After Father's death, we called a meeting of all surviving members of the family. Late in the evening, we sat around the fire blazing in the stove. The mood was sombre, dejected. Since we were all going to perish if we stayed in the *kolkhoz*, we thought, we might just as well try our luck on the road. We had no provisions, so we decided to steal a sack of wheat from the mill. Stealing it was not difficult at all; we immediately transferred the contents of the sack into two smaller sacks and buried them in a snowbank. Then we sat quiet for two weeks. No one noticed. It was safe to begin baking bread. If anyone asked where we got the flour from, we said we bartered it for some clothes we had brought from Poland. Once again we used shag to bribe the cart driver to take us to the nearest town, two days away. In the town, shag bought us a ride on a cistern to the nearest train station. On the train, we met some refugees from Stalingrad, who told us about terrible hunger in that city, so terrible that some resorted to cannibalism. Three days later, we were in Toshkent; unfortunately, we arrived in Guzar just after a convoy had left for Persia. We could do little but wait for another one, living in small tents, which we enlarged by digging a lower floor. That small improvement proved disastrous, for torrential rains soon flooded both the tents and all our belongings. Under those living conditions, exhausted by slave labour and hunger, we fell victim to numerous contagious diseases. Mother got seriously ill, and we took her to the hospital. I visited her there several times, but one day I found her bed empty. She had died. Then my youngest sister, Kazia, got sick, and once again we sought help in the local hospital. We never found her again. In the midst of such havoc, my older brother and sister Honorata joined the army, while my younger brother and I were sent to the Youth Corps. They dressed us up in adult-sized uniforms—they had no other sizes—so that to be able to walk, we had to roll up the sleeves and the pant legs. We sported that pathetic scarecrow look that seemed quite fashionable in those days.

Once, when I was in the Youth Corps camp, Honorata came to visit me. To cheer me up, she brought me an armful of fruit. Heedless of warnings, I stuffed myself with the fruit and ended up with dysentery. I was afraid to go to the hospital because there was talk of the corps leaving for Persia; the sick would not go. But in the end I was so weak that I was carried to the hospital, and the corps indeed left without me. A week later, my sister came to visit me again. I asked her to buy me a bottle of vodka, for I had heard it was a good remedy. She did, but the vodka did not help. Since the hospital, too, was being liquidated, I gathered my last ounce of strength and signed out. I had only one hour to register for the convoy bound for Persia. To make matters worse, it was getting dark, and I was suffering from night-blindness. On the verge of despair, I suddenly heard my brother's voice. He was looking for me. He helped me to register for the departure, put me aboard the train, and later the ship. Thanks to him I made it to Pahlavi, but Mother, Father, my grandmother, one sister, and one brother all died in that cursed land. Most of my other siblings managed to leave with the civilian refugees.

From Pahlavi we went to Khānaqīn in Iraq, and then to Palestine. There I registered for the Youth Corps school, located twenty kilometres from Gedera, which organized basic literacy courses for those who had not finished Grade 5 and vocational courses for those who had. I signed up for a mechanical course and spent an entire year in the huge British workshops near Haifa.

At the end of that year, I felt ready to join the regular army. I went before the recruiting commission and, to my delight, qualified for the air force. But my joy was premature: because many units needed reinforcements, it was decided that only those born in the first six months of the year would fly; the others would walk or ride. So on January 17, 1944, I was sent to Egypt to replenish the Carpathian Lancers Regiment, which had recently suffered some losses. When we arrived and presented ourselves to the lancers' commanders—all of us young and angry boys of seventeen—they burst out laughing. They called us "little mushrooms" because our backpacks towered above our heads. We did not mind; we had been through much worse. The regiment was just getting ready to leave for Italy, but we were first sent to Abadia for a six-week driving course. We rejoined the regiment in Italy, in March 1944.

In view of the imminent assault on Monte Cassino, we had to dismount our vehicles and train on foot in the difficult mountainous terrain. On May 2, we set out for the front, arriving at the gorge Inferno, which supplied the front line, two days later. Finally we took positions between Monte Cairo and Monte Cassino. We dug in and the waiting began. To break the monotony and tension, Corporal Oraczewski tried to catch a loose horse grazing on a grassy slope, hoping to present it to the unit commander. He moved slowly, talking to it gently in Polish, and patiently inching towards it. Suddenly several shots rang out, spooking the horse; Oraczewski shuddered, bent a little, and slumped to the ground. He was dead.

When the assault against the mountaintop stronghold finally began, the night grew lighter than the day. I had never seen a night like that. I was supposed to go on a reconnaissance mission, but Lieutenant Polkowski cancelled it because it was too bright. The following night, he identified me as a volunteer to check out a rocky formation—a "saddle," we called it—and draw enemy fire. We needed to know exactly where the enemy positions were. A chill ran down my spine when I realized that I was to be a live target for German snipers. But I survived that mission unscathed. On the way down, we came across a squadron going up in another wave of the assault. I was ordered to joined them as a munitions carrier. This turned out to be my baptism by fire. They loaded me with ammunition, and I began climbing step by step. Now and then I heard commands, "Ammunition forward!" and I scrambled to move faster. The load was awkward and made it impossible to dodge enemy bullets. Older colleagues hollered at me, "Take cover, get down, don't be such a hero!" The weight on my back was sapping all my strength, and eventually I collapsed from exhaustion. I got up, took a few more steps, collapsed again. Someone offered to help. Then I heard "Ammunition forward!" My feet and my back refused to move, but I did. I reached the drop point after some of the longest minutes of my life.

Going down, I carried a wounded soldier, Senior Lancer Piecha, who had taken a round across his back. He was crying in pain. We found him a stretcher, and this lessened his torment somewhat. (Two weeks later he died in the field hospital.) There was no time to rest; I was immediately sent back up with a supply of drinking water. On the way down, I brought a dead soldier. After a hasty meal in the field kitchen, I went up again with coats, because soldiers were freezing up there. I brought down another dead soldier. I spent the whole day going up and down, always with a heavy load, always under fire. That was my contribution to the battle of Monte Cassino, perhaps the bloodiest battle in which I took part. To this day, I think it was a true miracle that I went through that storm of bullets without an injury to my body.

I went into action for the last time around Bologna, this time in an armoured vehicle. Through no fault of our own, we drove into an ambush. The Germans, well camouflaged in their positions, let through our first two vehicles but then hit the third one. The burning vehicle blocked the escape route, which gave the enemy time to kill the cars trapped ahead of it. My platoon was in the rear guard, and we immediately opened fire, but to no avail. We lost many good men there.

Soon after taking Bologna, we received the news that the war was over. This joyous message came together with a tragic one, about Yalta and the surrender of Poland to the Soviets. First a toast, then a blow. Despite the mixed feelings, there was quite a lot of cheering and shooting in the air. There were even some casualties when the exuberance became too drunken.

I ended my Italian campaign in a tank unit of the 2nd Armoured Division. In 1946 I was transferred to England and eventually went before the commission qualifying for emigration as farm labourers in Canada. I arrived in Halifax in June of 1947. I was originally sent to Alberta, but my aunt, who lived in Saskatchewan, arranged for me to be transferred to her farm. I liked working there, and I lacked nothing, but the mosquitoes were such a nuisance that I decided to move to

Winnipeg. There I joined the Polish Combatants Association, and, with just a few interruptions, have remained its member to the present day, serving the organization in various capacities, including one term as president.

I did not know English at the time, so I found it difficult to find a permanent job. For a while I worked at Inland Steel, well known for hiring Polish veterans, but the company ran out of orders in 1951, and I was laid off. A friend of mine, Gienek Nowak, helped me find a job at a railway company, and I started there at $1.05 an hour. Three years ago I retired, after thirty-five years on that job.

My closest companion over those years was my wife, Lonia (neé Majewicz). She, too, was deported by the Soviets and, after leaving Russia, moved from orphanage to orphanage. In 1948 her uncle brought her over to Canada. We were married in 1951 and have two sons, Krzysztof and Tadeusz.

The rest of my family was scattered by the war around the world. One of my sisters ended up in Karāchi, then still in India; two others went to Masindi, in Uganda; one stayed in Siberia. My oldest brother remained in Poland. My sister Honorata, who served in a transportation brigade of the Women's Auxiliary Services, now lives in Chicago.

WŁADYSŁAW OLEJNICZAK

I was born in 1917, near Czempiń, in the Kościan county, district of Poznań. I began my military service early, for at eighteen I volunteered for the 2nd Training Battalion of the Border Guard Corps [KOP], in the 68th Infantry Regiment. The battalion sent me for a five-month NCO course; upon graduation with the rank of corporal, I was posted to Jarocin to train recruits. Soon afterwards, I was dispatched to Pleszew, for another five-month course. When I graduated, I was promoted to a professional NCO.

In 1938, we could feel the war in the air. In the spring of the following year, I was assigned to a special battalion that was sent to Delatyn [Delyatin], county of Nadwórna [Nadvornaya], in the Carpathian Mountains, not the friendliest of territories for the Polish army. Discipline was tightened to the point that we were not allowed to go to town alone. In May, we were detailed to Nowe Miasto on the Warta River, where we reinforced field shelters along the river. On August 1, we returned to Jarocin, and I was reassigned to a company of heavy machine guns. On August 22, the garrison commander announced covert mobilization. We were issued special activity booklets with detailed instructions. By the evening, my company was all reorganized; I found myself in a supply column consisting of nine carts. After live ammunition was distributed, we marched out towards Nowe Miasto, where we had built bomb shelters just a few weeks earlier.

The war began while we were on the march. Our slow advance soon turned into a quick retreat along the Pyzdry-Zagórów-Konin-Koło line.

Koło was bombed in the first days of the war, but we still managed to cross the damaged bridge in the direction of Iłowo. Shortly afterwards, German armoured units, moving at high speed, overtook us and cut us off. On September 17, they pounded our convoy for five hours—that was my baptism by battle. We lost five supply carts. On the night of September 18, we forded the Bzura River, fought through the German line, and fell back towards the Kampinos Forest. We dug in at the edge of the forest and improvised shelters. We held that line throughout the next day. Emissaries from the German command demanded that we withdraw or suffer the consequences, but our commander decided to defend our positions. In response, German artillery shelled us for over three hours, but we were well entrenched and did not suffer many casualties. After the barrage, the Germans threw at us their infantry, backed up by tanks. We destroyed two tanks with our anti-tank guns and generally held our ground. But that night we received orders to withdraw.

The instructions from our military command were that, should we find ourselves in a hopeless situation, we should surrender, preferably in medium-sized groups of several soldiers. On September 23, my unit of eighteen men was encircled by a strong German detachment, and we were forced to lay down our arms. The Germans collected the weapons and took us to their rear. They treated us fairly, in accordance with the conventions, and gave us a helping of rice each. Then they transferred us to Sochaczew, where more POWs had already been assembled, and on to a large arena in Żyrardów. There each prisoner was issued two loaves of bread and loaded into cargo cars to be taken by train to Ostrów Wielkopolski. The journey lasted two days. In Ostrów, the Germans pulled out all Silesians and Pomeranians and sent the rest to Krotoszyn, and from there to Germany, near the Dutch border.

I was in that latter group and ended up in Stalag 6c. We were disinfected and assigned to barracks; the food was poor. The Germans verified our records, and sent us to work depending on our former occupations. I did not mind working on a farm, so they transferred me to the so-called *Kommando*, consisting of sixty prisoners. Every morning we were escorted to individual farms, scattered in six villages. On Sundays, we had compulsory exercises and marching drills; when ordered to sing, we sang Polish military songs, of course. Working conditions on my farm were passable, and the food was decent. But after the French campaign, the Germans brought in French POWs and moved us to other farms. It was there that I met my wife-to-be, Nelli, then a fifteen-year-old girl from Silesia. I stayed at the same farm till the end of the war, but she was sent away to a farm eighteen kilometres away. This made our meetings more difficult, and we stayed in close touch mostly by mail.

The long-awaited freedom came with the arrival of British soldiers. Overnight, our fortunes changed: our masters went to sleep in the cellar, and we slept in their beds. The British treated us as allies; they gave me a motorcycle with the official papers and enough gas to go get my fiancée from her farm. We were married on June 3. At the time, I was working as a volunteer at an American field hospital; shortly afterwards, both of us were sent to a camp for former POWs in Fallengoster. There I became a member of the Polish Combatants Association. I also joined—and was placed in charge of—a company organizing high school courses for all ex-prisoners.

I had little difficulty deciding to stay in the West. At first, we thought to settle in one of the European countries because Canada was not accepting married couples. It was not until 1949 that I decided to go to Canada on a farm contract. My wife, Nelli, and our children remained in Germany while I explored the New World. I brought them over to Canada eleven months later.

When I first arrived in this country, I worked the sugar beet fields in Portage la Prairie and drove a combine at harvest time. After the harvest, there was no more farm work available so I was released from the contract. I moved to the city and took a job at the Canadian National Railway, for a dollar an hour. During summer months, I worked changing railway tracks; in winter, I cut ice on the lake, used for cooling railway cars. After that I went through a succession of jobs: in a tannery, in the gas department of the Winnipeg Electric Company (I quit that job because I developed an allergy to natural gas), and at Vulcan Iron (I worked there until the company was liquidated). Finally I got a job at the General Motors dealership on Main Street, where I stayed for thirty-three years, until retirement.

When my family joined me in Canada, our life settled into a comfortable routine. We bought a house in 1954, and when we grew more established, we built a new home in 1967. We sent our children to good schools and universities. Our oldest son, Dionizy, is a mechanical engineer and works in Montreal for Air Canada. Our daughter is married and now lives in Vancouver. Our youngest son graduated from university as a marine biologist, but, unable to find a job, he retrained as a real-estate professional and works in Vancouver.

In 1965 I rejoined the Polish Combatants Association and have remained an active member ever since. For ten years I was on the Auditing Committee, and for seven I served as its chair. I also served two terms as president of Chapter #13. Now contentedly retired, I hope to continue my involvement in various social initiatives of the association for years to come.

PIOTR ORLUKIEWICZ

I was born in 1919 near Brasław [Braslav], in the Wilno [Vilnius] region. I reached the Polish armed forces via the Soviet army. After invading eastern Poland, the Soviets conscripted all those born in 1917, 1918, and 1919. Thousands of Poles and Ukrainians found themselves, for the most part against their will, in the Red Army. I was drafted on May 5, 1940. Trying to comfort us, the Soviet recruiters assured us that the Soviet army was not at all like the Polish army: no one would smack us in the face or kick our butts or whip our backs. No, no one would do that to us; rather, as we soon discovered, the army would simply exercise us to death or have us shot for disobedience.

The recruits were soon shipped to Russia, where we got our first taste of true Soviet discipline. The rigour was inhuman, slowly choking to death any independent mind or body. Immediately after the reveille, we had to go—on command—to the latrines. Then our shirts were inspected for lice, strictly according to the regulations. If any were found (and usually there were), the owners were sent to the baths. The rest of us were off for a morning drill. Frequently during the march, we would get a command: "Sing!" If our singing did not please the commander, he would order us, "Run and sing!" A kilometre later, he would bark, "Crawl and sing!" Dripping with sweat, we had to drop into the mud without as much as missing a beat. We felt like screaming but had no breath left to scream with. More Soviet discipline: after the outbreak of hostilities with Germany, dozing off on duty meant a bullet in the head; the smallest infraction of discipline was immediately brought before the collegial tribunal, which could pass only one sentence—a firing squad. And all the while we had to attend—often in rain or snow—political lectures extolling the superiority of the worker state and its army over the decadent capitalist institutions.

When the news of the war with Germany reached us, many Poles sang for joy. Officially, we said that we were happy because now we could finally pay the Germans back for the lost war of 1939; but in our hearts we were thinking how we could get across the battle lines to the other side, as far away from the Red Army as possible. In the meantime, our general announced the need to intensify our sluggish training and emphasized the need for high political morale. Perhaps to boost mine, they made me second-in-command in my team, but the promotion did little to excite my enthusiasm.

The political commanders in the Soviet army must have read our hearts, for they never allowed us to reach the front. On June 29, we were called up to a special meeting, at which we were informed that we were being disarmed. All those born in western Ukraine were ordered to step forward. All personal records were verified. During a short interview, I declared that I did not belong to the Party and that, before the war in Poland, we had one cow (this was a lie, for we had twelve). What I said proved enough to classify me as a *kulak* [wealthy peasant]. They loaded us into cattle cars equipped with hastily constructed bunk beds, and sent us in the direction of the front line in Orlov. The capacity of the railway system was stretched to the limits, with hundreds of trains taking civilians and the wounded away from the battle zone. We spent days at a time waiting at sidetracks, giving them the right-of-way. We were issued no food and had to fend for ourselves, foraging in the surrounding villages. Several times we became targets for German bombers. At some point someone somewhere decided we should not get too close to the front, after all, and we turned back and moved inland. We spent a month on that train, moving aimlessly in various directions. The Soviet command clearly did not know what to do with us. Finally, in Sverdlovsk, a senior officer came to us and said, "Until now you have been our prisoners, but now you are free citizens." We could hardly believe that, and our doubts were confirmed when they sent us to what was essentially a labour camp. Officially, we were waiting for the arrival of Polish military authorities to transfer us to the Polish army, but in practice, we were being used as a slave labour force to build an airstrip. The Soviets did their best to exploit us as long as they could. The work at that airstrip was hard and lasted until November, when the ground froze up.

All the while we were sleeping in light tents, with only lice-infested straw for bedding. I caught a bad cold and became really sick. The only available medicine was hot water with salt. I drank it, briefly got even sicker, but by the morning I recovered. The medicine was indeed "worth its salt." When the danger of freezing at night became very real, they moved us to *zemlianki*, crude dugouts with even cruder beds. The ground under the beds was frozen solid. We had to heat the bed boards by a stove to be able to lie down on them. We shivered by night and we shivered by day, when we had to cart away barrelsful of earth in -40°C weather, wearing only threadbare Soviet-issue clothing. We worked that way for four months, the Soviets consistently refusing to release us to the Polish army. When they did move us, it was to a different camp where we loaded and unloaded freight trains. They kept telling us that if we worked well, they would let us go. But few of us believed them, and some even suspected that there was no Polish army and that the whole thing was a Soviet ruse intended to make us work harder. The work was so hard, in fact, that many fell sick, and some even died. One of my friends deliberately cut off his fingers with an axe so he could be sent to the hospital, where there was no work and the food was better. We were fed with a cup of soup and three slices of bread a day. Hunger, like cold, was our constant companion.

Our situation looked hopeless until someone from our group ran into a Polish lieutenant in Sverdlovsk. He passed on to the Polish authorities the information about the 2000 men languishing in our camp. Soon afterwards a Polish officer arrived, argued with the Soviets, and eventually secured our release. And all this through a chance meeting.

We went by train straight to Krasnovodsk, where we boarded ships bound for Persia. We arrived on the beaches of Pahlavi on April 4 and spent the night there. In the morning, Persian peddlers descended on the beach, trying to sell us hard-boiled eggs, but we proved a hard sell: we simply had no money. As far as I was concerned, all this made no difference to me, for I was not feeling well: while aboard the ship, I contracted typhoid fever. There were rumours that those suffering from the fever would be sent back to Russia, so I was terribly afraid and did not see the doctor for many days. I went with the troops to Tehrān, but there I collapsed. Barely conscious, I was taken to the Polish hospital tent. As if through dense fog, I heard the sergeant ask the nurse who brought me in, "Nurse, why have you brought this corpse here, to stink up the whole place?" He was apparently talking about me. Several days later, when I regained consciousness and took a close look at my face in the mirror, I understood the sergeant's remark: I indeed looked like the walking dead. But no matter how terrible my appearance, I still could not eat; I only drank huge quantities of water. When I forced myself to eat a meal, the fever returned. Every morning I could see bodies covered with white sheets, but I was determined not to become one of them. I did not eat, but I desperately wanted to live. My wish was granted to me: hardly anyone survived two bouts of typhoid fever, but I did. When the crisis was over, the nurses began to force some food into me, and gradually I returned to the land of the living.

When I had fully recovered, I was sent to Palestine and assigned to the 8th Battalion of the 3rd Regiment; we were stationed in Kastino. I shared a tent with seven other skeletons from Russia; our buddies called us "Russians"—good-naturedly, of course—and fed us well so we could put some muscles on our bare bones. Our superiors also understood we were still too weak for the rigours of intensive training. In fact, my health took a sudden turn for the worse when I came down with acute appendicitis. After emergency surgery, I was given six weeks of convalescent leave in Natanya. I ate well and finally regained my strength.

My next assignment was to a temporary company in Gedera, where I stayed until February 1943. Then a whole group of us went to Iraq, to a company collecting convalescents from various hospitals. Finally, I ended up in a transportation company and, after a six-week driving course, I was put behind the wheel of an ambulance and dispatched to Italy. I went through—or rather behind—all the major battles of the Italian campaign. I say "behind" because our task was to collect the wounded and take them to field hospitals, but I never fought on the front line. This does not mean that we had it easy. Once, our company, twenty-five ambulances in all, stood between Menafra and Campobasso. When the offensive started, we were overwhelmed with wounded, both our own and German. We shuttled them for twenty-four hours, no time for food or sleep. The Germans were the worst, for they screamed at us and demanded special treatment. As if they deserved anything! Our twenty-five ambulances must have ferried over 1000 wounded that day. During one of the last major offensives of the war, the battle for Bologna, I ended up in the hospital for the third time. It turned out my kidney stones were seriously rattled by my military diet; fortunately, I recovered without any surgery.

That was the end of the war. I joined the Polish Combatants Association [PCA] while still in Italy, so I am one of its oldest members. In November 1946, I was in the first contingent of Polish veterans leaving Italy for Canada. In the same group came Tomszak, Czubak, and Aksamit. We arrived in Winnipeg on November 15. Hearing so much Polish spoken in the streets of Winnipeg was a pleasant surprise for us. Unfortunately, we could not savour those feelings, for on the third day we were taken to a farm in Beausejour. The farmer immediately sent us into the forest to cut lumber near Seven Sisters and haul it to a sawmill. We were ill-clothed for such work—after all, we had just arrived from Italy—but we happened to run into Father Jaworski, who helped us get what we needed. Five of us lived in a small hut for a month, working from dark till dark, and making $45 a month. After Christmas, which we celebrated in Father Jaworski's church, we managed to get to Winnipeg, to the employment office. When we described our working and living conditions, we were transferred to a Polish farmer in East Selkirk. The work was still hard, but accommodation and food were decent. Through the winter, we cleared twenty hectares of bush and were paid $50 a month. In the spring, our pay went up to $70, and at harvest time to seventy cents per hour.

I did not complete my two years of the contract on a farm. After much persuasion, I managed to convince the Employment Office to issue me an insurance booklet, a necessary condition for any city job, and hired myself out as a carpenter. I worked at various construction sites for four years and learned a great deal about carpentry. In 1951, I got a more stable job at CPR, mostly repairing and maintaining railway cars, but in the evenings I continued to do some freelance carpentry. I was a loyal CPR employee for twenty-nine years.

I met my wife, Genia, in 1949 in Winnipeg. At the age of ten, she had been deported to Siberia with her parents, and she came to Winnipeg in 1948. I met her at a social organized by St. John Cantius Fraternal Aid Society, and we were married in 1950. The wedding ceremony was performed by Father Jaworski, who came from Beausejour especially for the occasion.

Our family life took the usual course. We bought our first house, on Austin Street, jointly with my brother-in-law, for $4200; the second, much larger, house, we purchased for $7500 jointly with my wife's uncle. Later I built a house in the Garden City area, sold it at a profit, and built another one, in which we live to this day.

Our immediate family grew as well. Our son Jurek was born in 1952, and another son, Tomek, a year later. We spared no effort to give them the proper education. Jurek finished law and has a flourishing legal practice in Winnipeg. Tomek graduated from Red River College and now lives and works in Saskatoon.

Both my wife and I have been active in Polish organizations in Winnipeg. I helped with the expansion of the PCA clubhouse, and in subsequent years served on the Auditing Committee. My wife was president of the Women's Auxiliary. As we are getting older, we have fewer and fewer worries. We are financially secure and live quite comfortably. Only from time to time, my peace is disturbed by some memories floating back from the past. I have helped my brother to immigrate to Canada with his family, and he now lives in Winnipeg, but I could do nothing for my two sisters who stayed in the Wilno region, or for my brother who remained in Russia. I have lost hope that I will ever see them again.

JERZY PISKOR

I was born on May 25, 1926, in Radom. My father, like his father before him, worked in a sawmill in the nearby village of Wsola. The sawmill and the manor to which it belonged were part of the estate owned by Jerzy Gombrowicz. Later, we moved to Starachowice, when my father got a job at a huge sawmill in the nearby town of Bugaj, in the foothills of the Świętokrzyskie Mountains. I started my schooling in Starachowice, and we were still living there when the war broke out in 1939. I remember that day: I woke up to the drone of German bombers over the city. At first, their target was the industrial complex, but soon they began to bomb the city itself. The explosions and vibrations shattered glass in window frames, even though we had taped the windows as advised by air defence instructors. It is mostly with the ringing of windowpanes that I associate the first day of the war.

I was too young to be in the army, but I was in the Boy Scouts. Our team organized special assistance for the soldiers in the military transports passing through the railway station in Starachowice. We brought them coffee and food, good conversation, and some laughs. They much appreciated it.

With the outbreak of war, all the schools were closed and my education came to a halt. But once the confusion and shock of the defeat subsided, we tried to make up for the lost time by attending clandestine classes organized by the teachers from our junior high. Perhaps most devoted to the cause of underground education was our teacher Zofia Lipko: working under her supervision, we covered, in the space of one year, the material usually taken in two; in just two years we passed all the exams and graduated from our underground junior high.

In the fall of 1939, heavy fighting took place in Starachowice and its environs, and many officers from the scattered Polish units took refuge in the nearby Świętokrzyskie Mountains. They wasted no time and almost immediately began to organize an underground army, or, rather, armies, for the anti-German resistance was highly politicized. In our region, we had not only the Home Army [AK], owing allegiance to the government-in-exile in London, but also Peasant Battalions, National Armed Forces [NSZ], People's Army [AL], and the military units of the Polish Workers' Party [PPR] collaborating closely with the Russians. School friends and Boy Scouts whispered about them to one another and encouraged one another to join various clandestine groups supporting the troops in the forest. Through one such school contact, I joined the forces of the NSZ. My choice was also prompted by the fact that my cousin had joined them already in 1943 and was active in the Lublin region, near Janów, Zamość, and Kraśnik. In the spring of 1944, when the front began to move eastwards, his unit moved into the vicinity of Zawichost, in the Świętokrzyskie Mountains. That was also the time when I began to take a more active part in the operations of the NSZ. At the beginning, my participation involved passing the information about the size of the German forces in Starachowice, about their movements, their quarters, and so on. I also helped find safe houses for the guerilla fighters staying in the city. From May until November 1944, I was a member of a special operations unit: we held regular jobs in the city or on farms, but joined in the armed operations if called upon. Our commander was Captain Gustaw; on his instructions we looked after compromised members of our resistance network, obtained false documents, and arranged for ammunition and food for the partisans in the mountains. We "procured" weapons by attacking individual German soldiers whenever they least expected it. My own safe house was located in the apartment of a Polish policeman ostensibly collaborating with the Germans but strongly sympathizing with the resistance. He was a good source of information, which I passed on to the guerilla units.

I joined the ranks of guerilla fighters in early November 1944. Life in a partisan unit was quite different from the more settled activities of my former special operations group. We prowled through the forests, sleeping in shelters improvised from tree branches, emerging in villages only when there were no enemy troops in the vicinity. The Germans were combing the wooded areas searching for us, but we usually stayed one step ahead of them. Not always, though. They caught up with us on November 12 near a place called Kępa. A strong detachment of German gendarmerie surprised us at the edge of the forest. A furious gun battle erupted, my baptism by fire. We threw against their superior force our superior knowledge of the terrain and guerilla tactics. In the end, we managed to capture two trucks with arms and ammunition but, expecting German reinforcements, had to immediately withdraw from the site of the battle. After this "baptism," I felt like a rat: dead tired, wet, hungry, and wanting only to lie down somewhere and sleep.

On October 29, the entire Świętokrzyska Brigade gathered in the village of Lasocin to celebrate the November 11 anniversary [Poland's Independence Day]. General Bogucki, commander-in-chief of the NSZ, was there together with all the brass and lots of invited guests from other resistance organizations. The leadership used this opportunity to discuss our options in connection with the expected Soviet offensive. Various rumours were afoot. Some claimed that we would withdraw to Silesia and be lodged in various safe houses there; others thought we would split into smaller units and scatter across the Polish forests; still others talked about the possibility of going to Yugoslavia and then to Italy to join the 2nd Corps. The leaders of the AK were invited to our celebration at Lasocin, and they participated in the discussions about the Soviet offensive and its consequences for the brigade. At the level of ground troops, our two organizations worked hand in hand, and I remember no talk about potential conflicts between our leadership and that of the AK.

Not long after the meeting in Lasocin, on December 17, we went into action near Raszków. I remember that operation well. People from nearby villages came to us asking for help against Russian bands terrorizing the countryside. In one of the villages, Węgrzynów, lived many women resettled from Warsaw after the uprising. The bands pillaged it, stealing what they could and raping the women. Our intelligence found out that the units of Vlasov's army* were responsible for

---

* Andrej Andrejevich Vlasov (1900-1946), a Soviet general captured with his army by the Germans in 1942. He later commanded the Russian Liberation Army, formed by the Germans and composed of Soviet prisoners of war, which fought against the Red Army.

this outrage, the same units that had earlier taken part in crushing the Warsaw uprising. So it was with some relish that we routed the thugs and effectively put an end to their rampage.

We felt it was our moral obligation to look after the surrounding villages. After all, those villages fed us and often gave us shelter. We tried to impose the onus of supplying provisions especially on those estates whose Polish owners had been expelled. Those estates were still typically managed by Polish administrators, who did not protest much when we requisitioned the foodstuffs needed for the troops. But when they could not supply us with the necessities, we went to the villages. The local German authorities tagged and registered all cattle and pigs, and farmers were responsible for delivering them to the approved sale stations. But the authorities did make allowances for provisions taken by the partisans. To help the farmers under those circumstances, we would kill, for instance, two pigs, one for us and one for the farmer. In a certificate we issued the farmer, we would state that both pigs were requisitioned for the troops. This way, though he lost a pig, the farmer had some meat for his own family (or for private sale), and the Germans, who strangely enough respected our certificates, did not harass him. So we were on good terms with the local population. Flour mills supplied us with flour; women from the villages baked bread for us. Vegetables were usually difficult to find, especially in the dead of winter, but not everyone complained about that.

There were cases, I admit, when some locals refused to help us, and even actively collaborated with the Germans against us. In those cases we sent our reports to headquarters, which reviewed the evidence and, if warranted, arranged field trials. If proven guilty, the collaborator was sentenced to death, and the sentence was carried out by the special operations section of the NSZ.

On December 22, 1944, we were billetted in three villages, Maciejów, Giebułtów, and Maciejowice. The villages were quite prosperous, so the entire brigade sojourned there, spending Christmas and meeting the New Year in the homes of the villagers. On January 12, a courier arrived from the headquarters in Cracow with the report that the Russian front had begun to move. They could offer us no further support, and the brigade had to cope on its own. Our commander immediately ordered a state of alert, and we set out that same evening in the westerly direction. The next day we crossed the railway tracks at a small station, Tunel. In the distance we saw a detachment of German soldiers, and they, too, must have seen us, but neither engaged the other. After a long night's march, we reached two villages, Pogwizdów and Kępie, and, exhausted from the long trek, were hoping for some rest. But just then the Germans attacked. They must have followed us at a distance, for they now surprised us under the cover of darkness. Fierce fighting erupted. We lost nine men and ten were wounded, most so seriously that they had little chance of survival. The battle ended the next day in the afternoon, after an agreement was reached between our command and the Germans. Soon we were on the move again, catching up with the retreating German units. In Żarnowiec, along the Pilica River, they had organized a line of defence and fortified the only bridge in the area. We had to act quickly. Our scouts captured a few German soldiers and officers, and the commander explained to them that we did not want to fight them; all we needed was the safe passage so that we could cross to the West and join the Polish army there. Then we set them free and Captain Zaremba went with them to the German headquarters. Two hours later, a German interpreter showed up and explained that they would let us through the bridge in the evening. He also gave us the appropriate warrants. We patiently waited for evening, but our scouts brought the news that the Russians were closing in on our rear. We had no choice but for the whole brigade to move quickly towards the bridge in Żarnowiec. We managed to cross it already under fire from the advance Russian units. We lost two carts with supplies but kept moving towards Solcz. The weak German forces could not hold the Russian offensive along the Pilica line, and soon the Russians forded the river and were again on our heels. They probably did not know whom exactly they were pursuing, but that did not matter in that lethal chase. What saved us was probably the deep snow, which soaked and froze our feet but also brought the Russian tanks to a near halt.

After several days of forced march, we were dead tired. I was dozing off in a hut, nesting a rifle between my legs, when an ear-splitting explosion tore off the roof and, half dazed, I was looking into the starry sky. The Russian artillery had found us out. We began to retreat, frantically, beyond the range of fire, across frozen fields, and over windswept meadows. We reached an alder grove, where our chaplain, Father Mróz, was waiting for us. Our situation was critical, and he began to administer the extreme unction, preparing us for death. We had not expected that the Russians would catch up with us so quickly, and the shock of surprise put us to flight and scattered us across the fields. The chaplain's deliberate, serious actions slowed us down, quenched the panic, helped us reorganize. Soon we were a unit again and moving quickly, just in front of the Russian advance troops and just behind the withdrawing Germans. The latter had enough problems of their own not to harass us; they seemed to respect the safe passage they had issued to us at Żarnowiec.

Resting no longer than a few hours at a time, we marched towards the Odra River. Near the town of Odmęt, we briefly stopped in the barracks vacated by American and British POWs. We were facing another big obstacle: the bridge on the Odra River. Once again Captain Zaremba, accompanied by an interpreter, Officer Cadet Topaz, went across the bridge to the town commander. He requested permission for the supply column to cross the bridge (without any mention of the troops). The commander was reluctant until Zaremba showed him the safe passage from Żarnowiec. This worked. The Germans agreed to an evening crossing, but history repeated itself: the Russians pressed on our rear, so without waiting for nightfall, the entire brigade—men, horses, and carts—rushed across the bridge on the Odra. This time we suffered no losses.

We were now moving inside German territory, and the Germans were aware of us. They demanded that we turn south, towards the Czech lands. The march through the Sudety Mountains was most difficult. We had to walk along side roads to avoid further risky encounters with German troops; at times we had to detour around their detachments, adding extra kilometres and tedious hours to our march. In Bohemia, we came across a column of prisoners from the Warsaw uprising, escorted by a small group of German soldiers. As we approached it, about 150 prisoners merged with our men and later joined the ranks of the brigade.

The Germans, who must have kept track of our movements, demanded that we march towards a place called Rozstání. When we arrived there, we realized it was right in the middle of a testing range. In the vicinity were only two abandoned villages, most of their buildings burned down. With some apprehension we set up camp, but hardly anybody got any sleep before our scouts returned with the news that large German units were surrounding the testing range. Our apprehension turned into frustration and anger that we had allowed ourselves to be led there like lambs to the slaughter. We waited at the ready, but the Germans delayed and delayed, making no move against us. Eventually, our intelligence people reported again that German troop movements were not related to our presence at the range. This brought us considerable relief, although the tension took some time to subside.

The people in the villages we marched through were friendly, and we established a good rapport with the Czech underground. Captain Tom, from the intelligence services, was our liaison with both the Czechs and the Germans. It was through him that we learned that the Czechs wanted to send their contacts to the Czech units of General Svoboda, fighting on the Russian side. The Russians, of course, could not know about this. The Czechs took advantage of a German offer to fly them beyond the Russian lines. Three of our officers, Captain Szaława, Captain Gnat, and Lieutenant Rumba, joined them as well to re-establish communications with the NSZ headquarters. The flight was successful, but near Zawichost, Rumba stepped on a mine and died on the spot. Szaława reached Cracow, and there ran into a former nurse from our brigade, Mańka Pędzel. She offered to put him in touch with the NSZ, but instead betrayed him to the Security Services. We knew that before she joined our brigade she had been a member of the People's Army, but we didn't know she had been recruited by the Security Services and was working for them. Captain Szaława was put on trial in Kielce and executed by a firing squad. Of the three emissaries, only Captain Gnat avoided capture and death, and later rejoined the brigade in the West.

The brigade stayed in Rozstání for a while; then we marched in the direction of Pilzno. Not far from that town, in a village of Všekary, we stopped again and began to organize a conduit for moving people from the east to the west and vice versa. The conduit was used not only by the brigade itself but also by the 2nd Corps of General Anders, the 1st Division of General Maczek, and the London government-in-exile.

While in Všekary, we got word from Czech intelligence that not far from us, in Holešov, was a German concentration camp for women from all over Europe. This was already the beginning of May 1945, and the Allied front was closing in. The commander of the brigade gave an order to capture the camp and release the prisoners. So on May 5, exactly at noon, our troops surprised the German crew and took the camp without any resistance. The women were free. One of them pointed out a shack standing to the side; she wasn't sure, but she thought there were more women there. The shack reeked of petrol, and when we opened it, we got a glimpse of hell: it was packed with women, Jewish women, all starved, suffocating, and barely alive. They were to be "disposed of" before the arrival of the Allied troops, but at the last moment fate grinned at them.

The women were so grateful for the freedom we brought that they presented us with a big heart with all their names written on it. One of those freed at Holešov was a Frenchwoman, Mrs. Michelin; after she returned to France, she sent a letter to the brigade, inviting everyone who had participated in the liberation of the camp to visit France at her expense. Each of us was welcome to spend two weeks enjoying her hospitality.

The taking of the concentration camp was perhaps our last major wartime action. On May 6, our patrols came in contact with the American reconnaissance units. When we learned about it, the brigade erupted with cheers and celebration. At last we would find some protection under the wings of the Allies! We began to take nearby German units prisoner, and one of our detachments even took prisoner an entire command headquarters of one of the German armies. Then, on May 8, the war was over.

Despite our joy and optimism, our situation was not enviable. Our uniforms were in tatters, food was in very short supply, and only lice were abundant. The brigade was still stationed close to the Russian front. The Russians demanded that the Americans hand over our brigade to them, but the Americans categorically refused. Just in case, General Devine moved us fifty kilometres to the west, near the town of Bernartice. Now that the war was over, we could rest a little, but with more time to think came worries about families back home. So from Bernartice, the brigade sent another reconnaissance team back to Poland. This team was made up of Captain Gustaw (former commander of the special operations in Kielce), Captain Białynia (who—as I later discovered—was an administrator of my uncle's estate in Wolica near Busko-Zdrój), and Captain Albert. Their objectives were to re-establish contacts with Poland and to help the families of the soldiers of the brigade. That latter task often involved smuggling family members to the West. Through the conduits they set up came the family of General

Bohun-Dąbrowski, except for his wife, who had died before we could get her out. Through Bernartice came also General Piskor's wife, Lucy Piskor, who spent two weeks with the brigade before she continued on to London. The brigade's underground transit points were even used by the wife of Stanisław Mikołajczyk, at the time premier of the Polish government-in-exile in London.

The political situation of the brigade was also difficult, especially after General Bór-Komorowski was named commander-in-chief of the Polish Armed Forces in the West. He and the leadership of the NSZ had had strong disagreements even before the war, and those misunderstandings resulted in the Świętokrzyska Brigade now being excluded from the Polish Armed Forces. Ordinary soldiers, like myself, were disappointed with the high command's attitude. We thought that the blood we shed in the fight against Germany fully entitled us to membership in the Polish Armed Forces. We could not understand—and didn't care much for—the politics behind the pronouncements of the high command in London, and our feelings of resentment continued until the old quarrels were put to rest and the Świętokrzyska Brigade's wartime efforts were acknowledged by London.

Towards the end of June 1945, the brigade was moved further inside the German territory, near Coburg. On the basis of an order that came from the headquarters of the American army, we were disarmed and reclassified as displaced persons. Only forty of us, all with some special training, were selected to join the Polish forces in Italy. I was one of them because I could drive. We were issued an Italian Lancia, and drove through Innsbruck, Brenner Pass, and Bolzano to Ancona, where we found the 2nd Corps. I was assigned to the 28th Supply and Transport Company of the 2nd Warsaw Armoured Division. I travelled with that unit throughout Italy and England, until the dissolution of the army and my demobilization in 1947.

In 1946, I sent a letter to my parents through the Red Cross. That letter proved both a curse and a blessing to them. A curse because soon after my parents received it, the Security Office arrested my father and interrogated him for days. They kept asking how I had made it to the 2nd Corps, and he kept answering that he didn't know. In the end they released him, but not without some patent threats. And yet the letter brought much relief to my family, for this was truly our first exchange of correspondence since my wartime peregrinations had begun; the only piece of news that had reached them earlier was that I was missing in action and presumably dead.

Around the time of our demobilization, representatives of the Warsaw government organized a campaign encouraging ex-servicemen to return to Poland. There were some who yielded to their clever persuasion and went back, only to bitterly regret their decision. I, too, was torn between the alternatives. My uncle, General Piskor, was then in London, so I visited him and asked for advice. Because of his own position in the Polish army, he could not go back, but he did not try to convince me to stay. When I mentioned to him the possibility of emigrating to Canada, he was most supportive and even admitted that he, too, was considering that option. I needed no further encouragement and decided to try my luck beyond the ocean. He did not have a chance to act on his intention before he died in London in 1952.

Three Western countries expressed willingness to accept some of the demobilized Polish soldiers: Australia, New Zealand, and Canada. Of those three, Canada indeed appeared the most attractive, not only to me but to a large number of my comrades at arms, as well. We went to the camp where the civilian and military recruitment commissions were located. The Canadians were accepting only men with some experience in agriculture. The initial qualification criteria were very strict: for every 100 applicants, only one was accepted. It took an intervention and a protest from General Rakowski, who said that in his units he had ordinary soldiers, not supermen, before the commission reviewed its recruitment policy and started again from scratch. The commission routinely asked about the size of the family farm, about acreages of cereals, potatoes, beets, about farming techniques, and so on. Prior to the interviews, the real farmers among us gave those from more urban backgrounds crash courses in agricultural practices to prepare them for the "exams." As for me, luck seemed to be on my side from the start: I got through the commission's sieve quite early and was spared the bouts of frustration, uncertainty, and disappointment experienced by many others.

Over 1000 of us left Southampton for Halifax on May 20, 1947, aboard the liner *Aquitania*. The passengers were a mixture of ex-servicemen and civilians. When we sailed into some stormy weather and the ship began to roll, many civilians came over to our quarters, probably feeling more secure among the uniformed soldiers. We put on brave faces, even though our hearts were sinking and heaving with the ship.

We docked in Halifax on May 25. We were issued our last military pay. The authorities demanded that we surrender our handguns, but a soldier never willingly gives up his weapons, so the boys began throwing their guns overboard, into the water. Many of them are probably still lying on the bottom today. Then we were transferred onto a special train. One group got off in Quebec, another in Ontario; mine disembarked in Manitoba, and the final group continued on to Alberta. The destinations and transport were all arranged jointly by the Ministry of Agriculture and the military authorities.

From the CPR station, where we first stepped off the train, we went by tram to the Fort Osborne Barracks. After two weeks of recuperating from the long journey and acclimatizing to Manitoba's dry heat, we were sent to three camps—in Roland, Emerson, and Letellier—to work in the sugar beet fields. In Roland, we lived in tents, had meals from a makeshift kitchen run by Rudolf Kozłowski, and enjoyed the light-hearted atmosphere and comradery. We made little money there, but it was enough for cigarettes and an occasional beer. One Sunday, we even organized a bus trip to Winnipeg to take part in the first meeting of the local chapter of the Polish Combatants Association. At the meeting, chaired by Lieutenant Czubak, Lieutenant Klimaszewski was elected as the first president of the chapter.

I worked in the sugar beet camp at Letellier for three weeks; afterwards I found myself, together with a friend of mine, Aleksander Świrski, helping with the harvest in Holland. We were no longer in a large, organized camp, which ensured us a degree of protection, but scattered among the farms and dependent on the farmers for food and lodging. And the farmers, used to the free labour of German prisoners, often treated us like slaves. They thought we didn't deserve food on days we didn't work, and tried to forbid us to go to a hotel for a beer, claiming we had no permit to do so. We felt sad and hurt by such treatment: was that what we fought for in the war? After two and a half weeks of wheat harvest, I returned to Winnipeg, but only for a while. In the fall I was again out in the fields, harvesting sugar beets for another farmer.

The farmers didn't need us in winter, so I looked for a job in Winnipeg. By word of mouth, several of my friends and I learned that the Abitibi Company, with offices in Sutherland Hotel, was hiring just then. It was a pulp and paper company, and it was indeed recruiting lumberjacks to cut bush in Ontario. Since strength was in numbers, a whole group of us decided to go. We occupied an entire barrack, ate at a local kitchen (the food was excellent, considering that we were in the middle of nowhere), and soon had a small community going. While there was daylight, we cut trees; but after dark, we entertained ourselves with many a silly pastime. One of them was an orchestra that played on paper instruments. Jan Konecki was its chief instigator and conductor. There was much clowning and silliness, but that was exactly the point, to fill the free time with laughter.

Working hard in the bush, one could make decent money, for the pay depended on productivity. But the Employment Office somehow found out that we were lumberjacking in the bush instead of slaving on the farms, as per our contract. We got word that employment officers would be waiting for us at the railway station when we got back. But we feared nothing: instead of staying on the train until the main station, we got off in St. Boniface, to their chagrin, no doubt.

We remained in Winnipeg till spring, living off our savings, for jobs were scarce in the city. Finally, pressed by need, we went to the Employment Office to file requests for unemployment insurance papers, without which no one wanted to hire us. The unfriendly employment officers began to threaten us with deportation for failing to fulfil the terms of our contract. But after protracted discussions, we managed to convince them that they were mistaken, and we got the papers.

Not long afterwards, Lieutenant Czubak and I were hired by a hotel in Winnipeg Beach. The owner, Mr. Radymski, was sympathetic towards the veterans, and tried to help rather than exploit us. The working conditions in his hotel were quite good: we were paid $65 a month plus food and lodging. Although the pace of the work was hectic, especially during the peak of the summer season, our tasks differed from day to day, and few of them were unpleasant. With the holiday season over, we returned to Winnipeg to look for something more permanent. Together with Jan Misiewicz and Jerzy Czyczko, I tried a clothing factory on Notre Dame. Clothing factories were—and still are—notorious for paying low wages. If we worked no overtime, our weekly wages did not exceed $18, hardly enough to live on. The room and board at

Mrs. Sobol's place on Selkirk Ave, which I shared with two buddies of mine, Świrski and Kociołek, cost me $45 a month. Add to that the cost of tram tickets and an occasional beer, and I had nothing left of my paycheque. We also received $10 to $15 monthly from England, as a demobilization supplement. Still, my monthly income was rather pitiful and sufficed only for a very modest existence. So I kept looking for a better paying job, and eventually I found one, with a dry-cleaning company.

Most of my army buddies were of the age when you start thinking of settling down and starting a family. Whenever possible, we tried to meet Canadian-born Polish girls. One such opportunity arose in 1949, when the Polish Gymnastic Association Sokół organized a choir. Many of us signed up right away, hoping to broaden our social life and meet some young, beautiful, warm Polish girls. Our conductor was Mr. Radian, who had once sung with the Polish Radio Choir. Since we needed someone to play the piano, Mr. Radian approached a young lady from the Polish community, Miss Adela Ufryjewicz, and she gracefully accepted the offer. That is also how I first met her: sitting at the piano, talking to Mr. Radian, and laughing. After several conversations, we became quite close. Our budding relationship was interrupted for a year, because she moved to Windsor, but we resumed it on her return. It flowered into marriage in 1951. At the time I was still quite poor, struggling to make ends meet; that she decided to tie the knot with me bespeaks the power of love and trust in the future.

My friends, too, were looking for love and marriage. Many maintained good relations with the local Polish families and were invited to various celebrations and parties, but relatively few of them, perhaps fewer than five percent, married Polish-Canadian girls. Fortunately, in the late forties and early fifties, many young Polish women came to Canada from German labour camps, from the Women's Auxiliary Services of the Polish Armed Forces in the West, and from the refugee camps in Africa, where they had been placed after leaving the Soviet Union. It was among these women that most of my buddies found their brides.

In 1951 I began to work for a dry-cleaning company called New Method Dry Cleaning. The company opened a new express cleaning outlet, Peter Pan Cleaners, and I became its manager. But soon New Method Dry Cleaning was sold to a larger firm. We had just bought our first house on Smithfield Street for $8500 (our mortgage was at 4.5%);

this price might seem insignificant today, but fifty years ago the wages were much lower. With some experience in the dry-cleaning business, I got a job at Quinton's, and managed one of their outlets for ten years. Then in 1964, I was ready to start my own company, Imperial Cleaners at Pembina and McGillivray. We both worked very hard, my wife and I, so the business was soon doing quite well.

I was also blessed with a happy family. We have two sons, Richard and Thomas. Both finished university. Richard, the older one, married an Irish-Canadian and moved to Victoria; Thomas also married into an Irish family but stayed with his wife and their two Polish-Irish-Canadian daughters here in Winnipeg. With a tinge of sadness, I must admit that neither son found Polish social life in Winnipeg appealing, but they are aware of their Polish roots and so, I hope, will be my two granddaughters, Kelly and Sarah.

On the whole, I have been fortunate in life: I have a stable family, grandchildren, and a secure future. True, our beginnings were very difficult: my wife was one of several children in a family of rather modest means, and we could count only on ourselves. We built our future—our comfortable present, that is—with hard work and fortitude. My start in business was probably hampered by the linguistic barrier. In those days there were no government-paid language courses; one had to work at the lowest paid jobs and climb the ladder step by step. When those courses did become available, I never took advantage of them, for I was already too busy planning my business empire. And besides, I had the best, gentlest teacher—and a native speaker of Canadian English—I could ever have hoped for right at home: my wife.

Over the years I have actively participated in the life of the Polish community in Winnipeg. I have been a member of the Polish Combatants Association [PCA], Chapter #13, since its inception. I was also involved in the various projects of the Polish Congress, took part in all Polish celebrations, and even danced in a Polish folk ensemble. But as my family grew and required more of my time, my involvement in community life diminished.

Although I may have retired from active professional and community life, I have stayed in touch with my friends and colleagues. Lieutenant Huba from the Świętokrzyska Brigade (and a cousin of mine) died not long ago in Ontario. I corresponded with Colonel Bohun-Dąbrowski, who kindly sent me a copy of his book, with a special dedication.* But it is the initiative of Henryk Lebioda, a comrade of mine from the Świętokrzyska Brigade, who now lives in Regina, that, in my opinion, deserves a special mention here. Some fifteen years ago, he started helping Polish hospitals that care for former guerilla fighters left invalids by the war. His wife, Dutch by birth, has also wholeheartedly espoused this cause. Since the Regina chapter of the PCA numbered only twelve members, Henryk has used his own personal contacts to gather medical equipment and send it to the needy Polish hospitals. With the approval of the provincial government, he collects the equipment no longer needed by the modernized Saskatchewan hospitals, such as surgical tables, hospital clothing, and wheelchairs, and ships it all to Poland. Recently, he dispatched, at the cost of $9000, a large transport of such supplies, worth about $200,000. I described his efforts to our Winnipeg chapter of the PCA and suggested that we help him cover the transportation costs. My proposal met with general approval, and thanks to the efforts of H. Kozubski, S. Kmieć, and W. Kuzia, we managed to send over $7000 to Regina.

That money was certainly well spent. Now and then, we get copies of letters Henryk receives from various beneficiaries, thanking him for the gifts. The latest, very moving, came from an invalid in Belarussia, who could hardly believe that his sacrifices in the struggle for freedom in the ranks of the AK were still remembered so many years after the war. So far, this reconditioned Canadian medical equipment has reached hospitals in Iłża, Starachowice, and Ostrowiec in the Świętokrzyskie Mountains, where the NSZ was engaged in the heaviest fighting. Currently, the medical supplies are being sent to the headquarters of the AK, which distributes them to the hospitals where the need is the greatest.

I had always maintained strong ties with Poland—after all, much of my family was still there—but visited it for the first time since the war only in 1968. I went with my older son, Richard. We started in Italy, where I showed him the traces of my wartime presence there. The stay in Poland coincided with the unfortunate events in Czechoslovakia and in Warsaw. My son was shocked by all the soldiers at the borders and by the strict border-crossing regulations. I did not enjoy them, either,

---

* *Byłem dowódcą Brygady Świętokrzyskiej Narodowych Sił Zbrojnych: Pamiętnik dowódcy* (London, 1984).

but then, I remembered much harsher times. During that trip, my son had an opportunity to meet his grandfather, who died soon afterwards. Most recently, I went to Poland in 1992 to take part in the international convention of the former members of the Polish Armed Forces in the West. The gathering was very moving. The former NSZ members stood side by side with the AK fighters and with soldiers from other military formations. The old misunderstandings between the leadership of the NSZ and the National Armed Forces had become the stuff of history books. After some fifty years, my own contributions to the fight against Nazism were recognized with two medals, the Partisan Cross and the NSZ Cross. After the celebrations, I retraced the old guerilla routes from Giebułtów through Żarnowiec and Koło to Odmęt, the route that was the most difficult experience of my life. From that trip I brought back to Canada some pictures of fields near Kielce, overgrown with blood-red poppies.

JAKUB PLEWA

I was on active service in the 16th Infantry Regiment in Tarnów when the war of 1939 broke out. Our regiment trained soldiers who supplied the ranks of the Border Guard Corps [KOP]. In March of that year, we had been sent to the 18th Battalion stationed in Brasław [Braslav] county, near the Lithuanian-Latvian border. Coming from the south of Poland, we were struck by the difference in climate: when farmers in Tarnów were starting to work in the fields, the fields near Brasław were still blanketed with over a metre of snow. In fact, we were training on a lake still bound by thick ice.

In April, when the Germans annexed Klaipeda, our battalion was woken up in the middle of the night and put on high alert. We stayed in combat readiness for three days. My company manned twelve heavy machine guns and four mortars; we were also issued long, armour-piercing rifles. Those three days were tense but uneventful, and in the end the alert was called off. After that episode, our battalion's man-power was doubled.

In late spring, we were transferred to Augustów in the Suwałki region and lodged variously in cottages, stables, and barns. When on duty, we wore full uniforms and complete battle kits. In July we moved again, to Białobrzegi, where we began building air-raid shelters. We passed the days carting sand, laying beams, setting up camouflage. We also con-structed machine gun sites and prepared stores of ammunition, partly on the sites and partly in nearby tents.

On September 1, we were ready for combat. We saw some German reconnaissance planes, but they did not engage us. We, too, were ordered to hold fire; instead, we remained in a constant state of air-raid readiness. We did practise shooting, but at made-up targets, often at night, when every tenth shell was a flare, so we could see how we were doing. On September 8, I was on my assigned post when two German airplanes appeared above the horizon. One of them was heading straight for our site. I kept my sights trained on that aircraft until it came so close that it was almost begging to be shot down. We had been ordered to hold fire, true, but I could not resist the temptation and popped off a short round in its direction. The plane staggered, then fired at us and circled back towards the German line. A few minutes later a messenger arrived from the platoon commander. He asked me if I had fired. I replied in the affirmative. So he ordered me to report to the company commander. When I did so, the commander ordered me to dress up and report to the battalion commander. I thought I would face the firing squad for disobeying an explicit order. Lieutenant-Colonel Nachowicz asked me again if I had shot at the German airplane. I admitted it was me, but I had done it because the plane came so close that I could not help myself. "Dismissed!" he said, nothing more. I returned to my tent full of anxiety. In the evening, it was announced I was being given an official reprimand for disregarding an order; but the very next morning I was publically commended for my marksmanship, for it turned out that I had brought that plane down. The pilot was injured but had managed to escape with his life. He jumped out of the plane, and saw some children running in his direction. He panicked and started shooting. When the peasants in the nearby fields heard the shots, they grabbed their forks and shovels and charged at him. They would have torn him to shreds if it had not been for the arrival of our reconnaissance troops.

We stayed at our positions until September 12. That day we loaded our equipment onto a train, but the train did not go anywhere. In the evening an order came to unload and return to our former stations. The following day the same thing happened. It was not until a couple days later, when we were almost convinced that the whole loading exercise was just a cruel joke, that the train finally started moving south. Along the way, we were attacked by German bombers, but we were not defenceless: our units were well armed with heavy machine guns, anti-tank guns, light field guns, and an assortment of other weapons. This time the commander ordered us to shoot at any flying object that appeared above the horizon. We were told that machine guns were not very effective against airplanes and that we would do better firing single but well-aimed shots. I am convinced this tactic was effective. Whenever German planes appeared, we tried to shoot with precision; they saw the danger and stayed high up. Dropping their bombs from high altitude, they did not cause much damage to the train. They tore up some tracks and damaged the engine, but no lives were lost.

After improvised repairs, we continued south through Baranowicze [Baranavičy] and Łuniniec [Luninyets] towards Równe [Rivne]. Late at night on September 17, the train stopped in the middle of the fields, and we got an order to unload. We formed marching columns and set out on foot along a side road, with all our equipment in tow. It was only then that we learned that the Bolsheviks had crossed the border and invaded Polish territory. There was no official announcement, but the news of the invasion quickly spread by word of mouth up and down the column.

Marching west towards the Bug River, we did not come across any Soviet troops or see any Soviet planes. What we did come across were arches put up by local Ukrainians at the entrances to their villages to welcome the Soviet troops, decorated with red flags and portraits of Stalin and Lenin. Once, as we were approaching a village, a cart drawn by a pair of beautiful horses galloped straight into our column. Our boys quickly seized the horses and pulled down the driver, who tried to explain that he came as an emissary to negotiate the conditions of our passage through the village. We were to negotiate with the locals to pass through a village in our own country: preposterous! We shoved him to the back of the column and marched on; I do not know what happened to him.

By nightfall we came to a small town called Kołki [Kolki], on the road to Łuck [Luts'k]. The town was eerily quiet and empty, except for a few older women. One of them was lurking in the shadows of the house assigned to us as lodging. As a precaution, we searched the house and—wouldn't you know it—discovered a cachet of machine guns and ammunition buried under the dirt floor. There was no point asking the woman about it: she saw nothing and knew nothing. Later, as we were squatting down to dinner, a group of armed Ukrainians fired at us and then vanished as quietly as they appeared. One of our guys got hurt. Immediately patrols were dispatched in all directions but found only the wind sweeping over the open fields.

At daybreak we moved on. The experience of the previous day should have taught us a lesson, but apparently it did not. Two Silesians, both good soldiers, developed a sudden craving for milk and strayed to a nearby village to buy some. When they did not come back, the whole company went to search for them. We found one drowned in a well; the other, stripped to his underwear, was nailed dead to a tree with his own bayonet, not far from the road.

The following day, shortly before noon, we heard artillery fire in the distance and spotted some saddled horses without riders. Soon we also found the riders: several Soviet corpses by the roadside. Further down the road we passed two Soviet tanks, one burned out and the other shattered. Clearly we were in the war zone. The column was put on full alert, and yet, around three in the afternoon, we walked right into a Soviet trap: in front of us was a whole Soviet division, its tanks camouflaged in ditches. They attacked at dusk with a hurricane of machine gun fire. We spread into an extended line. I hid behind some ammunition boxes, the best cover I could find. As it grew darker, we got orders to withdraw a few hundred metres and dig in. Around eleven at night, all hell broke loose again. Soviet artillery, we discovered, was behind our backs. In front was the infantry: we could see their shadowy units moving in the moonlight. Then, like human waves, they began to swell in our direction. Wave after wave, they came so close we could hear their frightened voices turning into screams as we brought them down with our deadly fire. That was the Soviet way of launching an attack: sending thousands after thousands to a certain death. We had plenty of ammunition and shot to kill, of course. Those wave attacks must have cost the Soviets hundreds of soldiers, but then life was cheaper than food to the Soviet leaders. We stood our ground until early morning. At dawn, the Soviet artillery fire intensified and their tanks moved into action, followed by more infantry. For us, it was time to move. We sent the horses and the wagons ahead and followed along forest paths towards the northwest. Unfortunately, we did not get very far. About eighteen kilometres from Kowel [Kovel], the Bolsheviks encircled us once again. This time they blocked all potential routes of escape, and our command had no choice but to negotiate. In the end, the battalion commander gathered us all and announced that we had to disarm. Tears rolled down our cheeks as we listened to him. I was feeling completely useless and helpless, and I am sure others were troubled by similar emotions. But we followed the orders, marched in twos down the road, removed the locks, and dropped our rifles in piles on either side of the road.

The Soviets marched us to Kowel. It was already night when we got there, so we settled down in a fenced square, sleeping wherever we could. In the morning, we got some bread and hot water. No one knew what was going to happen. A few of us jumped the fence and went to see what was going on in town. We saw plenty of newly appointed local militiamen with red bands on their arms. One of them, still wearing a Polish uniform with the badges of a platoon leader, walked up to a young Polish officer. He reached to the officer's shoulder and tried to grab his Polish insignia, saying in Russian—but with a heavy Jewish accent—"You won't need these any more. There is no Poland now." The lieutenant pushed him away, pulled out his revolver, and shot him squarely between the eyes. For a moment he stood motionless, then turned around, handed his gun to a Soviet officer who had witnessed the whole thing, and in silence walked into a nearby house gate. The whole scene lasted less than a minute, but that minute will stay in my mind for ever.

There was much confusion and uncertainty as to what would happen to us. Finally, several hours later, our captors announced that all Polish officers would be detained, but privates would be allowed to go home. Right away they formed us into a column and marched us to the railway station. On the platform, they pointed out to us which cars were bound for which districts or cities in Poland, and we took our seats according to our destinations. The train pulled out of the station but, to our consternation, it began moving east, not west. Slowly we realized that the Soviets had played a cruel practical joke on us: we were all bound for Shepetovka and labour camps, not for Poland.

I stayed in Shepetovka for about two weeks, one of some 22,000 Polish POWs assembled there. Food was scarce. Once a day we could get a bowl of weak soup, if we had a container and if we lined up for most of the day. Since few of us had any containers, we improvised as best we could. I found a large sugar beet and carved it out into a bowl. Lining up seemed less of a problem: after all, we had little else to do. Standing in lines, we watched the camp and talked. Within the first few days, we noticed that small groups of prisoners were sent out in unknown directions. We heard rumours that some went to work in the mines near the Zolotoy Rog by Vladivostok. All the guys from my unit stuck together, and eventually we were dispatched as a group to build the road from Lwów [L'viv] to Kiev. The Soviet soldiers and officers treated us relatively well. I remember only one incident when a Polish soldier was shot dead in the camp, located in an old hops-processing plant. We worked there for a whole year, till December 1940; then 1200 of us were transferred near Tarnopol [Ternopil'], where a new air-field was being constructed, and set to work digging ditches, levelling the terrain, and so on. This lasted until June 21, 1941. That day we marched out to work as usual, but around 9 a.m. we were told to gather our equipment and return to camp. On the way back, we spotted some German planes. Soon we learned that Tarnopol had already been bombed. The Germans had attacked the Soviets: our enemies were at each other's throats. We were overjoyed.

Some time later, we formed a marching column and set out for a twenty-one-day trek across Ukraine. After seven days, we reached Zolotonosha. From all that walking, I developed ulcers on one foot, and it swelled so much that I could not wear a shoe. I kept marching, with a shoe in hand, but fever was draining all my strength. I heard a Soviet colonel announce that an agreement had been signed between the Polish and Soviet governments and that we were now allies, but I was not sure that I was not hallucinating. Several kilometres later my strength gave out completely, and I had to lie down by the side of the road. I asked some colleagues to stay with me, but they were afraid because guards shot all marauders and pushed their corpses into ditches. So I thought I had reached the end of my life. But a few guards went by and none pulled out a gun on me, and when the supply wagons came close, they picked me up and placed me in one of them. Several others, too weak to walk, were already riding in it. At some point they transferred us into trucks, which kept moving steadily in the direction of Starobel'sk. Along the same road thousands of cattle were being herded eastwards. Many collapsed from exhaustion or were killed during Romanian air raids, so we had good meat to eat. Finally, our column of several thousand Polish POWs reached its destination, Starobel'sk.

For once the Soviets did not lie: a Polish army was forming in

Starobel'sk. Immediately on arrival we went through registration and verification formalities to determine our assignments to various services. I found myself again in a machine gun unit, part of the 18th Infantry Regiment of the 6th Division. We started training, which was rather rudimentary at first, for lack of proper equipment. From Starobel'sk we were transported to Totskoye, where in February we suffered terrible hardships in -63°C weather. The firewood we brought from the forest was not enough even to thaw the frozen shirts on our backs. We left Totskoye to train with new English equipment in Chirakchi, Uzbekistan, in Central Asia. Things looked good at first, but as the weather got warmer, many men came down with malaria and dysentery. I quickly succumbed to both. I suffered from high fever, a blinding headache, and running bowels. In this condition, going to the latrines always tested the limits of my endurance. I remember crawling on all fours to that smelly place and squatting with the help of those steadier on their feet. The fear was that someone might fall in and drown in one of the pits.

After a month of suffering in a tent, I was taken to the hospital. They had no bandages or drugs but at least they offered us some compassion, badly needed in that place of death. One woke up in the morning to see patients on nearby beds already covered with white sheets. Then came the orderlies who carried the corpses away. I stayed in that hospital, clinging to life, for about a month. Then the whole place was evacuated to Krasnovodsk, but I was too weak to be allowed aboard a ship. I weighed no more than thirty-four kilograms. They had to leave me in a Soviet hospital. After four weeks, although still exhausted, I decided to escape and rejoin the Polish army. With six others, we began to collect food supplies, taking the bread from those who had died or were too weak to eat anyway. We dried it into hard biscuits, easier and lighter to carry. Next we bought a bottle of wine. One of us, a handsome lieutenant, drank it with the nurse on duty, a plain woman who seemed to fancy him, and got her drunk. When she fell asleep, we took the keys to the storage room, where our uniforms were kept, and went to the station. We knew we had to make it to Ashgabad, a collection point for scattered Polish civilians and military. The train was crammed with Soviet soldiers, but we managed to squeeze in, standing most of the way on the steps or in the corridors. At the station in Ashgabad we found Polish hospital staff on duty. They were looking out for lost Polish souls—and bodies—like ourselves. They took me straight to the hospital, which was well supplied with medicine from England, and there I began a slow process of convalescence.

When I was deemed strong enough, I was loaded with others onto Canadian trucks and driven to Persia. It was a crazy ride. The drivers were all Persians, contracted by the British, and they drove, it seemed, with abandon. As we were climbing up the steep mountain roads, the only safe way to stop was to put stones under the wheels. This task was performed by special helpers, always at the ready with a stone or two. Breaks could not be counted on. My recollections of that trip are rather blurry, for the journey was very strenuous and my health still very poor. In fact, when we arrived in Tehrān, I was taken again to a military hospital, where I spent several weeks recovering from the vestiges of malaria, dysentery, and general exhaustion.

When I was sufficiently recovered, the medical commission assigned me to the 35th Workshop Company, not only because of my health but also because of my trade: by profession, I was a saddler, and saddlers were in great demand. By then I was also able to visit my former unit. When my friends first saw me, they crossed themselves as if they had seen a ghost, for it had been officially announced that I was dead. Afterwards we had a few good laughs on that account, for there is a superstition that if one has been buried once, he will enjoy a long life. Superstition or not, the saying came true for me.

Our advance workshop units soon left for Kirkuk in Iraq and moved on to Palestine, near the town of Rehovot. We usually followed the regular troops, repairing their trucks, making tarpaulins, and such. When we landed in Taranto, Italy, I was in the rescue platoon, which removed shattered or broken vehicles from the roads. Those that could still be repaired were towed to our workshops; others were simply moved to the side. Soldiers from my company often worked on the front line, and many were highly decorated. Our cranes worked, for example, near the "Doctor's House" on Monte Cassino. For a while, the base of our operations was in Medola, where the Americans had by mistake bombed French positions and killed some thirty soldiers; but most of the time we moved with the front-line units.

In our spare time, we often fooled around with Italian kids. There was always several of them hanging around, eager to learn a Polish song, such as "Antoni Kociubinski plays his double bass," in exchange for a bar of chocolate. At other times, we fooled around with their older sisters or with nurses. Wine was plentiful, and we drank it in large enamelled teacups, holding three-quarters of a litre. Needless to say, we were a cheerful bunch when off-duty.

We were stationed in Senigallia when the war came to an end, and we remained there until our departure for England. There was never a shortage of work for us: Allied drivers made sure of that. We went to England in the fall of 1946. It was a time of heart-wrenching decisions: should we return to communist Poland or stay in the West? British officers approached each soldier individually to declare himself. I remember some fellows signing up for the return one day, only to strike their names from the list the next, and ask to get them reinstated on the third. Since I had a brother in the United States with whom I had corresponded throughout the war, I wrote to him in 1945 that I wanted to emigrate. Strangely, he did not respond. I wrote to my family at the old, pre-war address and rather unexpectedly got a reply. Unfortunately, it was not encouraging. So I signed up for Canada. In the meantime, I worked as a saddler for a former British officer in a small town on the coast. I had no difficulty finding a job outside the military, and neither had those who could shoe horses or thatch houses. Intellectuals had a much tougher time.

I arrived in Canada by boat and then made it across half the continent by train, to Winnipeg, Manitoba. The group I was in, contracted by a sugar company, was sent to work in the fields, thinning sugar beets. We were supposed to get $40 a month, but in fact they paid us by the acre. Our backs were sore, but we still did not earn much. Once, at the end of the week, I did not even have enough to pay for my food, and I certainly was not a sluggard. Luckily, I managed to transfer from the fields to our communal kitchen, where the pay was indeed $40. At the end of the sugar beet season, I went back to Winnipeg and chanced upon a job as a caretaker in the Holy Ghost Parish. That was a start, and afterwards I worked making cement blocks in West Kildonan, and sewing shoes in a shoe factory, until I got a permanent job at a CPR shop in 1949. There I worked for thirty years, until my retirement. Never in my life did I sit idle or receive any unemployment payments. I was never a burden to my adoptive country.

Two weeks after I was married in 1948, we bought a house on Aberdeen Avenue. We paid $4400, with some help from my wife's parents. Another house, in Fort Rouge, we bought together with two of our friends, Stawikowski and Zbigniewicz. With a decent place to live, we started a family. As the children grew, they became involved in Polish Scouting, and I was drawn into various activities of the Polish Combatants Association [PCA], a generous patron of the Scouts. For the last three years, for example, I have served as president of our small credit union.

I am a proud old man now: proud of my years in the 2nd Corps (for all those years I have kept my uniform, although it does not fit me any more), proud of the achievements of the PCA, and proud of my children (my daughter got a doctorate in psychology) and grandchildren. A little healthy pride of this kind can add much zest to one's life.

PIOTR POLAŃSKI

I was born on November 28, 1910, in the town of Krasiłów [Krasilov], Starokonstantynów [Starokonstantinov] county, in Wołyń [Volyn]. I was the youngest of three brothers. My parents had a farm, and as a young boy I helped them with various seasonal chores. I did not really go to school because it was still wartime. Polish schools were closed, and my mother did not want to send me to a Russian school. Instead, she taught me Polish at home. Father died in the spring of 1916. Even before his death, my eldest brother was called up into the Tsar's Imperial Army. He served less than two years, in Poltava. After the Bolshevik coup of 1917, the Imperial Army disintegrated, and he came back home. He stayed with us for about six months before he joined the Polish army, which was then being revived. When he was tired of soldiering, some time after 1920, he settled in Poland, while Mother and two of us youngsters stayed in what became the Soviet Union. He visited us from time to time, crossing the border illegally. In January 1923, he decided to take us with him to Poland, and I was eager to go. We readied the horses and the sleigh well before dawn on January 9, and left when it was still dark and bitterly cold. We took only side roads to avoid Soviet patrols and reached the border near the town of Bazaliya. We crossed the border in plain view of two watchtowers, one Soviet and the other Polish, but no one came out to stop us. The Soviet soldiers knew that whoever rode with such brazenness was probably well armed, so they thought it better to stay put. And they were right: my brother had a revolver, a Mauser, inside his shoe top, and I, at my mature age of twelve, was cradling a *parabellum*, a heavy type of revolver. The guards on the Polish side were on the lookout for Soviet soldiers, not civilians, so they did not bother us either.

At first I stayed with my brother in Zbaraż [Zbarazh] county, and later in Białozórka [Byalozurka] in Wołyń, where he had a salaried position. Soon Mother and our third brother joined us, and we started farming again. Even though we worked hard, life was difficult and poor, so in 1927 our eldest brother decided to emigrate to Canada with his wife and two daughters, while we continued to farm until the war. In the meantime, I finished seven grades of elementary school and started attending a vocational technical-industrial school, but had to drop out for lack of money. Instead, I signed up for volunteer military service. For two years I served in a motorized squadron in Warsaw; then I returned to help on the farm. In the late 1930s, I also worked part-time over a period of three years as a secretary in our communal office.

Since 1938 the threat of war had been on everyone's mind; it was oppressive and almost tangible. By 1939 we knew it was only a matter of time. I was not surprised when my mobilization papers arrived. I had to report to the 12th Armoured Battalion in Łuck [Luts'k] on August 30. We were not destined for the German front—in fact, we did not take part in any fighting during the September campaign. My unit was placed at the disposal of the Supreme Commander and took orders from the very top. Around September 11, we were instructed to move towards Warsaw, but that order was soon revoked. Instead, we were to go south. We loaded our equipment onto a train in Dubno and made it to Radziwiłów [Chervonoarmeysk] without any incident. Then, on September 13, at dawn, German bombers found us out. Under heavy bombardment, we had to unload the tanks and make for the nearby woods. We never looked back, and drove across the forest towards Brody and Brzeżany [Berezhany]. Plagued by frequent air raids, we moved mostly by night. Near Kołomyja [Kolomyya] we ran into three Soviet tanks with a crew of eighteen who encouraged us to leave our equipment and weapons and go home safely while we still could. They were there to help and protect us. Their encouragements sounded almost like a provocation to us. "Why don't you fight the Germans?" demanded our commander. He received no response except for a false smile and a shrug of the shoulders. The Soviets were courting trouble:

our detachment of several dozen tanks could have easily wiped out their outpost. Now, in retrospect, I wonder why we did not. We had the latest French tanks designed for infantry support; they were rather slow, reaching only twenty-six kilometres per hour on a beaten track and eighteen kilometres in other terrain, but they were well armed with anti-tank and machine guns manned by a crew of two. The Soviets were no match for us, and perhaps that's why we ignored them and drove on.

Some time later, we realized that our supply company had gone missing. We waited for it for a couple of hours, but it did not show up. I found out what happened to our supplies only months later, in Syria, when I met two soldiers who had served in the supply unit. They told me their column had been stopped by the Soviet tanks, which had ordered the trucks off the road. The drivers had been told to park in different spots, according to their cargo. A few trucks from the back of the column noticed that things were going wrong, veered off into a side road, and crossed the Hungarian border. What happened to the men who obeyed the Soviet orders no one knows.

Cut off from our own supplies, we refuelled in Kołomyja and moved on towards Kosów [Kosov]. Food was scarce in that region, and we could not get anything except apples. On September 18, around midnight, we crossed the Romanian border at Kuty by going over the bridge on the Czeremosz River. We drove into Vizhnitsa and parked our trucks on one side of the road and the tanks on the other. In the morning we continued to Storozhinec, where it was announced that we would be disarmed. That was the hardest moment for us, for when a soldier gives up his weapons, he becomes a slave—at least that's how we saw it. We left our heavy equipment as we had parked it and dropped all personal weapons into a heap before a joint Polish-Romanian commission. Feeling quite defenceless, we boarded a train bound for the internment camp. But before the train pulled out, the Romanians realized they had no drivers for the tanks. Our commander agreed to loan them our drivers on condition that they would later rejoin our group. The Romanians made the promises, but we never saw our buddies again: with over twenty military detention camps in Romania, it was almost impossible to find them.

Our destination was Calafat, a small town on the Danube. We were lodged in the deserted military barracks; a few bales of straw scattered on the cement floor were our beds for the following two months. At first the weather was good, and we could even swim in the Danube, but as the autumn cooled into winter, our quarters grew chillier by the day. Our food rations were modest: a loaf of bread (one kilogram) for every two men plus three cauldrons of soup and two sacks of potatoes for the whole camp of 2000 men. The morning meal consisted of coffee brewed from dried sugar beets and some bread; for dinner, we had potato soup, garnished with onions fried in oil. After two weeks in the camp, the authorities organized an exchange of our Polish zloty into Romanian leje. They paid twenty leje for one zloty. Officers could exchange up to 300 zlotys, privates up to 200, but in the end they let us sell only 100 zlotys each. Those who had enough spare money could now buy fruit, mostly grapes, from the local people, but the locals were on an even leaner diet than we were and wanted to buy whatever bread we had left.

Soon after settling down in the camps, Polish commanders received instructions to begin organizing escapes, in the first round for the pilots, then for armoured personnel, and finally for the other services. The pilots had it easy: for a few leje, local boatmen ferried them across the Danube, and they were on their way to Yugoslavia and further, to Italy and Marseille. But the Romanian government became aware of this exodus and ordered local authorities to pursue and recapture all escapees. When our turn came, the Romanians were on the lookout for us. They quickly cornered several of my friends—I still remember their names: Kubacki, Szpakowski, Matacz, Nowak, Kopciuch—and sent them to a penal camp in Fagaras. This detention did not prevent them from escaping again, for I met them in Syria a few months later, but it certainly made the escape more difficult.

I, too, tried my luck twice. We were transferred to a large camp, housing some 12,000 soldiers. It was more closely guarded than our first location: barbed wire, lampposts every fifty metres, and guards every 100 metres were clear signs of the Romanian attempts to stop the flow of escapees. At first we could still get passes to go to town, and many soldiers simply did not return. That is how I was supposed to go, but unfortunately I got mixed up with a group of Polish officers who got arrested for carrying guns. At night, the officers broke out of the prison and ran away. It was several days before I could make new arrangements for my escape. This time I got as far as the Yugoslav border. Waiting for some means of transportation, we learned that the Italians had taken sides with the Germans, and we could no longer travel safely through Italy to Marseille. We had to return our passports and have our destination changed from Marseille to Beirut in Syria. An anxious week later, one in ten of us got back his passport plus a ticket to Constanţa on the Black Sea. The rest had to wait. We were advised to board the train in twos and spread across its length to avoid stirring any suspicions. For once, things went smoothly. In Constanţa we were met at the station by couriers who took us to a safe house, where we could eat and sleep. While waiting for passage to Beirut, we lodged for ten days in a small hotel in the town of Turnu Severin. The local chief of police, a shameless drunkard, knew about the whole operation. He would come to the hotel and demand food and vodka for free. When the hotel manager objected, the chief ordered the arrest of some of our men. We had to bargain with him to get them back. In the end, it was cheaper to slop and water him than to endanger the whole operation.

On May 30, at long last, we boarded a ship called *Besarabia* and left port for the Dardanelle Straits, so narrow that the ship's side almost brushed against the rocks. At dawn we entered the Marmara Sea. A Canadian warship patrolling those waters approached and signalled us to stop. Our captain complied, showed the ship's papers to the Canadians, and half an hour later, we were allowed to continue to Pireus, in the south of Greece. The Pireus harbour was run like a British port: at four in the afternoon, the longshoremen called it a day. It did not really matter that half our cargo was still unloaded. We were forced to spend the night in the harbour, aboard the ship. Since the authorities did not allow us to go ashore, we traded with the Greek merchants who surrounded our ship in small boats by lowering money down on long pieces of string and hauling up the merchandise the same way. The following day we finished unloading, took on a few more refugees, and, navigating with care to avoid mines, left port. We took the southerly course, heading for Tel Aviv in Palestine. The entrance to the Tel Aviv harbour was blocked by a sunken ship; the ten or so Jewish emigrants who needed to disembark were ferried to shore by barges manned by Polish-speaking Jews. We made another brief stop in Haifa before taking course on Beirut. We arrived there in the late afternoon, on June 4, 1940.

The registration services were already waiting for us. Cavalry

Captain Znaniewski read the names of those from armoured units and took us to the camp. After the medical checkups, we were assigned quarters in mosquito-infested tents. We were fed mutton in such quantities that we could not eat it all. The next four days were spent on verification and registration; then by train to Homs, about 400 kilometres from Beirut, where the armoured brigade was stationed in the barracks that had once housed the Foreign Legion. I was assigned to the reconnaissance of the Carpathian Brigade, and found myself in a motorcycle squadron (another squadron still used horses and mules for carrying their machine guns). Most of our equipment was French. In addition to the motorcycles with sidecars, we also had one-and-a-half-tonne Citroën trucks. Our machine guns, also French made, were set in the bases of 81 mm mortar throwers. I was in my element now and eager to learn everything there was to learn about them. All our uniforms were French, too: light clothing for the day because by noon the air was so hot we could hardly breathe, and much warmer for the night. At night, cold air seemed to stream from the snow-covered peaks of the Caucasus, visible on the horizon, and we had to dress for that cold. When on night duty, we wore thicker pants and jackets, sweaters, fur vests, and warm shawls to protect the kidneys.

On June 18, a radio broadcast announced that France had capitulated. Our Polish commanders did not know what the French intended to do with us. The general feeling was that if the French in Syria decided to keep on fighting the Germans, we would fight along with them. But if they decided to disarm us, we would try to break through with all our weapons to neighbouring Palestine. At first, the French commander, General Miterhauser, proclaimed that he would fight on, but a few days later the situation changed. The Germans demanded that the Vichy government surrender its Syrian troops, and the French complied: they ordered Miterhauser to lay down the arms. He, in turn, demanded that we, too, give up our weapons. That, of course, was out of the question. We would rather fight the French than once again suffer the humiliation of surrender. In the end, the French saw our determination and allowed us to depart for Palestine on condition that we leave behind our anti-tank guns. Most of our troops left by train. Our motorized squadron made its own way towards Damascus and then towards the border with Palestine. We spread out along a desert road, ready to resist any French attempts to disarm us by force. Every truck was armed with a machine gun and a mortar thrower. Motorcycles had machine guns fitted in their sidecars. If surprised by the French, each detachment could defend itself until help arrived. Fortunately, all these precautions proved unnecessary. We drove unimpeded until we reached Lake Gennesaret, where we stopped for two days. The weather was so hot that we bathed in the lake every half hour; to make some shade, we hung blankets on our guns. After a couple of days, we continued to the British camp in Latrun, thirty kilometres from Tel Aviv. There we set up our tents in the vicinity of a Trappist monastery: a wise choice of location on our part, for the monks were friendly and often treated us to a cool glass of wine.

On October 3, we were on the move again. We crossed the Suez Canal to Al Cantarah and continued across Egypt to the outskirts of Alexandria. The mounted squadron remained on the outskirts of the desert, while our motorized squadron was positioned near the channel connecting the Mediterranean Sea with a lake just beyond Alexandria. The channel had a strategic significance because during the rainy season the swollen lake threatened the city, and the channel was used to pump excess water out into the sea. Our task was to protect from sabotage the pumping station and the fresh-water intake for the city. We guarded those facilities around the clock for a few months, without any incident. In February, we were sent to the Libyan desert near Sīdī Barrānī, where an Italian army had been destroyed by the Allies. We salvaged whatever motorized equipment was in good shape: trucks, carriers, even guns. After two months under the desert sun, we returned to Alexandria, where we trained for a drop to Greece. We were almost ready to board the ships when, at the last minute, in the middle of the night, we got the news that it was too late: the Germans had overrun Greece as well. The whole operation was called off. Instead, we were shipped to Tobruk.

While the British had been busy taking Italian Somalia and then Syria, the Germans had entered Africa. An Australian division bravely withstood their repeated assaults on strategically located Tobruk, but after four months of heavy fighting, the Australians were exhausted. It was to relieve the Australians that our brigade was dispatched there. Together with a Czech battalion, we took over a section along the coast. The enemy was a fair distance away, but every night we went on patrols in that buffer zone. Within our squadron's sector, we always had two lookouts in a small tent constantly surveying the terrain. When on that duty, we had to scour the foreground with a pair of binoculars, noting every movement, recording every shot and measuring the angles. Around 5:00 p.m., a courier, crawling on all fours, took the lookouts' report to the reconnaissance officer; the lookouts stayed out for the night. That was one of the toughest duties: the sweltering heat of the day, the lugging of heavy machine guns, the stress, and the exertion quickly took their toll.

When the siege of Tobruk was finally broken, and the troops of General Rommel forced into retreat, our brigade took part in the pursuit. Unfortunately, my regiment got different orders, and we left for a training camp in Egypt. First we drove through the desert, and then, on December 22, we boarded a train to Kataba. There we got our first reinforcements, about 100 men from the Krechowiecki Lancers, trained on Marmons and Harringtons. From that camp, I was sent to a training course for driver-mechanics in Palestine and, when that was over, to Gedera.

In the meantime, the British withdrew all Polish troops from Africa, and I, too, eventually found my way to Qizil Ribat [As Sa'dīyah] in Iraq. Our regiment was assigned to training reinforcements from the Krechowiecki Lancers Regiment, comprised of Poles who had come from Russia. In their units I found several guys from Wołyń, my own home region.

[Piotr Polański passed away before he could complete his memoirs.]

JANINA POPKIEWICZ

I was born in Lwów [L'viv] one year before the outbreak of World War I, on May 13, 1913. As a child, I saw much wartime misery because my father, drafted into the Austrian army, was captured by the Russians. I was already three when he managed to escape and return to his beloved Lwów. That city was more than our hometown: it was our roots, our soul, our identity. My grandparents were born there, and so were my parents. Even after all these years, my feelings for Lwów are deep and tender.

My father was a building technologist. Right after the war, he was hired by the Polish National Railways to help rebuild railway bridges destroyed by the various armies. I attended primary school in Lwów; for part of my high school, I lived in Silesia, but it was in Lwów, in High School No. 8, that I wrote my extramural matriculation exam in 1934. Afterwards I started work as an accounting trainee for my father's company. With four years of experience on that job, I took a more responsible position in the accounting department of the Lwów Regional Power Authority [ZEOL], which employed over a hundred people. Power plants were considered to be military installations of strategic importance and were controlled by the military. The ZEOL management was required to keep detailed personnel files on all our employees, and it was one of my responsibilities to maintain them in good order.

When the Soviets invaded Lwów, shortly after September 17, 1939, our power plants continued to operate without any major changes. A Russian was named chief superintendent, but our former superintendent,

332

Mr. Dreszer, continued to manage the operations. In fact, he did much more: he organized an underground resistance network, which involved all his engineers and some support staff. I was aware of the dangers that came with membership in such an organization, yet I, too, quickly became an active operative. My pseudonym was "Elizabeth." Despite the compulsory secrecy, we knew more or less who belonged and who did not. Belonged to what? At first we did not quite know what our organization was called or what its allegiances were, but, eventually, it became clear that we were an integral part of the Home Army [AK]. Our main task was to maintain communications among our various units. We had listening and radio sets to receive messages, which we then passed to our field troops. One of my duties was to type precisely, in multiple carbon copies, the incoming instructions and correspondence, and then carry them to our outposts.

Under Soviet control, our lives took a definite turn for the worse. The Soviets made a concerted effort to "enlighten" us, meaning to indoctrinate us with communist ideologies. They announced that under their "humane" regime, each worker would get two whole weeks of holidays. When we pointed out to them that under the capitalist Polish rule we had four weeks, they dismissed our objections as hostile propaganda. With the Soviets came long lineups in stores. Staple foods, like sugar, became scarce, but, suddenly, gourmet delicacies, like crabs and smoked salmon, appeared in their place. Polish schools, both elementary and secondary, were allowed to function, but under Soviet supervision, with Russian as the official language. University professors, artists, and writers were tolerated, even respected, but only as long as they did not openly speak out against the Soviet authorities.

The new government even gave us an opportunity to express our joy at having been liberated from the oppression of Polish lords, and at becoming citizens of the socialist state. It ordered a referendum, participation in which was compulsory. The only tolerated vote was in favour of the new regime; any dissent was unthinkable—at least to thick communist minds, unused to thought—and meant instant deportation "to the polar bears," as we used to say. The referendum did not matter, of course, and voting "for" meant as little as voting against. In 1940, the Soviets began mass deportations of Poles into the heartland of Russia. Lists of people to be deported were compiled by local Ukrainians and included, in the first instance, families of the Polish military, policemen, and forest rangers. Mother kept our suitcases packed and ready in case we, too, were woken up one morning and ordered to go. Fortunately, weeks passed and we were spared, even though scores of my co-workers were not. The only explanation we could think of for this kind of luck was that we had moved into a new neighbourhood just before the war, and the local Ukrainians simply did not know us.

When the German-Soviet war broke out, the Soviets fled Lwów in panic. The Germans took over the city and our Power Authority as well. We had to tighten the rules of clandestine operations because one of the engineers was suspected of pro-German sympathies. In spite of those precautions, a Ukrainian employee informed on Mr. Dreszer, the head of the power plant and of our underground organization, and the Germans arrested him. He was replaced, in both capacities, by Julian Wiktor, also an engineer. My functions remained unchanged: officially, I was the power sales manager, but secretly I served as Mr. Wiktor's personal courier, taking his messages to drop-off points, often in local churches. I also helped with the logistics of airdrops of money and radio equipment, organized by the Polish government-in-exile. This meant collecting the goods and delivering them to our units in Lwów and its vicinity. One such airdrop took place in Krzywczyce [Kzhivchitse]. Finding the packages was relatively easy; it was bringing them into town that posed problems. Young men with heavy backpacks would immediately draw the attention of the Ukrainian police or German guards. So it was left to us, my girlfriend Kazia and myself, to carry the heavy equipment (probably radio sets) back to the city. Girls laden with bundles turned fewer heads. The equipment was all wrapped in canvas and placed in well-worn backpacks. We trudged back to town, pretending to be bending under the weight of food supplies or some such. No one stopped us. At one point we had to go past a building of the Gestapo. I could feel my soul settling on the tip of my shoulder, as the quaint Polish saying goes. We were scared, but, shaking and sweating, we safely made it back to my apartment and stashed the cargo in a hiding place. That place was cleverly designed by the pros from the AK, who carved out a space under the hardwood floor. It could be accessed only through a trap door, which was opened by inserting a hat pin into an almost invisible hole.

My involvement with the underground came to a crisis when my handbag was stolen on a streetcar. Inside that bag was a powder box with important messages for various units. We immediately called an organization-wide alert for fear that I had been exposed and compromised as a courier. Fortunately, the thieves turned out to be good Polish patriots. They stole all the valuables but, apparently realizing that the bag contained dangerous correspondence, returned it to my mother, with the papers intact. She gave them a generous reward, and we never heard from them again. After the arrest of Mr. Dreszer, this was the closest that our communications unit came to a disaster.

When the Nazis took control of Lwów, they allowed Polish elementary schools to stay open but closed down high schools and universities. In response, high school and university professors organized clandestine courses and entire programs, which operated despite frequent arrests. Those who fell into the claws of the Gestapo were never seen again. Julian Wiktor's mother and aunt were among those arrested and sent to Oświęcim [Auschwitz]. Two months later Julian Wiktor received an official, macabre query whether the family wished to be sent their ashes. A number of professors from the Lwów University met a similar fate. On the basis of a list prepared by some pro-German Ukrainians, the Gestapo rounded up several dozen Polish scientists and intellectuals and executed them by a firing squad. Only a few pro-German scientists were allowed to continue their research. One of them was the famous Professor Weigel, who ran a laboratory producing anti-typhoid vaccine. He paid Poles, usually women, for feeding lice with their own blood. It was a most unpleasant way to earn money, but for many this was the only way to stave off starvation.

As the Soviet offensive began to move, their bombers appeared over Lwów. I must admit they bombed the city with high precision, for their targets were usually the neighbourhoods settled by the Germans. Withdrawing from Lwów, Germans troops took their last, desperate parting shot by blowing up the power plant in Persunkówka. The entire city sank into darkness. Fortunately, the advancing Soviets brought with them a train carrying a portable power station and quickly re-established power supply. Throughout those stormy events, I continued to work for the Power Authority, accepting and reviewing requests for hook-ups to the power grid. In contrast to the Germans, the Soviets showed considerable respect for writers, artists, intellectuals, and scientists, and their applications were usually dealt with first. Whenever I could, I tried to support the applications of those sympathetic to our underground struggle, but the final decisions always rested with the vice-secretary of the communist party.

After the "liberation" by the Soviet army, our organization continued to operate underground. Some members of the Home Army identified themselves and began to wear white and red bands on their arms. But it did not take long before the Soviets rounded them all up, tried them, and deported them to labour camps in Vorkuta and Donbas. Our commander, Julian Wiktor, was more far-sighted and our communications unit never revealed itself.

My mother, too, was far-sighted, and in May 1946 decided to leave for Poland at all cost. She contacted the Resettlement Office and for 3500 rubles got us a spot in a convoy of some thirty trucks bound for Poland. Before we left, I transferred all my responsibilities as an AK courier, and all documents, to my replacement. We took our seats in the truck, not without some trepidation. Our anxiety was well justified, for we had heard what happened to one of my bosses, Mr. Romański. He and his family (his wife and two sons) drove to Poland in a truck assigned to him by the commander of Lwów. The truck was loaded with their belongings. But somewhere, in a forest along the way, the truck and all its passengers disappeared. We were afraid we could meet a similar fate, and, in fact, we almost did. At the last minute, several rough-looking Russians got into our truck. They demanded vodka and started drinking. Later they jumped off the truck with my suitcase. But the real scare came when we stopped in the middle of the forest, and the rest of the convoy disappeared far ahead. The driver and his helper got out of the truck and just stood there, as if waiting for someone. Luckily for us, just then several military vehicles drove up and asked what happened. The driver mumbled something about engine problems, got back behind the wheel, and we continued the dangerous voyage to Poland. In the end, we arrived in Cracow safely. We stayed with my cousin Stacha.

Some time later, the news reached me that our AK communications unit in Lwów had been discovered by the Soviets. They found the printing shop and the radio station. In June 1946, my entire former cell was arrested, including Julian Wiktor, couriers Kazia Dobrowolska and Jaś Skwarczyński, and many others. Mr. Wiktor courageously accepted all responsibility for the group's operation. He was sentenced to twenty years in a labour camp and sent to Vorkuta. He died there in 1953. The others got lesser sentences, from ten years up. Fortunately, in 1948 all those sentences were commuted into "expulsion from the Soviet Union," and they were all expelled to Poland.

In the meantime, I found a job as a sales manager in a paint factory in Cracow and worked there until we emigrated in 1957. It was my brother who prompted the decision to emigrate. In 1939 he managed to escape through Hungary to France, and later he served under General Maczek. After the war, he married and stayed in England for a while. My mother missed him so much that, in 1957, we went to England as tourists to visit him. But by the time we arrived, he had already gone to Canada and started arrangements to bring us over to the other side of the ocean. Our Canadian visas were delayed several times, and we were on the verge of being deported from England when we finally got those papers. Our emigration from Poland was almost as dramatic as our exodus from Lwów.

With our arrival in Winnipeg in March of 1958, a new chapter opened in my life. My English was pretty rudimentary, but I soon managed to find a job in the Children's Hospital. Two years later, my friends helped me to get a better job in the Medical College, where I was trained as a pharmacology technician. After two years in Kingston, where I worked in Dr. Loventhal's biology lab, I returned to Winnipeg and to the Medical College. I continued to work in the college's pathology lab until I retired in 1980. I enjoyed my professional life, both the challenges of daily routines and the many friendly and good-hearted people I met over the years. I stay in touch with many of them to this day.

I was also heavily involved in various social initiatives in Polish community organizations. I was a member of the Federation of Polish Women since my arrival in Winnipeg. With the help of the talented actress Jadwiga Domańska, we organized, for example, the very popular "evenings with a mike"; the meetings were held in the hall of the Polish Combatants Association [PCA] #13. In 1980, I was elected president of the federation. For many years I was protocol secretary of the Manitoba Chapter of the Polish Canadian Congress. I also helped with the production of a Polish television show in Winnipeg, hosted by Kazimierz Patalas; taught in the Polish school in St. Andrew Bobola's parish; and ran the Polish library for the PCA. I am satisfied that I have done my share of work for the Polish cause.

And through the years, I have never stopped dreaming about Lwów.

JAN SAJEWICZ

I came to Canada from Poland in 1939 to work as a priest with the Polish community here. For the first three years I served in St. Stanisław parish in Toronto. But the war was raging around the world, and I felt I could be of more use somewhere on the front, so I approached Bishop Gawlina, in charge of the army chaplaincy. To my chagrin, he told me that he had enough chaplains, yet he recommended that, if I wanted to help, I could go to the families of the Polish military relocated from Russia to camps in Africa, Asia, and the Middle East. I followed his advice and chose Africa.

The year was 1943. I was to sail from Washington, DC, a warm and friendly city. I arrived there by train. In those days you could not phone for a taxi; you had to wave it down in the street. So I waved one down, and the driver, a woman, noticed my foreign accent and clothes and asked if it was my first time in Washington. I said yes. She immediately suggested that she drive me around the city and show me its sights. And, indeed, she took me on a tour of Washington. In the end, she charged me only for the trip from the railway station to the Polish Embassy.

The sea passage to Africa was long and dangerous but also exciting in many ways. I had already gained some experience with seasickness on my voyage to Canada. Now, on the way to Africa, I turned that experience—plus some advice from an old steward—to good advantage, and did not suffer much from upset stomach. But the danger was almost palpable. The ship I was on formed part of a military convoy crossing the Atlantic, the Straits of Gibraltar, and the Mediterranean Sea. We survived several attacks by German submarines, but God's providence must have taken us under its wings: other convoys at the time lost as many as ten to fifteen ships, whereas we lost only two.

In the midst of that danger at sea, there was also much joy. I was on friendly terms with many sailors; so much so that I even converted two of them to Catholicism. One was of Slovak stock; I baptized and prepared him for the First Communion. The other was a typical Anglo-Saxon American: Lloyd Brown, the most popular fellow aboard the ship, the best boxer, and the best swimmer. Friends called him Brownie. We had cabins beside each other, and we became as close as brothers. We used to sit under the barrel of the biggest gun (he was the commanding officer of a defence unit), share photographs of our families with each other, and talk about things close to our hearts. At one point he asked me about my religion. He didn't remember if he had been to the First Communion and didn't even know if he had been baptized. But his wife was a Catholic, and he could recite "Our Father. . . ." So we had several lengthy discussions about God and salvation. I baptized him and admitted him to the First Communion on a Sunday, just as we were entering the Strait of Gibraltar. He came to Mass neat and shining in his uniform, visibly moved by the experience. His friends were surprised by the transformation, yet they, too, were glad: in the evening they presented him a large cake and sang him "Happy Birthday." I think he experienced a true conversion.

The sea passage took two months. When we disembarked in Suez, the group of priests with whom I travelled was driven to an American military camp and then transferred to Cairo. The American high command looked after us there but could provide no immediate means of transportation, so we had to wait. We used that delay to visit Bishop Gawlina in Jerusalem. While in the Middle East, we also went for a quick tour of the Holy Land and of a few camps of Polish cadets in Palestine. Those were my first encounters with Polish exiles. The meetings with the cadets moved me profoundly. In the middle of a desert camp, I heard their confessions and said Mass for them. Those youths, many of whom should still have been by their mothers' sides, were dressed in uniforms, solemnly readying for war. For two years they had wandered through Russia; they knew hunger, they knew the struggle for bread, often brutal and dishonest. And yet, when I later got to know others like them in the African camps, I was amazed at their high sense of right and wrong, despite the depravity they had witnessed. I think their high moral sense was due in part to our pastoral efforts but in an even larger measure to the influence of their Christian mothers. Young women were in the African camps, too. Most of them were honest and courageous, but there were also others, depraved and demoralized. One must understand that it was not really their fault: they had to survive in Russia, they had to cling to life whichever way they could. No doubt many of them had been mistreated, molested, and raped by evil men. To help them rehabilitate, the representatives of the Polish government-in-exile scattered them among several African camps and gave them work.

There were five of us in Nairobi who came to work in Polish refugee camps. Four were priests, three from the United States—fathers Śliwowski, Wierzbiński, and Górka—and myself from Canada; the fifth was a captain who had been sent to organize and teach in the camp schools. All of us met with Prelate Władysław Słapa, our superior and director of pastoral care for the refugees. He was a jolly highlander from the Polish Carpathians, and he had a heart of gold. After the camps closed down in 1948, he went to Morocco, then to the United States, and finally to Canada. He died in Calgary. It was he who suggested our assignments to individual camps. I had always wanted to work with young people and had long set my sights on the camp in Masindi, Uganda. Masindi was the second-largest camp, with some 3000 people; the largest was Tengeru, with over 4000. In other camps the number of refugees fluctuated between 500 and 2000. All together, twenty refugee camps in the heart of Africa gave shelter to some 20,000 Poles, most of them women and children. The camps, including Masindi, were financed by the Social Agency of the Polish government-in-exile, but the commanding officers were British. On the day-to-day basis, the camps were run by Polish superintendents, supported by teams of workers and institutions. There were teachers, food services, cooperatives. There was also pastoral care. Tengeru, for instance, had three priests, but some smaller camps, like Kondoa between Tengeru and Ifunda, relied on the local mission for spiritual help and instruction. The missionary there was an Italian, Father Dardanelli, who had learned Polish in a few months to look after the spiritual needs of our exiled flock.

Much as I wanted to go to Masindi, I was not in a position to choose. Father Śliwowski, as the oldest among us, was assigned the parish in Ifunda, Tanganyika [Tanzania], a bit of a trouble spot, but he would not or could not take up that post. So Prelate Słapa named me in his place.

I did not go to Ifunda right away. The camp was in a state of unrest—some called it "a women's revolution"—and I had to wait until the animosities and emotions subsided a little and allowed for a peaceful change of spiritual advisors. In the meantime, I was sent to Makindu, between Mombasa and Nairobi. Makindu used to be a camp for Italian POWs, but was adapted to the needs of the displaced families of Polish soldiers. Seven to eight hundred girls and women found refuge there, and some 300 families passed through the camp before they were transferred to England. But Makindu had also another sort of population: female troublemakers ejected from other camps. Strangely enough, their presence was rarely noticeable, they blended in so well with the other refugees. No doubt the superintendent of the camp, Mr. Dołęga Kowalewski, had a hand in moderating their excessive behaviours. A former landowner, a family man, a writer, and a poet, Kowalewski was a charming man, with a gift for talking people out of all silliness. He was always rational and fair, and even the worst delinquents showed much respect for him. Some of them did not want to leave the camp when their turn came. One of the women went so far as to hide herself to avoid transfer to England. When the camp police found her, she had to be taken to the train by force, in her nightgown, with her suitcases thrown in behind her: an unpleasant scene that should have been avoided, although I'm not sure how.

The Makindu camp was blessed with other dedicated administrators besides Superintendent Kowalewski, such as the commanding officer, Major Kałuska. I hold her dear in my memory and often pray for her. Mrs. Stefania Garlicka was another; she worked in the education department. She was a wonderful person, a friendly soul who knew how to reach and appeal to other women. She cared for them deeply, as much for their physical needs as for their spiritual well-being. A deeply religious woman, too.

Many women held various jobs in the camp. Some helped with the administration, some with teaching, some in the kitchen or on the camp farm, some with cleaning. All who were paid for their work taxed themselves voluntarily at thirteen percent to establish a fund for social services. The fund was used to support those women who had children but were receiving no help from the army.

My chief responsibility was pastoral care, but I tried to help with other tasks, too. Mr. Kowalewski was very effective when dealing with individual people and their problems, but he did not care much for larger organizational issues. The camp was often in a state of creative disarray. One of its symptoms was the lack of even a single radio receiver in the camp and a chronic lack of up-to-date news from the war fronts. To make up for that deficiency, I used to post cut-outs from recent newspapers on the bulletin boards or just read the news to groups of women. To enliven those dry newspaper reports from the world at war, I sometimes told jokes and humorous stories, which kept my audience's spirits up and made them come again to hear more.

I worked in Makindu for six months, until all the refugees left for Britain. Then I was moved to Ifunda. It was a compound of simple houses built of raw bricks rather than the logs common in other camps. The first chaplain there was an Italian who quickly mastered enough rudimentary Polish to talk to people and hear confessions, but he stopped short of preaching. He fell in love with our people. He was replaced by Father Krawczyk, an army chaplain. At that time the conditions in the camp began to deteriorate, and conflicts erupted. Many refugees accused the administration of immoral conduct and of unfairness in the distribution of American gifts. They claimed the administrators gave the lion's share of those gifts to their friends in the camp. Unfortunately, Father Krawczyk sided with the administration, which cast a long shadow on the integrity of our pastoral enterprise, for it seems the administration was indeed to blame for the disturbance in the camp. I think the representatives of the Polish government should have acted sooner and of their own accord. But they did not, and it took a virtual revolt, under the leadership of Mrs. Cybulska, a simple yet brave policewoman in the camp, before changes were made. Together with other women, she came to the superintendent of the camp and demanded that he leave. Nine other women were also expelled from the camp. Mrs. Cybulska took over the day-to-day supervision of the camp until the government sent a replacement for the superintendent. But this fellow made all the errors of his predecessor, whose side he openly took. He did not last long. Only when Aleksander Czerny came did the emotions in the camp subside. He knew how to work with people and managed to restore order and a degree of trust in the camp.

I was parachuted into the camp when it was still in the throes of change and discontent. I was supposed to take over the functions of Father Krawczyk, and eventually I succeeded and lasted until the camp's dissolution. But the beginnings were difficult. Despite Father Krawczyk's support of the administration, the women did not want to let him go. Some were so bitter and irrational they teetered on the brink of hysteria. "Blood will flow before we'll let him go," they screamed. It took me some time before I managed to calm those extreme feelings and understand the reasons for them. Priests played a crucial role in every camp. They carried moral and spiritual help and often devoted themselves utterly—most of them, anyway—to the spiritual welfare of their flocks. A priest kindled hope if there was no news from the husband on the front, consoled at the news of death, helped find sources of strength when sickness struck. A priest became part of those women's lives, a vital part, which they could not afford to lose.

The camp in Ifunda was located 1800 metres above sea level. It had a highland climate, with warm days and cool nights. We only had two seasons, dry and wet. Once, during the wet season, torrential rains caused some flooding, and I had to evacuate the children to another camp. We were driving at night through the jungle, torrents of water cascading from the low clouds, when our truck slid into one of the deep ruts and got stuck. It wouldn't go forward or backward. We spent that night under the tarpaulin, listening to the rain and to the wild and frightening noises all around us. Only in the morning did help arrive. But even in the wet season, Africa's bane, malaria, did not bother us much.

There was little political life in the camp: the focus was on survival in the past and in the present. The survival of Soviet deportations, prisons, labour camps, hunger, and brutality were still a fresh, painful memory. Some tried to keep that memory from fading, even exacerbating it for whatever private reasons, with speeches and papers and inflammatory rhetoric. I remember one captain, who wanted to speak on May 3rd* about the wrongs we had suffered at the hands of the Soviets. "I'll end the speech," he told me, "by saying that a day will come when we drive the Polish ensigns into Stalin's carrion. . . ." He

---

* The anniversary of the first Polish constitution of 1791.

wanted to play on people's emotions, oblivious to their already brittle state. I don't think this was right.

What was needed was not inflammatory rhetoric but calm documentation of the Soviet crimes. The people in the camp were a mine of information about the labour camps in Siberia. Yet no historians came, no journalists. In fact, the British did not want to hear what happened to those people. One of our commanding officers, Captain Douglas, was very sensitive to any mention of Soviet crimes. He forbade us to speak ill of the British allies, not that anyone complied. And when a woman showed him scars and bruises she was still nursing, he told her to "cover up and shut up." I tried to gather some of that information, but most people did not open up easily. They did not want to return to those painful memories, probably wishing that they could forget them all.

The survival in the present took many forms. To revive spiritual life, we built a church in Ifunda. There had been only a little shrine, and people had had to stand outside during Mass. So we built a brick church, with the floor made of bricks and the roof of long African grass. Inside, we had small folding chairs. One of the refugees, Mr. Adamiak, who was mute but gifted with paints and brushes, painted for us a picture of the Blessed Virgin. (Later we took that picture and, in a procession, carried it to the mission cathedral and hung it there on the wall in memory of the Polish refugees.) The church was dedicated by the bishop in a beautiful ceremony. Afterwards, all church and national celebrations were held in it. It was used for funeral services at least thirty times: that many people, from the community of 1000, died and were buried at the local cemetery. To commemorate them, we inscribed a plaque and placed it near where they had been laid to rest.

Daily life in the camp was well organized although that organization took no stock of the camp's geographical location. Children went to school Monday through Saturday. Mothers prepared them for school, and then many went about their paid or volunteer duties in the kitchen, on the camp's communal farm, or elsewhere. But our conception of the school day was still rooted in Polish traditions and failed to take into account the African climate. Classes started at eight in the morning and lasted till noon or 1:00 p.m. The poor kids had to study (or at least pretend they were doing so) in unbearable heat. We seemed oblivious to the fact that noon in Africa is suitable only for rest, not work. Our rationed meals were also mismatched: the noon dinner was too rich and the supper too skimpy for the climate and for the way we worked. But we were stubborn and persevered in our Polishness.

We were on good terms with the local population. They often came to the camp, and some even worked there. They carried water for us and boiled it, so we could drink it. They also did most of the heavy chores on the farm because men were as scarce as medicine in the camp. What was our attitude towards them? The British thought they knew them well and kept their distance. But I thought this was not very Christian, so they were welcome in our camp, and we considered them friends. But even church authorities urged us to be less open. The bishop of Dar es Salaam suggested that I be more careful how I acted toward them. If you give a Black something for free, he'll start taking whatever he wants without even asking; he'll think you don't need those things, he warned me. Best to give him a job and a decent pay. There was no problem with baptizing their children, which I often did in our church. But the bishop advised me that those who came asking for the sacrament of marriage I should send to him. Given their way of life, he argued, it was often difficult to know who was already married and who wasn't.

Our children learned the local dialect quickly from their Black peers, and sometimes used it at school if they didn't want the teachers to understand. They also learned some tribal dances and superstitions. Needless to say, I did not approve of this.

We had many children of various ages in the camp. Some of them were quite young, probably born in Siberia; others must have accompanied their mothers through the inferno of exile. We tried to offer them as much cultural stimulation as we could: they had a common room in the rectory, religious organizations, Scouting, even folk theatre. Our teacher organized a Christmas play, with Joseph and Mary and little Jesus. Herod was styled as Stalin, despite strong objections from the English officer in charge of our camp.

I knew all the children because I taught them religion and spent a lot of time with them. I remember teaching grade five students the seventh commandment, thou shalt not steal. Suddenly a girl stood up and asked permission to speak. "Father," she said, "was it a sin when we stole bread in the Russian camps?" I had to explain to her that under certain circumstances taking what is not ours is not a sin. People should be paid for the work they perform; it is one of our basic rights. But if one doesn't get paid, which was the case in Russia, and faces starvation, taking bread cannot be treated as a moral transgression. Perhaps my explanation was too lofty or long-winded, but a boy interrupted me and offered an alternative explanation, one that convinced the children much more readily. "It couldn't have been a sin, Father," he said, "because when we were going to steal, a priest came along with us and showed us how to do it."

Some children remembered the Soviet schools well. In the camp in Tengeru, I met a little girl who often played with the three daughters of my cousin, who happened to be quartered there. That little girl must have liked me, for she gave me a primer she brought with her from Russia. The primer was printed in Polish but by the Soviet authorities and in the spirit of communist propaganda. On one page it described how in the past workers had to labour in terrible, demeaning conditions; on the other was a description of the bright and joyous Soviet "reality." And to whom do we owe our welfare? To Lenin and Stalin, of course. The children's reaction to this propaganda was apparent in the book. The portraits of Lenin and Stalin had eyes scratched out, and below a childish, clumsy hand wrote: "Two blind worms." The last page of the primer admonished the children that they should love Stalin and adorn his portraits with flowers. The same child crossed out "flowers" and put in "shit."

Children also told stories of what it was like in Soviet schools. Here is one such story, as told by another girl. I have no reason to suspect that she made it up. A teacher in school had asked the children if they were hungry. The children, of course, cried "Yes." "So let us pray to Lord God that he may give you some bread," the teacher said. The class prayed, and the teacher asked again, "Well, did Lord God give you bread? No? Then maybe we should pray to Father Stalin." And she turned towards a portrait on the wall and started a prayer. As this prayer drew to an end, Stalin's hands began to spread, and a shower of candies and tarts fell to the floor. A stupid contraption for primitive atheistic propaganda. Even children saw through it and never faltered in their Christian faith; I can attest to that, having met so many of them in the camps.

The entire camp in Ifunda was surrounded by a fence, and, for security reasons, children were not allowed to go outside its perimeter. In particular, they were not allowed to go into the lake, infested with croc-odiles. Despite the ban, we did have one tragic accident when a croc pulled in a careless boy. We did not manage to save him. The grass around the camp was cut down and always kept short so that any intruding animals would be immediately spotted. Two miles away from our campsite was a national park with a nature preserve for lions, giraffes, and African buffalo, but none ever encroached on our territory. Neither did I see a live snake throughout my stay in the camp.

On occasion I took the children outside the confines of the camp to see the farms of our Black neighbours. We were walking through a vil-lage when the children suddenly ran towards a small hut and surrounded something on the ground. They became very animated, then amused, then positively laughing their heads off. I walked up to them and saw a famished dog, just skin on bones. So I asked the children, "What's so funny? The farmer probably has nothing to eat so he cannot feed his dog." And they replied, "That's not what we were laughing about. We were wondering how this dog came here from Russia." In the minds of those children, all starvation and poverty sprang from Siberia.

There weren't many toys for the children in the camp, but the chil-dren often found them in nature, playing with birds and small animals. Once a bird hobbled into the camp; it looked like a heron. It was hurt and hungry, and the children cared for it and fed it. The bird took a spe-cial fancy to one girl from the grade school. It walked her to school and then back home, and played with her in the evening. And when she slept in, it knocked on the door with its beak to wake her up. It doesn't take much to be a friend. Another source of great fun for the children was riding one of my bicycles. But even more than the bicycle, they liked my she-donkey. I bought her to have a means of transportation, but she was soon appropriated by the children. They called her "Lala." An Italian POW who still lingered in the camp made a little wagon for me, and they rode in the wagon drawn by the donkey, parading through the camp.

When the camp could spare me, I took every opportunity to travel in Africa. Perhaps the most interesting expedition was to the top of Mount Kilimanjaro, towering 2000 metres above sea level. The expe-dition took five days: three for the climb and two for the descent. We set out from a hotel in Moshi, a small group including Mr. Czerny, our superintendent, myself, a guide, and a few porters. Ours was not the first Polish tour of the mighty mountain, for there had been many others; it seems that all Poles passing in its vicinity wanted to conquer it. I must admit that my conquest had a distinct quality of a Pyrrhic victory: on reaching the top, I was so exhausted that I fainted. The porters had to pick me up and practically carry me to a shelter down on the mountainside. There, after ten glasses of tea, I recovered. Still, a victory it was, and I did win a garland of immortelles,* with which the guides crowned all those who climbed to the top.

Altogether, I stayed in Africa for five years, until 1948. We left behind many traces of wartime sojourn there. The churches we built were taken over by missionaries. The one in Ifunda became the focal point of the parish cared for by an Italian priest, Natale Euzebio. He learned some Polish from us, and later invited us to the cathedral to hear a Black choir singing Polish Christmas carols translated into Swahili. We also left behind some 700 people in Tanganyika. The end of the war was not a joyous occasion for all: some had nothing to go back to, no reason to go to England. The British were unwilling to issue permits for them to remain in Tanganyika, and only those with some financial resources or attractive professions could secure them. Those who left for Britain and later scattered across the world remained forever bound by their African past. Occasionally, they organize reunions to remember those years and keep the old friendships alive. The last such meeting took place in Orchard Lake, near Detroit, in the United States.

After the dissolution of the camps, I returned to Canada, bringing with me several trophies, including a large snakeskin. For a while, I worked in Toronto; then in Winnipeg, where I edited the *Gazeta Polska* [*Polish Newspaper*], which later merged with the *Głos Polski* [*Polish Voice*] published out of Toronto; then in Ottawa, where we established a Polish parish of St. Hyacinth [Jacek], which now numbers 500 families. I spent seven years in the Toronto parish of St. Casimir. When Poland was celebrating a millennium of Christianity, I travelled throughout Canada with a replica of the famous painting of Our Lady of Częstochowa, which we called *The Visitation*. This was the most gratifying period of my pastoral work in Canada. We displayed the painting in several cathedrals, and people from far away brought their

---

* Flowers that retain their colour when dried.

sick and ailing to pray with us for hope and strength. I also took that opportunity to present lectures on the history of Polish Christianity and on the history of the miraculous painting. After a hiatus of two years, during which I edited a Polish Catholic monthly in France, I returned briefly to Winnipeg, then to Edmonton, and then to Saskatoon. A car accident cut short that last posting, and I finally settled in Winnipeg, taking residence with the Benedictine nuns and serving as chaplain for the Polish Combatants Association.

STANISŁAW SMOLEŃSKI, JUNIOR

I was born in 1919 in Warsaw, and we lived there until I was ten. Then, as my father's job took him away from the capital, we moved with him to Sierpc, then to Vilnius, changing homes and schools. In 1939, when the war broke out, I was doing my practicum in a sawmill in Broszniów [Broshnev], in the district of Stanisławów [Ivano-Frankivs'k], where my parents lived at that time. I had followed in my father's footsteps and was attending a wood-technology high school in Łomża. As part of my program, I had to spend some time working in a mill; I was lucky to get sent to Broszniów. But my luck ran out on September 1, when my father was mobilized and I, as the oldest son, had to start looking after the family. This proved quite a challenge, especially in late September, after the Soviets came in. We had heard a lot about them at home from Father, who had served in the Russian army and often told us about those days. If what he told us was not flattering to the Russians, the Soviets went far beyond the ruthlessness he remembered. Soon after they invaded, they nationalized the mill where I was working, so I became a regular state worker. Our house caught the fancy of some communist bureaucrat, so we were thrown out and given a single room in an attic instead.

We lived there until April 1940. On a cold spring day, the Bolsheviks banged on our door and told us to gather some things. They led us to the railway station, where they put us onto a freight train. The cars, each crowded with some fifty people and their scanty belongings, had primitive cots on the sides and a stinking hole in the middle, which served as a latrine. Seventeen days we spent on that train, going in an unknown direction. We hadn't heard from Father since he was mobilized in Grodno [Hrodna]; we didn't even know if he was alive. Now we were being taken nobody-knew-where. Everyone was confused, frightened, and exhausted.

When we got off the train, we were in a Kazakhstan *sovkhoz* [state farm]. The whole transport was divided into smaller groups and distributed among various farms; we were assigned to a milk farm. The good thing about this assignment was that occasionally we could get some de-fatted milk. Soon after our arrival, we were photographed and issued new passports valid for five years but with a special note that we were forbidden to travel outside the region. Much good those passports were!

"Your occupation?" they asked me on the first day, or at least I thought that was what they were asking, for I didn't know Russian. I had once trained to be a carpenter, and I said so. That's dandy, they said, or maybe they didn't, but they sent me to a local carpenter anyway. He was a man of few words: he gave me a small birch tree and an axe, and told me—as much with gestures as with words—that I was to make a cart shaft out of it. I didn't work long for him: as the weather got warmer, I was sent haymaking. Out into the fields at sunrise, back from work at sundown. The days were long and sweaty, but the food was decent. For breakfast, to give an example, we would get bread and sour milk; for dinner, soup, with a piece of meat from time to time. But my mother and brothers were not so lucky. They all had work assignments but were getting cash wages, with no food allotment. They were supposed to buy the food themselves; the problem was that there was no one to buy it from, and even if there had been, the money was not enough to feed all of them.

Once in a while, letters and even parcels from Poland brightened our hapless existence. We managed to get in touch with our grandfather in Warsaw through the Red Cross. He, in turn, gave us our father's address in Kozel'sk. We were relieved that Father was alive and wrote to him many times but never got any reply. We were hoping that one day one of our letters would reach him. Instead, it was his letter that reached us, more or less at the same time that we learned about the formation of the Polish army. The letter brought us the good news that Father was in Tatishchevo, where a Polish military camp was being set up. It also brought us some money and urged us to come join him.

But joining him was not that easy. I went and pleaded with the superintendent of the milk farm, but he agreed to release us only after all harvesting and storing had been done. This was much too late, we felt, for it meant that we couldn't go until winter at the earliest. So we decided to go on the crook: Mother managed to hire two oxen and a cart, and we drove to the station about ten kilometres away. Mother went in to buy the tickets; after she shared the contents of her purse with the ticket clerk, she emerged wielding four tickets to Ural'sk. That was as far as we could go as civilians because Tatishchevo had been declared a military zone and only military personnel were allowed in.

When we got to Ural'sk, we tried again to get tickets to Tatishchevo, but again without success. So we started sending telegrams to Father, letting him know where we were and hoping he could arrange passage for us to the Polish camp. In the meantime, we took up residence at the station, the only place where we could spread out some newspapers on the floor and thus spend the night. After a few days with no news from Father, a transport of volunteers for the Polish army pulled in. I talked to the transport's commander, and he agreed to take me on, but he had reservations about my mother and brothers. Finally, he agreed to take all of us on condition that they would never get out of the train at any station. He was afraid that the NKVD [state security police] might spot us, putting him and his whole transport in jeopardy. So with extra precautions, I put my mother and brothers into a car and went back for one of the suitcases still at the station. But when I got back to the tracks, the train had already gone. I was left with a suitcase but with no documents. I had no other option but to wait for my father to come and pick me up. Mother would soon be with him, and she knew where I had been separated from them. I stayed at the station for another two days, dodging the NKVD and military police. When Father finally came, he was delighted to see me, but most distressed when he learned about my mother and brothers. They had not yet arrived in Tatishchevo when he left. He bought us tickets without any difficulty, and we were soon on the train. The trip was tense, both of us worrying about the rest of the family. But our worries turned to joy as soon as we arrived: they had already reached Tatishchevo and were settling in at the military camp.

Unfortunately for us, more or less at that time, the camp's headquarters decided to send all military families south because there was not enough food for all in the camp. Although I had intended to sign up as a volunteer, I decided—as the oldest son in the family—to go with my mother and brothers and look after them. After a tiring journey we found ourselves on the Amu-Darya River. They wanted to put us on barges and send us up the river. That meant that we would be almost completely cut off from the rest of the world. But the women, much bolder than a few young men who were among us, myself included, objected, quarrelled, cried, and said they would not go. So they put us back onto the train and sent us in an unknown direction.

We ended up in Kyrgyzstan, in a *kolkhoz* [collective farm] near Frunze [Bishkek]. They lodged us in a small pigsty, a foul and dirty place, but at least it kept the rain out. Soon after arrival, I went to work on a tobacco farm. I was getting one meal a day, a hasty noodle soup, but after a month, it turned out that I would get no money and that, in fact, I owed them for the meals I ate. I was furious and stopped going to work. My mother and brothers had been getting no food, and although we were assigned rations of half a kilogram of bread per person, we had no money to buy them. We were starving and growing so weak that we could hardly walk. Fortunately, after a short while, Father came to take us away from that miserable place. We took a train and returned to the army camp. By then the Polish army was much better organized and supplied, and we were quartered near the camp and given sufficient food.

Now I could finally join the army myself. I volunteered for the 4th Armoured Battalion, stationed in the town of Chernaya Rechka. At the beginning, we had no uniforms, and only a few of us got new boots. Later, some Estonian uniforms arrived, but they were all ill-matched and in odd colours, and we looked more like clowns than soldiers. Our unusual appearance did not interfere much with our various soldierly activities. I was sent to the officers' college for armoured units. The training took two years, much of the time in the most primitive of conditions. We began with the basics of infantry training, which included digging wells, ditches, and the like. Only then did we get some theory of armoured warfare. Our first practical experience with tanks came only after we had already left the Soviet Union.

We went to Krasnovodsk with the first transport, in March or April 1942, and waited there for the sea passage. The local people often came asking for help in fixing their tractors and other machinery; our mechanics—and we had quite a few of them in our unit—helped them out willingly, in exchange for grain or cereals. Thanks to those outside jobs, we ate much better than other detachments, and even shared with those less fortunate, some of whom arrived lean and barely walking.

Finally the day came when we were loaded onto a tanker and sailed for Persia. Conditions on the ship were brutally primitive: the only latrine was the wide sea on the other side of the railing, and we were afraid that someone would fall overboard. We disembarked in Pahlavi on a dirty beach and were sent to the disinfection tents. There the orderlies shaved us up and down and disinfected us with Lysol. All our clothes were burned, and new underwear, uniforms, and boots were issued. The first British food rations, after the scarce and monotonous staples of the Russian army, caused much joy and lots of stomach cramps. And no wonder, for I saw guys devouring sardines with raspberry jam and asking for extra helpings of both.

Our next stop was Ahvāz, much hotter than anything I had experienced in Russia. There I was promoted for the first time. Once again, we were put aboard a ship, this time a passenger liner adapted for military purposes, and we sailed for Gedera in Palestine. At last we felt almost at home: everywhere we went, we could speak Polish and everywhere we were understood. This camp was intended to help us recover from the ordeals and malnutrition of Russia. Those ravaged by typhoid fever needed even more time to regain their strength.

My officers' college continued intensive training throughout that time, although not in the same place. From Palestine, we were transferred to Main near Cairo, in Egypt. We took over a camp from the Carpathian Brigade, whose soldiers gave us not only some equipment but some tips about Cairo as well. Cairo was swarming with all kinds of armies: had some German soldiers wandered in from the desert, probably no one would have noticed. There were scores of restaurants, places for entertainment and for shopping. If you knew whom to ask, you could buy anything, from raspberry juice to pure alcohol (and sometimes even both of them already mixed together). It was in Main, in the shadow of that boisterous city, that we got our first tanks of Mark 4 type, armed with one heavy machine gun. Later we got Valentines, and finally Matildas. Our armoured equipment arrived just in time, for General Rommel was on the offensive, and we nearly got sent to the African front as regular infantry.

When I learned that my father and brother Julian were in hospital in Tehrān, I asked the commanding officer for a leave of absence. Much to my surprise, I was granted my request. I made my way to Tehrān, mostly by car. I stayed with my mother and my other brother, Andrzej, in the camp, while visiting Father and Julian. Fortunately, both of them got better shortly afterwards and recovered completely in a matter of months.

I stayed with my officers' college, towards the end located in Khānaqīn, until the departure for Italy. For that occasion, I was assigned to the 1st Squadron of the 6th Armoured Regiment in the rank of corporal. We were taken by boat to Naples and then marched to a transition camp, where we had to wait for the equipment. My first days in Italy were a disappointment: I had been expecting sunlit landscapes and azure sky, but instead we were greeted by heavy clouds and incessant rain. And yet I was lucky, for I was one of the very few who had decided to bring along rubber boots. They proved invaluable for getting out of my tent, surrounded by a large lake of water and mud. Sometimes we wished one of the German bombs that were being dropped on Naples would fall in the vicinity of the camp and drain all that water from under our feet. But none did. The Germans probably did not know we were there.

We went into action for the first time at Monte Cassino and Piedmont, not the entire regiment but only selected teams that joined New Zealand units. Those units had some immobilized tanks, used primarily for shelling, and our task was to use them to provide fire cover.

As we moved towards Piedmont, the explosions died down, and we entered a zone of calm, peace, and quiet. We wondered why the Germans were not firing at us, and finally decided that they must have been engaged in other sectors. We were lucky. We went into that charge without having refilled our tanks, and soon we had burned most of our fuel. Had the Germans chased us with heavy artillery fire, we might have been in trouble. But they gave us lots of space to manoeuvre. We were going slowly along road number 6. My platoon received an order to enter the town, but it was getting dark, and we had encountered a large bomb crater. Going through or around it in the dark would be risky. Also, our infantry was far behind, so we had to withdraw for the night. The next day the Germans became aware of our approach, but, despite heavy fire, we moved closer to the city. On the third day, pushing forward, we got stuck in yet another crater. We set up the machine gun and took shelter under the tank. Throughout the day we were under heavy mortar bombardment. At about six in the evening, one shell exploded so close that pieces of shrapnel shot under the tank and wounded all of us. I myself got three of them: one in the knee, one in the thigh, and one in the groin. After dark, our guys pulled us out and sent the entire team to a hospital in Casamassima. They also tried to salvage the tank and found that it was so scarred by shrapnel that the hatches couldn't be opened. I stayed in the hospital for a month. The doctors removed two metal fragments from my leg, but they did not want to mess with my groin. That souvenir I carry in me to this day.

My wounds were relatively light, but this was not obvious to the medical personnel at first. They arranged for me an invalid's pension and a release to Britain. But when they realized that the piece in my groin was not moving, they gave me eighty pounds, and that was the end of it. Two of my buddies, who were more seriously wounded, were indeed sent to Britain for more intensive medical treatments. They never returned to our detachment; instead, they signed up for university in London.

I eventually decided to leave the hospital and return to my regiment. I didn't bother to ask anyone for permission. Soon after I reported my return to the colonel, warrants for my arrest arrived. Someone in the hospital administration thought I had deserted. To go where, I wanted to ask them. My superiors had a few good laughs at my expense, and the matter was quickly cleared up. Unit commanders were proud that soldiers preferred to return to their front-line posts instead of drifting through convalescence units. We heard horror stories about those convalescence units: they forced soldiers through so many therapies, gymnastics, massages, and exertions that lugging boxes with ammunition through knee-deep mud seemed like a child's play. That was, in fact, the duty assigned to me on my return to the regiment, then stationed near Loreto. All the tanks were already fully manned, so I was assigned to an ordinance supply unit. In my entire army career I had never been so scared as on that duty. Our task was to deliver ammunition to the regimental depot, from where it was picked up by front-line units. On one occasion, we were unloading a truck in the middle of the depot when Germans began to shell our positions. We could see explosions churning up the earth, but none touched any of our ammunition piles. Still, by the time we were leaving, I was drenched with sweat. Fortunately, I did not stay long on that nerve-wracking duty, but was transferred back to a tank.

We were riding on the left wing of the offensive, without much resistance from the Germans. We were taking them prisoner in cohorts, just waving them to move back towards our infantry lines. They were completely disoriented and devoid of any will to fight. When we reached the environs of Bologna, the war came to an end. By then I was an experienced tank driver, with battle wounds and the Cross for Bravery (for the Piedmont campaign) to prove it. So I wasn't surprised to be sent to Gubio as a Sherman tank instructor. Although my English was still poor, I had to translate technical instructions into Polish—not much fun, but an order is an order. I held that position until we left for England.

From Southampton, where we docked, we were taken by train to the paratroopers' camp in Hardwig. Looking out through the window as we passed through the densely populated areas, with a house clinging to house and a town hugging town, I wondered if there would still be enough room for us in this country. In the following weeks, I consulted with my father, then in the 9th Maintenance Company, and decided to sign up, like many of my colleagues, for the Polish Resettlement Training Corps.

While I stayed in close touch with my father, contact with the rest of the family was more difficult because my mother and brothers were in a refugee camp in Africa, in northern Rhodesia. They arrived in England only in 1948; I think the British deliberately delayed their return, hoping that the majority of ex-servicemen would decide to go back to Poland. Mother sent us word from one of the ports-of-call that they would be arriving in Southampton, and we waited for them in the harbour. Father, with tears in his eyes, at first didn't recognize my brothers—after all, five years had passed since he last saw them—but soon we were celebrating the reunion.

That same year, both my father and I finally took our demobilization papers. We were in no hurry to sweat in a factory, but eventually we had few other choices. I rented a furnished apartment, and we all took jobs in a plastics factory. The working conditions there were so bad that no one wanted those jobs; that's why we got them. The locals put it quite plainly: they will hire a Pole only where an Englishman didn't want to work. But, after a while, even we couldn't stand it, and found new jobs in a textiles factory, making between £4 and £5 a week. With four of us in the family working, we had enough to get by and even some to spare. With an eye to professional advancement, I took an evening course in draughting, and on its completion got a cleaner, though lower-paying, job in the same factory.

By then we could see that Britain itself held no future for us, and so we applied for emigration to Canada. The process took a whole frustrating year, but it ended with a letter from the embassy advising us we had been admitted. An immigration officer suggested that the three of us brothers should go first, and then, after we settled down, we could bring our parents over. It sounded like good advice, and we agreed. We also followed the advice of the immigration office when it came to deciding where in Canada we should settle. Originally, we had been thinking of Toronto, but everyone we talked to tried to convince us that Winnipeg was the place for us. We knew little about Winnipeg, so we tried to read up on it. We discovered it had the greatest number of sunny days of all the major cities in Canada, and that caught our fancy. That it is the coldest city in Canada somehow escaped our attention.

When we got off the train at the station, we knew not a single soul in Winnipeg. All we had was an address of a friend of a friend. We got in touch with him that very first day, and from him we learned about a meeting of the Combatants Association [PCA] that same evening at the restaurant (rented by Adam Mossakowski) in the Empire State Chateau. It was our first evening in Winnipeg and our first meeting of the PCA, the first of many.

Soon we began to settle in Winnipeg. My brothers landed jobs in a textiles factory, and I got hired as a machine operator by Pioneer Electric. But I kept looking for a draughting job and eventually found one in an industrial-consulting company. Three months into my new job, the superintendent called me up to his office. On my way I nearly panicked, thinking that he was going to fire me. He didn't; on the contrary, he offered me a raise. This was one of many pleasant surprises that made my work for that company richly satisfying. I worked for it for several decades, watching our team grow from several people to several dozen, until I retired a few years ago.

With a steady job, I began thinking of starting a family of my own. I met my wife-to-be while she was visiting from Regina. Her visit turned into permanent residence when she got a job at a local hospital. We courted for a time, then were married, had children—a daughter and two sons. Now our daughter is already married and has two children of her own; she graduated from Red River College and works for the University of Manitoba. One of our sons has also finished his post-secondary studies, and the other is close to finishing. We are very proud of them. In varying degrees, they all speak Polish and continue to participate in both cultures in which they grew up.

STANISŁAW SMOLEŃSKI, SENIOR

My memories reach back to the time before the October Revolution of 1917. I was conscripted for military service in the Russian army in 1915 with a blue draft card, which identified me as the only child in the family. When the actual mobilization was announced, I chose not to appear before the commission. From the army's point of view, I became a deserter; but I saw things differently. If I reported as a conscript, they'd have consigned me to the infantry, to be meat for machine guns. There had to be a better way. Well, there was. My father, who worked for the railways, found an acquaintance, an airplane pilot in Gatchina near St. Petersburg. His name was Krzyżanowski, and he agreed to help me get into the Imperial Air Force. So my father and I boarded a train in Moscow and went to St. Petersburg, where we had to stay the night. Since we had no friends or relatives there, and since we couldn't go to a hotel because, as a deserter, I had no proper papers, we spent the night pounding the pavement. In the morning, when we no longer had to show our documents, we took a hotel room to wash and rest. Then we got on the first train to Gatchina. As per pilot Krzyżanowski's instructions, I reported as a volunteer to the 1st Auxiliary Battalion under the command of a Pole, Captain Bołsanowski. An insider's backing forced open some doors for me, and I was admitted. Not only that, but I was admitted as a member of the school's permanent staff. No doubt my full matriculation certificate from a commerce high school in Warsaw and my training in airplane engines had something to do with this appointment. For three years after my graduation, I worked, first as a helper and later as a fitter of such engines, in a French-owned engine factory in Moscow. All Russian army airplanes flew with our engines. So I was given the rank of corporal and sent to the classroom to teach engines to prospective airplane mechanics, most of them commissioned and non-commissioned officers. My Russian was still very shaky, so I had to prepare detailed notes for every lecture and then read them to each of my two classes. I taught in that school for a whole year, until 1916; by the twelfth month of my appointment there, my Russian was fluent.

In my spare time, I began to dabble in the art of flying planes. Two Polish pilots at Gatchina, captains Piątkowski and Malczewski, gave me lots of advice, but it was usually with the platoon leader Arsynev, a Muscovite, that I took my lessons on the Farman IV. He let me hold the controls and corrected my errors until I got the hang of it. The Farman IV had its depth rudders in the front; it was powered by a simple six-cylinder rotary engine, "Gnom," which turned around with the propeller and burned huge quantities of fuel. The propeller was made of wood and had to be started by hand. I recently saw one of those engines at the Winnipeg Aviation Museum. The plane could begin ascending at sixty kilometres per hour and could reach the speed of 120 kilometres per hour.

While I was teaching and flying, the army administrators were busy looking for me. The imperial bureaucratic machine may have been slow, but it was excruciatingly thorough. Eventually, a warrant for my arrest arrived in Gatchina. Gatchina replied that Corporal Smoleński had indeed been enlisted there as an instructor. This reassurance that I had not escaped my military duty and the extensive efforts on my father's part (mostly financial in nature) to hush the matter seem to have placated the military authorities, and they did not pursue me any further.

The October Revolution, as I remember it, was a time of utmost confusion and chaos. As a member of the Socio-Revolutionary Party, I belonged to a battalion revolutionary committee and was even its delegate. I was bending with the winds of chaos, you might say. My sympathies and loyalties were divided, which at times placed me in a vulnerable position. At one point, for example—I don't remember the exact date—the revolutionary committee decided to put our Polish commander, Captain Bołsanowski, on trial. As a commander, he was very strict and demanding, and the punishments he often meted out were thought to be inhuman. So he was brought before the revolutionary court martial, and I, as a committee member, sat among the judges. The prosecutors demanded the death penalty. There was nothing unusual about it: if an officer was found guilty, his epaulets were immediately ripped off, and he was shot in the head. But Bołsanowski did not deserve it, and, besides, he was a Pole, so I tried hard to get him out of that mess. Finally, I made a motion that instead of the death penalty, he should be sent to the front. It was a wise suggestion, everyone nodded. The problem was that, at that moment, there was no obvious front. After some further discussion, one was found, and he was sent away. I'm sure I saved his life, but I paid for it, as I later found out from my cousin who had access to military files, with a note entered in my file suggesting my unsuitability for further promotion.

Because the times were dangerous and armed bands of marauders roamed the countryside, we had to organize some form of self-defence in Gatchina. We had the organization and discipline, but we needed guns. So I went to the Forest Institute in Petersburg, forty kilometres away, where Lenin held his temporary office. It wasn't difficult to see him. I spoke to him in Polish, which he knew quite well since he had studied in Cracow. I explained why we required those guns. He wasn't convinced at first, "Comrade," he said, "why that urge to have guns? No one's murdering you." But in the end he agreed, tore off a margin from a newspaper, and wrote on it, "Vydat' tovarishchu Smolenskomu 50 vintovok" [Issue fifty rifles to comrade Smoleński]. We went to the magazine and picked up fifty brand-new Japanese rifles. Back in Gatchina, we armed our guards with them; fortunately, they never had to use them.

Gatchina had only one branch of the military, the air force, so the pilots and their ground crews had to take on all garrison duties. As a platoon leader, I was often in charge of a troop guarding the railway station. One night I was sitting in the station bar, drinking tea, while my men, a few dozen of them, stood guard around the station and along the tracks. Suddenly I heard some shouting and arguing outside the building. The Russian troops loyal to Kerenski* had quietly approached my men, disarmed them very politely, and taken over the posts.

---

* Alexander Kerenski (1881-1970), head of the Russian Provisional Government from July to October 1917; forced to flee Russia after the October Revolution.

Eventually, I, too, had to surrender my arms, and we were all sent home. These were the troops that Kerenski sent to rescue St. Petersburg from the Bolsheviks, but the Bolsheviks wheeled out some big guns against them and blasted them to hell. Thus we recovered our rifles and our sense of duty.

It was easy in those days to get killed for no apparent reason. That's what happened to Bogusławski, a university student, who was on his way to relieve me from duty as the commander of the guard. He was riding in a hackney coach, a *droshky*, when he chanced upon a patrol of the counter-revolutionary police. He probably did not even see them, for they were shooting from a window. I was lucky: if he had come a bit earlier, I would have been in that *droshky* and taken that bullet. But it happened to be him. Bogusławski, as it turned out, was a nephew of the Moscow Orthodox church archbishop, and I was delegated to take part in his funeral in Moscow. The service was very solemn and elaborate, with the wake and reception afterwards. Despite the revolution raging outside, the reception was both exquisite in its cuisine and traditional in its rituals. We were served caviar in fancy saucers and Russian pancakes and many other foods that I no longer remember. With every course—and there were many—the archbishop made a short speech, which always ended with the same formula, "God, accept the soul of your servant Bogusławski. Gospady, pamylui" [Lord, have mercy]. The drinks were also unusual for, although served in wineglasses, they were non-alcoholic, a lemonade of sorts. I found myself thinking that had that bullet been mine, the ceremonies would have been much simpler, but the drinks definitely much stronger.

Around the time of the October Revolution, I founded the Polish Military Association in the Gatchina garrison. Most of the Poles in Gatchina were railroad employees, and their families had been evacuated from Poland by the Russians. That was how my family had found itself in Moscow. My association gathered, at least for a while, over a hundred Poles, mostly non-commissioned officers. I rented an empty store and set up a teahouse, where I served good tea for a token fee. The establishment soon became a Polish clubhouse and attracted not only the military but their families and friends as well. I bought some dominoes and chessboards to give them some entertainment, and even organized special events connected with various Polish national anniversaries, such as the commemoration of Tadeusz

Kościuszko.* The Russians, so absorbed in their own internal problems, did not seem to mind my little Polish initiatives.

Since I had started my military career as a deserter, it was only fitting that I should end it the same way. It may have been already 1918, and the unrest and confusion were reaching their crescendo. Summary trials and executions had become the order of the day. Even being a Bolshevik did not offer much protection: Korytowski, a Polish mechanic, was one, but he was shot anyway. So when it was getting too hot for me, I packed my sack, slung the rifle over my shoulder, and went to my parents in Moscow. It may have been the only time in my life when I really enjoyed shopping: wherever I went in my military uniform and with the rifle on my back, people respectfully (or fearfully) stepped aside and let me buy whatever I needed. I did not have to stand in line or haggle for a price.

While staying with my parents, I joined the Polish Muscovite Revolutionary Regiment named after Bartosz Głowacki.† My cousin was already a member. The regiment was made up of common soldiers and officers from all services, all of them Poles. We wore distinctive epaulets, with the number of our Polish regiment. The Bolshevik authorities considered us part of the regular army, but for us, the regiment was a form of self-defence and a refuge from the revolutionary chaos. We stayed in the barracks most of the time, spending time on idle talk and games. It was during those weeks of boredom that eight of us, including my cousin, decided to risk the return to Poland. We went to the military border between Russia and Germany and, showing the Germans our railroad IDs—for we were all sons of railroad employees—managed to get across the checkpoints. The Germans assumed that we were Polish POWs returning home. Since they needed railroad workers, they put us on a train and sent us to Mińsk and later to Warsaw. In Warsaw, we had to report to the police daily, then once a week, finally once a month, until the Germans were disarmed. At that moment, we immediately revealed our military identities and joined

---

* Tadeusz Kościuszko (1752-1817), Polish and American hero, led the 1794 Polish insurrection against Russia and fought in the American Revolution.

† Bartosz Wojciech Głowacki (ca. 1758-94), a peasant who fought in the 1794 Polish insurrection against Russia; made an officer after the battle of Racławice.

the then-forming 36th Infantry Regiment of the Academic Legion of the Polish army. I had been a platoon leader, and they needed non-commissioned officers. Thus I began my career in the Polish military. Soon I transferred to the 1st Air Force Regiment as a senior mechanic, and was given the rank of master 1st class, which corresponded to staff sergeant. There were only two of us bearing that rank in the whole army.

I began my post-secondary education in the early 1920s at Warsaw Polytechnic, in the department of Mechanical Engineering. I studied there for a few years, but only half-heartedly, waiting for the Aviation Engineering Department to be opened. But my hopes never materialized, so I decided to change the focus of my studies entirely and transferred to the Szkoła Główna Gospodarstwa Wiejskiego [Central School for Agriculture], department of Wood Technology. I wrote my thesis on harvesting resin from the common pine in the district of Warsaw, under the direction of Professor Szwarc. Years later, on the occasion of the 175th anniversary of the school's founding, I received, on the basis of my thesis, the degree of Master of Science and Engineering.

While a student at Warsaw Polytechnic, I worked nights at the editorial offices of the daily, *Rzeczpospolita* [*Republic*]. I was responsible for receiving domestic wires by phone, dictating them to a typist, and passing them on to the editors. During the three years I spent there, I met lots of interesting people. Kornel Makuszyński, the literary editor, had his office next to mine. I owe him a great deal. At the time, my wife was seriously ill, but the doctor demanded cash for the operation she needed. We had no cash and no savings. The only object of any considerable value I owned was an exquisite samovar from Bukhara, which the doctor would have accepted as payment, but with which I was reluctant to part. When Makuszyński learned about my problems, he asked me into his office, closed the door behind me, and offered me a loan, spontaneously and unpretentiously, without asking for details or for reassurances that I would repay. He was a very decent man, and he had his own share of grief, for his wife was also unwell.

I also remember others from the editorial staff of *Rzeczpospolita,* many of them leading intellectuals of the interwar years. I knew people like the writer Adolf Nowaczyński and the poet Kazimierz Wierzyński. A name-day party for the editor-in-chief, Stanisław Stroński, always attracted the cream of the capital's intellectual elite of all political stripes, including the representatives of the leftist daily *Kurier Poranny* [*Morning Courier*]. The discussions were fascinating and often heated but never rude, in deference to the ladies and especially Stroński's wife, who was English but spoke Polish well.

The May coup d'etat of 1926[*] happened just as I was finishing my studies. I saw what was happening in Warsaw with my own eyes: my cousin and I spent hours roaming the streets and collecting bits of news. There weren't as many casualties as was often claimed afterwards. And certainly no one was killed at the Military College, which took the side of the government.

Soon after graduation, I went into business for myself. Together with a friend, we began a consulting business, preparing forest management plans. The money was good, especially when we did everything ourselves, including the drawings. But after three years, the work grew tedious, being always in the woods at the mercy of the elements, so I accepted a job in a sawmill in Czarna Wieś, near Białystok, which later became an experimental mill of the Forestry Research Institute. Our mill employed about 400 people, among them many refugees from Russia granted political asylum and the right to work in Poland after the October Revolution. When a group of Russian officers was threatened with expulsion, I had to intervene with the ministry to ensure they were allowed to remain in Poland. The mill employed not only former counter-revolutionaries but also, as it quickly became apparent, a large number of rabid communists, the majority of whom were Russian as well. They organized armed gangs to carry out acts of sabotage and terrorism in the vicinity of the mill. For example, they attacked and ransacked the buildings of the District Forest Administration, wounding the chief forester and killing his secretary; they murdered the priest who harangued communists from the pulpit; and they broke into the mill's safe, which, fortunately, was empty at the time. Some of those acts of violence were clearly ordered and directed from beyond the eastern border. I, too, kept getting death threats and sentences from the communists, so many, in fact, that I could have wallpapered my house with them. For that reason I always carried a gun on me, and they knew

---

[*] A military coup led by Józef Piłsudski, which overthrew the government and installed a regine controlled by him.

it. They never risked carrying out those threats. After a rash of murders, the authorities sent in an investigator and the police. I pointed out to them those communists I suspected of crimes. They put fifteen of them in chains and sent them by train to Białystok, where they were put on trial. Two were sentenced to death. One of them was called Hlabicz, a Russian; the other's name I don't remember, but he was Polish. They found a cache of arms in the latter's house, including some machine guns.

In the late 1930s things settled down considerably, except that my own health began to fail: I came down with pneumonia, and the doctor recommended a gentler climate. So after ten years in Czarna Wieś, I accepted a transfer to Broszniów [Broshnev], district Stanisławów [Ivano-Frankivs'k], where I managed a mill employing 800 workers. The mill had its own power plant, which ran on sawdust and wood refuse. There I worked until 1939, until the mobilization.

Through some lucky coincidence, a fragment of a diary I kept at the time has survived, and it describes my September tracks with considerable detail. So I will let it speak for me:

"August 31, 6:30 p.m. Mobilization posters have just appeared. I must report in Grodno [Hrodna] on the first day of mobilization, so I have made the arrangements to hand over the mill to the sole engineer who will stay in charge.... I went home to kiss goodbye my two little boys, Andrzej and Julian, and asked my oldest one, Stanisław, to look after his mother. I kissed my wife and went by car to Lwów [L'viv]. I got here at 2:00 a.m.

"September 1. We are finally leaving Lwów, after a one-hour delay. The train is crammed with people, the station crowded with reservists and their families. Everywhere heartbreaking sobbings, shameless tears. . . . We've arrived in Warsaw late at night. I'm going to see my parents, and to say goodbye.

"September 2. At 6:00 a.m. I said goodbye to my mother and sister; my father and nephews wanted to see me off to the station. We took a hackney coach, but after a few hundred metres we were halted by the air-raid sirens. I had to bid my father and nephews farewell in the middle of the street and go to the station alone. At the crowded Warsaw-East railway station, the reservists were boarding the train through the windows. I got a place standing on a seat in a second class compartment. We're going very slowly, stopping at every station. . . . In Ostrów we got our first taste of war: German airplanes dropped eighteen bombs on our tracks. Fortunately, none of them actually hit the tracks, so there was little damage. We reached Grodno late at night; it, too, had already been bombed.

"September 3. I've seen the cathedral; one of its walls has been torn open. Another bomb left a hole in the roof of the workshops where I am supposed to work. Many were wounded. . . . In the morning I was given my assignment as assistant superintendent of the assembly plant in the armoured weapons park. Work begins at 7:00 a.m. and goes on till 5:00 p.m., with a one-hour break for the midday meal.

"September 9. Every day we have three or four air raids. Once, when some 300 of us, soldiers and officers, gathered in the field in front of the workshops, a German airplane swooped down, blazing with machine gun fire. Miraculously, no one suffered an injury. But during the raid on Czechowniczyn, the Germans hit the ordinance depot, blowing up lots of ammunition. Yesterday, walking to the workshop during a raid, I found a packet of candies, apparently dropped from a plane. I took them to the lab for analysis, wondering if that "gift" was lethal. Our efforts in the assembly plant are yielding impressive results. Despite the bombings, both the civilians and the military are working quickly and efficiently. We believe that victory will be ours, and confirm one another in that belief.

"September 10. I was summoned to the headquarters and learned that I and several other officers had been reassigned as commanders of motorized columns, destined for the front, at the disposal of the high command. Our entire complex is to be evacuated to the south. We must quickly repaint and refurbish the vehicles, and need all the civilian help we can get.

"September 14. It's taken us four days, but my column is now ready for departure. We have been changing our location every day, afraid that German spotters might catch sight of us and later blow us to pieces.

"September 17. At 8:00 a.m., a courier from the civic county headquarters arrived with a message that I was to report immediately. When I arrived, I learned that Soviet troops had crossed the border. We were being squeezed from both sides. I was ordered to wait by the phone. Meanwhile, the headquarters was a hub of frantic activity. Civil servants were being paid three months' wages. At 8:30 a.m., the county chief administrator left. The clerks wandered through the empty rooms aimlessly, in despair. At 9:00 my orders came: withdraw towards Wilno [Vilnius]. I returned to my column at the edge of the forest and began dispatching vehicles, three at a time. I'm riding in the last one, a passenger car. . . . I have just received a report that the Soviet troops are only fifteen kilometres away. . . . The road to Wilno is crowded. The military, postal, and police vehicles are moving fast. Anti-aircraft guns are much slower. Above us, airplanes fly in the direction of Wilno: this time they are Polish planes. Chaos in the making.

"September 18. We arrived in Wilno late at night and stopped at the anti-tank blockade. The streets are jammed with people and vehicles. I sent the column to the rallying point and made my way to the headquarters. The commanders of the other columns were already there. What next, nobody knew. I was feeling depressed. Have we been defeated? What can we do? No answers, of course; no one knows anything. I left the headquarters and, after a long search, found this hotel room. There is no food, but I managed to get some tea. I finished my soldier's ration of bread. I must get some sleep. . . . I can't sleep. Thoughts are swirling within my skull; I'm feeling dazed. What's happened? What's going to happen? I can't, I don't believe we are finished. It's only a temporary setback. Yes, it's only temporary.

"September 19. In the morning, we reported again at the Wilno headquarters. We were informed that we'll receive six months' wages, but for the time being we were put on alert along with our units. At 2:00 p.m., I was relieved from duty and went to town for my midday meal. Since I hadn't had a decent hot meal for three days, I drove to my wife's relatives and admitted that I was hungry. After I ate, I changed the dressings around my ankles; long days in stiff boots have given me painful blisters and sores all over my feet. I soaked them in warm water, and put on new bandages. I have returned to the unit and am awaiting further orders. . . . At 6:00 p.m. a telephone message from the headquarters ordering all columns to move out. We tried to carry it out, but the security commander, a major of the Border Guards Corps, would not let any vehicles out because the Soviet tanks were already in town. Finally, I got an explicit order to go with my column to the Zielony Bridge and wait there. The city was all lit up, crowds of people in the streets. This commotion was caused by the news being broadcast on the radio, too good to be true, of a coup in

Germany. Suddenly panic erupted, I'm not sure why, and people were scrambling in all directions. Vehicles sped across the bridge. We're stuck in the traffic of cars, horse-drawn carts, marching infantry, artillery. Foul drizzle and bone-chilling cold. At the bridge, a machine gun and a soldier beside a truck blocking the way. The drizzle has muffled all sounds. Silence. While I talked to the commanding officer, we heard a short burst of machine gun fire, then a few explosions. The Soviets are coming. Our orders are to withdraw towards the Lithuanian border."

Immediately after crossing the border, we were interned. Lithuanian troops transported us to a summer resort on the Niemen [Nemen] River called Kołotowo. The houses there were typical summer cottages, without any heat. That worried us, for winter was drawing nigh. Fortunately, they moved us to Kalwaria [Kalvarija], a small Jewish town with a large asylum. They cleared half the asylum for the Polish officers: the irony of this did not escape us. We were placed in rooms, each with cots for four people. The doors had no knobs, only bars in the windows; the bathrooms had no taps, nothing to hang oneself on.

The other half of the building still housed the mentally ill. Lithuanians were not any different in the way they treated them from most other societies at the time. Every now and then the sick were taken outside by the orderlies for a walk. From our windows we could see their small yard and the baths. The orderlies always carried big sticks and beat the poor, lost souls at every turn and seemingly without restraint. I still remember the time when they were taking a woman to the bathhouse. She didn't want to bathe and was howling like a wild thing. The orderlies beat her up and pulled her by the hair to the baths. A terrible, painful memory.

The camp's commander was Major Jaksztas. He probably spoke Polish, for in those days I never met a Lithuanian who couldn't, but he never used it in front of us. One of my friends, a young Lithuanian 2nd lieutenant serving in the Polish army and interned together with us, was probably his nephew. But Jaksztas treated him like the rest of us, strictly but fairly. My young friend was an artist, a painter, freshly graduated from the Academy of Fine Arts. Once he drew me a caricature of a Lithuanian soldier, which I still have somewhere in my files. He spoke Polish like a Pole; as for myself, although I spent more than a year in Lithuania, I never learned much beyond *negalima*, "not allowed," a favourite phrase of our guards.

Those common guards treated us with the utmost contempt. I don't know why they hated us so much, why they treated us as the vilest of criminals. They didn't openly beat us up, only because this was not allowed by the Geneva Convention, but hitting us with rifle butts was commonplace. One of them even went so far as to feign willingness to organize an escape, for a fee, of course. But this was only a vicious ruse. One of the officers who fell for it was shot dead, another wounded. We knew this had been a provocation so we went on a hunger strike, every single officer in the camp. We set down the rules: smoking cigarettes and drinking water was allowed, but no food. We endured some ten days to a fortnight, and the Lithuanians gave in; they did not try to force-feed any of us. They accepted our demands that the provocation be investigated and those responsible punished. Whether they actually punished anyone, I don't know; but I know that they promised.

The camp was run under strict discipline. We couldn't, for instance, go outside, except in a line into a small yard and under watchful eyes of the guards. But we could freely move among the floors and were allowed a certain degree of freedom in some respects. We governed ourselves through a council, which communicated and negotiated with the Lithuanians on our behalf. The council was led by retired General Przeździecki, an old, quiet, amiable man. Through it, we brought some cultural life into the camp by organizing concerts and lecture presentations. We had among us two violin virtuosos and a piano player, who on two occasions delighted us with music. Since our officers came from a variety of professions, we also set up, under their direction, various self-education circles.

Another form of our self-governance was a system of peer justice, with two courts, one for junior officers and one for senior officers. I was elected member in one of those and participated in several proceedings, mostly dealing with officers who willingly collaborated with Lithuanians. In some cases we sentenced them to banishment, which meant that no one talked to or shook hands with them. They lived in the same building but were expelled from our community. This punishment was real; so much so, that some thought it preferable to risk an escape from the camp than endure this sort of ostracism. Another case

I remember had to do with an officer, a Jew, who received food parcels from home full of aromatic bacon. He fried that bacon—maliciously and ostentatiously—on a small camping stove for all to see and smell. The smell wafted throughout the building and exasperated those on the lean camp fare. The court convened, considered the matter, and passed the sentence: his bacon was thrown out and his stove smashed. I think his was the only incident of this sort. I remember that he was a Jew because he was an aberration (well, there may have been another, the collaborator Melniker): throughout our internment, the Jews showed themselves true and loyal Poles. In fact, even when some of our senior officers turned collaborators and talked to the Bolsheviks, the Jews conducted themselves blamelessly.

Our camp fare may have been lean, but we never really starved. The servings were decent, but all the food was, of course, Lithuanian style. So, for instance, we were served cabbage boiled in milk; I had never eaten it before and, despite the experience, never acquired a taste for it. For Christmas and Easter, the meals were tastier, though still far from gourmet. But after our hunger strike, the Lithuanians were so considerate that they served us easily digestible porridge with milk, to make sure we didn't all get sick. And, to their partial credit, no one did. The other part of that credit must go to the excellent doctors who were among us: they supervised the strike and made sure that everyone drank enough water to stay reasonably healthy.

We stayed in Lithuania for an entire year, from 1939 to 1940. When the Bolsheviks came, the Lithuanians transferred our camp to the Soviet military authorities and the NKVD [state security police]. Once again the Lithuanians showed their decent side. Major Jaksztas called up all the officers and openly announced: "I must hand you over to the Soviet 'convoy'. If you have any dark points in your past for which the Soviets might want to sentence you to death, you'd better escape to Poland now." About twenty people took advantage of that offer, among them former prosecutors. Their names were not included in the lists of prisoners surrendered to the Soviets.

The "convoys" were special military units at the disposal of the NKVD. When they came to Kalwaria, they lined us up and, as a Lithuanian read out the names, the Soviets received us one by one, arranging us in groups of ten, and surrounding each group with guards. They warned us that one step to the left or to the right and the "convoy" would shoot. They walked us out from the asylum and into town. In the streets, the hostility of the local people came to me as a shock and burned itself into my memory: Jewish children threw mud and refuse at us, called us names, and screamed obscenities. Why, I never knew.

At the local railway station we were loaded aboard a train, a passenger train, I think, and taken to Kozel'sk. I don't recall how long that journey was, but I remember an exhausting march from the station in Kozel'sk to the monastery a few kilometres away. Many people, myself included, took quite a lot of baggage with them. I was no longer young at the time, forty-two years of age, mobilized as a senior reservist. I was carrying warm coats and blankets, for one could already feel winter in the blasting wind. After a while, I began to sweat and bend under the weight and was most grateful to several friends who took portions of the load off my shoulders—literally—and helped me carry the stuff. But not all were so fortunate in their friends. There was one major who had taken much more than he could handle. Like the majority of staff officers, he was not much liked by the rest of us, and I watched him discard one package after another, and no one offered him any help. This was symptomatic of the rift between the career officers and the reservists. The latter often felt that the professional officers behaved disrespectfully towards them, especially staff officers, who did not hide their condescension for the reservists. And yet despite this rift and the sporadic incidents it caused, the relations among the internees, both in Lithuania and in Kozel'sk, were on the whole friendly and mutually supportive. So in my experience, the oft-repeated sentiment about the lack of comradery or fellowship among Poles is plain wrong.

In Kozel'sk, there were two monasteries, one that used to be male and the other, much smaller, female. Four hundred of us, all officers, were herded onto the courtyard of the female monastery. We were ordered to sit down, or, rather, to squat. In the four corners of the yard we could see heavy army trucks, with machine guns mounted on top, all aimed menacingly at us. It occurred to me that this could be my end, and I started praying. Others must have been troubled by similar thoughts, for some looked deathly pale, and some even fainted (they were carried away on stretchers by the medical personnel in white coats). After this show of terror, they led us into an oppressive-looking cement prison building. Carrying out orders, we squatted along a wall. And then, in contrast to our cold reception, they brought out pots with hot barley soup, a characteristically Bolshevik gesture. After the meal, we were led to the bigger monastery, which, as it turned out, consisted of a number of smaller buildings, typical Eastern Orthodox chapels. Inside, cots had been readied for us, all traces of those who had come before us—and had been murdered at Katyn—swept clean. The cots were stacked one on top of another, four cots high. I got one of the fourth-storey cots and had to climb to it on a ladder; but when I lay down and looked at the wall, colourful saints gazed back at me from the murals. My neighbours were Captain Łabanowski and his sixteen-year-old son, who had joined the youth corps in his father's regiment. The Bolsheviks took them both, father and son, but for once they showed some decency by keeping them together both in Kozel'sk and in Gryazovets, where we were eventually shipped. They managed to stay together until they rejoined the Polish army. Good neighbours they were, and good friends.

The Kozel'sk monastery was devastated; all the trees in its orchards had died from freezing during cold winters and were overgrown with weeds. One of our tasks was cutting down those trees for firewood and for other uses; we often used pieces of that wood for carving figurines. Since carving required sharp implements, we needed whetting stones. We quarried them from the marble steps that connected the upper level of the monastery, with all its churches and chapels, and the lower level, where the monks' quarters used to be. The Soviets insisted on confiscating our whetting stones, but I could never understand why.

I also honed some other practical skills at Kozel'sk. The Soviets turned one of the monastic buildings into a car repair shop. There I learned an efficient way of recycling motor oil: you drain the used oil from the engine, strain it through some rags to remove any grit or dirt, and pour the filtered oil back into the engine. I saw this done many times and was assured that the engines would work just fine. Elsewhere in the camp, I learned some electrical wiring using barbed wire. It was easy to twist together and, where we were, its supply was plentiful. Care had to be taken, though, to keep the lines at some distance from one another to avoid shorts. I had never before seen naked barbed wire used for such a purpose, but then all my technological know-how had been profoundly bourgeois.

Our sojourn in Kozel'sk had as a goal our re-education. We had a cinema, a reading room, and a library—all in Russian, of course.

Unfortunately, many officers came from Galicia, and they knew no Russian at all. My Russian from the Gatchina days was still decent, so I did indeed spend some time in the library.

In a sense, the books offered me a way to escape, at least temporarily, the most unpleasant reality of the so-called *doprosy* [interrogations]. I understood (and still remember) the questions they were asking, but to this day I cannot see the point of those interrogations. They would lead us individually into a room, where a three-person NKVD committee was already in session. They showered us with questions, usually in Polish. They asked details of my private life, what I did for a living, how many workers I employed. Why they needed that information, I don't know. They accused me of joining the Polish army in 1920 and fighting against the Bolsheviks. Their information seemed to be more accurate than my memory. They knew I had served in the Russian army and where, and one of the *politruks* [propaganda officers] kept asking me why I hadn't remained in Russia. They knew I had taught in the aviation school in Gatchina, and even brought up some names of my former comrades-in-arms, who, until recently, had held senior positions in the Soviet air force. But perhaps worse than those interrogations were the times when I was ordered to act as an interpreter at the *doprosy* of my fellow officers. Then I felt as if I had been forced into the hateful role of a collaborator. My friends, however, understood the situation, and no one laid any blame on me.

When we were moved to Lower Kozel'sk, we began to suspect that some major changes were coming, especially after the arrival of a young doctor, a woman from some nomadic Mongolian tribe. She started conducting medical examinations, dividing us into those fit and those unfit, except that no one knew what we had been judged fit or unfit for. Those deemed unfit—there were only four of them among almost 400 examined—all suffered from advanced tuberculosis and were immediately taken to a hospital. And the rest of us, as it turned out, were fit for a long and strenuous journey. They loaded us into freight cars, and we set out in the direction of Arkhangelsk. Just outside the city, at a small station called Gryazovets, we got off and marched several kilometres to what used to be a camp for Finnish POWs. The camp was small, and there wasn't enough space for all 400 of us, so they quartered us in a garden among the trees, under the cruel sky. Each of us got a blanket, and almost immediately we began building cots with rickety roofs above them; still, most of us caught colds and fell sick. My cold turned into a nasty influenza, and I became so weak and feverish that they took me inside and made me a bed on the floor. I was far from comfortable, but certainly better off than those outside at the mercy of the elements. After a few days my fever came down, and gradually I recovered.

In Gryazovets, we met about ten survivors of the massacre in Katyn. Among them was an elderly gentleman, Dr. Szarecki, a professor of surgery from Warsaw University. There was also another surgeon, whose name escapes me now, who specialized in appendicitis. Those two, my brother-in-law, Siennicki (the father of the architect Siennicki from Montreal), who was a professor at the Warsaw Polytechnic, and myself formed a sort of survival partnership. My three partners were mighty minds, but I had an enamelled bucket, which I had saved from the medical unit of our transport and which soon became crucial to our survival.

From the moment we arrived in Gryazovets, we were starving. Things turned from bad to worse when the Soviets started a propaganda campaign to encourage us to join the Soviet army. Since there were no volunteers, they gradually cut our rations down to twelve grams of bread and a bowl of watery soup for a whole day. They thought hunger would force us to do what words could not. And that's when my bucket became so precious. We used it to cook soup from pigweed over an open fire to supplement the starving rations. I was the cook. Sometimes I would scrounge some salted skin of a beluga whale from the camp kitchen, add some potatoes, and boil it all together: the meal tasted foul but gave us some nutrition. At other times, Dr. Szarecki would bring scraps of fat he got as payment when he agreed to operate on a Bolshevik. Thus my enamelled bucket of soup helped us ward off hunger, at least for a while. Eventually, the Bolsheviks noticed that we competed with their gourmet kitchen and forbade us to cook outside.

We stayed in Gryazovets for a few months. The daily hardships left us little energy for any cultural initiatives. But even there, we tried to keep our minds alive: after all, there were quite a few wise men among us. My three professors and myself, the bucket owner, formed a science club— "White Bucket Club," we called it—which organized informal science talks and discussions.

It may have been fall when we got the news of the amnesty. The camp commander announced that he was setting us free and would be sending us to the then-forming Polish army. Our sentences—I had been given twenty years for taking part in the Bolshevik war of 1920—were nullified. What's more, they also gave us 1000 rubles each as restitution, except that rubles were mostly worthless, and the only way to buy something was to barter clothes for it. They put us on a train and took us to Tatishchevo, one of two rallying points of the Polish army. The military camp had already been set up when we arrived to join it, a small city of tents. We spent that winter under tents, keeping warm around wood stoves, which set quite a few tents ablaze. The wood came from a nearby forest, and everyone took part in collecting it, from privates to officers, to generals, including General Anders.[*] We carried the firewood, dry branches and logs, to the camp on our backs, wading through deep snow to the tune of Polish soldiers' songs.

The 400 of us from Gryazovets were assigned as officers to various units. I found myself first in the 5th Infantry Regiment, and then in a motorized group. The Soviets issued us no arms, except for a single anti-tank gun (God only knows what it was for), so we drilled with sticks instead of rifles.

The food in Tatishchevo was bad and in short supply. In the officers' mess, they served us a glass of vodka with dinner, but this was a small consolation. But one day there was an abundance of bread and butter, all coming from a nearby well-run German *kolkhoz* [collective farm] that was being dissolved by the Soviets. People stuffed themselves with that butter, which they hadn't seen for a long time, and afterwards some fell sick with yellows from eating too much fat. The British did not send us any food or arms in Russia, only first-class uniforms, wool and leather. The Russians looked at us with envy. They coveted good western clothing so much that for a leather belt you could get a sack of flour. That's why we had to watch that soldiers didn't sell or barter their uniforms away.

We languished in Tatishchevo for almost a year while the Polish high command negotiated with the Soviets the conditions of our departure for Persia. Finally, they moved us to Baku, brought in the tankers,

---

[*] Władysław Anders (1892-1970), commander of the Polish army in the Soviet Union (later the 2nd Polish Corps).

and ordered us aboard. The NKVD conducted no special checks; they simply verified the name lists and did not even bother to search us. We could take all our possessions, but few chose to hang on to the Soviet money. The euphoria at the prospect of finally leaving behind that "inhuman land" and everything that was of it blinded us all, and we burned our rubles in heaps, only to regret it later, when we found out that they had real value in Persia. I carried with me a diary from my Russian exile, which would have been confiscated by the NKVD, had they found it. Unfortunately, most of it perished in the course of my later wanderings. If the treatment by the NKVD seemed mild, the sea passage itself, lasting just under twenty-four hours, turned out to be a true ordeal. Everyone was seasick, scrambling to get to the latrine on time, with some not making it. The night was the worst, for you had to jump over those asleep on the blankets spread out on deck while the ship kept rolling from side to side and your stomach kept churning. But many of us had been through worse things in Russia.

How I was reunited with my family, well, that's a good story in itself. While I was still in Gryazovets, I received a letter from my father in Warsaw, telling me my wife had been deported to a *sovkhoz* [state farm] and giving me her address. So when I got my 1000 rubles of compensation, I immediately put 500 into a letter and sent it to her. Her job was tending pigs; my eldest son worked as a carpenter and in the fields, and the middle one broke in asses. For their work, they got no food, only some cash. But what they got was not enough to survive on, so they lived mostly on what they managed to steal. When she learned that I was in the Polish army, my wife bribed the local authorities and ran away from the *sovkhoz* to Tatishchevo. They got stranded in Ural'sk and sent me a telegram from there. I immediately arranged for a letter from the NKVD authorizing me to search for my family and set out. But when I got to Ural'sk, I found there only Stanisław; my wife and the other two boys had left for Tatishchevo with a military transport. Stanisław got left behind, a young man of draft age and without any papers. He was lucky the NKVD did not take him for a deserter. When we got back to my camp, the others were already waiting for us there.

When my family arrived in Tatishchevo, my wife was completely emaciated and my sons weak from hunger. But in Tatishchevo, too, food was scarce, and the military personnel had to share their food rations with their dependents. To relieve the situation, the camp commander, General Boruta Spiechowicz, decided to send our families to the south. He summoned me to his headquarters and gave me his officer's word of honour that he was convinced they'd have much better conditions there. I am sure he truly believed that. But the Soviets could not be believed. On their way south, the convoy was stopped and the families sent back to various *kolkhozes*. My wife was so bitter that she wrote a letter from the *kolkhoz* to General Spiechowicz, in which she called into question the worth of his word of honour. I have kept this letter to this day. Spiechowicz responded by handing me a document from the NKVD, giving me free passage and permission to bring my family back to Tatishchevo. I was immediately granted a leave of indeterminate duration, collected some food and medicine from the camp hospital, and set out to search for them. By train, I reached a small station in the middle of nowhere; then I walked several miles through a desert, until finally, after many natural and man-made obstacles, I found them clinging to life in terrible conditions. They were living in a pigsty, sleeping on dried reeds. All of them were sick, with obvious signs of avitaminosis and starvation. They were too weak to leave immediately, so I stayed with them for two weeks, trying to strengthen them with some food. To get it, I bartered my army boots and my English belt, and was even prepared to barter my uniform if it became necessary. Fortunately, it wasn't. Even after two weeks my wife was so frail that there was no way she could walk the few miles to the railway station. After asking around, I found a man who, for 100 rubles, agreed to take her there on a cart. The horse, its ribs showing, could barely pull the cart's weight along the soft desert road; we walked on foot by its side. When we finally reached the station, the ticket clerk demanded certificates that we had been de-loused. Of course, we had no such certificates, but 100 rubles easily removed that obstacle. On the train, I had to hush my wife, who reviled every NKVD officer we met. In the end, I managed to send her and our two younger sons with a staff transport to Persia. With the same transport went my brother-in-law and a former member of the White Bucket Club, Professor Siennicki.

I stayed behind in Russia, and, once again, because of my knowledge of Russian, was chosen as an interpreter for the NKVD, except this time I assisted in negotiations concerning the transport of our troops to Persia. One of the perks of this job was that my provisions came from a special NKVD store. It was supplied with a dizzying abundance and variety of foods, with almost anything you could imagine in those wartime days: dairy products, meat, fish, caviar—you name it, it was there.

After three months, we, too, left for Persia, where I re-established contact with my family. They were lodged in the Shah's gardens: they had cots, and a roof over their heads—relatively decent conditions. My wife was working as a clerk for the refugee camp police. Shortly after my arrival in Tehrān, the months of malnutrition and anxiety took their toll. I fell ill with tropical fever and pellagra. At first I stayed in a very good hospital for British officers, and later in the hospital of the Polish Red Cross. At the same time, my youngest son came down with typhoid fever, so he, too, ended up in an isolation hospital. Luckily, we both recovered: he went back to stay with his mother, and I was assigned to a convalescence unit, with lighter duties. Despite our health problems, we have mostly pleasant memories of Tehrān. As did all officers, I had to pay for my personal provisions, but I had the resources for it. My salary was quite high because of my years in service, even though I was only a lieutenant. My wife and children also had a good income so they could support themselves.

When I returned to active service, I was relocated to the camp in Qizil Ribat [As Sa'dīyah], some 400 kilometres away from Tehrān. Despite the distance, I remained in close touch with my wife because getting leave was not difficult. The Qizil Ribat camp was built especially for the Polish soldiers. There we finally got our long-awaited weapons and began training. I found myself in the 2nd Armoured Brigade. At first we trained with old, primitive, frustratingly slow tanks, the Valentines, but eventually we received the superbly equipped Shermans. We also got a corresponding number of carriers and armoured vehicles. Those vehicles had automatic transmission, with five forward and five reverse gears. They could drive forward and backward with the same speed and were extremely manoeuvrable. We were impressed.

I remember one unusual episode from that time with particular clarity. I went to the registrar's office of the infantry regiment to do some work on the personnel records. The registrar took out a cigarette holder and offered me a cigarette. He pulled out a box of matches and was just about to strike a match when out of the blue sky a blinding flash of lightening struck, burning a hole in the tent and hitting the ground right between us. The sky was cloudless and sunny, no signs of a storm or thunder. The registrar was killed on the spot. One officer cadet and myself were knocked senseless for two hours. We were taken to hospital, and when I came to, I was completely paralyzed. It took me two months to recover the feeling in my hands and legs and start moving again.

The training and exercises in Iraq took over a year, enough time for our British liaison officer, Taylor (we called him "Krawiecki," or "taylor-ski"), to learn passable Polish. Since our day-to-day operations and training were all done in Polish, we needed people like him to help us stay in touch with the outside world.

Well trained, we were sent to the front in Italy. We went straight to Monte Cassino. General Anders undertook the task on which the British and Hindi had already broken their teeth. I was assigned to the maintenance company of the 2nd Tank Brigade, which serviced three regiments, the 1st, 4th, and 6th. We had a special unit, which used huge, fourteen-wheel tractors to pull the damaged tanks to the shops. Sometimes we could hardly believe the tight places into which our tanks managed to manoeuvre themselves. If they broke down or got hit there, we did not try to extricate them; we left them as mementoes of the hard war.

In May 1945, we were in the vicinity of Bologna. I don't remember the moment or circumstances when I learned that the Germans had capitulated. We knew that Poland had been cheated by the Allies and that the end of the war did not mean freedom for Poland. There was much talk among the officers whether we should all resign in protest against this betrayal. That's what the Yugoslavs did and why they had been interned in a camp in Italy. The irony was that it was the Poles who had to guard them. I'm not sure whether there was much point to those, sometimes heated, arguments, except that they gave us a vent to release some of our frustration at the unfairness of the world.

After the war's end, we were shipped to Britain, where the British set up the Polish Resettlement Training Corps, whose mission was to train officers and regular soldiers for various civilian occupations. Because of my experience, I was seconded to a training camp, in which the commanding officer was Major Masztak. He named me director in charge of instruction. In this capacity, I sought out among our soldiers masters in various trades, who assumed the duties of instructors. This way I set up courses in locksmithing, tanning, shoemaking, tailoring, cooking, and other occupations. Those courses lasted about three months; they gave no official papers, but they taught the basics of a trade. Many officers took them. I knew one colonel who finished a cooking course and later worked as a cook; another trained as a tailor. In the context of those courses, we also published a range of booklets, and even books, dealing with such topics as metallurgy, ironworking tools and machines, technological materials, and so on. We had a few dozen men in each course, among them my sons; the whole camp numbered several hundred people.

While I was quartered in the barracks, my wife rented an apartment in town. As an officer's wife, she was receiving a military pension, and she didn't have to struggle for the basics of life. Since my work in the corps counted as regular military service, I, too, was receiving my usual lieutenant's pay. Unfortunately, having served its purpose, the corps was dissolved, and His Majesty formally dismissed us all from military service. We received our civilian papers and a monetary recompense of £700, much less than what the British officers received. Still, the money was welcome, and it helped us purchase a house and settle down.

My sons and I went to work in factories. I started in a textiles mill, where my job was to prepare wool for processing; dirty and hard that labour was, but the pay was good. Later I managed to get hired in a metal works, even though the Trade Union of Metal Workers was against hiring any Poles. The union did not like foreigners because they worked too fast and too efficiently; seeing their productivity, the directors cut the bonuses for the less efficient British workers. But the union made an exception for me and took me on for a trial and training period, with a minimal pay of £4 per week. The British workers were both friendly and helpful. Working beside me on a large lathe was an elderly man. At the beginning, when I still lacked the experience, he often left his own tasks and came to explain to me how certain things worked. He did not begrudge me his time or knowledge. On my part, I tried to fit in and stay on friendly terms with the union. A union representative used to come to me to warn me that on such and such a day, they would be measuring my efficiency. "Do this much and no more. That's the union norm," he would say. And I did as he asked, for they were decent towards me. Eventually, when I gained more experience, I received a regular wage of £9 to £12 per week plus a substantial bonus, the same as other British workers.

After a few years, we decided to apply for emigration to Canada. Life must be easier for immigrants in a country where everyone is an immigrant, we thought. I wrote to my father in Poland, asking for advice. He wrote back, "It's a wise decision, son, perhaps your wisest." So we sold the house and sailed for Canada. We were fools to have delayed our emigration, I was thinking during the passage. If we had signed up for agricultural contracts, we would have saved money and the government would have found us jobs. But everything worked out for the best. My sons, who left for Canada a year ahead of us, had already established themselves in Winnipeg. They had found jobs in factories, and by the time we arrived, they had already bought a house on Pritchard Avenue, one of those insubstantial houses built for ex-servicemen returning from the war. The houses had no basements, but they were inexpensive.

When we came to Canada, I was already over sixty. The employment bureau accepted my papers and classified me as having a university education. I waited for any offers, but finally a secretary told me openly that I was too old and should not hope for a job. But I couldn't live off my children, so I hired myself out as a night watchman at a construction site. I got a minimum wage, but our needs were small. I worked there for three seasons until I finally retired.

KAZIMIERZ SMOLIŃSKI

To this day, so many years after the war, I still cannot but wonder whether it was mere luck that led me through those countless fields of death or whether it was the very hand of God, his providence, that was shaping my destiny.

I was born in 1918. At the age of twenty-one, I volunteered for the Polish army and reported for service on March 21, 1939. I went through an accelerated recruit training and took my oath just three months later.

I was stationed with the 54th Infantry Regiment in Tarnopol [Ternopil']. In early September, we were loaded onto a train and sent westwards. Soon we met the first victims of the war: the refugees from Silesia, trains full of youth slowly moving to the east. At one of the frequent stops, I noticed an old couple, as grey as doves, sitting sadly in a corner of a railway car. I walked up to them and gave them my emergency food ration. This was strictly forbidden by military regulations, but the shadows of smiles that flitted across their faces took away my fear of any consequences.

Of course, there were no consequences. As soon as we crossed the Vistula River, a German warplane appeared. Bombs exploded the tracks ahead of us, and the train stopped. Then it shuddered as it took several direct hits. My car was shattered into splinters. I felt no pain under a pile of twisted metal and mutilated bodies, and slowly crawled towards light. When I got out, I noticed a young cavalry captain with his leg blown off. I covered him with a blanket, and said that the medics would be there shortly and everything would be all right. He looked at me with death in his eyes and said, "Friend, I know I have no leg." I do not think he survived.

We ran from the train, chased by the warplane's machine guns. I found refuge in an abandoned barn. I was alone. At night I made my way to Kraśnik and further to Lubomla [Lyuboml'], where I found a military unit getting ready to break through to Romania. I reported to a lieutenant by the name of Hitler, but he assured us he had nothing to do with Adolf. He assigned me to the regimental command as a courier.

Eventually, we began to move towards the east in a long column of trucks. Once again a solitary German aircraft swooped down from the cloudless sky. We ran for cover, but this plane dropped no bombs, only leaflets announcing that we were surrounded. This must have been true, for shortly afterwards we received orders from our command to lay down our arms. We began to disassemble our rifles and handguns and scatter the parts in ditches. The fighting was over for us, but our fate was uncertain, so I decided that no one would save me but myself. As a courier, I had a bicycle, so I jumped on it and began pedalling in the direction of Włodzimierz Wołyński [Vladimir Volynskiy]. I intended to ride my bike home. At some point, a man with a red band on his arm and a rifle waved me down. He asked me, in Ukrainian, where I was from, and demanded that I give him my leather belt. "You didn't give it to me, so why I should give it to you?" I retorted in Ukrainian. That instant gut reply may have saved my life, for he must have assumed I was a Pole and did not expect me to speak back in his language. Visibly discomfitted, he let me go. I was very close to Włodzimierz Wołyński when I heard a whisper from behind a bush, "Hey, Mr. Soldier!" When I stopped, a young Boy Scout emerged from the thicket. His name was Zbyszek, and he may have been ten years old. He told me not to go through the town because they were murdering Poles there. "I'll take you to the barracks through the back roads," he offered. He did, and I never saw him again. I have no doubt that he saved my life.

At the barracks, I was issued a new uniform. Then we located several buses of the Silesian Bus Lines parked throughout the town, unscrewed their floors, and got out a considerable quantity of heavy machine guns. I have no idea why they were there, but they were exactly what we needed. We cleaned them and put them together. Armed to the teeth, we left the barracks to "clean out" the town, but by then the town was almost totally deserted. On September 16, one of our officers announced that Hitler was dead and the war was over. This must have been part of the Soviet misinformation campaign, for the very next day a Soviet tank roared into town, followed by some infantry. They disarmed us and took us prisoner.

At first, we were shipped from one detention camp to another. When the Soviet-German war broke out, we were sent to help with the building of the Kotlas-Pechora transit route. I remained there, in camp number 54, until the amnesty. Under the terms of the amnesty, we were released to join the Polish army in Tatishchevo near Saratovo. I was assigned to an NCO school and transferred with the school to Dzalal'-Abad. There I graduated at the rank of corporal and got my assignment to the 2nd Regiment under the command of Lieutenant Sędziak. Fresh from school, I was given the task of training some old-timers, well past the usual recruitment age. I must admit that marshalling them around gave me no pleasure, and I did not much enjoy that posting.

The transit to Persia I remember well. Who could forget the crazy Iranian truck drivers, who sped with abandon along the narrow mountain roads? Each driver had a helper who clung to the step of the cab, a stone in hand. Whenever the driver pulled over on an up-slope, the helper jumped down and stuck the stone behind one of the wheels. A labour-intensive but effective way of braking. When we reached Khānaqīn, I was placed in the 4th Brigade of Colonel Grobicki. The unit dispatched me to a special training course for repair-shop technicians in Musayba near Baghdād. All our instructors were British, so willy-nilly I learned some passable English there. Afterwards I was set to work on a lathe in a workshop repairing military equipment. During our stay in Basra [Al Başrah], we were issued trucks: my team got a heavy combat-engineer truck, complete with turrets and pneumatic brakes. Each of us had to be able to command it, drive it, and use its guns. Versatility was the rule. We drove in it through Trans-Jordan and Palestine. I did little sightseeing along the way—we were always too busy repairing something—until we got to Port Said and Cairo.

From North Africa, boats ferried us to Taranto in Italy, where we set up camp in Campolieto. We engaged the Germans for the first time at Lacroche. At Monte Cassino, we left our carriers behind and moved to our assigned positions on foot. Once a British supply officer drove over to our positions. Lieutenant Lech, our platoon commander, chose me to take him to the front line because I knew some English. It was already getting dark. The Brit was driving along the tape that marked the road. Suddenly he pulled over and said his eyes were hurting and he could no longer see the tape. He pulled the handbrake, and we exchanged places. I sat behind the wheel, put in the gear, and on we went. A few minutes later, we could smell something burning underneath the vehicle. As we pulled over to find out what was going on, a shell exploded just metres ahead of us. The force of the explosion almost pushed us over the edge of the precipice. The Brit, unperturbed, looked up into the dark sky and said, "Someone loves us up there." Indeed, had we not stopped when we did, that shell would have landed smack in the middle of our carrier. And the smell was from the burning handbrake, which I had forgotten to release. Ridiculous as it sounds, it was the Brit's blindness and my absent-mindedness that saved our lives. As we drove on, we noticed two of our soldiers by the roadside. My Brit leaned out of the window and shouted, "Would you like a lift?" One of the soldiers shouted back in Russian, "Net, net, my zdes nedalochko" [No, no, we're not going far]. We were so startled that I pulled over beside them. It soon turned out that these two had spent time in Siberia and, hearing a question in a foreign language, they answered in the only foreign tongue they knew, Russian. Their Polish, by the way, was impeccable.

Time has dimmed in my memory the exact sequence of events from the Italian campaign. But I still vividly remember a number of episodes that at the time shook my heart—and my pants—to the core. One of them was my last reconnaissance patrol. I had been on patrols all day and was dead tired when we came to Predappio Novo. I was hoping for some rest, but the platoon commander ordered me to check out a German machine-gun site up the mountain. I took a few gulps of wine and up we climbed again. The gun site, overlooking the valley, was deserted. Relieved, I sent a courier down to the commander, set up guards, and let the rest of my team and myself get some well-deserved sleep. I slept so well that I heard none of the heavy barrage of German artillery fire that shook the valley for hours. Fortunately, no one from my team got hurt, but the onslaught took a heavy toll of death lower down on the mountain.

On another occasion, when we were fording the river Senio,

Lieutenant Lech gave me an order to get across the river and drive up the de-mined road marked by white tape to the town of Santa Vita. I was supposed to check the town out and return with a report. With a small company, we reached the town without any mishap. We found there a handful of old houses but nothing suspicious. Afterwards, I drove along the same route several times until one day I had to brake hard to avoid the wreckage of a Polish carrier torn into shreds by a mine. A mine in the middle of a safe road marked by the sappers! I was shaken by that sight, but I drove on. Just around another bend, we came across one of our tanks, a Sherman. The driver was waving his hands at us and shouting, "Hey, kids, get out of here! Look out, a mine!" I felt very hot at first, then cold, and then streaks of sweat rolled down my back. My God, I have driven along this road more than five times, I thought. Then I looked up through the windshield towards the blue sky and muttered, "Thanks." It must have been Him.

Night patrols always held the most surprises. Once I took with me two Italians and a couple of other young tigers, and together we went out to nose around in a village ahead. I could not decide whom to put in the lead—the worst place to be in if you step on a mine called a "jumping-jack"—so I took the position myself. We walked for a while until we came across a deserted machine-gun site. The Germans might still be around, so we readied our weapons and cautiously approached a dark house nearby. Then, on command, we sprang forward, kicked in the doors, and shone the lights inside. What we saw stopped us right in our tracks: a roomful of young Italian women in negligees as frightened as we were surprised. But soon their fear and our surprise gave way to laughter and conviviality. We quickly checked out the backyard, and, finding it secure, we sat down to a delicious supper of salami and wine, gracefully served by our young hostesses.

Towards the end of the war, I was transferred back to my home unit, the 4th Wołyń Battalion. From the original battalion very few were left, so it fell to me to train the reinforcements, mostly Poles who came to us from the German army. Shortly before we were sent to the front, my trainees made me take an oath that, if one of them got wounded, I would never leave him alive where the Germans could capture him. They feared German interrogators would beat confessions out of them and then punish their families back in German-occupied territories for their desertion. In this situation, they preferred to die, they said. I had no choice but to take that oath, and it was that oath that eventually earned me a Virtuti Militari Cross.*

Our orders were to give combat support to the 1st Infantry Company, which had lost lots of blood on the dikes along the river Senio. We reached the assigned sector by jeeps, then moved on foot. The Germans were firing illuminating shells, which exploded with blinding intensity. I tried to close my eyes but had the sensation that a missile was about to strike me right on the forehead. So I kept opening my eyes to make sure it was not. We spread out and followed the captain. Suddenly I noticed that there was no one ahead of me. Then I heard moaning, and when my eyes adjusted to the darkness, I noticed a soldier on the ground. He was not from my platoon. I ran to him and saw that his side was one big bloody mess. He was bigger than I, but I could not leave him there, so far ahead of our front line. I also remembered my oath. So I gave him some wine from my canteen, crawled under him, and, holding him on my back, began to withdraw. The Germans were still lighting up the sky, so every now and then I had to lay him down, run away to fire some rounds, then run back and drag him another hundred metres. I was hoping this would confuse the German sharpshooters, and I was right. Finally I reached our positions, left the wounded man behind the only bush I could find, and ran to alert the medics. By the time I got to our meeting point, my captain was convinced I had either let myself get killed or else deserted to the Germans. He greeted me with threats of court martial for attempted desertion. I tried to explain that I was taking a wounded man from the field, but he replied, "That's the medics' job, not yours." "Yes, when we are advancing, not when we are withdrawing," I foolishly tried to argue, but my colleagues hushed me down.

I almost completely forgot about this incident unti,l a few months later, I was advised that I should report to the headquarters to be decorated. To my surprise, I was awarded the highest Polish military distinction, the Virtuti Militari Cross. I still wonder if I would have had the courage and stamina to drag that soldier from the field if I had not taken that oath. Probably not. An oath is a holy thing, and luck—or providence—would no doubt have abandoned me if I had abandoned that soldier.

[For personal reasons, Kazimierz Smoliński could not continue his memoirs.]

---

* The highest Polish military distinction, comparable to the British Victoria Cross.

ANTONI TOMSZAK

I was born in 1920 in a town called Bestwinka, in the county of Bielsko Biała, district of Katowice. I learned about things military in my mid-teens through the paramilitary youth organization Strzelec [Rifleman], which I joined at fourteen. At fifteen, I stood in the guard of honour during Marshal Piłsudski's funeral. By the time I was drafted in 1938, I thought of myself as a well-trained soldier.

In September 1939, we were being transferred to a military unit in Kielce, but the Germans bombed the railway line, and we did not get past Tarnów. Those who survived the air raids were reorganized into a company that withdrew towards the Hungarian border. We crossed it on September 22 and were interned, with 5000 others, in a large internment camp in Szomabathely. Altogether, there must have been some 40,000 Polish soldiers in Hungarian camps at the time. Ordinary Hungarians helped us organize escapes to the West. They took us to the baths, where they provided us with civilian clothing and took our uniforms back to the camp. We crossed the Yugoslav border, usually at night, with the help of local guides. The first to go this rout were the professional military. As an ordinary conscript, I had to wait my turn until April 1940. I used that time to better myself by attending the educational courses organized by our military authorities.

When it was my time to go, I went through Zagreb and Split to Greece. About 300 of us gathered in Athens. Some were shipped directly to France, but I ended up on a boat called *Warszawa*, bound for Syria. Eventually, I found myself in one of the units organized by

Colonel Kopański under the French command. After the French sur-
rendered to the Germans, they wanted to disarm us, but Colonel
Cieszkowski refused to cooperate. Instead, he contacted the British in
Palestine. Shortly afterwards, we left Syria, joined by many Poles from
the Foreign Legion, and made our way to Latrun, near Emmaus in
Palestine.

There I was reassigned to an anti-tank artillery unit of the Carpathian
Brigade. At first we continued to train with French guns, but soon the
British supplied us with their uniforms and equipment. When Rommel
threatened Alexandria, we were transported to Egypt, where we assumed
the positions prepared by the Australians. Then one night, we boarded a
destroyer, as per orders, and sailed out into the darkness, completely
ignorant of our destination. It turned out that we were heading for
Tobruk, once again to relieve the Australians. The harbour had been
completely destroyed, so we were ferried to the shore by barges. We
hardly had time to settle into our new positions before the Germans and
Italians began to shell us. We responded in kind. After 8:00 p.m., this
exchange of fire died down: there was an unwritten understanding with
the enemy, as we soon found out, that we kept truce at night. As if daily
bombardments were not enough, nature herself turned against us and
flooded the lower-lying positions of our cavalry. And yet we were consoled in our misfortune by the sight of the Italians scrambling out of
their bunkers to escape the same deluge. We could then see quite
plainly that their numbers were about six times greater than ours. They
were so close we could hear their chatter, but they kept their heads low.
They were more cautious than a guy from my unit who stuck his head
out of the trench to light a cigarette and had his head blown off by a
sniper. We stayed in Tobruk for five months and did not cede a foot of
land to the enemy.

Finally, the long-awaited offensive of the 8th Army, from
Alexandria, reached Tobruk. Along the way they lost many good boys,
most of them at Ghazālah, where the Italians played a nasty trick on
them. They began to wave white flags, but when our troops
approached, they opened murderous fire. In response, our light tanks
and carriers swooped on them, taking few prisoners. They paid dearly
for the treachery. By Christmas, our offensive reached Dérna [Darnah],
where we captured well-supplied storehouses. Exuberant, some of our
soldiers overindulged in drink and began shooting in the air. This

brought on us a deadly air raid, which killed some twenty men. After that, the offensive did not make much progress. Our Polish units were withdrawn to Alexandria and then to Palestine. There we met our colleagues from Russia, who were being organized into the 2nd Corps. We used to call them, in jest, "Buzuluks," because that was where they had come from. They, in turn, referred to us as "Tobruk rats." The real rats in Tobruk were excellent jumpers: they jumped with their hind legs, for their front legs were very short. They reminded us of Australian kangaroos. We did not mind them at all; in fact, we liked them quite a bit: they ate with us, and slept with us, and entertained us with their acrobatic jumps.

Experienced and proven in combat, we soldiers of the 96th Anti-tank Regiment of the 3rd Carpathian Division were now entrusted with the task of training the newcomers from Russia. I got a group of officers from other services and taught them how to use their new British equipment. They were later formed into the 5th Anti-tank Regiment. We spent some time training in Syria and Iraq, and then returned to Egypt. Our commander was then Major Doroszewski because General Kopański was needed at the headquarters. Before Christmas, we landed in Taranto in Italy and, as combat-experienced units, almost immediately went into action in the mountains of Asterfieraldo. At Monte Cassino we fought as an anti-tank regiment, but some of our units were equipped with mortars. We stood by the "Doctor's House," and the mortars by the road to "Spectre," both positions of strategic significance. After Monte Cassino, our regiment was reinforced and sent to the Adriatic coast, near Osimo and Loreto. The end of the war found us at Lake Como.

Although the fighting was over, we remained in the army for another year, handing over our guns to be cut into pieces and turned into scrap metal, and deciding whether to return to Poland. I had no news from my family back home, so my decision was easy. We also went for a special audience with the Pope, arranged by General Anders.* Our officers carried the Holy Father in a litter, which made us all very proud.

In due time, I went before the Canadian commission recruiting agricultural workers. The Canadians wanted only young, healthy, and

---

* Władysław Anders (1892-1970), commander of the Polish army in the Soviet Union (later the 2nd Polish Corps).

strong men; they had no use for the wounded or the disabled. I got through the interview without a hitch. Altogether, they selected 2800 men in Italy for work on Canadian farms. In Naples, they put 1500 of us on the *Robinson*, a liner bound for Halifax. The rest came soon after in a second contingent.

The idea of organizing the emigrating ex-servicemen into a civilian association was born in Italy, and the Canadian chapter of the Polish Combatants Association [PCA] was founded in Falconara. We elected Lieutenant Czubak as our first president, with Turzański, Kaczmarek, and others serving on the board. During the week-long passage to North America, Czubak named messengers for every province. Since he was the only board member going to Winnipeg, in Manitoba, he asked Wlizło and me, heading for the same destination, to help him with organizational matters. We brought with us, from the 2nd Corps, some books and two typewriters, which served us well for the next fifteen years.

Each of us coming to Canada had to sign a contract, which bound him to work on a farm for two years. I was sent to the homestead of a Scottish family in Cypress River near Holland, in the southeastern corner of the province. Four kilometres away, on another farm, worked a friend of mine from the same regiment. I slept in a draughty loft, and when the wind got too cold, I had no choice but to sleep in the barn. For Christmas, my friend and I bought a case of beer and wanted to celebrate a bit in my loft. But the Scottish farmer got angry with us and kicked us out to the barn. We did not even open that beer: we just cried over our miserable lives. Later that winter, I drove the farmer's children to school in a sleigh. Once I bought a loaf of bread while waiting for them in town; on the way back, they found it and devoured it, crumbs and all. I could not even be angry with them, for they were as hungry as I was. In the summer, the farmer fed us better, but the work was much harder and always from dawn to dusk. We were paid $45 a month plus room and board, such as they were. On one occasion, my farmer took me to the movies and even paid forty-five cents for my ticket. At the time I wondered at his generosity but, as I soon discovered, quite needlessly: he deducted the same amount from my next pay.

Some of my colleagues could not stand such working and living conditions in the long run. They left the farms and headed for Winnipeg. But all too often, they were greeted at the station by the police, who had been alerted by the farmers. The runaways were hand-cuffed and sent back to the farms at the expense of Mr. Czubak. After two failed escape attempts, they were sent back to Italy. At least thirteen of our colleagues were deported that way. A few, in despera-tion, even decided to return to Poland, persuaded more by the terrible conditions in Canada than the propaganda of the communist authori-ties sent to us from Poland. How the Polish regime got hold of our addresses, I do not know.

I worked on a farm for a year. For the second year, I signed a con-tract with a friendly Polish farmer from Beausejour, who needed my help only in the spring at seeding time and in summer for harvest. The rest of the time I could work wherever I wanted. I did not help him much: the year was very wet, so seeding was slow. And later, driving a tractor during harvest, I came down with appendicitis and was rushed, straight from the field, to a hospital in Selkirk. Four days after the sur-gery, I ran away from the hospital and went back to Winnipeg on foot. In the fall, I found a job in a sewing shop as a presser of winter coats for forty-five cents an hour; in the summer, I worked for Mr. Ślązak as a construction labourer. I also worked as a mechanic in a body shop, making about eighty cents an hour. It was not much, but a loaf of bread used to cost seven cents and an egg one cent. I was not making a for-tune, but I had enough to make ends meet.

In my spare time, I helped with various initiatives of the Polish Combatants Association, such as sorting the mail from the veterans in the offices of *Czas,* or sending them encouragement, and sometimes books, which could make their time on the farms more bearable. The president of our chapter was then Mr. Czernik, with Adolf Wawrzyńczyk serving as a secretary. We were the first chapter to organize in Canada, and to this day I have a running argument—in jest, of course—with Chapter #1 in Thunder Bay about who was really number one. Winnipeg lost its pre-eminence because the General Assembly of the PCA moved the headquarters of the association from Winnipeg to Toronto, and the current chapter numbers do not reflect the order in which they were founded.

Throughout my years in Canada, my primary responsibilities within the PCA revolved around disabled veterans. I have always thought it was our duty to remember the colleagues who did not have our good luck to go through the war unscathed. Soon after my arrival in Canada, local medical authorities discovered that forty-six veterans were infected with tuberculosis. The Canadian government decided to deport them to their country of origin, Italy. We immediately launched a campaign, led by Lieutenant Czubak, to reverse this decision. Thanks to our determination and to the support of some influential people sympathetic to our humanitarian cause, we succeeded. All the sick were sent to a sanatorium in Brandon, and our association offered to pay for the treatment. At the time there was no public medical insurance, so Lieutenant Czubak appealed, through the Ministry of Agriculture, to all those working on farms to donate a dollar each to help with those medical bills. That was the beginning of our mutual aid society. We also tried to help those left disabled by the war and unable to support themselves through work. Czubak appealed to Britain in this matter. Eventually, various military commissions determined the degree of their disabilities and to this day some of my colleagues receive a war disability benefit.

Every year our Disabled Veterans Section collected donations at various specially organized functions. We threw parties and socials and balls, and used the revenues to help the less fortunate veterans. Over the last forty years, we have collected more than $100,000, and sent that money to hospitals and veteran agencies in Britain, Argentina, France, Germany, Italy, and Poland. In return, we receive hundreds of letters with heartwarming words of thanks and, not infrequently, with pleas for desperately needed help.

When the farm contracts were over, many men returned to Winnipeg and began looking for suitable life companions. Most of them were nearing thirty, which in those days was considered high time for getting married. I, too, had such thoughts on my mind. On New Year's Day, as I was coming back from church with a friend of mine, we noticed two attractive young women on the streetcar. They were looking in our direction, laughing, and saying in Polish that our gait showed we must be *Polusy* [Poles]. And indeed, we were still not quite steady on our feet after the highly spirited welcoming of the New Year. One of the women was Bronia Turowska, my wife of several decades. She lived not far from me, as it turned out, which helped when we started courting. She was working as a housemaid for a Ukrainian dentist, who did not treat her very well. She had no room of her own but had to sleep with the children, and he rarely let her go out, not even on New Year's

Day. I found her a better job, and we were eager to marry as soon as possible. To get her out of her contract with the dentist, I had to pay $70 to an employment agency, a large sum in those days, almost enough for a down payment on a house, or at least on a building lot. We have kept the receipt for that money and years later joked that I had bought myself a wife, like a rich sheik.

We lived on Magnus Street, not far from the PCA headquarters located in the basement of the Polish church of the Holy Spirit. We had a library and a reading room there; it was also there that we began organizing various social and cultural events, especially after a number of Polish women who immigrated here from Germany became involved. As our audiences grew, we began to rent halls from other organizations and quickly realized that what we really needed was our own building. That idea became our goal, which we achieved a few years later.

My wife and I also needed more permanent accommodation, so in 1950 I bought our first home. I gave $250 as a down payment and borrowed the rest from Mr. Dubienski. One of our first social gatherings in our new home was a tea party. All the money gifts we received, we donated to war invalids. Not that we could not have used some money ourselves: as our children began to arrive—first daughter Zosia, then son Czesław, and later two more daughters, Krysia and Wanda—we did not always have enough cash to buy them milk. But somehow we survived and perhaps grew stronger for want of luxuries. Zosia and Czesław attended the Polish school in the parish of the Holy Spirit, and both were active in Polish Scouts; Zosia was even a team leader. All our children finished university and all are fluent in Polish. They are proud of their Polish roots, and we are very proud of their accomplishments.

FRANCISZEK WAKERMAN

I was born in 1916 in Zimna Woda, near Lwów [L'viv]. In 1939 I was in active military service in the 5th Anti-tank Regiment, based in Skniłów [Sknilov], not far from Lwów. After basic training, I was sent to the NCO School, and, upon graduation, I was assigned to the ground crew of the 6th Reconnaissance Squadron. My duties revolved around servicing and maintaining airplanes. Our reconnaissance pilots flew mostly Czaplas and Rs. Czaplas were reliable and economic Polish-made planes, with star-shaped, five-cylinder engines. At the time, the Polish Air Force also used Karaśes, P7s, P11s, as well as some older types, such as Potters 25, 27, and 15.

Just before the war broke out, my regiment was on manoeuvres in the vicinity of Leżajsk, and then in Brześć [Brest] on the Bug River. On August 20, we returned to Lwów, but only to be dispatched to an airfield in Pabianice near Łódź. Our squadron cooperated with the army of General Bortnowski. We had not had a chance to fly many missions when, on September 14, we were ordered to withdraw towards Kołomyja [Kolomyya]. The move was easy for the pilots, but we, the ground crew, had to make our way under constant bombardment by German planes. During one of the air raids, I was wounded in the leg, but not seriously. I was still able to ride a motorcycle to Lublin, where the medics dressed my wound. From there, we were taken by trucks to our rallying point. We arrived just in time for the commander's last briefing. He announced that the war was over for us and that our entire unit would withdraw to Romania. We crossed the border in

Kuty, amid rumours that some soldiers were so distressed by this defeat that they had taken their own lives. Needless to say, we travelled in a sombre mood.

On the Romanian side, we were billetted for a while with local families until they transferred us by train to the camp in Calafat. I was not much taken with the idea of wasting time in an internment camp, so I and four others decided to run away. We left in the evening and walked throughout the night towards the west, in the direction of Turnu Severin on the Romanian-Yugoslav border. At dawn we reached the transfer point, where a sergeant from my regiment recognized me, so verification of our identities was quite straightforward. The crossing of the Danube to Yugoslavia had already been tried out, so everything went very smoothly. The Yugoslavs received us warmly. For a time, they lodged us in hotels and with families; later they took us to the Greek border where we said our farewells in the presence of an honour guard and an orchestra playing the Polish national anthem.

Our next transit point was Athens. We waited there for a month until a Polish ship—I think it was the *Pułaski*—ferried us to Marseille in France. From there we went to Lyon, where we were quartered in the military barracks. We arrived in Lyon around Christmastime, our first Christmas outside the country. To help us deal with homesickness, particularly intense at this time of the year, our command organized various cultural and social events, but we celebrated the season in our own way: with lots of good champagne.

Shortly after Christmas, we were transferred once again, this time to Le Bourget near Paris, and from there to the coast, where we boarded a destroyer bound for England. On arrival, we went through some language training and were assigned to various British units. At first our fighter pilots were distributed among British squadrons, but eventually two Polish fighter squadrons were formed, 303 and 302, and a few bomber squadrons as well. I was sent to Blackpool to Squadron 505, but we were moved to the south of England to train with Ferivato bombers. Only later did we get heavier machines, Wellingtons, and were moved to an airfield near Nottingham. There we started regular bombing missions to the continent. Although, as a member of the ground crew, I did not actually fly, we were very close with those who did. Their lives often depended on us, and we always anxiously awaited their return.

When our unit was reorganized, I was retrained and reassigned to

Squadron 300, which flew Lancasters, the new four-engine machines designed for heavy bombing. Many of my friends from the maintenance volunteered then for flying missions. Some of them got themselves killed, some earned the highest honours. But I was a down-to-earth kind of fellow and preferred to keep my feet on the ground and my hands in the engines. I had developed a taste for adventure, though, so I volunteered for an assignment to Italy, in Squadron 301, which flew special missions. I sighed a deep sigh of relief when we landed in Brindisi, our Italian home base. Throughout the flight I could not stop thinking of the first group of ground personnel—I was in the second—whose plane, a Halifax, was apparently overloaded and crashed on its way to Italy, killing all aboard.

Squadron 301 flew mainly Halifaxes and Liberators. Our destinations were often various points behind the enemy lines. During the Warsaw Uprising, we supplied the insurgents with weapons and ammunition. Our commander was Captain Król, who was clearly blessed with what Poles call a soldier's luck. We could hardly ever meet him in person because he was always in the air or asleep. And from all his missions he always came back unscathed. After a year in Brindisi, we welcomed the end of the war. We returned to England by boat and were greeted by General Ujejski. A few weeks later, we were back on the airfields, servicing planes that flew supplies to the occupation armies in Europe.

At that time there was also much talk about the future of the Polish soldiers in the West, much of it sponsored by the Polish Resettlement Corps. My heart wanted to go to Poland, but my mother had died and my sister did not encourage me to go back, so I decided to bide my time in London. I found a job in a furniture factory, whose products were in high demand after the devastation of the war. Later, a friend of mine, who used to fly as an onboard mechanic, convinced me to come to Canada. I came to Montreal in 1951, but he found me a better job in Winnipeg. I started at $1.15 an hour as a mechanic for the MacDonald Company. Later I worked for Bristol, relocated to Cambridge Bay to work on a radar station, returned to Bristol, and eventually settled down at CAE Company, where I stayed until retirement. In the meantime, at thirty-five, I decided to marry. I met a young lady from a respectable family, Domszy, whose father had come to Canada in 1912, and we were married in 1952. We had five children, three daughters (Teresa, Janina, and Halina) and two sons (Antoni and Tomasz). All of them were members of the Polish Scouts. Two of my daughters are now licensed nurses; one son works as an engineer for the city of Winnipeg, and the other has done quite well for himself as a merchant. I am now a proud grandpa of two granddaughters.

Since I retired ten years ago, I have actively pursued my hobby of growing raspberries: I have a ten-acre plantation and have spent there many sunny hours. I believe in healthy eating and vitamins, and my plantation is a delightful source of both. And when there is nothing to do on my plantation, we like to rest in our cottage on Lake Winnipeg. Over the years, I have maintained contacts with my family in Poland and visited them in 1979. I would still like to go back to Lwów, the city of my youth, and I remain hopeful that one day it may indeed be possible.

I have belonged to the Polish Combatants Association since the early 1950s. I have served as a board member and participated in its various initiatives, such as organizing the very successful Polish pavilion during Folklorama.

ADOLF FRANCISZEK

WAWRZYŃCZYK

I do not relish my memories of the war. I prefer to pass over those years, especially since I joined the Carpathian Lancers Regiment somewhat later than most of my friends.

My return to civilian life began before the Canadian commission recruiting agricultural workers for Canadian farms. We were still in England then. To this day, I chuckle every time I remember how an old professional farmer, Piotr Siedlecki, tried to teach a bunch of us city rats the basics of agriculture in a couple of afternoons. He told us how much oat seed is needed to seed a hectare of land and patiently explained the difference between oats and barley. We asked him plenty of dumb questions and, although he answered them all with admirable composure, his answers did not always allay our fears. I worried most about milking cows. I had never before touched those things under a cow's belly, and I trembled at the thought of pulling on them in front of the commissioners and, even worse, in front of other cows. Fortunately, I was spared that embarrassment in the examination room; and on the farm, too, I worked in the fields rather than in the barn.

After we arrived in Canada, seventy of us were sent to Letellier, Manitoba, to work in the sugar beet fields. Since I was one of the few who could speak English, I was frequently called upon to interpret, which meant that I could stretch my back more often than others. The sugar beet season ran for two months in the spring and two in the fall;

during the summer, we worked for individual farmers. It may have been June when the farmers came to pick their men. They judged us by our appearance. Those who looked sturdy and able were picked first. I was the last one to be taken—there was nothing to pick from by then. A little scrub of a farmer, looking pretty much like myself, finally asked me if I would like to work for him. How could I say no? I worked for him throughout the summer, helping as best I could with harvest and later with threshing.

Many of those who found work in the vicinity of Winnipeg came to town on the weekends, not to live it up in bars, but to organize. We needed to establish and maintain communication among colleagues scattered on farms across the vast Manitoba prairie. The basic structures of our Combatants Association [PCA] had already been laid down, in no small measure through the efforts of Mr. Czubak, who came to Manitoba with the Italian group of veterans. Our challenge was to adapt the organization to the specific Canadian conditions.

The help we received at the time from the local Polish weekly *Czas* could not have been more timely and effective. The newspaper gave us a place to work, where, together with Czubak, Wlizło, Czernik, and Ilkow, we could respond to the correspondence and attend to the administrative needs of our fledgling organization. Mrs. Waleria Szczygielska, very familiar with Winnipeg and its environs, helped us with various local matters. I assumed the functions of an official scribbler: my desk was always covered with scores of letters from and for our members on the farms. Our "office" was in fact a clearing house for all their correspondence, and sometimes the only time they could come to collect it was in the middle of the night.

At the time, most of us had decided to settle down in Canada. Good jobs were hard to find, but most of us were young and eager to start building our new lives. But there were a few who found it almost impossible to adjust to the harsh Canadian reality. I remember one man who came to the offices of *Czas* in a state of heavy depression and tried to commit suicide right in front of us. He pulled out a bayonet and pierced himself with it. At the sight of blood, Mrs. Szczygielska went into shock, but we grabbed him before he could inflict more damage on his body and called an ambulance. He was rushed to the hospital, where the doctors managed to save his life. I am not sure if he was grateful for it, and I do not remember what happened to him afterwards.

I considered myself lucky because I could always find work in the vicinity of Winnipeg. For a while I even had my employment papers signed by a farmer, Mr. Pundyk, although I never actually worked for him. He remembered that years later, and, in a conversation with the *Czas* editor, Mr. Mroczkowski, complained that he had sponsored a veteran who had not even showed up on his farm. That I did not work on his farm did not mean that I sat idle. I did hold various jobs to support myself and spent most of my free time in the offices of *Czas*. We had plenty of work dealing with complaints about living and working conditions on various farms and with maintaining communication among veterans and with government agencies. In winter, we did most of that work on the weekends because during the week a number of us, including Mossakowski, Klimaszewski, Kirulyk, and Gardziejewski, worked as lumberjacks. We worked for an enterprising Mazovian, Mr. Rog, who had come to Canada around 1927 and settled down along Highway 94. His wife was Ukrainian, but for the most part they cultivated Polish traditions at home. We lived and worked in the forest. We had to start by building ourselves a shelter: a rather primitive hut from roughly hewn boards, basic but adequate. We cut trees all day and spent the evenings talking, singing, reading. Working and living in such close quarters did occasionally get on our nerves. Once, when I was stubbornly hacking at an old tree with little visible effect, Tadzio Gardziejewski told me to stop. I did not, so he lost his cool and threw an axe at me. Thank God he missed. Later that day we made up, and he even helped me bring down that same tree—a tall spruce. We cut off its top and placed it between our beds as a sign of peace.

One weekend, towards the end of the cutting season, our little hut burned down. I came back from Winnipeg to find only a heap of ashes and rubble. In its midst, I saw an open book, partly charred, but much of the text still legible. I bent down and read: "Do not regret the roses when forests are afire." Well, we did not, and we did not try to rebuild the hut. It was the end of the season, anyway.

Around that time, it became apparent that several of our colleagues, including Białecki, Czernik, and Biernacki, were suffering from tuberculosis. The Canadian authorities were very concerned about the spread of that disease, and even threatened deportation to Italy of all those infected. Our association had no choice but to take a strong stand, and it paid off. Not only did we prevent Canada from acting on its threat, but we also managed to place those infected in a sanatorium in Brandon, where they were nursed back to health. This was the first significant achievement of the PCA.

We did not let this communal success blind us: we all had to build our individual lives in Canada. During one of the breaks from the forest, a few of us decided to try our hand at running a restaurant. We did quite well for a while, although socially rather than financially. The restaurant made it possible for us to remain in Winnipeg and get the coveted permits for permanent residence in the city. In addition, we could use our facilities, whenever available, for various PCA functions. The association made our restaurant its official headquarters, where it held its monthly meetings, organized parties, and even hosted Santa Claus. But our business did not prosper, and eventually we had to close it down.

By then I had discovered two things about myself: my future did not lie in the restaurant business, and Canadian cities were too claustrophobic for me. I could not find a place for myself in Winnipeg or in any other city. As the saying goes, a wolf is drawn to the woods. So after some serious soul-searching, I applied for a job in a paper mill in Marathon, on Lake Superior. Shortly afterwards, my wife and I moved to a small town on the edge of the forest. I worked at the mill as a lab technician, assessing water content in cellulose samples. The work was monotonous but left me much time for thinking and learning, and I was indeed thirsty for knowledge. During the eight years we spent in Marathon, I obtained a university degree in chemistry and gained much experience in my field. But above all, I enjoyed living a stone's throw away from the forest, where you could go for a short walk at noon and come back with armfuls of fresh wild mushrooms for dinner. We were visited there by friends from Winnipeg, especially Gardziejewski and Klimaszewski (Klimaszewski even worked in Marathon for a short period), but over time our ties to Winnipeg grew looser and less constraining.

Eventually, we were ready to move. I got a better job in another paper mill in Turso, thirty kilometres from Ottawa. I was soon promoted to supervisor and later superintendent of the technical department. We spent thirteen years there, happy and productive. Only when the children needed better schooling did we move closer to Ottawa. All our children, Marysia, Urszula, and Andrzej, attended both English or French schools at various times, which gave them excellent command of the two languages. In fact, they are all multilingual, for at home we always spoke Polish, and the two girls also studied Spanish. All three of them studied medicine and are now practising physicians.

In recent years, I have travelled quite extensively, visiting Japan, for instance, over twenty times in the last ten years. Our firm supplies the Japanese photographic industry with cellulose for photographic paper. My company also retains an apartment for me in London. I use it as a base for short trips to the continent, where I supervise the quality of raw materials for our best quality papers. A while ago I had developed a method of mixing wood from deciduous trees with that from coniferous, which has become an international standard. That is why my expertise is both trusted and desired around the world.

I am already sixty-five and intend to retire in two years: there are also other values in life, besides professional work. In many respects, I have probably become a typical Canadian; after all, I settled here, raised my children, had a career. But whenever I go to Europe, I always rediscover my European roots. I speak English, of course, but also Polish, French, Italian, and German. I even tried some Hebrew. And the fullness, the energy, the breadth of cultural pursuits I encounter there never fail to wake me up from my Canadian slumber.

I visit Poland almost every year, dropping in for weekends from London. I take a keen interest in my brother's boys, the young generation, whose lives are so tough and future prospects even poorer. Until Solidarity shook up the country, I did not feel inclined to get involved in any collaboration with Polish industry, but since 1980, I have established scientific ties with the Paper Institute in Łódz.

What am I going to do with the rest of my life? To be honest, I am drawn back to the ideals of my youth. I strongly believed that to live fully is to help others. In my golden years, I am hoping to find more time for the young, especially those who lost their paths through life and ended up in prisons. I believe that many of them can be brought back onto the beaten track, but to do so would take much time and patience. I am hoping to have much of both. This kind of work with young people fascinates me. Some thirty kilometres from where I live is a youth detention centre. I have some contacts there, and I know some priests who work with troubled youth. It is my dream to spend the rest of my life helping them discover themselves and return to useful, active life.

TOMASZ WIELGAT

I was born in 1918 in Wołyń [Volyn]. Our settlement, Osiecznik, was halfway between Kowel [Kovel] and Łuck [Luts'k]. My father had been serving in the Polish Legions under J. Piłsudski and settled in Wołyń to run a 350-hectare landed estate. I had five siblings.

Soon after the Soviet invasion, in September 1939, I was called up before a Soviet recruitment commission. A *politruk* [propaganda officer] told me to show him my hands and probably liked what he saw: I had large hands, calloused and scarred from hard work. They asked me if I belonged to the Strzelec [Rifleman, a paramilitary organization]. I felt I had to admit it, for they probably knew it anyway. The interview was over, and I was sent to join a group of recruits. We saw another group go to the baths as we were being ushered to a railway car. Later we were joined by a number of older men, all over forty. It all looked suspicious to me. They took us by train to Kołomyja [Kolomyya] and then escorted us on foot to a landed estate, Kornicza. We could rest in the barns. Next morning, the guards threw shovels at us and ordered us to dig. Then it dawned on us: we were in a labour battalion.

We stayed on that estate until the Germans attacked the Soviets. Then, one day, we were loaded onto carts and taken east, beyond the Dniester River. Along the way, half my unit got lost, taking advantage of the general disorder and confusion. I, too, wandered off from the column and, on my own, walked back to Kołomyja, where a priest I knew gave me shelter. In such situations, one's instinct is usually to return home, and that is what I was determined to do. So one night I set out in the direction of Włodzimierz [Vladimir], stealing my way mostly at night. When my parents saw me, they were overjoyed, for they were convinced I had been killed.

One unusual circumstance stands out for me from that period. Its roots, though, went back to the times before the war. My father employed on his farm several Ukrainians, including a man by the name of Michajlo. Michajlo, as Father discovered, was an active member of the communist party. When Michajlo realized that his secret was out, he pleaded with Father not to report him to the authorities. Father liked the man and felt sorry for him, so he promised he would keep it secret, but he advised Michajlo to quit those activities. As it soon turned out, Michajlo did not heed my father's advice, and my father lived to thank him for it. When the Soviets invaded, Michajlo became reeve. He remembered my father's good will and repaid in kind by not allowing Father's deportation to Siberia.

But few Ukrainians were as charitable towards us as Michajlo. As newly formed detachments of the Ukrainian police turned into roaming guerilla units of the Ukrainian Insurrection Army, Polish settlements found themselves in real danger. Attacks on the Polish population, even massacres, became common. We had to be constantly on the lookout for signs of approaching trouble. My brother Mietek followed and kept an eye on one such bloodthirsty band led by a Ukrainian priest. He incited his followers to cut the throats of all *Lachs* [Poles] and Jews to make Ukraine "as pure as that blue-grey sky." Eventually, my family could no longer take the stress of constant danger and moved westwards, to the district of Lublin.

I stayed behind in Wołyn as a member of a Polish self-defence unit. About a hundred of us became the core of what later became a division of the Home Army [AK]. Our leader was a commando who had been parachuted to join us. He was a good tactician. Once, when a large Ukrainian unit was spotted in the vicinity, we took the initiative and came down on them at night, instead of waiting for their attack, for they, no doubt, knew about us. Groggy from sleep and confused, they were completely destroyed. As the murders and repressions against Poles intensified, our unit grew in strength, and similar detachments began to form near Łuck, Włodzimierz, and Kowel. Together, we formed the 27th Division of the Home Army, and our numbers quickly swelled to 6000.

Protection of the Polish population against the Ukrainian Insurrection Army was only one of our objectives. Another was the sabotage of German transports to the eastern front. Warsaw sent us a special group of explosives experts who taught us the basics of their art. Usually an explosion was triggered by pulling on a piece of string after the train's engine had passed the mines. We did not want to hurt the engine drivers, who were usually Poles and often joined our ranks. Most of our supplies, including food, arms, and ammunition, came from such blown-up German transports. We established a reliable intelligence network on the major railway stations, and we always knew whether a transport was worth the risk. After one of our most successful sabotage operations of this kind, I saw eight Tiger tanks roll off the shattered cars and slowly sink into a bog.

Most of our activities took place around Kowel, our home base. So when the Soviet armoured units of General Guderian surrounded the city, we were trapped in it. To get out, we had to fight our way through under heavy bombardment. There was talk that we lost almost 1000 men, either killed or wounded. The forests around Szack [Shatsk] gave us some relief from German air raids, but all higher ground in the forest was well guarded by enemy tanks. Under constant sniper fire, we had to plod through wetlands and bogs, losing another 100 men. It was then decided that, to survive, we had to split: one group went towards the Prypeć [Pripyat'] River, another towards the Bug River. We crossed the Bug River near Łęczna and disappeared into the forests around Parczew just before the Soviet offensive started, the offensive which pushed the Germans all the way back to Warsaw.

My unit, some 3000 fighters strong, was on the move again, led by Colonel Żegota, with reinforcements for the insurgents in Warsaw. On the way we stopped by the beautiful castle in Lumbartów. The Soviets had been there before us, and we saw beautiful galleries littered with torn and devastated paintings. When we actually ran into the Soviets, they let us through, but only to surround us with heavily armed units a few kilometres later. The Soviet commander demanded that we lay down our arms. He said, "You don't need your weapons any more. I won't let you get to the uprising; you'll all be slaughtered there. Go home." And he indeed let us go free. Our guerilla fighting was over. Some joined the Soviet-backed Polish army, others went home, but all felt somehow let down.

After the war, I married a girl I met in the Lublin district. My parents moved again, near Grudziądz, where they got an abandoned German farm. Since my wife was Czech, we decided to settle in Czechoslovakia. It was easier to make this decision than it was to live with its consequences. I did not speak Czech and had to pretend that I was a Czech from Wołyń. We also got a deserted German farm and ran it for two years, but in the end the Czech security services began to suspect something about my past in the Home Army. A friendly policeman warned me about it and advised that I disappear. We had no choice but to run. I arranged for some detailed maps, and, with their help and after many adventures, we made it across the border to the town of Cheb in Allied-occupied West Germany. We walked into a police station and asked for asylum. Some of the interviews felt almost like interrogations. One of the officials, a Ukrainian, when he saw me pull out a cigarette with the name "Partisan" on it, confided that he, too, had been a guerilla fighter, but in the Ukrainian forces near Kowel. I froze for a moment, for here I was sitting across the table from my former enemy, and now my future depended on him. Fortunately, the rest of the formalities went smoothly, and we were sent first to Ludwigsburg and then to Murnau, a former camp for Polish officers (we still saw their beautiful paintings in the cellars). There we waited for eight months for an official invitation from my brother Adam, who had emigrated to Canada some time earlier. Since he could not send it himself, he arranged for a friendly farmer to sign it in his place. After we arrived in Canada, the farmer never insisted that I actually work on his farm.

We landed in Canada—my wife, our daughter, and I—in 1950, the year remembered for a devastating flood in Manitoba. Good jobs were few and far between, and it took me some time before I found decent long-term employment. My first job was making wooden shelves for $3 a day. Then I worked on the construction of a drive-in theatre, but I quit this job to cut lumber for Mr. Rog on the 85th mile north of Winnipeg. We were making $100 a month there in the bush, had plenty of food, and even hunted moose. When I came back to Winnipeg in the spring, I worked for a while in a dairy and later for the city. As another winter was drawing near, I tried my luck in a foundry, but that labour was so back-breakingly hard that I had to resign. In the end, I got a job with the Canadian Pacific Railway, and worked for this company until my retirement.

Five years after we came to Canada, we bought our first home. Our daughter was ten by then. Four years later, our son was born. Now both are university graduates. My son is an engineer-geologist and is involved in drilling for oil.

I joined the Polish Combatants Association soon after our arrival here, when Mr. Mossakowski was president. I have been an active member ever since.

HENRYK WIKTOROWICZ

I was born in 1919 in the town of Świsłocz [Svisloch], county of Wołkowysk [Vawkavysk], district of Białystok. When the war started, I was a student at an agricultural school in Dowspuda, Augustów county. We heard some shooting beyond the Prussian border, and we all knew what it meant. We ran to the train station and managed to jump onto the last train leaving for various local towns. Later that same day, September 1, the German army was in Augustów. My peacetime education was over.

When I got home, I learned that four of my brothers were fighting in the Polish army; three others and my two sisters were still helping to run our farm, not large but sizeable enough for the Soviets to consider us *kulaks* [wealthy peasants]. Soon after they invaded Poland, Soviet cavalry rode across our fields to where I was working. An officer rode up to me and asked, "Where is your *pameshchyk* [estate owner]?" I told him that my father owned the farm, but I could see in his face that he did not believe me. Why should the son of the owner sweat with a scythe in the fields? The NKVD [state security police] who came later seemed to be more open-minded: they only wanted to know exactly what we had and how much of it. We were forbidden to sell anything, and they inventoried all our land, goods, and chattels every month, until February 1940.

On February 9, around 4:00 a.m., we heard banging on the door. When my father opened it, we saw a Soviet officer, his revolver drawn, and behind him four *boitsy* [guards] with rifles at the ready. They pushed us up against a wall with our hands up. They searched the house, looking for guns, but found nothing. So they ordered all the men to get dressed and take enough provisions for one day. They led us to a local police station, where they kept us in a cellar until the following day. We worried more about the rest of the family than ourselves. But in the morning, they put us onto a sleigh and took us to the railway station. In one of the cars, our family was already waiting for us. This way of splitting a family at the moment of its expulsion and deportation was apparently a well-tried NKVD technique for intimidating the victims and thus avoiding potential trouble.

We did not know where we were being shipped. In Baranowicze [Baranaviçy], they transferred us onto the wider Russian tracks, and we continued the sad journey until we reached Kyshtym, a small town in the Chelyabinsk region, beyond the Ural Mountains. There they switched us back onto the narrow tracks and dispatched us to a copper and sulfur mine in Karabash. Upon our arrival, we were assigned our quarters: one small room, perhaps three by four metres for two to four families. Promises that we would be moved to better houses in the spring gave us little comfort.

The following day we were issued work clothes, sorted into work teams, and led to the mine. There, the foremen instructed us in what we were supposed to do. My task was to use a pole to slow down the carts loaded with ore and sent down an incline towards the shaft; if they went down too fast they could derail. Empty carts were pulled back to the loading area by horses. Two weeks of that work gave me painful ulcers all over my back. I had to see a doctor, on whose orders I was assigned to a different job, drilling the ore with a heavy machine propped on three legs. Every now and then I had to change the drilling bit. The work was hard and dirty, especially when the ore was soft: oil and dust streamed from the drilled hole, almost choking me at times. Hard ore was much easier to work with.

In the spring we were indeed moved to new quarters, and each family was given two rooms. By then we were all experienced, but tired, miners. Even Father, who was over seventy, had to work on the surface; only Mother was allowed to stay at home. We usually worked ten-hour shifts in the mine, followed by a compulsory bath. During the shift we had one break for a meal, but beyond that we were not allowed to waste any time, not even for a smoke. If caught idle, one risked a loss of half the day's pay, and in some cases could even end up in jail for up to six months. Despite the gruelling pace of the work, we had only one day a month to rest.

The pressure on us to increase production was unbearable. We had to "voluntarily" extend the length of our shifts, but the pay remained minimal. The Russians who worked alongside us were treated the same way. To survive, one had to sell whatever valuables one still had, a watch, a wedding ring.

Our first Easter in the camp was both painful and hungry. I wanted to get an extra day off, so I knocked myself in the leg with a log. Unfortunately, I did it a touch too hard and really hurt myself. On the plus side, though, I got a whole week off on account of that injury. We celebrated Easter the best way we could. Food was scarce, so we had no eggs or sausage, as was customary in the old days. An extra slice of bread was all we could muster. Sometimes when we could get a bit more bread than we needed, Mother dried it in the oven, for "the blackest hour." Yet this kind of frugality did not always work because the camp commander made rounds through the shacks and confiscated any stored provisions he could find.

I worked in that mine for eighteen months until the news reached us of the Sikorski-Mayski agreement.* We heard about it through the loudspeakers in the common room, the same room where we were subjected to so much political propaganda and indoctrination aimed at turning us into good communists. The news about the agreement made people jump and sing for joy. The Russians who happened to be there at the time envied us our patriotic fervour and our imminent release from the mine.

Without waiting for any official announcements, seven others and I decided to take our chances and leave the camp immediately. If we asked for an official permit, the commander would probably deny it; after all, half the miners were Poles, and if they all went, the mine would cease production. Before we left, we sent a telegram to the Polish embassy in Moscow, in Polish and in Russian, informing them that we were eight young men wanting to join the Polish forces. We

---

* An agreement between the Polish government-in-exile (W. Sikorski), and the Soviet Union (I. Mayski), signed in 1941, which provided for the formation of the Polish Army in the Soviet Union and the release of Polish political prisoners and deportees.

found a rich *kolkhoz* [collective farm] some ninety kilometres from the mine and offered our labour. The *kolkhoz* badly needed extra hands in the fields, so the superintendent agreed not to let the NKVD know about us. He even let us build a shelter in the field where we were supposed to harvest peas.

Two weeks later we needed to find out if the Polish embassy had replied to our message. We drew lots to decide who would go back to the mine, for that was a risky and dangerous business. If caught by the NKVD, we would be charged and tried as deserters. As fate would have it, I drew the marked lot. I packed a sack of split peas and some flour, and set out for a forty-kilometre trek and a fifty-kilometre train ride. Everyone in our old *pasiolek* [village] was happy to see me, but I was even happier that a day earlier a telegram had arrived from Moscow, with the following message: "Please go to Buzuluk, where the Polish army is being assembled." I did not stay in the settlement for more than a day but said my farewells and returned to my friends in the *kolkhoz*. The last leg of my trip led through a wild Siberian forest. It was getting dark, and I heard noises all around me. The worst was the howling of wolves, coming from either side of the road. I was getting ready to climb a tree for the night when I saw the lights of an approaching truck. The driver would not stop, but he slowed sufficiently for me to jump onto the back. This ride shortened my way considerably. When I rejoined my companions, they could hardly believe I had made it back alive, and with such good news.

When we showed the telegram from the embassy to the superintendent of the *kolkhoz*, he solemnly thanked us for our work and supplied us with some flour. To keep the spectre of starvation at bay, we supplied ourselves with an additional sack of peas. Thus, well provided and joined by several other Poles from the *kolkhoz*, we left for Buzuluk. Along the way, at every station, we saw hundreds of Poles going in the same direction. I was travelling without any documents confirming that I was a free citizen; such documents were issued only one per family, and I had had to leave it with my mother and sisters. What I did have was the telegram from Moscow, which worked like magic in lineups for bread. "Rebiata v armiu idut" [The boys are joining the army] always got us to the front of even the longest line.

It was autumn when we reached Buzuluk, damp and cold. On arrival, we were registered, assigned quarters, and fed. The lack of soup bowls was a minor irritant, but need is the mother of invention, as they say. We carved bowls out of halved water melons or from any other suitable material. Spoons, as precious instruments, we kept, well licked, inside our bootlegs.

After two weeks, we were transferred to the 5th Division in Tatishchevo. Our provisions for the two-week trip consisted of two dried, pressed fish per person. This was not enough even for a couple of days, let alone for a week. When hunger began to twist our guts, we had to forage for food on our own. At one of the stations, someone smelled sausage in a locked car. A few of us chatted up the guards and entertained them with some unsavoury jokes, while a couple of strong guys broke the locks and threw out a most delicious-smelling crate. Pure Cracow sausage. Later that night we all stuffed our bellies with that delicacy, and all got sick with dysyntery afterwards, probably from drinking the water from the steam engine.

In Tatishchevo, we were issued tents, one per ten recruits, which we had to put up in the middle of a muddy field. There were no beds; I was lucky to find an old plank, and I slept on it for several nights. Dirty and tired, we went before the recruitment commission. The secretary read out the names, ages, and education, while Colonel Sulik, standing on a raised platform, decided which service each of us would join. I was sent to an infantry communication platoon, and so was one of my brothers (he later died from disease while still in Russia); another brother was assigned to anti-tank artillery. At long last we were transferred to warm quarters, but we still had no uniforms; everyone wore what he had brought on his back, many—especially those who came from prisons—little more than tatters of indoor clothes. I was lucky in this respect, for I still had my high boots and a jacket from Poland.

After a few weeks of initial training, I was assigned to a newly organized NCO school. I was not particularly happy about this development. The trainees were housed in a primitive shack without a roof, and their guns needed constant cleaning from the exposure to the elements. My company's commander was Captain Gnatowski. He tried to convince us that the army is like a religious order: a soldier should be celibate (as he was), self-disciplined, and nothing should be impossible to him. Self-denial was definitely part of our daily routine, for we voluntarily halved our meagre food portions to feed the civilians who followed the army. Other daily routines included fifteen minutes of working out in the morning, with nothing but shirts on our backs even though it was mid-winter; the singing of a religious hymn, followed by a short prayer; and a breakfast of coffee and 100 grams of bread issued the day before. Afterwards, training sessions and gruelling exercises accounted for the rest of the day.

In February, we made arrangements to go south, to Dzalal'-Abad. In its warmer, almost pleasant, climate, we continued practising discipline and marching but did not learn much about communications. On graduating, I was promoted to senior rifleman and returned to my communication unit to brush up on radio and telephone equipment. While still in Dzalal'-Abad, I got news from my sister that my father had died from typhoid fever; I also learned that one of my brothers had died of dysentery on the way to Krasnovodsk. He had been so close to freedom, real freedom from Russian hunger and misery. I do not know where, or even if, he was buried. They may have had to simply throw him off a moving train. Polish corpses by the tracks were not an uncommon sight.

I went with the army to Pahlavi in Persia, and further into the Middle East. In Kirkuk, I was transferred to the 5th Communications Battalion, and with that unit left for Italy. At Monte Cassino, I volunteered for a unit supplying ammunition to the front line. We drove jeeps, always at night and always without lights or any other signals. The trail was marked with a tape, but on a dark night, the tape was hardly visible from behind the wheel. One of us had to lie on the hood and whisper directions to the driver. When we drove in a convoy, we attached a white towel to the jeep in front of us and followed this moving white spot. The main danger was the machine gun nests perched above the trail. When the flares caught us driving along a riverbed, the machine guns above showered us with bullets. Somehow we always managed to dodge both the bullets and the artillery fire, which usually intensified before dawn. Only one jeep from my unit was destroyed. After every successful return from the frontline, my partner, Major Majorowski, used to make a sign of a cross and say, "Daddy's home, the kids rejoice."

When the war ended, the mood in my unit was far from cheerful; in fact, we felt cheated and depressed, for most of us had no home to go back to. The propaganda encouraging Polish soldiers to return to Poland had no effect on us: our homes were now on the Soviet side of the border. When we learned that Canada had agreed to accept 4000 Polish ex-servicemen as farm labourers, I signed up without hesitation, and on November 20, 1946, I set my feet firmly on Canadian soil. I was originally marked for British Columbia, but in the end that province did not accept anyone, and I ended up in Winnipeg. From Winnipeg I was sent to a farm in Assiniboine, Saskatchewan, and spent the following two years working for several farmers. When the contract expired, I returned to Winnipeg in search of work. Good jobs were hard to find, for Canadian ex-servicemen had returned from the army as well, and they had an obvious advantage over us. I spent one winter cutting lumber for the Abitibi company, making $7 for a cord (128 cubic feet) of chopped spruce. This was considered good pay, for one could cut two such quantities a day. Afterwards, I worked for the railways for eighteen months, but the labour was so hard I decided to look for something else. In the Employment Office, I chanced upon a friend of mine, who, in a similar predicament, had decided to sign up for an upholstering course. I did the same and have been upholstering sofas ever since. I have never been a burden to Canadians and have never taken any unemployment payments.

I was married in 1951. My wife had a job in a sewing factory and was making $12 a week; I could make $17. Although not much, this was enough to start us thinking of buying a house, which we did a year later. With a good roof over our heads, we started a family. In the years that followed were born Basia, Franek, Celinka, Marysia, Pawełek, and Jadzia. I am very proud of my children. Basia and Celinka are both married, and I have two delightful granddaughters. Franek took a degree in geology at university, but he works in my company and intends to take it over when I retire.

I have been a member of the Polish Combatants Association for over thirty years. For the last five years, I have been on the board of our Chapter #13, and at the moment I am serving as its president.

KAROLINA WIKTOROWICZ

My family was settled not far from Lwów [L'viv], in a place called Kłodno Wielkie [Klodno Velikoye], where my parents owned a farm. I had four siblings: three sisters and one brother, Józef. In May 1939, he left home to join the Franciscan brothers of Father Maximilian Kolbe in Niepokalanów, near Warsaw. But his novitiate lasted for only a few months: when the war broke out, all novices were sent home. The day my brother returned from Warsaw left such a deep impression on me that it stayed with me all my life.

Even more vividly than the outbreak of the war, I remember our expulsion and deportation into Russia on February 10, 1940. I was eleven years old then and a fourth-grader. In the morning I got up as usual to ready myself for school. We lived outside the village, and it took about an hour to walk to school. Around 6:00 a.m. I heard knocking on the door. My mother suddenly became very anxious, for neither my father nor brother was home, only my two aunts. One of them, Aunt Marysia, walked to the door and talked to the Soviet soldiers outside. They told us to dress up and get ready for a trip. They did not say where to, but we all knew. We quickly gathered enough food to last us a few days. Mother asked one of the soldiers about her husband, but he only laughed and said, "Don't worry, they'll find you another." My youngest sister was only six months old, and my grandma, a very old woman, was ordered to come as well. Aunt Marysia was not allowed to go home, but she rejoined her family at the railway station, where the soldiers took us by sleigh.

A few hours later, we were loaded into cattle cars but did not move out of the station for almost a day. In the meantime, Father came with his dogs, which led him straight to our car. Our journey, once it started, lasted for three weeks. As the train was pulling out of the station, we began singing "He who trusts in the protection of his Lord...." We subsisted on *kipiatok*, hot water, which we could get at train stops, and on what we had brought with us from home. The car was equipped with a primitive stove, but after a while there was nothing to cook. Our final destination turned out to be a settlement four hours away by sleigh from Sverdlovsk.

In the settlement, or *pasiolek*, shacks had already been prepared for us. We were lodged in one shack with four other families from the same convoy. The locals, who had been forcibly resettled there a few years earlier, were very kind to us. A Russian woman, seeing Mother with an infant in her arms, brought us a glass of milk and an egg. She shared what she had. Soon after our arrival, my mother, together with another woman who had a small boy the age of our Sophie, decided to buy a goat. This decision probably saved the two children's lives, for in the middle of winter an epidemic of measles swept through the settlement. My little sister also got sick but survived, she and the little boy who drank the goat's milk. I remember saying goodbye to all the others who perished: forty little coffins in a row above a ditch dug in the frozen earth. Among them lay the Soviet commander's son: death played no politics.

Our life in the settlement had its routines. When I was not tending Sophie, I went to school. My older siblings worked in the forest cutting and gathering lumber; in the summer, they cut incisions on pine trees to harvest resin. At home in the shack, we spent much time inventing new ways to kill the resistant bloody pests we could in no way get rid of. Lice, too, were a constant nuisance, and all-too-intimate companions in our misery.

When we first heard about the amnesty—some time in the fall—we fell to our knees and sang religious and patriotic songs. Settlers of other nationalities, Germans and Russians, envied us our joy. The local authorities tried to persuade us to stay. They needed workers and warned us that hunger would kill us long before we reached Poland, but we did not listen. We decided to go in search of the Polish army. We went southwards by train, starving most of the time. Finally, when we could not fend off hunger any longer, we got jobs picking cotton for one of the southern *kolkhozes* [collective farms]. There we got more news about the Polish army, and Father went to look for it. Before leaving, he got us one sack of onions and another of turnip cabbage. They would not have lasted us long if my two older sisters had not gone to work in exchange for *lepioshki*, a kind of bread pancake. I, too, went out into the fields to pick cotton but fell seriously ill and suffered from hemorrhage. The doctor told us I had pneumonia, but somehow, with the Lord's help, I survived. When I was no longer in any immediate danger, I was sent to an orphanage in Jizzakh; my youngest sister came with me, too.

One day, a sergeant from the Polish army came and took our orphanage closer to the military camp. The army looked after civilians and whenever possible arranged for their exit from Russia. And so my little sister and I went with the orphanage to Pahlavi, where we arrived by boat. Walking down the gangplank and dazzled by the sunlight, luggage in one hand and Sophie in the other, I almost fell into the water. Someone held me up, and someone else helped me to the shore. There we were safe, and there was plenty of food to eat. Perhaps even too much, for many children became violently sick from cating fat mutton.

We did not stay in Pahlavi long: the orphanage was moved first to Tehrān and then to eastern Africa. All the while I looked after my little sister the best I could, but I really missed Mom. Our camp in Africa was called Masindi. Most children there were orphans. There was a school for us, and special activities, such as Scouting. I started attending Grade 6, and then the first grade of high school. After a year in Masindi, we were shipped—literally—to Bwana Mkubwa, in southern Rhodesia, where I was finally reunited with my mother. I continued to attend high school in Lusaka. Our teachers were brought from Cyprus. Many of them were engineers, lawyers, and other professionals who had managed to escape the storm of war in Poland. One of the subjects we studied was English. Unfortunately, our teacher was an old lady, very gentle and caring but without any pedagogical talent. Needless to say, we did not learn much English then. At the time I lived in a dormitory, sharing a little hut with three other girls. Every morning and every evening, all the girls from the dormitory gathered on the central square to sing a prayer and hear the good and bad news. I remember how shattered we were at the news of General Sikorski's death.* Even worse, for me personally, was the news of my brother's death. He survived the battle of Monte Cassino only to burn to death in his tank near Loreto. I spent many sleepless nights crying for him.

We stayed in Africa for four years; in 1948, all of us—Mother, my sisters, and myself—left for Britain. We saw no future for us in Poland, and England's economy was depressed by the war, so we made arrangements with our uncle in Canada to sponsor us. After we arrived in Winnipeg, I found work in a garment factory. I met my husband in church, after an evening service, some time in May. He took me out to the movies, and not long afterwards, we were married. We have six children, four daughters and two boys. The oldest daughter, Barbara, finished sociology and works as a social worker. Marysia is a biochemist; Cecylia is still studying in Quebec. All my children graduated from high school and went to university. As for myself, I am still running a busy household, but I find time to work with other women in the Emilia Plater Women's Auxiliary, associated with the Polish Combatants Association.

---

* General Władysław Sikorski, premier of the Polish government-in-exile and the commander-in-chief of the Polish armed forces, died in a plane crash near Gibraltar in 1943.

TADEUSZ WILTON

I was born on September 2, 1919, in Lwów [L'viv]. We lived on Kasper Koczkowski Street, and I began my schooling in the elementary public school on Father Kordecki Street. Later I attended a high school with special emphasis on mathematics and the sciences. These were the most beautiful years of my youth. I was a fan of the soccer teams Pogoń and Czarni, and took a keen interest in car racing, organized in Lwów on a grand European scale. I knew the looks, the makes, the top speeds of all car makes. Those kinds of trivia were what really mattered to me then. And now, from the distance of years, I wonder why, in the sixth, seventh, or eighth grade, when the ominous clouds were gathering all over Europe, I never heard from my teachers or from other adults around me that a storm of catastrophic proportions was heading our way. Maybe I was just not listening. In any case, the outbreak of the war and the tragedies that followed took me largely by surprise.

Having passed my matriculation exam in 1938, I volunteered—as was the custom—to work for a period of one month for the good of the nation. We were sent to build roads in the environs of Łuck [Luts'k], in Wołyń [Volyn]. After this exertion, I holidayed for a month before joining the Youth Labour Corps. Then I faced a choice: I could either go to university or join the army. I chose the latter, hoping that a year of military training would open for me the doors to other careers. That a war might close them all never occurred to me then. I signed up for the Officer Cadet Artillery College in Włodzimierz [Vladimir], the school of choice for many graduates of my high school. Our military instructors taught us the art of war, but even they never openly spoke of the threat of war. And yet the signs of impending trouble were plain to see: Hitler had annexed Austria, Czechoslovakia was reduced, Zaolzie was aflame. Perhaps our instructors were afraid the talk of war would distract us from our studies. Or perhaps they failed to realize the seriousness of the situation.

In early spring, general mobilization was briefly announced but soon, in May, it was revoked. My cadet college went on manoeuvres. In Rembertów near Warsaw, we were assigned to various infantry units, which then engaged in joint exercises with the other services. An English general by the name of Ironside was an outside observer of our war games. Afterwards, I was sent to the 5th Light Artillery Regiment in Lwów and was stationed there until the outbreak of the war. We slept in the barracks, rose early for morning exercises, and did the various soldierly chores—all of this to give us, the officer cadets, a better insight into the daily routines and challenges in the life of ordinary soldiers, whom we were learning to lead and command.

I was still in Lwów when the war broke out. The command must have had enough officers in the line units, because they left us in the barracks. I was at the other end of town, near the Central Train Station, when it was announced through the radio that Germany had attacked Poland. I immediately decided to return to the barracks. Along the way, I could see people stopping in the streets to comment on this development, not quite sure what it meant for them. They soon discovered, when several German bombers appeared above the city and first explosions shook the ground and the air. A woman I vaguely knew was killed by one of them. The citizens of Lwów quickly realized that this war meant nothing good for them. The news reached us of Germans advancing very quickly across the Polish territory. My unit was engaged in the preparations for the defence of Lwów, but before the Germans could reach us, the Soviets swooped on the city and took it on September 20.

I am trying to remember my first encounter with the Bolsheviks. We were held unarmed in the barracks of the 6th Anti-aircraft Regiment on Palatyńska Street. Soviet soldiers came along the tenement houses and entered the barracks. They looked slovenly and dishevelled, not at all like conquerors. And yet they took us prisoner. We were ordered to get outside and line up along the street. I happened to stand beside the gate of one of the tenement houses. Things did not look good, so at first opportunity, I slipped inside the gate, where some good people helped me to change into civilian clothes. I stayed in hiding for a while, and when the Soviets were no longer in sight, I shrank my neck into the high collar of my jacket and started home. I walked through the city for close to an hour and no one tried to stop me. I was spared the Soviet captivity, at least for the time being.

My life took a turn for the worse when the Soviet authorities announced general conscription. It was preceded by a referendum in which all citizens of Lwów "voted" whether to ask Stalin to protect them from all the unpleasant things that were happening in the world, or, in other words, whether we wanted to be annexed to the Soviet Union or not. Participation in the referendum was—in the tradition of Soviet democracy—compulsory. What would happen if someone voted against annexation? Probably nothing, but most of the people I knew simply did not fill out their ballots. On the basis of this referendum—according to the Soviet authorities ninety-nine percent of voters opted for the annexation—we all became Soviet citizens. Shortly afterwards, the regional commander issued a conscription decree stating that all young men born in 1919 were called up to serve in the Red Army. Those conscripts whose last names began with letter "w" were ordered to report in mid-December. I could not imagine myself in a Soviet uniform, so, with a small group of like-minded men, we decided to escape to Hungary. We had heard that Polish units were being formed there and sent over to France to fight the Nazis.

We quickly put that decision into action and took a train to Stryj [Stryy], near the Hungarian border. Each of us boarded a different car to avoid creating an impression that we were an organized group. Despite the various precautions we took, I constantly had the impression that everyone was looking at me and knew where I was going and why. We arrived at Stryj late in the evening, and, because strangers in that town were very conspicuous, we set out into the mountains that same night. The way up was quite easy and we saw no sign of being in the border zone. But our guide, a scoundrel if ever was one, led us straight to the Soviet watchtower. He was clearly working for them, but he did take our money, of course. They caught us all before dawn and we found ourselves behind barbed wire in Skole. My dream of escape to the free world burst like a soap bubble.

Skole was a small town known mostly for its winter sports. The Soviets made it into a transition camp for those captured crossing the border. Our numbers grew by twenty to thirty a day during the two weeks I was kept there. My mother learned somehow of my plight and sent me a small food package, some buns or bread, if I remember properly. The contents of the package was thoroughly inspected and the bread cut up into small pieces to make sure that no instrument was smuggled inside that could harm the great Soviet Union. After two weeks, we were sent by rail via Lwów to Krasnovodsk, and then further to Dnepropetrovsk. There I sat in the can, without a trial or sentence, for eight months, awaiting the outcome of the "investigation." That "investigation" consisted in trying to convince me to admit to the worst crimes and to sign my name to whatever the twisted imagination of the investigating officer had dreamt up. Signing such a document usually ended the investigation. Fortunately for me, I was never beaten up during the interviews, perhaps because I looked very young for my age. Even though I had already served in the army, I still did not need to shave, and they must not have taken me very seriously. I came up with a story that I was going to Hungary to continue my education there since most schools in southeastern Poland were closed, and I stuck to that story for a while. Eventually the Soviets announced that we were all guilty of violating paragraph 84/14 pertaining to illegal border crossing. I got a lenient sentence of five years, while most of my friends got ten for the same crime. From the moment those sentences were announced, prison authorities began to show us more respect: we became incarcerated "citizens," with some civil rights, including the right to larger portions of soup and sugar.

Two weeks after the sentencing, we were sent up north, via Moscow, near the Peczora River, where we spent a year, until the fall of 1941, building a railway track to the White Sea. It was perhaps the hardest year in my life, and I still wonder how I managed to survive. Perhaps because I never met my work quota. Those who worked harder quickly lost their health, and often life, too; only the men from Trans-Carpathian Russia seemed to be unaffected by the exertion required to meet the required daily norm. As for myself, I swung the shovel as little as possible, enough to keep me warm but not enough to drain my energy. My inefficiency was not, of course, without a consequence. Every morning the foreman sang into my ear: "Tadeush Piotrovich trista gram" (Tadeush Priotrovich 300 grams), the smallest ration of bread.

We had little outside news in the camp, but eventually we learned about Hitler's declaration of war against the Soviets and about the German invasion of the Soviet territories, and about the talks between the Polish and Soviet governments. At last a ray of hope. Then one day the camp commander gathered us all and announced, "And now we are all going to kick the ass of our common fascist enemy. We are friends now." Shortly afterwards, a military commission came to the camp, and each of us was asked if he wanted to go to the Polish or the Soviet army. A majority chose the Polish. We got some money, the right to move freely, and the permission to buy food for the road. About 300 of us boarded a train, and many others joined us along the way. When we finally reached Kermine, a rallying point for the Polish army, we were told that they were sorry but they had too many people arriving daily and could not register us at the time. Instead we were sent in barges along the Amu Darya River to work in a *kolkhoz* picking cotton. The locals were quite friendly towards us, and the *kolkhoz* administrator even asked us if our bellies were full or empty. Some time later, they took us back to Kermine, dressed us in uniforms, and, after two weeks, just before Easter 1942, shipped us to Pahlavi. It is difficult to describe our joy at escaping the Soviet Union. We were bathed and freshly clothed and given white bread to eat! These simple things were almost as exotic to us as figs and dactyls and the very notion of Persia. I had read about that country in my geography and history textbooks, never dreaming that I would ever see it with my own eyes. Every day brought new, exciting experiences. Certainly not the least of them was the ride across the mountains to Palestine, where the Carpathian Brigade was already taking shape. Our trucks, driven by Persians, groaned with exertion and squealed with terror on the twisting mountainous roads, but never lost contact with the beaten track. I sighed with relief when we finally descended towards the fields of undulating wheat, fragrant orchards, Jewish kibbutzes, and Arab villages. I was spellbound by the abundance and richness and freedom that seemed to me almost out of this world.

In Palestine, I was assigned to the 2nd Light Artillery Regiment in the rank of corporal officer cadet because of my year in the officer cadet college. I spent most of my time moving between Palestine and

Iraq, polishing my already decent knowledge of the art of war. By the time we left for Italy, I had earned the rank of 2nd Lieutenant.

We landed in Taranto, Italy, on December 24, 1943, but hardly anybody noticed that it was Christmas. I have read many beautiful accounts how people melted into tears at Christmastime with memories of happier days, but most of my colleagues and I experienced nothing of the kind. We were soldiers and had a bloody job to do; there was no time for sentiments. We moved to a new site, and barely had time to set up camp before the command ordered us to the front line on the Sangro River.

We took our positions deep in the valley. We could see German patrols up on the mountains, peering at us through binoculars. When they got close enough, we shot at them, not to achieve any strategic objectives but to get some front-line experience. In late March or early April, we moved to battle positions at Monte Cassino. Our guns were well camouflaged but the monastery stood before us in plain view. When I visited the site many years later, I could easily find the firing position where the battery I commanded was located.

From the actual assault, I remember a few tragic moments. The artillery barrage started in the middle of the night, with dozens of batteries firing at the same time. The mountain and its environs lit up with an eerie yellowish-red glow. We loaded the guns, fired, loaded, fired, eight 25-pound shells a minute, for hours on end. When the barrels grew too hot, we cooled them with wet blankets. I saw a shell explode in the hot barrel of a gun and rain death all around. But a worse tragedy was caused by human fatigue and nonchalance. To fire a shell, a soldier had to get very close to the gun and load the shell gently into the hatch. As the guns got hotter and the muscles more tired, soldiers began to throw the shells into the guns from further away. They did that hundreds of times, grew smug about it, and then one of the guns blew up, igniting a store of ammunition. That's what hell must be like, I thought at the time. The entire crew was killed, torn into small pieces by the force of the explosions. One soldier jumped out of a nearby ditch, his clothes on fire. We threw some blankets on him, but could not save him. The next morning, we collected bits of human flesh scattered all over the site, none big enough to identify the victim.

After taking Monte Cassino, we were moved to Monte Cairo, to give artillery support for the Carpathian Lancers going against Passo

Corno. Then we advanced northward along the Via Emilia and the Adriatic coast until we reached the Forli region, the birthplace of Mussolini. There we wintered, facing the Germans dug in just outside our firing range. In the spring, the Allied offensive against Bologna gathered momentum, where we went into action for the last time.

How did we learn that the war was over? We were still in our battle positions. Around us, the wheat fields were already knee-high. We did not think about the end of the war, for we were still on active duty. The day before I had lost a good telephone operator. He had heard something outside the door of the cottage we were resting in, opened the door, and been blown up by a German grenade. The next morning, on that sunny April 25, the division commander came to us and announced, "Gentlemen, the war is over." What a waste of life, what a senseless death, we all thought about the telephonist; it seemed as if he had given his life for nothing. And yet, in some way, we all felt quite relieved, hoping that the ordeal was over.

When the war was definitely over, we went south to the vicinity of Ascoli Piceno. The local people were warm and friendly, and they lodged us in a former agricultural college. It was a spacious building, with a wide hall, perfect for parties and other forms of entertainment. Our parties attracted also many local young women. In a short time, there was much talk about getting married, and a number of soldiers indeed tied the knot. The villagers did not mind those international marriages; in fact, the local priest held us as an example to the local youth: "Look at the Poles," he said from the pulpit. "The war is barely over, and they are already thinking of starting families. Why can't you do the same?" As for myself, I was not so thrilled by the prospects of marriage. Regular soldiers who came to me for advice quickly found that out. I was an officer and a battery commander, but I was very friendly with my charges. After all, we had gone through many battles together, and we trusted one another with our lives. (Garrison officers are usually much more detached from their subordinates, whom they merely train in the art of show marching.) So when soldiers came to me asking whether they should get married, I used to tell them, "You'll always have time for that, and in the meantime enjoy life." Unfortunately, my advice was rarely effective, for when a man loses his heart, his mind usually goes with it, too. And yet I must admit that those who married and stayed in Italy have been for the most part quite satisfied with their lives.

Other soldiers came to ask whether they should go back to Poland. One of them said to me, "Lieutenant, how is it that we volunteered to fight all the way to Poland, and now have been cheated like that? You've heard what Churchill said. He made a deal with the Russians and surrendered Poland to them. What are we going to do now?" What could I say, I was as bitter and disappointed as he was. "I'm not going back," he said, "I've been in Soviet prisons." And so had I. I only told him that my orders were to allow each soldier to reach his decision; I was not supposed to convince them one way or another.

Although my two brothers, my sister, and my mother had remained in Poland, I chose to stay in the West. I was not alone in my decision to stay; in fact, not a bachelor from our regiment decided to go back. But there were some who could not bear the thought of leaving their wives and children behind; those chose to return, sometimes with tears in their eyes. Now, I know that their return had nothing to do with politics and that they cannot be blamed for it. But at the time most of us thought of our decision to stay in the West as a protest against the Soviet takeover of Poland; those returning were viewed as betraying the Polish cause. We thought that we would go back as soon as Poland shook off the Soviet yoke. In the meantime, we settled wherever fate cast us, slowly acclimatized to new conditions, found jobs, started families. No one contemplated going back to the political tyranny and poverty in Poland, but the hope of return was always with us. When one of our friends accepted Canadian citizenship, we thought he was crazy. Why would he do something so anti-Polish? It took us some time to get used to this idea of becoming citizens of another country, but one by one we followed in his footsteps. For one thing, we needed all the rights of citizens to get organized, to influence foreign policies that could have an impact on Poland. Living from suitcases no longer made much sense. The die had been cast, we had chosen a new homeland, and that was where we had to live and work for our own good and for the good of Poland.

We were still in Italy when it was announced that volunteers could sign up for two-year contracts as farm labourers in Canada. I signed up right away. Now, from the distance of years and experience, I do not think it was such a wise step. I should have gone to England, and spent a couple of years preparing for civilian life. Many of my friends went that route and were the better for it. But at the time I felt I needed to cut the umbilical cord to the army with one quick decision. My commander told me, "What's the hurry? You want to milk cows in Canada? You'll always have time for that." I did not listen. At the first opportunity, we presented ourselves before the Canadian commission. They showed us a couple of samples of wheat and asked us if we knew what it was. That was the extent of agricultural knowledge they required. Once accepted, we were transferred to a demobilization camp. Later, we boarded the liner *Sea Robin* and sailed for Halifax. We arrived there in the fall of 1946 and continued by rail to Winnipeg.

Why did I choose Canada? When I was still a schoolboy, I had read Arkady Fiedler's *Canada, the Land of Fragrant Resin*. That book had enchanted me. The ragged mountains, wild rivers, roaring grizzlies—a country of breathtaking beauty. And I do not think I was the only one searching for a childhood dream: Fidler's images of a wild and noble country—a compulsory reading for Polish schoolboys—influenced many Polish veterans to seek out that vestige of paradise on earth.

Immediately after my arrival, I discovered that while this vast land was indeed wild, its urban centres spoke mostly English, a language I did not know at all. My knowledge of Italian did not help much. Once, when we were still in the Fort Osborne Barracks, the regional commander, Brigadier-General Morton, invited all officers to the officers' club. Our conversation consisted mostly of him and his assistants talking and us smiling politely. At one point he asked us—and this must have been translated for us—why we did not wear our military medals. We all had various distinctions (I had the Cross of Courage, the War Star, the Star of Italy, and the Star of Africa), but many of us did not wear them because we saw no point to parading in them in a foreign land. I do not wear them even today. He seemed puzzled.

Thank God the Polish community in Manitoba, led by Mr. Dubienski, welcomed us with open arms. Mr. Dubienski organized for us a meeting with Mr. Christianson, from the local employment office. We were hoping we might convince him to let those involved in organizing the veterans in Canada remain in the vicinity of Winnipeg. Mr. Christianson invited us for tea, attended also by Mrs. Panaro, Mrs. Szczygielska, and the children of Mr. Dubienski. We first drank some whiskey and then presented to Mr. Christianson our plans for setting up an organization of Polish combatants, the Polish Combatants Association [PCA]. Our leader, Bolesław Czubak, had to remain in the city, we argued, and our arguments must have been quite convincing, for they let him stay. Most other organizers, including myself, got farm jobs in the vicinity of Winnipeg.

Soon the farmers came to collect their new employees. I went to a farm on Highway 9, just before Lockport. My farmer had about 300 head of cattle, so my job was bringing hay from the stacks in the fields to the barn. In a sleigh drawn by a pair of horses, I had to drive out into the thick of a snowstorm, load the sleigh, and drive back to the barn. That was my chore twice a day. It was hard physical labour, perhaps too hard for my rather weak physical frame. But overall the conditions on that farm—there were ten of us working there—were probably better than on most other farms. Everyone was paid $45 a month plus room and board, a minimum the farmer was obliged to pay. But the food was something else. After so much physical exertion, I was always ravenously hungry. When the ten of us sat down for breakfast or lunch, and the farmer's wife brought us a stack of toast, jugs of coffee, and heaps of pork and bacon, the mountain of food was so high I could hardly see my colleagues on the other side of the table. It usually took us twenty minutes to eat the table clean. And six hours later, we were ready for another meal. We communicated with the farmer through his Ukrainian workers, who knew English much better than we did. My own job was pretty simple: load, drive, unload, so my need for English was pretty minimal.

I worked for that farmer from November until spring. Then I moved to a farm in Springfield for another four or five months. Finally a friend of mine gave me the name of a farmer who would sign my papers and not require that I actually work for him. I made the arrangements and moved to Winnipeg, where I had no money but at least had more time for organizational work.

When I was still on a farm, I usually came to town on the weekends. Only Czubak was permanently in Winnipeg, and most organizational responsibilities rested with him. We were greatly helped in our efforts to organize by the Polish weekly *Czas*. Those in charge of it, the editor Synowiecki and Mr. Chudzicki, gave us free access to the offices of *Czas*, located at Dauferine Street. They also let us use their telephone and often interpreted for us, as when the Mounties came to ask us about our political orientation and plans for the future.

It took us about a year to let our colleagues, scattered on farms across the province, know about our Combatants Association. They send us money asking for Polish newspapers, books, correspondence, and membership in the association. They began to send us letters complaining about being stuck in God-forsaken holes. "The farmer is torturing me. Please help me to get out!" some letters read. We often heard such cries of despair and urgent pleas for help. Those letters we had to translate for Mr. Christianson, who could intervene on a veteran's behalf with the farmer, or even move a veteran to a different farm. Sometimes those interventions were absolutely necessary, for there were farmers who treated their workers worse than slaves. Mr. Dubienski advised us to "sit quiet and not stir trouble because the Canadian government will refuse to take in more veterans," but in some cases we felt morally obliged to speak out.

The Polish weekly *Czas* was also an important contact point for those seeking family members or friends who moved from farm to farm. Seeking out new addresses and answering the letters was time-consuming, but I do not remember a single letter that remained without reply. We understood how important it was for our men to stay in touch with one another in this vast and still-foreign country, and how important those Polish ties were for their morale and will to survive.

When my own farm contract expired, I found a job in the construction firm of Mr. Chudzicki and Mr. Szarzyński. For fifty cents an hour, I mixed mortar and carried it to bricklayers. The pay was better than on any farm, for I made $4 a day and over $80 a month. The down side was that I had to pay for my own accommodation and food. I worked this way for two construction seasons, side-by-side with Czubak and other veterans. Later I got a job in a ladies garment factory, which also employed many Poles. Łodzia-Michalski worked there as a presser, and I got hired as a cutter and held that job for ten years. Eventually, I found a job at the post office and stayed with it till my retirement.

I was thirty-three years old when my closest friends started getting married and settling down. It was time for me, too, I thought. It so happened that I had just met an attractive young woman, Stefania Rajfur, so after a few months of courtship we tied the knot. We began our life together happy but poor. We could not afford any luxuries. It took us ten years to save for our first car, and furnishing our home took even longer. In the meantime, we brought to the world three children, two sons and a daughter. Some of my friends, Stanisław Ilkow for instance, went to university and later landed excellent jobs. I toyed with this idea but was afraid I would not cope with both work and school. After I got a job at the post office, our standard of living and my satisfaction with the job definitely increased. Unlike some of the veterans, I did not have much education or technical skills and cannot speak of great professional accomplishments in Canada. What I can say, though, is that I honestly provided for myself and my family.

I had become a member of the Polish Combatants Association while still in Italy. Our first board of organizers here in Winnipeg was comprised of people like Czubak, Klimaszewski, Mossakowski, Kalaska, Wielobob, and a few others whose names now escape me. We were the first and the strongest organization of Polish Combatants in Canada. The second strongest group was forming in Port Arthur, and Czubak sent me to one of their board meetings to convey his greetings and offer some practical advice. After Czubak's departure, Klimaszewski became the first president of our newly formed Chapter #13 in Winnipeg. Following his resignation, I took over the reins. It was a difficult year. People were busy working and looking after their families; only a handful could still afford to remain actively involved in the combatants' affairs. After a year of presiding over Chapter #13, I, too, had to limit my involvement to take care of various family matters. All of us, it seems, went through such low periods, but most of us returned to volunteer work when personal circumstances allowed.

The Polish community in Manitoba needed our volunteer work, and we needed it, too. We brought a fresh dose of Polish language and culture into the fading memories of immigrants from almost half a century earlier. After one of the concerts we organized with the Polish choir Sokół, people commented that they hadn't breathed so much homeland in a long time. For me personally, and probably for many others, our volunteer work on behalf of the combatants was a real school of civic life. The association became our second home, and its meetings and various functions were almost as important as family affairs. Some became so attached to our organization that they could not imagine life without it. To this day, they meet in the association's clubhouse over a glass of beer, remember former days, and chat about the future.

I am retired now and quite content with my life. I have three children and four grandchildren. One of my sons graduated from university with a degree in biology; he now works as a customs officer.

My daughter finished nursing at the University of Manitoba and works as a registered nurse in a hospital. My oldest son is a sales manager in an agricultural equipment dealership. All my children have done very well for themselves and live much richer lives than I ever did. And that is how it should be.

The majority of Polish combatants' children have graduated from universities and now occupy important positions in Canadian society. I never heard of any major disappointments. Their parents had to struggle to give them food and education and could not themselves afford any luxuries in life. But none of them regrets investing in their children and giving them a head start. After all, our children are our future.

TADEUSZ WOJCIECHOWSKI

I was born in 1925 in Jabłonowo, in Pomerania, as one of four siblings, all boys. When the war broke out I was only fourteen, and my brother Kazimierz even younger, so both of us stayed at home. My father worked for the railways, and he came back two weeks after Poland's defeat. My brother Leon also returned from a military hospital in Warsaw. For a while only Maks was missing: he was an officer cadet in the Polish army, was captured, and sent to a German POW camp.

In June 1940, I was sent as a forced labourer to a farm in Germany. I worked for a farmer, a *Bauer*, for three years. There were two of us boys from Grudziądz on that farm: I looked after the horses, and he after the cows. The farmer treated us very well. Of course, we had to work from dawn to dusk, but at least I never went hungry, eating five times a day. In 1943 the German authorities introduced a new national category in Pomerania, the so-called "Germanized" population (also called "list #3"). Mother decided to sign up for that classification to help my brother Maks, who still languished in a POW camp. I was technically underage and had no say in the matter. In 1943 I was called up before a German recruitment commission. In July of that year, I was drafted into the *Arbeitsdienst*, an organization similar to the Polish Youth Labour Corps. The Germans sent us to an island in the estuary of the Panemünde river, where they were making their V-1 missiles. I also saw there the first airplanes with jet engines. Two companies, each 200 youths strong, were employed there for moving earth and camouflaging the production facilities (we painted them green). In the middle

436

of August, air-raid warnings began; the whole island was blacked out, except for the concentration camp. Soon the island was heavily bombed, but the key installations, where missiles were assembled, were not damaged. After those raids, while we were filling in bomb craters with dirt, the entire Nazi elite from Berlin, headed by Himmler, came to survey the damage. Later they moved us from the compound to tents in the forest. At the end of September, after three months of service, I returned home to Grudziądz.

In November of that year I turned seventeen and was immediately called up for regular military duty. I was assigned to the infantry and sent for training to Fulda in Bavaria and then briefly to France. The German army was full of people like myself, Poles from Pomerania, from Silesia, and even from western Poland. When we were in our own company, we spoke Polish, and our German commanders had no objections. In fact, relations among ordinary soldiers of Polish and German origin were quite friendly. We tried not to interfere with one another, each group celebrating Christmas its own way: they had a minister on one Sunday, we a priest on another. Polish soldiers in the German army could earn the rank of corporal, but in my company, the corporal was Czech. He encouraged us to sing Polish songs on the march. He also knew that my brother was a POW in a German camp but made no bones about it.

After a period of intensive training, they dropped us on the Atlantic coast, near the Spanish border. The town was called St.-Jean-de-Luz. Our outposts were located every three kilometres along the coast. Shelters were built on the sand dunes and each was manned by twenty soldiers. Our orders were to patrol the coast, around the clock, seven days a week. Patrols changed every eight hours, and once a week we were allowed sixteen hours of rest. The food was lousy: half a loaf of bread, one warm meal, and three cigarettes a day. I slept outside in the sand because the shelters were full of rats that danced on the beds at night.

After the Allied invasion of Normandy, in June 1944, we began to withdraw, marching mostly at night. We were issued sixty bullets and one hand grenade each; the company also got a Polish machine gun, the kind cooled with water. The Germans did not know how to handle it, but three-quarters of our company were Poles from Pomerania, and we found someone who had used it before. We marched towards Paris and then turned southwards. It was becoming obvious that the end of the war was not far away. We could hear the hum of Allied airplanes overhead. One night we came across a building with lights in the windows. We got inside and were ordered to cover the windows. Then I heard an old lady say to some children in Polish: "They'll probably take us now." I told her in Polish not to worry, that there were no more German troops behind us, and that they would soon be free. She offered us some food and later gave us a loaf of bread and some bacon for the road. We kept moving towards the Swiss border. In the evening three American tanks appeared ahead. One of the German commanders ordered fire, and the tanks disappeared. The following morning we found ourselves under heavy fire, which continued until midday. We were still hiding in the cellar when we heard several American tanks, and a few minutes later, an American soldier shouted through the doorway, "Get out! *Hände hoch!*" We were talking among ourselves in Polish, and it turned out the American was a Pole, too. He asked us some questions, and I gave him the maps I had on me giving locations of German headquarters. He took the maps and went back to the tank. We were sent to a local collection point, and from there to a temporary POW camp. The following morning we were issued a can of pork each and taken to the regional collection point on the Mediterranean Sea, near the Riviera. A soldier with a Polish eagle ensign on his arm lined us up and announced: "Those who feel Polish and want to volunteer for the Polish army, go across the road to the meadow." More than three-quarters of us jumped across the road without any hesitation. The rest were Germans, and they were taken to another camp. We were first fed, then taken by boat to Naples and by train to the south of Italy. We were joined there by some Poles from the army of General Vlasov. We could finally bathe, put on new Polish uniforms, and feel Polish again. Without much delay, we were assigned to various services. I was selected by Lieutenant Jasiński for armoured cavalry. We moved to Matera, and then to Galatona, Calabria, and Gubio. I visited the monastery of St. Umberto and saw the glass coffin under the altar. In Gubio, I went to officer cadet college and trained as a driver, radio operator, and gunner. Afterwards I was assigned to a regiment of the Carpathian Lancers. In the end it turned out that all my training was for nothing, for the war was over. I was transferred to Macerata and a while later to Scotland.

I learned through a friend of mine from Grudziądz that my parents and one of my brothers were killed during the Soviet offensive at the end of February 1945. Grudziądz was heavily fortified, and the Germans had put up strong resistence there. As a result, most of the city was destroyed and many civilians died during the Soviet assault. The Red Cross also let me know that my brother Maks, after being freed from the *Oflag*, had joined a guard unit of the Polish army. Kazimierz, like myself, was in the German army and has been sent to Africa, where he was taken prisoner by the Allies. Later he joined the division of General Maczek. He was already fighting the Germans when I was still one of their soldiers. He earned the rank of platoon leader and the Cross of Virtuti Militari [the highest Polish military distinction].

I saw no point going back to Poland, especially since my parents were dead. A good friend of mine did return, but soon afterwards his sister wrote me that his lungs, kidneys, and liver had all given out and he had died a short time later. Maks had been in Canada since 1947, and he sponsored my coming here in August 1949.

After arriving in Winnipeg, I quickly became an active member of the Polish Combatants Association. I also joined the Polish amateur theatre and the Sokół choir. Together with Tadeusz Gardziejewski, we sang second bass. Between the theatre and the choir, I had rehearsals almost every day, right after work. At one of the choir rehearsals I met my future wife, Stefa. We were married in 1952 and had four children: Teresa, Ludwig, Barbara, and Urszula. Teresa graduated from the University of Manitoba and works for the Department of Finance in Ottawa. Ludwig is still studying computers and electronics at Red River College. Barbara finished high school and works in an optical store. And Urszula has just started her third year at university.

I got my first job at Weststeel in St. Boniface, but since 1951 I have been employed by the Canadian Pacific Railway. At first I worked in a team that lay down and repaired the tracks. The work was very hard, cold in winter and sweaty in summer. In 1963 I was temporarily laid off, but they later recalled me to paint railway cars. I am due to retire in seven days. I have a good pension plan, and I feel financially secure. My future looks bright, and I am looking forward to it.

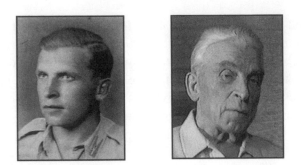

ADAM ŻURAD

I was born in 1915, during the First World War. Our town was surrounded by deep ravines, flowing down into the valley below. Tsarist troops were sliding down those ravines, pounded by Austrian artillery, when I was about to utter my first cry. The artillery fire set trees and some buildings ablaze. In the midst of that chaos, I was born. "Son, you've been born at the wrong hour," my terrified mother moaned. Only Grandma was with her, as the rest of the family had run away into the forest, fearing capture by one or the other of the warring sides. Grandma and Mom took me down into my uncle's cellar because it was made of stone and gave better protection from stray shells. They put me in a barrel of oats, trying to make me as safe as they knew how.

In my fifth year of life, I lost my sight for six months. Fortunately the doctors identified the cause of my blindness, and after a successful operation I could see again. I remember that moment as if it happened yesterday. I opened my eyes and, through a haze, I saw some pigeons. The sensation was apparently too much for me, for I fainted.

I went to primary school in Budziwój, and, after four years, I took the high school entrance exams. There were six of us siblings in the family, and our parents tried to give each of us a chance at proper education. My sisters and I started attending the high school in Sambor, but the railway connection with that town was cancelled, so we had to move to Drohobycz [Drogobych]. Commuting to school was most tedious, and perhaps even a bit dangerous, as we had to walk four and a half kilometres through the woods to the station.

After the matriculation exam, I was called up for military service. Initially, they assigned me to artillery, but I ended up in the infantry officer cadet college in Kielce. The discipline there was of the strictest kind, and our muscles often bore the brunt of it. After graduation, I was sent to the 4th Legionnaire Regiment in Kielce, to a communications platoon. I enjoyed that line of work, especially after I was offered some specialized training. I remember that, by the end of that course, I could telegraph seventy signs a minute.

After my military service, some friends of mine convinced me to move to Lwów [L'viv] and to sign up for university, in the faculty of law. In the spring of 1939, I took a lodging with some friends of mine from Drohobycz. My financial situation was rather precarious, so I found a job in Borysław [Borislav]. Fortunately, my employers appreciated my thirst for knowledge and tried to help me in every way they could. They even let me leave earlier so I could get to my lectures on time.

Sadly, both my work and studies were interrupted on August 28, 1939, when I received my mobilization papers and was ordered to report in Drohobycz, to the 6th Podhale Regiment. I did see some military action. We went to Sambor and began to withdraw from there under constant German air raids. But on September 12, we mounted a counterattack to take Sambor back. Unfortunately, the Germans must have been expecting that and were well prepared for us. In the end we had to fall back. At one point I took a detour to go home, see my parents, wash, and have one last good meal. When I returned to our temporary barracks, my unit had already moved out and the buildings were empty. With a few other stray officers, we managed to find a Fiat, and we chased after our withdrawing troops. I caught up with my unit in time for another skirmish with the Germans near Stryj. We went through Morszyn [Morshin], towards Stanisławów [Ivano-Frankivs'k]. Soon our scouts discovered that the Soviets had taken Stanisławów, and Stryj [Stryy] was in German hands. We had no choice but to head for the mountains.

We reached Wyszków on the Hungarian border. The troops, by now a collection of survivors from various units, waited on the Polish side, while Colonel Dębicki negotiated with the Hungarians the conditions of our passage. In the end, they agreed to let us pass, provided we gave up our weapons. Parting with our guns was difficult for many of us—more than one had a tear in his eye—but we followed the order, threw away the rifle locks, and surrendered the rest. The Hungarians took us in with pity, maybe even compassion. We marched on foot to Munkacs, where we boarded trains going in various directions. In my transport, there were also Polish women and children. We passed through Budapest, and continued almost to the Austrian border, on the Danube.

Our pipeline to the West was well organized. Those with some knowledge of Hungarian and southern Slavic languages went ahead to make the necessary contacts and arrangements. Then specialists from various services were smuggled out. All of this had to be done in conspiracy because the Gestapo sniffed around the camps; they did not have the authority to arrest anybody, but they could call in the Hungarian police to do the dirty work for them. I was sent to Split, whence the Polish ship *Warszawa* took us to France. After a tedious process of registration and verification, I signed up for a course in military law, interesting but rather useless. In the meantime, General Maczek had begun to form his division, and I was transferred to it. After some intensive and quite rigorous training, we faced the Germans again. The French did not want to fight, so we covered their rear as they withdrew. General Prugar-Ketling, with his division, crossed over to Switzerland. His men were lucky: they were well-looked-after there, and many of them went to university during the war. We kept fighting. Near Montbard, some of our tanks ran out of gas. We destroyed them, and continued with the rest through the mountains. Near Dijon, the Germans tightened their noose around us. The orders came to destroy the rest of our weaponry. General Maczek then explained the situation to us and ordered that whoever was able should find himself civilian clothes and try to make it home.

This was, of course, easier said than done. The Germans were already all around us. I stumbled into their patrol with a friend of mine. We could both speak German pretty well, so we told them we were students who had got into the army by mistake. They took us to one of their internment camps, but we managed to escape with a small group of others. We hid in haystacks and later walked to the railway station and took a train to Montbard, where we had fought several days earlier. We were still wearing our Polish uniforms. When we stopped in a house by the roadside to ask for some water, the owner, a Polish woman, immediately recognized us as Polish soldiers. She told us not to show ourselves in the streets because the locals were angry with

Poles: if we had not put up so much resistance, their town would not have suffered so much damage. So we waited until the night and then scattered, in twos, in various directions. I went with a sailor, Józek. The following day, we came across a farm that employed POWs from Morocco. The farmer offered us jobs, so we stayed there for several days. Then we set out again in the direction of Paris. We walked into a German patrol, but we told them we were looking for jobs, and they let us go. In Melun, we did get arrested, but we escaped for the second time. After a few days of walking, we found some good people who took us in. We started preparations to go to that part of France that was still free, but we learned that this would help us little. In the end, we stayed in hiding where we were until 1944.

After the Allied invasion, I rejoined General Maczek's division. At first we were told we would be retrained as reinforcements for the paratrooper brigade, but we ended up training with an armoured unit in the south of France. From that transition camp, I was sent to the 10th Hussar Regiment of the 2nd Corps. Every soldier in that regiment sported a moustache, so I, too, had to grow one. We went though more training in the south of Italy and in Egypt before they sent us into action during the assault on Bologna. Shortly after that the war was over, but we continued sporadic fighting with pockets of German resistance along the eastern coast of Italy.

When all the fighting was long over, a Canadian commission came to recruit agricultural workers. I signed a two-year contract to work in the sugar beet fields. Later I was sent to a cattle farm, where I cut bull horns, branded cattle, and did all the cowboy duties. I also worked on other farms, including one near Edmonton. In 1952 or 1953, I got a job in Shilo, during the construction of a new military base. The pay was quite decent: $1.10 per hour plus room and board. When that job was over, I was hired by the Canadian National Railway, and travelled quite a bit around the country. I lingered for a while in British Columbia, but eventually returned to Winnipeg, where most of my friends were.

I never married. I guess I was looking for an angel, but they are hard to find. I was quite active in the Polish Combatants Association, for a while serving as a treasurer of our self-help fund. I have many dear friends and have been asked to be godfather to their children many times over. Three of my godchildren are still in Winnipeg. In recent years, I moved to a seniors' residence and feel quite content here.

INDEX OF PLACE NAMES